PERSONALITY DISORDERS AND STATES OF ALONENESS

VALUE INQUIRY BOOK SERIES

VIBS

Volume 246

a volume in
Philosophy and Psychology
PAP
Mark Letteri, Editor

INTIMACY AND ALONENESS

A Multi-Volume Study in Philosophical Psychology

Volume Two

PERSONALITY DISORDERS AND STATES OF ALONENESS

John G. McGraw

Rodopi

Amsterdam - New York, NY 2012

Cover Photo: www.morgueFile.com

Cover Design: Studio Pollmann

The paper on which this book is printed meets the requirements of "ISO 9706:1994, Information and documentation - Paper for documents - Requirements for permanence".

ISBN: 978-90-420-3494-5
E-Book ISBN: 978-94-012-0770-6

Printed in the Netherlands

Philosophy and Psychology
(PAP)

Mark Letteri
Editor

Other Titles in PAP

Amihud Gilead. *The Privacy of the Psychical.* 2011. VIBS 223

John G. McGraw. *Intimacy and Isolation* (Intimacy and Aloneness. A Multivolume Study in Philosophical Psychology, Volume I). 2010. VIBS 221

Fernand Vial. *The Unconscious in Philosophy, and French and European Literature.* 2009. VIBS 203

Amihud Gilead. *Necessity and Truthful Fictions.* 2009. VIBS 202

Mark Letteri. *Heidegger and the Question of Psychology.* 2009. VIBS 200

Steven M. Rosen. *Dimensions of Apeiron.* 2004. VIBS 154

Christine M. Koggel, Allannah Furlong, and Charles Levin, eds. *Confidential Relationships.* 2003. VIBS 141

Sandra A. Wawrytko, ed. *The Problem of Evil.* 2000. VIBS 90

Amihud Gilead. *Saving Possibilities.* 1999. VIBS 80

Jon Mills and Janusz A. Polanowski. *The Ontology of Prejudice.* 1997. VIBS 58

CONTENTS

EDITORIAL FORWARD

I am pleased to present John McGraw's *Personality Disorders and States of Aloneness*, Volume Two of his multi-volume project *Intimacy and Aloneness: A Multi-Volume Study in Philosophical Psychology*. His extended focus on the subject of loneliness offers many fresh vantages, and unfolds the intricacies of this seemingly simple phenomenon. McGraw's work forces us to confront the inevitability of loneliness in the human condition, but also to see the real prospect of immeasurably enriching affiliation. While autonomous in its attention to the question of personality disorders, Volume Two complements Volume One's devotion to the broad issue of intimacy.

McGraw grounds his claims and considerations in psychological research and current culture as well as in traditional philosophy, so readers of various persuasions will find a foothold. Those who have a background in abnormal psychology will understand readily his use of the concepts and criteria in the *Diagnostic and Statistical Manual of Mental Disorders*, touchstones that he reinterprets as part of his comprehensive articulation of the phenomenon. McGraw links loneliness to prominent social and political configurations of our era, more specifically, a rising tide of divisive individualism and related features of the North American ethos that aggravates the permanent problem of loneliness. In this second volume, he "concentrate[s] on how [this societal reality] fosters negative personality traits, types, and disorders, especially in reference to various species of aloneness, above all the kind known as loneliness." McGraw's first and second volumes together stand as a novel and wide-ranging account of an issue of basic importance that we too often overlook or consider only in a superficial manner.

Mark Letteri
Philosophy and Psychology Series Editor

PREFACE

This volume is the second in a series that predominantly concerns personality, especially abnormal, chiefly in the context of states of aloneness. Like the preceding volume, *Intimacy and Isolation* (McGraw, 2010), this one concentrates on that negative sort of aloneness known as "loneliness," the unwanted absence of shared intimacy. Throughout this volume, references to *Intimacy and Isolation* will be cited as "vol. 1."

Each of the volumes has been designed to be integral in itself so that reading either will not be dependent on the other for its comprehension. Nonetheless, the two are highly interrelated, indeed, interpenetrating such that the reader is encouraged to examine both volumes and in their proper sequence for a more complete understanding of their contents.

In Volume I, I discussed at length five trends in the United States of America that have been highly instrumental in contributing to the proliferation and exacerbation of negative states of aloneness. I have called this quintet of undesirable social institutions SCRAM since it causes human relatedness to rush away and un- or disconnectedness to rush in and usurp its place. In this volume, I concentrate on how SCRAM fosters negative personality traits, types, and disorders, especially in reference to various species of aloneness, above all the kind known as loneliness. The components of SCRAM are outlined in Chapter One and succinctly summarized in Appendix A.

My discussion of disordered personalities is principally carried out in the context of their primary and associate diagnostic criteria as delineated by the American Psychiatric Association in its *Diagnostic and Statistical Manual of Mental Disorders* (*DSM-IV*, 1994). I have also consulted the Association's revised third edition (*DSM-III-R*, 1987) and its revised fourth edition (*DSM-IV-TR*, 2000). Please see Appendix C for a brief summary of the *DSM-IV* personality disorders. Unless otherwise stated, all citations of the *DSM-IV* will be referenced simply as the *DSM* or less frequently the *Manual*, with only the page number(s) as locator.

As a primary objective of this project, I have interpreted the three *DSM* editions' personality disorder criteria especially in light of the Five Factor Model (FFM) of personality, above all as articulated by Paul T. Costa and Thomas Widiger (*DSM-III-R*, 1994a, p. 329; *DSM-IV*, 2002a, pp. 461-467). See also Appendix B for a brief summary of the FFM.

The lexicons employed herein are *Webster's New World Dictionary of the American Language* (1980) and *Merriam-Webster's Collegiate Dictionary* (2002). For the sake of brevity, each of the many instances of their utilization will not be formally cited.

I wish to thank Désirée Marielle McGraw for her invaluable comments and support of this project. For his continued assistance in this endeavor, I am grateful to Mark Letteri, the editor of the Studies in Existentialism and the

Philosophy and Psychology special series in the Values Inquiry Book Series of Rodopi. In addition, I wish to recognize Elizabeth D. Boepple for her devoted editorial input in this undertaking. Finally, I am obliged to Patricia McDermott O'Connor, not only for her critiquing this, but past projects. It is to her that I have dedicated this study in its entirety.

One

INTRODUCTION

1. The *DSM* Personality Disorders

Insofar as this book explicitly focuses on abnormal personalities, it will employ their *DSM* general and specific definitions (see Appendix C). The *Manual* states that the general diagnostic criteria for a personality disorder includes an enduring pattern of inner experience and behavior that deviates markedly from the expectations of the individual's culture. This pattern is manifested in two (or more) of the following areas:

> (1) cognition (or ways of perceiving and interpreting self, other people, and events);
> (2) affectivity (or the range, intensity, lability, and appropriateness of emotional response);
> (3) interpersonal functioning;
> (4) impulse control.

Thus, a diagnosis may reflect, but does not necessarily require, impaired interpersonal functioning. (See Appendix C for the full list of general diagnostic criteria for a Personality Disorder.)

Contrary to the *Manual*'s conception of personality disorders in general, mine maintains that a grave deviancy in interpersonal functioning is not merely a possible but a necessary condition for their composition. Whereupon, it is the leitmotif of the present investigation of personality that it is quintessentially made up of its sociality, meaning its relatedness—or failures thereof—to other persons. This connectedness has as its nucleus shared intimacy and intimate sharing.

Therefore, it is my view that every individual who persistently succeeds in establishing and sustaining genuinely intimate attachments to other persons is to be considered a normal personality. Correspondingly, every individual who is gravely remiss in doing so is a failed personality qua personality. So understood an abnormal individual is one who profoundly and habitually does not fulfill the demands of intimate *interpersonality* and does so either by a quantitative deficit or a qualitative defectiveness, primarily the latter.

While I contend that a serious shortage of shared inwardness is the gist of every personality anomaly, I do not claim that all *personal* shortcomings, such as those, for example, involved in dishonesty and vanity, are owing to a lack of such intimacy. Clearly they are not unless by *personal* is meant what is *intimate* or vice versa.

Although deficiencies in intimate connectedness need not ipso facto be detrimental to occupational and other important areas of human interaction, they often adversely affect them as well. For example, many individuals with abnormal personalities are unable to obtain or retain employment due to their undesirable personality traits, ones that negatively impact their fellow workers.

As to the definitions of the ten specific disorders of personality, they are now listed in terms of what I will argue is the gravity of their departures from normalcy and their unamenability to therapy:

The schizoid involves a "detachment from social relationships and a restricted range of emotional expression in interpersonal settings." The schizotypal manifests "social and interpersonal deficits marked by acute discomfort with and reduced capability for close relationships" and by "cognitive or perceptual distortions and eccentricities of behavior." The sociopath—also known as the antisocial, the dys-social, and sometimes the psychopath—evinces a "disregard for and violation of the rights of others" in what the *DSM* designates a "Conduct Disorder"; it includes "aggression [toward] people and animals, destruction of property, deceitfulness, or theft." The paranoid emits a "pervasive distrust and suspiciousness" of others' motives as being "malevolent." The narcissist demonstrates a "grandiosity, a need for admiration, and lack of empathy." The obsessive-compulsive—henceforth the obsessional or, and less commonly, the compulsive—displays a "pattern of preoccupation with orderliness, perfectionism, and control." The borderline shows an "instability in interpersonal relationships, self-image, and affects, and marked impulsivity." The histrionic reveals an "excessive emotionality and attention seeking behavior." The dependent presents "a pervasive and excessive need to be taken care of." Lastly, the avoidant is marked by "social inhibition, feelings of inadequacy, and hypersensitivity to negative evaluation" (ibid., p. 629).

In contrast to the ten specific personality disorders, the *DSM* distinguishes, first, a "Personality Disorder not Otherwise Specified;" second, simple personality traits; and, third, personality types, the kinds that manifest personality disorder patterns but do not in themselves constitute such aberrations (ibid., p. 633).

2. Personality Disorder Units: Groups and Clusters

I will argue that personality disorders are a blend of mental and moral shortcomings predominantly undergirded by a surfeit of egocentricity. Consequently, I will customarily refer to these personality illnesses as psycho-ethical aberrations. So understood, this interdisciplinary study pertains to the psychology of ethics but even more to the ethics of psychology above all insofar as each is pivotal to the notions of personality and aloneness and their respective properties and typologies.

With especially these mental/moral kind of anomalies in mind, I have divided the ten disorders into three units that will be referenced as sets, aggregates, but ordinarily groups. They are the schizoid and schizotypal (Group I); the sociopath, paranoid, narcissist, and obsessional (Group II); and the borderline, histrionic, dependent, and avoidant (Group III.

Based on what it deems their descriptive likenesses, the *DSM* also relegates the ten disturbed personalities to three units, which it calls "Clusters." Cluster A contains the paranoid, schizoid, and schizotypal who, the *Manual* states, "often appear odd or eccentric." Cluster B harbors the antisocial, borderline, histrionic, and narcissist who, it maintains, "often appear dramatic, emotional, or erratic." Lastly, Cluster C features the avoidant, dependent, and compulsive who, the *DSM* says, "often appear anxious or fearful" (pp. 629-630). Consequently, it has possibly seven foundations for its three clusters, depending on how these words are defined.

Alternatively, I have but one ground for my groupings: their negative disposition concerning interpersonal relatedness. In addition to this single basis for my varying from the *DSM*'s aberrated personality taxonomy, I will provide more than ten other reasons, especially in Chapter Seven, for my departing from its division. In some cases, I differ from the *DSM* in the sense that I disagree with it. In others, I vary from it simply by adding considerations the *Manual* does not explicitly if at all address.

3. SCRAM: Five American Societal Illnesses and a Facilitator of Pathological Personalities

Personality and, more specifically, its disorders, while they are genetically based in varying degrees, are greatly influenced by social factors. Though they may not be actual causes of personality disturbances, these social factors act in predisposing, precipitating, sustaining, and exacerbating manners vis-à-vis these aberrations. I have singled out five detrimental social institutions, which, I submit, have, especially since the 1970s, increasingly ruled the United States of America. I formed the above quintet of societal arrangements into the acronym "SCRAM," the constituents of which are the following five quasi-fixations: "*S*uccessitis"; "*C*apitalitis"; "*R*ivalitis"; "*A*tomitis"; and "*M*aterialitis" (see Appendix A; vol. 1, chap. 1, sec. 2).

When the SCRAM factors are present, intimacy "hastens" away and in its absence loneliness and other sorts of unwanted aloneness invade this vacuum, filling it with painful and stressful emotions, such as anxiety and anger, in addition to negative self-ascriptions, such as self-worthlessness. Instructively, Americans' penchant for "haste" is itself frequently both a cause of loneliness and a method of coping with and covering up this and other negative kinds of aloneness.

All five of these societal sicknesses—hence, the suffix "itis" attached to each of them—engender obstacles between individuals and groups thereby variously isolate them in assorted kinds and levels of egocentrism.

Egocentricity is a kind of addiction to one's self. With many other students of ethics, I view selfishness, or greed, as the ultimate source of all immorality. To use theological discourse, it is the most egregious of capital sins, meaning moral transgressions. While pride, or inordinate self-valorization, is often reckoned the ultimate origin of all immorality, I would argue it is better understood as an effect of an underlying selfishness. Greed permeates all five elements of SCRAM but its hyper-individualism is the foundation, fabric, and goal of the other four. Aldous Huxley indicts current social institutions as constituting "organized lovelessness" (Goleman, 2006, p. 252). No present set of nationwide conventions is, I believe, more systemically geared to generating lovelessness—meaning not loving and being loved in positive manners—and to inducing social hostility than the self-centeredness of SCRAM.

SCRAM, especially via its social atomism, inculcates or at least activates egocentric tendencies in both the public and private spheres, in the second, by its promotion of privatism. This mentality entails being uncommitted to anything except the self's immediate and purely private, meaning individual, interests. Concomitantly, privatism avoids anything that might recognize and, a fortiori, serve the good of others and their communal well-being.

Judith Jordan stresses how cultural factors, often unconsciously, influence our view of personality aberrations. She claims that the culturally dominant American notion of personality, the independent, hyper-autonomous sort, "is often assumed to be normative and 'best.'" She insists that this belief "goes unexamined and unquestioned." In its wake, this assumption, Jordan contends, can lead, in the mental health sphere, "to the pathologizing of difference," such that, for instance, the dependent type of person is considered sick or more so in comparison to the independent. Hence, Jordan argues, "the marginalized groups of 'difference' are often seen as less 'mature,' less evolved" than mainstream personalities (2004, p. 124).

It is instructive that the *DSM* and Western "scientific" psychological literature in general seldom explicitly speak of there being an independent disordered personality but only a dependent sort. I believe that this omission is largely a legacy of the West's, especially America's—above all insofar as it is subject to SCRAM's hegemony—over-emphasis on autonomy and individualism and, correspondingly, its downgrading or simply neglecting homonomy— to use Andras Angyal's term (1958)—and communalism.

Granted, children must learn to be on their own. Nevertheless, the more they become adults, the more interdependent or, more exactly, interindependent, they must become. Thus, maturation is a process of growing autonomy being anchored in a growing homonomy, the essence of which is the intimate relationship. This constructive union is a condition which women of most if not all societies appear to excel at attaining and especially maintaining more than men. Cooperation, an homonomous undertaking, helps get human beings to become civilized and keeps them so.

SCRAM's social institutions, therefore, encourage Group II hyper-independent personality traits, styles, and types to proliferate and to be construed as culturally normal. Correlatively, what is dependent and different is deemed the incarnation of the immature and abnormal. Whence, in being proficient at generating or at least magnifying hyper-independent attributes, SCRAM is instrumental in promoting the inception and flourishing of antisocial and narcissistic personalities.

Because social atomism, with its apotheosization of autonomy and its anathematization of homonomy, has saturated the American mind-set insofar as it subscribes to SCRAM, the highly but negatively autonomous Group II aberrants are often thought to be less sick individuals than Group III. Nonetheless and objectively speaking, it is less ill, psycho-ethically considered, to fail by being overly homonomous than by being overly autonomous. In short, it is less undesirable to attempt to be hyper-related to others (Group III) than to be hypo-related (Group I) and, a fortiori, dis-related (Group II).

Hence, I underscore that SCRAM is directly contributory to the rise and reinforcement of Group II pathologicals, all of whom have varying gradations of malevolent selfishness as their underlying motivational force. In part and as a reaction to them, these four hyper-independent aberrants can also readily contribute to and sometimes even cause the actuation and actualization of the hyper-dependent Group III aberrants. Group II psycho-ethical deviants, due to their inveterate antipathy toward others in general, can also easily escalate, though not as a rule if ever generate, the extreme introversion and social isolation of the Group I abnormals.

Pathological personalities are, in my judgment, pre-eminently the exceedingly complex combination of three ingredients: first, the mainly biologically based negative psychological traits; second, negative ethical qualities that, in turn, are predominantly rooted in egocentricity; and third, harmful social conditions such as those produced or at minimum promoted by SCRAM.

To the extent that such aberrants freely initiate or, at least, perpetuate their negative psycho-ethical attributes, some disturbed personalities can be the result of volition. A caveat: though the notions of the volitional and voluntary are usually employed interchangeably to signify free acts, they are not so utilized in this study. The volitional will be understood as entailing deliberate acts and, thus, they pertain to the chosen characterological aspects of personality. The voluntary will signify more or less prereflective spontaneous acts that, at least initially, are unchosen in that they are legacies of constitution and temperament.

4. Personality Disorder Classification Models: The *DSM* Categorical and FFM Dimensional

It is widely held that the two main paradigms for personality aberration classification are the categorical and the dimensional. In employing the categorical model, the *DSM* contends that disturbed personalities have essential (primary) and associate (secondary) criteria that entail discrete diagnostic divisions, or taxonomies. These criteria in the form of taxons are envisioned by the *Manual* as being "qualitatively distinct clinical syndromes," meaning relatively unique packages of personality traits (p. 633; see vol. 1, pp. 12–13). The ten *DSM* personality disorders and three clusters into which they are grouped are described in Chapter Five.

In adopting a categorical, or non-continuous (discrete), paradigm of pathological personalities, *DSM* subscribes to the position that these disturbances differ in kind. They do so not only from one another but—and, a fortiori—from non-psychopathological types of personality, namely from the normal and by implication from the supranormal. Hence, in qualitatively dividing these personality abnormalities from one another and, a fortiori, their Clusters, the *DSM* appears to suggest that there are well-differentiated boundaries between them. However, the fact that the *DSM* groups the ten disorders into three clusters indicates that it construes them as not being completely distinct from one another.

With reference to the dimensional, or continuous (non-discrete), paradigm, the one chiefly invoked in the present study is the Five-Factor Model (FFM) of personality (see Appendix B). It maintains that variations with respect to personality traits can be plotted on a continuum that ranges from the lowest to the highest degree without any categorical, meaning any qualitative, or discrete, breaks within this quantitative sequence.

The FFM assembles personality traits into a quintet of broad factors: Neuroticism, Extraversion, Openness to Experience, Agreeableness (Humaneness), and Conscientiousness. These supertraits, also known as dimensions, classes, and domains, are looked upon by the FFM as the building blocks of personality in all its normal and anormal, meaning abnormal and supranormal, variations. Each of the five supertraits is made up of six traits.

Therefore, the FFM construes individuals with abnormal personalities as differing only in degree—meaning relatively relatively but not absolutely relatively—from one another and from normal and by implication and, a fortiori, from supranormal individuals.

Philip Erdberg states that supertrait "scales provide an overall picture of an individual's personality style," or, as existential philosophers say, of persons' "being-in-the world" that is unique to each of them. On the other hand, Erdberg remarks that "the facet [trait] scales allow more specific descriptions which detail the individual differences that occur within the domains" (2004, p. 81), meaning supertraits, dimensions, or classes.

Erdberg further stipulates that, with respect to the thirty facets, individuals can rank very low, low, average, high, and very high. Citing a study by Paul T. Costa and Robert R. McCrae, he reports, "approximately 7% of individuals fall in the two extreme categories, 24% in the high and low ranges, and 38% in the average range" (ibid.).

Each of the FFM's five classes is independent of the others in that the rating of individuals in one domain does not necessarily reveal anything about its standing in any of the other four dimensions (vol. 1, pp. 13–14). Some, including myself, would disagree with this view since, for example, lack of Humaneness and in particular its Altruism arguably eventually affects other supertraits such as Neuroticism's Angry Hostility and Openness to Experience's Positive Emotions. (Henceforth, the supertraits but not the traits will be capitalized.)

Patently, many of the above FFM traits are not only psychological in nature but explicitly ethical in composition, such as Openness to Experience's positive emotions, including and above all love, Conscientiousness's dutifulness, and all six of Agreeableness's attributes such as its altruism. Or, at minimum, the traits have implications of the ethical, like Neuroticism's impulsiveness, or preconditions, such as Conscientiousness's self-discipline and deliberation. Ergo, while the mental and moral qualities of disturbed personalities can be differentiated in theory, in practice, namely concerning the aberrants as they actually exist, these traits converge and are inseparable though distinguishable phenomena.

As a result, it will be put forth, especially in Chapter Ten, that therapy for a disordered personality necessitates the inclusion of moral considerations. Accordingly, such treatment itself can be considered a kind of ethical alliance, or partnership, requiring trust, truthfulness, cooperativeness, and other similar characterological qualities. This combination of psycho-ethical attributes is grievously remiss in pathological personalities, rendering them notoriously difficult to improve and, a fortiori, cure.

Individuals with personality disturbances diversely display an absence of the above thirty traits insofar as they are positive in makeup and a presence of them insofar as they are negative. They do so in a manner that differs in degree, according to the FFM, or in kind, according to the *DSM*, from that of normal individuals.

In this volume, I attempt to show how FFM traits are related to the *DSM* diagnostic features of its ten disturbed personalities, and how these qualities are situated relative to states of aloneness.

Two

ALONENESS

1. Introduction

I remember a cartoon that depicted two men swimming by an individual, who, though sitting in the water, still rose above it by six or so feet, whereupon one of the swimmers asked the other, "whoever said 'no man is island?'" Of course, it was John Donne, who declared, "No man is an *Island*, entire of itself," meaning absolutely independent from all others, because, he insisted, "every man is . . . involved in mankind" (1953, p. 186ns27–28). Begging to differ with his English compatriot, Matthew Arnold bewails the fact that all human beings, if not islands unto themselves, are, have been, and will forever remain at minimum islets of unwanted aloneness (1967, p. 125n5).

However, for Donne, love and its unifying powers can perpetually endure and even surmount any insularity and dissolution to which all human beings are otherwise inevitably subject:

> All other things to their destruction draw,
> Only our love hath no decay;
> This, no to-morrow hath, nor yesterday,
> Running it never runs from us away,
> But truly keeps his first, last, everlasting day. (Ibid, p. 184n6)

Again differing with Donne, Arnold decrees that not even the most foremost unifying faculty that we "mortals" possess, namely love, can save us from being insuperable alonenesses (1967, p. 125). Notably, in referring to human beings as mortals, Arnold anticipates Martin Heidegger's (1962, p. 304n53) description of them as "beings-toward-death."

Arnold contends that, whereas people yearn to be "parts of a single continent!" especially via the fusing force of love, they, nonetheless, ultimately persist in being apart from instead of being a part of one another. Consequently, Arnold mourns the fact that love's "longing fire" to merge hearts, even as it is "kindled," is "cool'd" by "an estranging sea." The result of this alienation is that all human hearts—the organs symbolic of their affectivity and personality as a whole—are shut-ins, marooned and landlocked on the reefs of an insurmountable isolation (1967, p. 126).

Yet, Arnold does not disclose precisely what he means by this invincibly alienating and literally mortifying insularism—from which, instructively, are derived the words "isolation" and "island"—save to say it is some sort of aloneness. However, Arnold might be interpreted as implying that all human beings are alone simply due to their sheer entitative (ontological) separateness from one another. This individualness, in turn, is owing to their separate and separating bodies, minds, souls, and whatever else is held to radically differentiate human beings and putatively cause them that kind of affective isolation that is loneliness (vol. 1, pp. 19–20).

2. Loneliness: Its Notion

Loneliness is due to an unwanted absence of interpersonal interactions and especially ongoing relationships, the nucleus of which is meaningful intimacy. It involves a lack of personations: primarily persons and secondarily personfications (for example, pet animals) and personalizations (for example, mother- or fatherlands). It is a negative type of aloneness since it contains painful emotions, including sadness, shame, depressiveness, and pessimism in addition to stressful affects, such as guilt, anger, frustration, and desperation. This tribulation also involves feelings of self-negation, such as self-vacuity and self-worthlessness (ibid., pp. 60–65).

As to its content, intimacy involves, for instance, not only the erotic of the romantic, sexual, and genital, but entities such as affection, compassion, nurturance, and fellowship. With respect to its genuine modes of expression, intimacy can be conveyed, for example, ardently and graciously but never coldly and unbenignly (ibid, pp. 171–173). Though such inwardness primarily refers to the private realm (for instance, the confidentialities of friendship), it is also germane to the public (for instance, civil amenities, such as friendliness) (ibid., p. 70; pp. 273–274).

Whenever loneliness is characterized as an "isolation" without qualification, it is to be understood as emotional in composition instead of social or physical. These two latter types of aloneness may trigger and intensify loneliness, but they are not this affliction nor are they its necessary, let alone its sufficient, causes. Loneliness is, therefore, a negative kind of felt "oneliness," whether a person is socially or physically all alone or with others. Hence, an individual can be lonely or not lonely whether in the presence or absence of another (ibid., pp. 151–152).

When loneliness stems from the absence of particularized company, it will be titled "person-loneliness"; when from the absence of human companionship in general, "species-loneliness." These kinds of loneliness are predicable principally of individuals and secondarily of groups. Whatever be the kind of loneliness, its locus is subjective in the sense of its occurring within some individual subject, the latter being understood as possessing a mind, or consciousness.

Loneliness, which is brought about by subjective qualities such as shyness or lack of self-worth, is known as "trait," or "endogenous"; that effected by objective factors, such as poverty or lack of education, is known as "state," or "exogenous."

This said, only personal qualities are considered in and of themselves sufficient to generate loneliness. Still, objective conditions are fertile and often formidable elements in producing a situation instrumental in generating trait loneliness. For instance, abusive or neglectful parents or other caregivers are tremendous sources of transforming state into trait loneliness such as that marked by sadness and shame.

Unless otherwise stated, when allusion is made to loneliness without qualification, it means trait instead of state. Also, when loneliness is mentioned without a proviso, it is to be understood as "chronic," the sort that persists more or less intensely for at least half the days of two or more consecutive years (ibid., p. 102).

3. Loneliness: A Classification

In *Intimacy and Isolation*, I distinguish ten forms of loneliness (vol. 1, pp. 107–152; for alternate divisions, see Weiss, 1973; Sadler, 1978). The first is the erotic, or the absence of romantic, sexual, and genital intimacy.

The second form is the cultural, or the longing to be connected to the societal mainstream or at minimum its most significant representatives and symbols. Gender, racial, religious, and ethnic groups are among those especially subject to this type of emotional segregation and lack of felt belonging. So also are the mentally and sometimes the physically challenged subject to feelings of non-inclusion, exclusion, and indifference (vol. 1, pp. 89–90; Leary, 1990, p. 22).

Third is the metaphysical, or the lack of feeling meaningfully and intimately attached to other beings in the world instead of being undesirably separate and separated.

Fourth is the cosmic, or the longing for some personation—ordinarily conceived as a person, especially a divine sort—or some supremely friendly or hospitable power or force that would give ultimate meaning/intimacy to individuals, their world, and the world as a whole.

The fifth form is the epistemological, or the longing to be known, understood, and appreciated.

Sixth, (in)communicative loneliness, is the self's inability to elicit and express its interiority to others or to access and grasp theirs.

The seventh species of loneliness is the ethical, which includes the various sorts of affective segmentation experienced in the attempt to become psychologically mature and morally authentic.

Eighth is the aforementioned existential loneliness, or the emotional segregation born of the inevitable shocks and stresses of life. They are especially traceable to the unhappy isolation feared in dying and perhaps surviving in some putative miserable post-mortem existence. Existential loneliness may be reckoned the loneliness *of* life—or, even more harrowing, loneliness *as* life—

in contrast to the loneliness *in* life due to one or more of the other nine species of emotional isolation.

Ninth is intraself loneliness, or the lack of self-intimacy. It occurs when, for instance, there is a felt absence of self-intimicization via cognition such as self-understanding or of a close connection with what people believe are their real, true, or authentic selves. So defined, intraself loneliness is, to put it in rather paradoxical language, intimately related to ethical loneliness. Intraself loneliness is a secondary and derived species of unwanted isolation since intimacy and its absence thereof are primarily interpersonal phenomena.

The tenth form of loneliness is the social, or the lack of a satisfactory societal network and a larger community that can range, respectively, from a person's boy or girlfriend, family, and friends to the "fellowship" of all human beings. "Sociality" can be conceived as the radical drive of human beings to associate with one another above all in terms of reciprocal interiority. "Socialness" can be construed as the actual realization of sociality via social networks, which range from family, relatives, friends, and acquaintances to the fellowship of all living beings. "Sociability" pertains to private and especially public (civil) amenities, such as amicability and affability, and other social interactions (ibid., p. 20).

Social loneliness is the most significant kind of affective apartheid. Accordingly, it is the central concern of this study insofar as it is pivotal to (inter)personality and states of aloneness. Hence, whenever loneliness is unspecified it should be understood as social or, at minimum, inclusive of it.

All persons, be they abnormal, normal, or supranormal, are subject to that kind of loneliness known as existential since it is reckoned intrinsic to human nature. Still, not all people experience this loneliness of life as such on an explicitly conscious basis.

I contend that some *DSM* aberrated personalities, namely the schizotypals and especially the schizoids of Group I, do not experience any loneliness save possibly existential.

Other disturbed personalities, to wit the sociopaths, paranoid, narcissists, and obsessionals of Group II, may undergo some types of loneliness other than existential, but, if they do, these aberrants are subject to this affliction mainly on a nonconscious level. These pathologicals frequently have a very narrow notion of intimacy but, at any rate, one that is always entirely self-serving, all of which accounts, in considerable part, for their being psychoethically disturbed in the first place.

Some abnormals, namely Group III, are subject to all forms of loneliness, though not usually simultaneously, on an exceedingly conscious basis. Indeed, I hold that borderlines, histrionics, dependents, and avoidants may become disturbed personalities precisely because they are habitually subject to the anguish and apprehensiveness of emotional segmentation.

4. Fundamental Interpersonal Motivations

I look upon those with personality disorders as being psycho-ethically abnormal, a deficiency that proximately stems from their lack of benevolence. This goodwill is the sine qua non of all genuine connectedness and its nucleus, namely intimacy, especially love. Benevolence, the backbone of Humaneness, along with equalization, acquisition, acquisitiveness, and malevolence, can be considered the basic motivations of human beings toward one another.

The differences among these five kinds of intention are extremely complex. However, they are vital not only to understanding inwardness and its unwanted absence in loneliness but to grasping personality in its normal and anormal variations (vol. 1, pp. 173–185).

Pure benevolence signifies intending solely the good of another; mixed refers primarily the good of another and secondarily that of the self (Hazo, 1967, pp. 22–28). From a psycho-ethical perspective, habitual mixed and especially pure benevolence are arguably the customary motivations of supranormal individuals.

In motivations of equalization, the self wishes to give and get on either an equatable (quid pro quo) basis or on one that is equitable (proportional) vis-à-vis needs to which the individual is commanded by justice to fulfill. Justice itself can be motivated simply by duty or benevolence and can be construed as the customary motivations of what might be considered, respectively, as lower and higher level normal individuals.

In contrast to the self and other-centered equality motivation of justice and the mainly or purely other-centered benevolent modes of intention, I distinguish three largely or exclusively self-centered patterns. In the order of their mental-moral deviation from normality and, a fortiori, from supranormality, they are the acquistional, acquisitive, and selfishly malevolent, each of which has various species.

With respect to intentions of acquisition and its pure species, the self desires to give solely in order to get some good; in mixed acquisition, the individual gives but ultimately to get some benefit. Unlike those of equalization, motivations of acquisition do not involve any strict duty to benefit the other, at least not directly and proximately.

The acquisitional refers to willing a good intended solely for the self, but there is no deliberate intention to overlook, much less oppose, the welfare of others. Such motivations do not fall directly within the parameters of justice let alone benevolence much less love. Even though acquisitional motivations are not deliberately opposed to the good of others, they do not include it such that people who are of this disposition can fail others by omission.

Concerning intentions of acquisitiveness, the individual is either culpably ignorant of or, worse, simply ignores the legitimate needs of others to which self is bound in justice to heed. Whereas acquisitionally based behavior is at least indirectly inimical to starting and sustaining intimacy, acquisitively based is directly injurious to doing so.

As to malevolent motivations, just as benevolence's wishing (velleity) another some good is distinct from willing it (volition) and, a fortiori, from enacting it (beneficence), so also is malevolence's velleity to do something bad or evil to another distinct from its volitionality and maleficence.

Selfish individuals seek a good—which, as in the case of benevolence, can be physical, mental, or spiritual—solely for themselves. If such egocentrics also deliberately desire to contravene the good of others to get their own, they are also ill-willed (in my view, selfishness is always at least potentially malevolent). Selfish people intend to gain their goals, if possible, by not only getting without giving but simply taking what they want regardless of its cost to others. In which event, greedy individuals may resort to manipulation, mendacity, aggressiveness, aggression, and violence.

Universalized benevolence, especially when actualized via beneficence, is a kind of altruism and also a sort of philanthropy. Correspondingly, an all-embracing malevolence, especially when it becomes maleficence, is a form of anti-altruism and a type of misanthropy. Obviously, maleficent actions are devastating to relatedness (vol. 1, pp. 173–185).

5. Personality Disorders and Motivational Modalities

Group I, II, and III abnormals are, respectively, habitually non-, anti-, and insufficiently benevolent individuals. More specifically, Group I are habitually acquisitional and, thus, are at least indirectly opposed to intimate relatedness, since its indispensable condition is goodwill.

Group II are chronically malevolent and often maleficent and, accordingly, are directly inimical to the exigencies of intimate connections. Maleficent behavior can vary in gravity from being mean-spirited to being vicious and maliciously so.

Group III are habitually acquisitive and, therefore, also act in a manner directly detrimental to intimacy requirements. These pathologicals especially do so when their acquisitiveness is deliberate. Still, such opposition to the demands of shared interiority is clearly not as damaging to relatedness as Group II malevolence.

Consequently and concerning interpersonal relationships, all aberrants fail in terms of benevolence, and, thus, with respect to love since the first is the sine qua non of the second. Abnormals are also remiss with reference to justice, especially the sort motivated by goodwill. The reason is that they fail to provide what is owed others, for example, respect, empathy, and arguably benevolence if not actual beneficence. In these ways, abnormal personalities exemplify mental trait disorders, construed as both psychological and ethical deviations.

Group I abnormals are, in my estimation, the most disturbed psychologically, although ethically they can be construed as the least deviated in terms of actually committing immoral actions. Therefore, the schizoid and schizotypal will usually be termed "nonmoral" in that they fail mainly by the omission of the ethical, which, in my judgment, is predominantly social in nature. These aberrants do so if only because, as absolute loners living at the fringe or beyond of emotional, social, and often physical relatedness, they have as little to do with others as possible. Group I may also be classified as "premoral" since they seem to lack a necessary condition for morality, namely freedom, insofar as they are biologically necessitated by factors of constitution and temperament.

Group II are the second most aberrated in terms of the psychic but are first in the area of ethical abnormality. So interpreted, they can be characterized as habitually "immoral," that is in conflict with accepted morality. This aggregate's sociopath can be not only immoral but "amoral," meaning lacking awareness and sensitivity to basic ethical principles and practices, in addition to being "antimoral," meaning deliberately unethical.

Group III are the least psychologically abnormal of the ten *DSM* pathologicals. They are also the least morally abnormal if acts of omission are considered more ethically reprehensible in principle than those of omission; if not so reckoned, then Group I are morally worse than Group III. Correlatively, if acts of commission are held as being the more morally deviant, as they ordinarily are, then both Groups III and II are ethically worse than Group I. In whatever case, the immorality and above all the amorality and anti-morality of the Group II sociopath represent the gravest deviations from the ethical.

Beyond listing the three aggregates in terms of their psychological and ethical variation from normality, I have done the same with respect to each personality disorder within its grouping. For instance, the sociopath is the most deviant of Group II and the obsessional is the least.

Within an aggregate, one disorder may be psychologically or ethically more aberrant than another but each is ranked according to the ensemble of its mental and moral departures from normality, the notion of which is especially examined in chapter five. For instance, the sociopath is morally more deviant than the paranoid but is less disturbed psychologically, if indeed the second is viewed, and it often is, as being on the psychotic spectrum along with the schizoid and schizotypal. Yet, in terms of the moral and psychological combined, the antisocial is more ill than the paranoid.

Group I, in their extreme incapability and non-hostile indifference to socialness, above all intimate, may be said to be "non-connected" to others both generally and specifically.

Group II, in their highly limited capability and disdainful indifference or direct hostility toward intimate relatedness, may be deemed as being "disconnected" from others in general. Nonetheless, they may be affiliated with specific others, albeit usually relatively few in number and then only for more or less selfish motives.

Group III, while extremely desirous of intimate relatedness, are not correspondingly capable of it, largely traceable to their extreme FFM Neuroticism. This huge gap between their aspiration for and attainment of "connectedness" leaves these aberrants exceedingly lonely unlike Group II but especially Group I. As a totality, disordered personalities tend to err on the side of introversion instead of Extraversion, a penchant that accounts for their lack of relatedness. This proclivity also accounts, first, for these abnormals' self-absorption and overall egocentrism; second, their absence of a sense of belonging; and, third, their lack of social network density specifically in terms of size, number, overlapping, and centrality (the component concerning the fulfillment of social benefits and needs) (vol. 1, pp. 315–323; Derlega and Margulis, 1982, p. 157).

Recall that Group I aberrants may be thought of as being premoral or nonmoral to the extent that they lack a sine qua non of morality, namely freedom. Insofar as they are not necessitated but simply highly influenced genetically, these rather "non-hearted" aberrants may be held responsible for their actions and especially their inactions.

Negligence vis-à-vis moral duties may be also envisioned as the standard ethical shortcoming of "normals," meaning statistically average. For when it comes down to it, ordinary human beings rarely act relatively directly contrary let alone malevolently so to the perceived welfare of others, especially if these average human beings believe that they have alternatives to doing so.

Group II aberrants are immoral in the way that malevolently "hard-hearted," arrogant, envious, and selfish people are. Nevertheless, in their conceitedness, they may fancy themselves as being highly moral—even impeccably so, especially the obsessional—given their habitual self-deception.

Group III abnormals are immoral in the manner that "soft(weak)-hearted" individuals are. They may aspire to being moral, but their abiding acquisitiveness and Neuroticism keep them from being sufficiently ethical to be classified as normals. Traceable in prominent part to their low sense of self-worth, Group III often think of themselves as being immoral.

Group III borderlines may be convinced that they are thoroughly bad—even evil—individuals and incorrigibly so (p. 651). As unethical as they may be in terms of ignoring the good of others or acting deliberately contrary to it, borderlines are seldom as bad toward others as they are toward themselves. Nor are they as hostile as are Group II, especially sociopaths and paranoids, toward all others but indulgent and lenient toward themselves.

I contend that normals can be regarded as those who are inclined to justice and possibly to a goodwill that prompts them to treat each other in a fair manner. Though benevolence is not a necessary requirement of justice—since people can treat others fairly without necessarily wishing them well—it is of love and other forms of intimacy. Naturally, all these positive human inclinations are substantially sabotaged by negative societal institutions, like those of SCRAM, but are significantly stimulated and supported by positive ones.

Consequently, I do not claim that human beings innately love one another or are even inherently disposed to do so. Nevertheless, there does appear to be to some extent the necessary though perhaps not sufficient evidence to hold that people naturally tend toward a non-benevolently motivated justice or possibly even one that is benevolently induced. In any event, the reader is notified that, first, my claims with respect to personalities, abnormal or otherwise, in terms of motivational molds are ordinarily to be interpreted as generalities and not exceptionless universalities.

Second and both following and yet proceeding from the first, depending on how all these terms are notionalized, such motivational patterns are to be understood as provisionals and probabilities. They are so because discerning, defining, and dividing the intentions behind human conduct is exceedingly problematic for many reasons.

One difficulty is that finding, collecting, and appraising the necessary, not to mention sufficient, data to allow accurate judgments in these matters is enormously demanding and perhaps impossible de facto. Individuals with personality disorders are especially resistant to providing such accuracy given their lack of self-understanding, especially Group I, and, in some cases, the deception both of self and others that characterizes these aberrants, paramountly Group II.

All such aberrants are isolates of one sort another be it social, physical, or emotional, and isolation is by definition the antithesis of association. Group I schizoids and schizotypals in addition to Group III avoidants have infrequent interactions with others and even less permanent attachments.

Group II may or may not have had frequent social contacts with others, though they usually have less than more. In any case, such interactions tend to be unpleasant for all parties given that sociopaths, paranoids, narcissists, and obsessionals are exceedingly unlikable and uncaring individuals. They are so predominantly traceable to their derisiveness, antipathy, and overall selfishness.

As to Group III, only the borderline and above all the histrionic of Group III are outgoing types. However, their gregariousness is ultimately due to their being ingoing in the sense of being self-centered.

Genuine intimacy is what the self most possesses in the sense of having more or less total jurisdiction as to its bestowal and reception. Forced intimacy is involitional by definition and, hence, not shared inwardness except in name. Group I aberrants try to elude others and if necessary compel others to be distant so as circumvent closeness. Group II also tend to distance themselves from others, except those they use to fulfill their needs. Yet, with respect to those individuals they desire as intimates, Group II will try to attain connectedness even aggressively sometimes using physical aggression to do so. Group III seek intimacy with others on both a temporary and lasting basis. In order to secure attachments, they habitually resort to angry threats and actions (borderlines), seduction (histrionics), possessiveness (dependents), or they simply elude such connection if they feel they are or will be criticized (avoidants).

6. Aloners

Loneliness is distinguished from other states of aloneness, including "aloneliness," "alonism," "lonism," "lonerism," reclusion (reclusiveness), seclusiveness (seclusion), solitude, isolation, and desolation. Those who belong to such groups will be titled, respectively, lonelies, alonelies, alonists, lonists (loners), lonerists, reclusives, seclusives, solitaries, isolates, and desolates, all of whom can be called "aloners" (for a discussion of loneliness and aloneliness, see vol. 1, chap. 2).

A. Alonelies, Alonists, and Lonists (Loners)

Aloneliness relates to the fear of feeling or being alone in some negative fashion, including and especially loneliness (vol. 1, pp. 17–23).

Alonism refers to an individual who resides alone. An alonist may in fact be highly sociable and, accordingly, is not necessarily given to being a lonist, meaning the individual who prefers being and acting in lone fashion.

Lonism pertains to a person, often titled a loner, who evades others to be *by* her or himself whether, for example, at work or leisure (unlike loners, solitaries circumvent others predominantly to be *with* themselves).

Loners (lonists) can be absolute or relative types. Those of an unrestricted sort by definition seek being socially alone under any circumstance. They take little if any pleasure in social interactions, are not pained by their absence, and, accordingly, are termed social isolates (ibid., p. 23). Group I aberrants are absolute loners, and they also tend to be alonists since they have a propensity to dwell alone. However, they are not alonelies since they do not fear being alone in any sense. On the contrary, the more aloneness, the better the schizoid and schizotypal like it (ibid., pp. 23–24).

Some loners are also reclusives, meaning herein that they segregate themselves not only socially but physically from others. They may do so even if they reside in the vicinity of others or even amidst them in the same dwelling.

Relative loners prefer being socially and often physically alone unless circumstances are perceived as conducive to their being with others in a manner predominantly beneficial to the former. Total relative loners favor interaction with people as a whole and in particular and, consequently, they bear others no habitual hostility, at least none that is a priori or virtually so. Nonetheless, because they are afraid that such interactions—and especially ongoing relationships—may prove negative, total relative loners refrain from social intercourse with others, both in general and in particular. Consequently, these sorts of isolates are subject to both species and person loneliness. Among the abnormal personalities, the avoidant is the total relative loner, although this aberrant is fundamentally a lonely and, hence, is classified as a Group III pathological.

Partial relative loners endeavor to be socially separated from others in general but not from all of them in particular. Hence, these lonists are at risk of person but not species loneliness, unless they are somehow prohibited from associating with any other human being whomsoever (for example, the criminal antisocial who is kept in solitary, meaning physical and social confinement) (ibid., pp. 24–26).

Unlike absolute loners and some partial relative loners, like avoidants, who manifest little or no antagonism toward others in general, there are some relative loners who do. I call them "lonerists." They display not only contemptuous indifference but also extreme hostility vis-à-vis others as a whole. Among the pathological personalities, those of Group II are the lonerists (ibid., pp. 26–27).

B. Recluses and Secluses

A recluse (reclusive) can be characterized as anyone who voluntarily or volitionally habitually withdraws from society. Such a definition can be applied to all the states of aloneness and their members, namely aloners. However, unlike some aloners, recluses habitually disengage themselves physically and socially from others. Therefore, recluses are, for instance, necessarily alonists, though the reverse is not always the case (ibid., pp. 35–37).

A secluse (seclusive) can signify the aloner who volitionally keeps apart, ordinarily socially and physically, from some or even all others. A secluse can also pertain to that type of aloner who lives in enforced isolation such as one who is quarantined due to a contagious disease. However, the quarantined may willingly consent to this isolation since it is to their and others benefit. However, there are individuals who live in enforced isolation who are not seclusives, strictly speaking, such as prisoners in solitary (lone) confinement for whom their segregation from others is involitional (pp. 37–43).

C. Solitaries

Of all the kinds of aloneness, only solitude is intrinsically considered both subjectively and objectively constructive. Solitaries require at minimum social aloneness and often physical aloneness as well—both of which can be known as "external" solitude—in order to perform or best perform some activity, such as praying, meditating, reflecting, researching, and writing. Such efforts demand constant concentration and other qualities of mental aloneness, known as "internal" solitude (ibid., pp. 28–29, 32–33). These endeavors also necessitate a considerable emotional detachment from other desired human beings, both those in general and in particular. In such instances, solitaries perpetually risk being at the decidedly not so tender mercies of, respectively, species and person loneliness.

Solitaries can be total or partial in addition to permanent and temporary (ibid., pp. 28–32). However, the most important distinction is between their being primary or secondary. What chiefly characterizes this kind of aloner is creativity, which can be defined as the artful production of something new or in a new fashion. In primary solitude, the product is something internal, especially a relatively new self. Of course, no self is absolutely new as if it were created *ex nihilo*, meaning, so to speak, "from scratch." In secondary solitude, the product is something external, like a novel.

Primary solitaries have as their governing goal the creation of self in terms of psychological but especially ethical improvement. Characterological creativity is arguably the most important kind of inventiveness since it entails ameliorating the person qua person, the most necessary, desirable, and demanding of all tasks. Producing a more virtuous subject is more humanly significant than devising a bestselling book, movie, song, or other object, all of which represents inventions of secondary solitude.

This said, primary solitude is not the principal vehicle for achieving personality—insofar as it is not a given—since this process, for example, demands communing with actual, meaning extramental, persons instead of purely mental types (for instance, fictional characters in a novel). This external communication involves an array of moral qualities, such as the all-around caring for others (ibid., pp. 30, 34).

All normal human beings can, to some extent, harmonize the needs for sociality and solitude or, more precisely, this kind of constructive aloneness that necessarily occurs within an ever expanding togetherness, namely from the dyadic to the largest of the communal. Many, if not most, normal adults prefer being in the presence or at least the proximity of others but simultaneously having external solitude accessible, provided a return to socialness is readily available as well. Still, any such positive aloneness occurs within the confines and context of togetherness.

Much of current didactic literature holds that the positive state of solitude is conducive to positive states of being with others (Tillich, 1980, pp. 551–553). Thus, solitude (primary), to wit being alone with one's self in a constructive psycho-ethical fashion, disposes—but does not guarantee—the individual to be with others in a positive manner. Hence, the ability to achieve company when and within one's self helps the individual do so with others (the reverse is also true though arguably less so).

To illustrate this reciprocity between being alone with one's self and being together with others, the intimacy with self that is needed in solitude necessitates a similar sort of openness, attentive listening, and respectful silence required for intimacy with others. Carin Rubenstein and Phillip Shaver state:

> Solitude is fully rewarding only for someone who has attained intimacy—with a close friend or lover, an imaginary companion or audience, or with nature itself. . . .To be healing [instead of] frightening, solitude requires the same open, trusting willingness to listen, which we've associated with intimacy. This is one reason why solitude and intimacy are so closely linked. (1982, p. 170)

Therefore, people who relish being together can use their shared intimacy to nourish their solitude that entails a kind of self-intimacy, especially if it is a question of primary solitude. Correspondingly, substantive trait loneliness—or those lonely "in and out of season"—insofar as it is a negative way of being alone with self, disposes an individual to be with others in undesirable fashion and vice versa.

Resultingly, those who cannot be intimate with themselves will have a harder time being so with others and vice versa. Alternatively, those who are lonely solely due to objective circumstances, to wit those suffering from state loneliness, will not as a rule continue to be lonely within relationships. At least they will not if they have adequate sources of intimacy, an inwardness that is primarily emotional and secondarily cognitive in nature.

Emotional isolates are often caught in a vicious circle since they seek the presence of others in part because of their habitual dissatisfaction with themselves. Thus, constantly expressed self-displeasure drives away both actual and potential intimates, all of which increases the lonelies' self-discontent. Self-dislike and all the more so self-hatred and other kinds of self-disgust are frequent factors in the lonely person's lack of worth and worthiness that, in turn, augment self-dissatisfaction.

D. Solitude and Pathological Personalities

Individuals with highly negative psycho-ethical personalities make extremely poor candidates for primary solitude. One pivotal reason for this inability is that the solitary life requires, among other things, a developmental kind of independence. However, all pathological personalities are either negatively independent or negatively dependent types of individuals.

Furthermore, primary solitude demands FFM Openness to Experience, especially as to its facets of ideas and values. In addition, it necessitates FFM Humaneness, such as its traits of altruism and modesty (humility), with respect to which pathological personalities are woefully remiss (Costa and Widiger, 2002, p. 461). These aberrants are, in short, too ego-centered to be involved in the kind of ego-transcendence needed to become primary solitaries. Moreover, both internal (subjective, or mental) and external (objective, or physical) solitude present the danger of riveting the attention of the pathological personality even more on itself.

The self-absorption of the individual with a personality disorder, which reaches its conscious culmination in the narcissistic aberrant, therefore, is not to be confused with the solitaries' self-reflexion and self-reflection. They utilize such self-scrutiny to understand themselves in objective manner, meaning as others perceive them. Nonetheless, the solitaries' self-focus is ultimately used as a means to connect with others. They go into themselves to get their selves out to others so as to benefit them. Disordered personalities, like narcissists, go out to others to get them into consciousness for egocentric reasons.

i. Solitude and Group I Pathologicals

It has already been set forth that schizoids and schizotypals are absolute loners, but by no stretch of the imagination are these Group I aberrants solitaries. Concerning schizoids specifically, for one thing, they usually simply lack the desire and cognitive aptitude to be, for example, a meditative solitary, given that these aberrants are deficient in terms of comprehension, clarity, and cohesiveness of thought.

Though they are introverted, schizoids are not introspective, as is the case with primary and often secondary solitaries. Moreover, schizoids are not only oblivious to the world inside but outside themselves. This behavior differentiates these pathological loners from solitaries who have not only a propensity for self-reflexion and introspection in general but for "extrospection," meaning reflectiveness upon the external world.

While they are almost always alone at home or at work, at least whenever they can be, absolute social isolates such as schizoids are seldom if ever at home in their own solitary company. The reason is that these loners do not befriend themselves just as they do not others. Unlike solitaries, schizoids are *alone by* themselves but not alone together *with* themselves. They are companionless with respect to both themselves and others (hence, they are not "alone together with others" in any intimate sense). Contrastingly, solitaries are companions to themselves and potentially to others. In any case, social isolation neither much pleases nor pains schizoids, though they consider it far more desirable than being with others, especially on an intimate basis.

Therefore, schizoids use social and often physical isolation to escape from others but for all that they do not wish to encounter themselves in solitude (internal). These pathological lonists are so impoverished that there is preciously little interiority within them to meet and share with others or to meditate upon by themselves.

All this notwithstanding, the *DSM* states that schizoids "*may* do well when they work under conditions of social isolation" (emphasis added, p. 639). Still, the evidence appears to indicate that doing well does not include solitary inventive or creative work of any sort let alone any directed toward creation of self in a mental/moral manner. In their aloneness, schizoids may, according to the *DSM*, engage "in mechanical or abstract tasks, such as computer or mathematical games" (p. 639). Such non-existential activities well suit these most odd and "out of it" android-like individuals, but these functions are irrelevant and even antithetical to solitary originality and ingenuity.

Pierre Teilhard de Chardin observes that some individuals shut themselves off from others such that they are rendered "impenetrable to one another and incapable of exteriorizing themselves" (1965, p. 163). This description admirably fits the inscrutable and incommunicative schizoids. Still, it behooves re-stressing that these pathologicals are cut off not only from others but themselves. They have at most a meager interest in their own interiority, one which, in any event, is cognitively, emotionally, and conatively, at least in terms of volition, meaning free choice, minuscule.

All the above suggests that schizoids are trying to hide from others and from themselves, though they have preciously little self to conceal. In contrast, solitaries (primary) do not attempt to hide from self but to find it. Nor do solitaries strive to seclude themselves from others save in the case of their needing external solitude to realize their projects, be they inwardly or outwardly directed.

Schizoids evince such an extreme non-interest and an emotional distance regarding their own company and that of others that, compounded with their behavioral quirks, they are like automatons. Or, they can be construed as zombie-like individuals, dead to both the interior and exterior worlds. To say the least, this schizoid dividedness precludes cognitive intimacy with self and emotional intimacy with others. The first kind of inwardness is directly essential to solitaries (primary) and the second at least indirectly.

As for schizotypals, they are so chaotic, and in idiosyncratic fashion, in their thought structures—if they can be called such, given their mumbo-jumbo contents—that, according to Theodore Millon, these individuals are "cognitively autistic." Accordingly, he characterizes the schizotypal mind-set as being replete with "metaphorical" irrelevancies, or asides," in addition to being "ruminative" and dispersed in daydreams and in "a blurring of fantasy and reality" (1986, p. 708). Individuals with such a fragmented, capriciously fanciful mentality can never be a solitary, though they can be and are, along with the schizoid, consummate loners.

Creativity can be approached from several perspectives, one of which is through the Apollonian and Dionysian archetypes of which there are higher and lower forms. The higher kind of Apollonian, for example, is dispassionate and restrained, whereas the lower is impassive and rigid. The higher Dionysian is passionate and spontaneous; the lower, intemperate and impetuous. The supranormal person synergizes the higher Apollonian and Dionysian (for expanded discussion, see vol. 1, pp. 86–88). The abnormal person is either lower Apollonian, like the schizoid, or lower Dionysian, like the schizotypal, issues taken up anew in Chapter Seven.

The solitary may require a Dionysian kind of imaginativeness but it must be Apollonian disciplined if it is to be productively creative, especially on a protracted basis, none of which is in the reach of the wildly meandering mentality of the schizotypal. Unlike the schizoid, the schizotypal does have an active though utterly fragmented and fanciful imagination, one that is immersed, according to the *DSM*, in, for example, "magical thinking" and ideation of a paranoid nature (p. 645). Contrariwise, solitaries engage in systematic and critical thought, in which case, they represent instances of the higher-level Apollonian archetype.

In being absolute social isolates, both the schizoid and schizotypal are unrelated to others as they are to themselves. The schizotypal is more secretive and suspicious than the schizoid and in this respect is more dis-related. The schizoid is a kind of paralytic loner; the schizotypal, a frenetic one. Neither is autonomous in a mature manner, all of which precludes becoming a solitary, above all a primary sort.

ii. Solitude and Group II Pathologicals

Group II pathological personalities evince not only profound anti-intimacy with others but with themselves and as such are anti-solitary (primary) sorts of individuals. Antisocials, paranoids, narcissists, and obsessionals do not relish being alone in their own company albeit they enjoy that of others even less. No individuals who have so much contempt for and animosity toward their fellow human beings can be content not to mention elated with and within themselves. Such individuals are inundated by the agitation inimical to the internal repose required for primary and often secondary solitude as well.

Group II score low in gregariousness and in warmth but these traits do not mean they like being alone with themselves. They may not be unhappy in their own company—given that their personality traits are not dystonic, meaning they do not cause them much if any displeasure. Still, these aberrants cannot be said to truly happy when they are all by themselves (and even less are they so when with others). Of course, not being unhappy is hardly the same as being happy.

The extreme egotism of Group II individuals is antithetical to the kind of self-reflexion, which characterizes primary solitaries. Their self-focus is undertaken precisely to liberate their selves from any egocentrism, while the aloneness of Group II pathologicals is used to increase their self-absorption.

Group II can be exceedingly pleased with themselves in a smug, vain, or arrogant manner. Again, they are hardly happy individuals—no one with a disturbed personality is—since they experience neither love nor its effects, such as serenity and joy. These emotions are routinely experienced by solitaries (primary) but foreign to all pathological personalities, especially sociopaths and their fellow Group II deviate personalities.

Solitaries (primary) are socially detached by choice, though they long to be with other persons—including, for the theistic solitary, God—both in general and in particular. Consequently, anyone who does not long for—meaning yearn for, miss, or mourn others—cannot be a primary solitary. Group II aberrants, as lonerists, are also socially detached by choice from others in general. However, they do not as a rule consciously long to be with others as a whole due to their derision and animus vis-à-vis their fellow human beings.

Despite being pathologically self-absorbed individuals, Group II's minds, whether these aberrants are physically with others or not, are generally fixated on them. This preoccupation is due to the desire to use their fellow human beings in some opportunistic fashion such as by manipulation and domination (sociopaths, narcissists, and obsessionals) or to defend themselves against these supposed enemies (paranoids).

Such self-serving practices preclude Group II being primary solitaries but not necessarily secondary sorts. Still, if an individual is constantly concerned in a negative manner about others, as is the custom of Group II abnormals, doing so hampers writing an article, composing a song, or engaging in other secondary types of solitude.

Hence, whether alone or with others, the consciousness of individuals with Group II disturbances is trained on duping and exploiting others (the antisocial), maliciously counteracting their alleged ill will (the paranoid), cajoling them into glorifying them (the narcissist), or controlling others to fit their own preconceived views of abstract perfection (the obsessional). These psycho-ethical defects are, to say the least, inimical to being alone in solitude as they are to being with others in socialness and sociability.

In these respects, paranoids deserve special comment. While they are consummate lonerists and mental/moral isolates like the other Group II individuals, their singularly mistrusting makeup is, like no other aberrant, forever malevolently honed in on others' suspected malevolence. This mania is due to paranoids' arrogant conviction that they are the core of others' consciousness, especially that of their enemies who are virtually everyone.

Consequently, paranoids are forever scanning the social scene for anyone who might discredit and in general do disservice to them. It is the paranoids' own embittered malignity that endangers not only others but themselves insofar as people might take action against these psycho-ethical deviants for their condescending and callous treatment of them. Again, no one who is so litigious, rivalistic, and belligerent, like the paranoid, can ever have the inner peace and outer concord that the solitary needs to function at all much less well.

Paranoids, then, may be inner-focused, such as internal solitaries, but they are never emotionally detached from others, which solitude (primary) necessitates. Paranoids' venomous and vengeful cauldron of hostile feelings toward their fellow human beings precludes such positive isolation. Still, paranoids' FFM "cognitive" competence may allow them to be secondary solitaries (see Costa and Widiger, 1994, p. 329; 2002, p. 461).

Nonetheless, paranoids often imprint their animosity and aggressiveness on whatever they undertake, for instance, their speech and writing. These traits usually limit paranoids to being third-rate, if that, secondary solitaries. These same qualities are even worse in terms of their moral character since they constrict paranoids to being fifth-rate human beings and, hence, individuals unfit for primary solitude.

In any event, whatever inward direction paranoids' mind-set takes, it emerges from their insufferable and usually insuperable monomania. In as much as all four Group II aberrants tend to megalomania, they are constantly seeking exclusive attention to themselves. Though paranoids resent being the alleged abiding object of others' consciousness, they relish it even more. They do so since they imagine that such concern attests to their prominence when in reality it testifies to others' repugnance for these odious personalities.

The truth is that people are likely to avoid having any thoughts about paranoids whatsoever, much less having anything to do with them. They eschew these pathological personalities given their gross in Humaneness, as evidenced in the paranoids' extreme jealousy, enviousness, arrogance, cantankerousness, hard-heartedness, cynicism, and, in general, their omnipresent obnoxiousness (pp. 634–638; see also Costa and Widiger, 1994, p. 329).

Indeed, paranoids might well fear that if others and their perceived ill-will toward them did not exist, they might themselves cease to be. Since paranoids can hardly avoid not realizing at some level that they are extremely unliked and unloved individuals, they may conclude that such intense feelings toward them proves they must exist. As a result, paranoids may avoid being alone lest they be deprived of the one thing that assures their reality: the presence of others' negativity toward them. It also gives paranoids a sense of importance since being the object of others' loathing must be due to their superiority.

Not even narcissists are persistently pleased with themselves and their own company; they frequently vacillate between revering and reviling themselves. This self-repudiation is generally a result of their lack of respect and esteem from others, that, according to the *DSM*, leaves these repugnantly pretentious individuals feeling "humiliated" and "degraded." Indeed, narcissists ordinarily form relationships, including those of a friendship and erotic nature, to "enhance" their self-worth. If it is not forthcoming, they react, as the *DSM* states, "with disdain, rage, and defiant counterattack," qualities hardly conducive to the equanimity needed for solitude or socialness (p. 659). These traits are typical of the other angrily and bitterly hostile Group II pathologicals as well, though such attributes are often suppressed or otherwise denied in the case of compulsives (obsessionals).

Lonerists, such as those of Group II, in not being happy in the company of others, are not so in their own company either, in that satisfactory and unsatisfactory relationships with others and self as a rule run parallel with one another. Given the disturbed personality's surfeit of negative psycho-ethical traits, normals do not like associating not to mention bonding with any such self-absorbed individuals.

Though Group II aberrants do not enjoy being with themselves, they even less like being with other human beings save to use them in one way or another. However, least of all do they like the company of those most like themselves, such as paranoids with other paranoids or other Group II individuals as a whole. None of the ten pathologicals is gregarious, save the Group III histrionic and borderline. In fact, as a totality, abnormal personalities are non-gregarious or anti-gregarious but being so does not make them prefer being alone with themselves in solitude.

Still, negatively independent individuals, such as paranoids, may seek out negatively dependent types, since they are more easily amenable to their self-serving objectives than are other independent people. Individuals can be positively or negatively independent, in the sense of autonomous, on the one hand, or positively or negatively dependent, in the sense of homonomous on the other. Similar to Group I, Group II exhibit a negative sort of independence that culminates in isolation from others but, dissimilar to that of the first, the second is based on dislike and disgust for people in general, all of which makes them consummate lonerists.

Individuals with Group II anomalies, if they do spend time alone, it is in the kinds of privacy and seclusion that are eventually harmful to others. To paraphrase Denis Diderot, it is mainly if not solely those who are negatively alone in some fashion or other who are or become evil. If this judgment applies to anyone, it does to Group II and above all to the most inhumane of them, the sociopaths followed by the paranoids. In their kind of perverse aloneness—one that reflects a negative type of seclusion—these two types of deviants, especially the sociopaths, are constantly pre-occupied about how they can be injurious even ruinous to others. Correlatively, their attention, especially the paranoids, is more or less affixed to ways to defend themselves against allegedly being maltreated by others and then to revengefully retaliate.

Hence, both antisocials and paranoids are always in the attack mode, though the second is especially convinced that known and unknown others are assailing them. Their assumed assaults are almost always the paranoids' projections upon others of these pathologicals' own malevolent mistrustfulness. Again, given their inHumaneness, others may, in fact, respond to this aberrant's animosity with their own animus, all of which reinforces the paranoid's suspiciousness and vengefulness.

In their ill-will, then, antisocials and paranoids are consumed with thoughts of causing harm to others. The paranoids translate their spite into malicious words and sometimes into aggressive deeds, while the sociopaths are given to inveterate malice often in the form of violent aggression. Such behavior hardly bespeaks the conduct of solitaries (primary) who employ the fruits of their mental aloneness to deepen benevolent and peaceful bonds with others.

One of the goals of solitude is to uncover truth about reality and to become truthful within the self and between self and others. Antisocials, however, are the enemies of truth(fulness), for they not only persistently lie but have become lies, though some of them are said to be literally "born liars." Normals become anxious when lying because of the cleft between what they say and know to be (un)true. The abnormals who are dyssocials, especially sociopaths, lack such apprehensiveness because they have become the very lies they tell or otherwise manifest. Accordingly, their very *being* is a lie and, as such, they *are* ontological lies. In this fashion, they may pass lie detector tests since their falseness has become their "truth(fulness)."

All this said, Group II aberrants, in that they are customarily free from experiencing species loneliness, at least on a conscious basis, may be able to achieve considerable success in terms of the creativity concerning secondary solitude. For example, a person with a paranoid or narcissistic personality disorder can write a seminal treatise on metaphysics, mathematics, or music without having to fear undergoing the pain of being emotionally or otherwise isolated from other human beings in general. For example, the eminent opera composer Richard Wagner, while he may not have had a full-blown narcissistic personality *disorder*, was arguably a highly narcissistic personality *type*.

iii. Solitude and Group III Pathologicals

Group III pathologicals err by excessive dependence on others and, as a result, solitude is largely inaccessible to them since, for all its potential for serenity, this kind of separation is a highly active and independent state. Therefore, their inability to stand alone when being by themselves renders the borderline, histrionic, dependent, and avoidant poorly equipped to become and above all remain (primary) solitaries.

Individuals with a dependent personality disorder are classic illustrations of those who are absolutely terrified of aloneness in any form. As their name implies, so much do dependents fear being on their own that they latch on to others, irrespective of the price they might have to pay for doing so, including their loss of inventive psycho-ethical originality, identity, and dignity.

Though dependents tolerate abuse and might sometimes even masochistically seek it as a sign of being "loved," they are even more afraid of neglect and the absence of nurturing that it portends. As such, these disturbed individuals are utterly incapable of being primary solitaries, since they find or forge no home within themselves. Consequently, dependents are terrified of noninclusion and exclusion, especially via abandonment, with which solitude, both internal and external, would forever threaten these most negatively homonomous individuals.

This said, dependents are the quintessential conformists who indiscriminately barnacle themselves on others, owing to their apprehensiveness of being alone physically, socially, and above all emotionally. Accordingly, they are easy prey for the proverbial wolf in sheep's clothing, such as the slick sociopath, including the kind of impostor who passes himself off as saint-like (for instance, charlatans such as Jim Jones, Jim Bakker, Jimmy Swaggart). Thomas Browne declares, "he who must needs have company"—that is one who cannot be alone and at home with self, as is paradigmatically true of dependent types of personality—"must needs have sometimes bad company" (such as the sociopath and narcissist) (1970, p. 95n3).

Dependent types never become themselves but only what others desire them to be. Such submissiveness reflects a constant attachment to others that is inimical to the diversified detachment necessary for solitude. On the other hand, overreaction to the fear of negative homonomy, or hyper-dependence, characterizes the negative autonomy, or hyper-independence, of Group II individuals.

Existential aloneliness is partially due to the ontological fact that all human beings are ultimately alone in that they are by necessity separate, and as such, vulnerable entities. Consequently, all persons must be reliant upon others for their safety, security, and stability. Not fulfilling these basic needs drives the dependent to a fright of pathological proportions in the form of total terror at the prospect of being alone or left alone in any manner whatsoever, including external and internal solitude. In these respects, dependent types, which include all Group III abnormals, are just the opposite of Group I who are afraid that they will not be alone and remain so.

According to Russian personalist philosopher Nikolai Berdyaev, most individuals try to immunize themselves against loneliness by partaking of a negative gregariousness which, he says, is "the primitive collective and its generic mode of life." He insists that only when human beings face up to the agonizing aloneness of emotional isolation, a torment that besets people in the depths of their hearts, can they begin to become aware of their "originality, singularity, and uniqueness." In Berdyaev's view, they are the defining dimensions of the creative person, a resourcefulness, which especially flourishes in solitude (1938, pp. 91–92).

The loneliness experienced by dependent personalities drives them toward others and away from being alone in solitude, a condition that itself is a main means of overcoming the fear of emotional isolation. In their ethical loneliness and existential aloneliness, the excessively dependent type of persons may opt to live inauthentically in what has been termed the pseudo-existence of "the crowd" (Søren Kierkegaard), "the herd" (Friedrich Nietzsche), the anonymous "they" (Martin Heidegger), "the mass man" (José Ortega y Gasset), and similar depictions.

These kinds of parasitism and negative symbiosis are manifestly opposed to solitude. In allowing themselves, for example, to be swept up by a group such as a crowd, dependents lose any sense of propriety and responsibility. In which event, they do things they would otherwise be too ashamed or afraid of doing when all by themselves.

This kind of cowardly dependence can lead to the occurrence of what Edgar Allan Poe portrays in the *Man of the Crowd* (1978). This person is unable to enjoy being alone but is thrilled to be with others in a situation of bedlam and pandemonium wherein violence and criminality are always at the verge of erupting. Poe essays that the person who "refuses to be alone" can become a "genius of deep crime" (ibid., p. 515). In this vein, he cites Jean de la Bruyère's proclamation, "the great evil [is] the inability to be alone" (ibid.).

Thus, a thoroughly (com)pliant personality, epitomized by the dependent aberrant, a type of lower Apollonian, can readily become a willing participant in the activities of mobs and gangs as well as members of lawless movements. All such riotous individuals are lower Dionysian types patently antithetical to the mental/moral makeup of solitaries and their aspirations. Hence, the lower Apollonian dependent personality can at least momentarily identify with and participate in lower Dionysian activities that the dependent often struggles to repress.

All Group III aberrants, not only the dependents, have difficulty in being by themselves—especially positively so. The borderline pathological is even more afraid of being excluded and in particular of being jettisoned than is the dependent aberrant; but the first less fears not being included than does the second. Lorna Smith Benjamin states that borderlines have such a craving "for protective nurturance" that they need to be in "constant physical proximity to the rescuer (lover or caregiver)" (1996, p. 122). Their insatiability for a defense against aloneness clearly rules out both external and likely internal solitude for borderlines. Then, too, in their habitual fits of abusiveness, they often cause their own exclusion and non-inclusion by and of others. This behavior is largely foreign to dependents who, in their pseudo-altruism, may include all and exclude none due to their spinelessness.

As for histrionics, no one so completely riveted on being center stage all the time can be a solitary. These paradigmatic social and erotic pathological butterflies would find solitary retirement from others harmful to their quest of being the axis of others' attention. Histrionics are uneasy and often horrified at the prospect of any type of situation wherein they are out of the limelight such that being alone is like being dead for this most extroverted of the diseased personalities.

Concerning avoidants, they may, on the surface, appear to seek aloneness given that they are loners. However, they are social isolates only in a relative sense because avoidants thoroughly dislike being all by themselves. Like other Group III aberrants, they tend to "fantasize about idealized relationships with others" (p. 663). Nevertheless, avoidants prefer being alone in comparison to a situation in which they are shamed by others whom these pathologically anxious individuals feel are always ready and willing to reject and otherwise embarrassingly exclude them. Avoidants fear aloneness in general but not as much as they do being with those who do not uncritically accept and approve them. These aberrants' withdrawal, therefore, is a defensive device to elude or escape reproof and outright repudiation.

Avoidants have a desperate desire to be loved by others, and if they feel safe with them, they will relinquish their self-enforced social and often physical isolation. Contrariwise, (primary) solitaries feel secure within themselves and generally do so with others whose company they value. Their isolation is volitional, usually tranquil, and by definition inwardly productive. Avoidants' isolation is involitional, agitated, and un- if not counterproductive. However, their withdrawal may be voluntary to the extent that these individuals are genetically (pre)disposed to being loners. This disengagement may contribute to the fact that some avoidants, such as author Franz Kafka, can excel in secondary solitude.

Any number of creative individuals such as Kierkegaard have been quasi pathologically shy in small groups and socially anxious in large. These traits of the avoidant ought not to be confused with being reserved understood as the kind of privacy wherein the individual endeavors to govern the revelation of personal data. Nietzsche, for instance, was highly reserved in the sense of being private, but he was neither shy nor socially anxious. Contrary to a common view of him, he was a very sociable (and kind) person when his multiple illnesses and devotion to his solitary pursuits prevented him the opportunity for social contacts.

Both Nietzsche and Kierkegaard admitted to being profoundly and persistently lonely. But each was a monumental solitary, both primary and secondary, in part due to their ability to use the suffering of their extreme emotional isolation to their advantage as persons and as philosophers.

Group III are chronically lonely people and prone to an abysmally low sense of self-worth. This lack of self-esteem, especially self-respect, tends to make these aberrants reluctant to seek the very social contacts they need to overcome or at least manage their loneliness (the avoidant). Or, it makes them desperately clutch those connections they have (the dependent and avoidant).

Histrionics' self-abasement may be masqueraded by an outward insouciance, bravado, and flair for the theatrical, as the etymology of their name indicates. Histrionics cling to others but only momentarily for they then pursue other potential admirers.

For their part, the borderlines' self-deprecation makes them successively cleave to others, condemn them, re-fasten on them, and then, repeat the self-defeating cycle over and over again.

Those who have such poor self-image, like Group III, are not fond of their own company. Since they are not at home with themselves, they make supremely unsatisfactory candidates for (primary) solitude. If they could be more autonomous and alone in a positive manner, Group III would be less irrational in their neurotic demands regarding being intimately with others.

In general, Group III abnormals are too wrapped up in themselves, albeit less so than Group II, and too emotionally defenseless and vulnerable to be (primary) solitaries. Group III are, therefore, overly caught up in their own emotional instability, insecurity, and other aspects of neuroticism to be companions to themselves and, therefore, to others.

Some FFM neurotic traits, for instance, vulnerability and hypersensitivity, are highly amenable to being rendered positive, including furthering creativity. As such, potentially constructive attributes may contribute to the development of solitude, especially but not only secondary solitude. Nevertheless, if people are, for instance, too self-conscious and thin-skinned, they will lack the concentration and dedication to be a (primary) solitary or at least these negative qualities will greatly prevent them from reaching their creative and self-creative potentials.

Fundamentally, not only the dependent but the borderline, histrionic, and avoidant are all negatively homonomous, or dependent, all of which is another reason for putting them into the same aggregate. Borderlines oscillate between pseudo-autonomy and pseudo-homonomy, but at bottom, they are excessively dependent types of person. Histrionics are imprisoned by others due to the first craving the attention of the second. Avoidants are seemingly independent but not by desire, for they long to be able to count wholly on others. However, their anxiety regarding being expelled from a relationship keeps them from forming one.

Hence, all ten aberrants err by excessive detachment and autonomy (independence), excessive attachment and homonomy (dependence), or both, as in the case of the borderline; although this aberrant is at base pathologically dependent. In essence, therefore, all the disturbed personalities are failures at both (primary) solitude, a type of positive autonomy, and sociality, a type of positive homonomy. Groups I and II miscarry more with respect to being together with others than Group III, while the latter misfire more regarding being alone than the other two aggregates of aberrants.

In sum, no individual with a personality disorder is a promising prospect for the kind of mental and often physical detachment exacted by primary solitude, especially permanent and total types. However, save for the schizoid aberrant and ordinarily the schizotypal as well, the pathological personality may be capable of the secondary sort of solitude. Famed American author Thomas Wolfe is often held to have displayed many borderline and even schizotypal features (Rosenhan and Seligmann, 1989, pp. 512–513). Notably, Wolfe excelled—in great part due to his own first-hand experience of them—in themes about loneliness, solitude, and other states of aloneness, such as homelessness and homesickness that, along with alienation and ennui, will be featured in a future work.

Anyone with a disordered personality is also extremely subject, at least on a subconscious level, to the various negative states of aloneness. They include the fear or dread of these conditions, to wit, aloneliness, with the exception of the absolute loners, the Group I deviants.

As stated, I view personality aberrations as being principally departures and failures in interpersonal relatedness, above all in terms of ongoing relationships in contrast to periodic interactions. Still, as disturbed individuals' psycho-ethical condition improves with age, as sometimes happens, especially to those with a Group III aberration, so also does the possibility for their being on their own in positive fashion, including solitude, both internal and external. So also and concomitantly does the possibility for their being constructively with others.

E. Isolates

I have endeavored to demarcate lonelies, alonelies, alonists, loners (lonists, social isolates), and solitaries in abbreviated and archetypal fashion. In actuality, human beings are blends of these kinds of aloneness insofar as they are not antithetical to one another as are, for instance, lonerists and primary solitaries. All the above sorts of aloneness pertain to the phenomenon of isolation, which now merits further inspection.

Throughout this volume, I have alluded to emotional, social, and physical isolation. The emotional type, insofar as it refers to loneliness, is always reckoned to be negative, since no one seeks to be in the clutches of this most agonizing and stressful aloneness in and for itself (vol. 1, pp. 43–48).

i. Social Isolation

Social isolation is generally understood as a withdrawal from social interaction. So conceived, this disengagement, whether voluntary or volitional, is usually deemed positive by absolute loners, some relative loners (for example, lonerists), and recluses, the last mentioned being those who seek physical isolation on a more or less permanent basis. Contrarily, social isolation is necessarily held to be negative by lonelies and alonelies in as much as this distancing prevents, respectively, emotional connectedness and inhibits feelings of positive aloneness.

Internal and external solitaries may regard social withdrawal as a sine qua non for their goals, though they do not look upon this separation as something necessarily free from the negative. The reason is that loneliness due to the absence of their fellow human beings almost invariably eventually looms on the horizon for the authentic solitary. I say human beings because, for instance, religious solitaries may maintain that their communion with a nonhuman being especially of a god-like sort precludes their being lonely or as lonely as they would be without such "divine presence."

On the other hand, absence of the divine is felt as the worst of all loneliness according to theists in general. For theistic mystical solitaries, the habitual absence of God constitutes "the dark night of the soul" with its cognitive obscurity and emotional aridity. Loneliness itself is dark in that it is a lack of light both in the form of an absence of the meaningfulness of enlightenment and in the form of an absence of heat and warmth. Loneliness is also a lack of light in the form of lightness in that it tends to be darksome or heavy-hearted, or depressive. In short, this ordeal involves a dismal absence of meaning/intimacy.

ii. Physical Isolation

With reference to physical isolation, it is usually viewed as negative by lonelies insofar as it prohibits their being socially with desired others. Spatial isolation is deemed positive by absolute loners, like schizoids, since it allows them to be socially separated from all others. Objective isolation is also looked upon as constructive by some relative loners, like lonerists, such as paranoids and narcissists, since it rules out their being with others in general. Yet, these kinds of lonists may also look upon physical isolation as negative since it impedes their being with those few individuals with whom they wish to interact.

Physical isolation by definition is viewed positively by total, or absolute, recluses. It is also perceived as positive by relative recluses, such as external and internal solitaries insofar objective aloneness furthers mental aloneness. Those physical isolates known as "nature solitaries" seek objective remoteness from others in and for itself. They do so instead of seeking it as a means to attain social segregation, as is the case with external solitaries, or to increase mental isolation, as is the case with internal solitaries. For absolute recluses, the greater the physical segregation, the better (ibid., p. 35).

As for seclusion, recall that it can imply willingly keeping apart, usually both socially and physically, from some or even all others, as when the bereaved seek being alone save perhaps from select others. Seclusion can also mean being unwillingly kept apart from others, as when people with a contagious illness are compelled to being quarantined (ibid., pp. 37–43).

As a verb, "to isolate" can mean to maximally exclude such as divorcement and disconnectedness in general. These words ordinarily suggest negative sorts of aloneness, if only because they usually imply both involuntary and involitional kinds of severance. However, involitionality does not necessarily insinuate the negative. Being quarantined to prevent the spread of a contagious illness is unchosen in the sense that the subjects experiencing this segregation most probably wish that their situation were otherwise. However, relative to their predicament, being quarantined is chosen in the sense of being condoned as a lesser evil to self or others.

Those with mental trait illnesses, such as individuals with a personality disturbance, cannot, as a rule, be isolated in the sense of being quarantined as such. These aberrants cannot be confined in this fashion if only because, according to various surveys and studies, for instance, the *DSM*, they number anywhere from 10 to 20 percent of the general population. As well, people with personality disturbances are not usually regarded as being mentally ill to the extent that they must be involitionally socially and physically segregated from society, except for the dangerous criminality of Group II sociopaths.

Isolation can also signify a kind of moral divorcement, to wit an exclusion or non-inclusion from normality due to various degrees or levels of egocentricity, the basis and barometer of the unethical. Abnormal personalities can be envisaged as isolates who vary in their lack of ethical probity and integrity according to their quotient or grade of self-centeredness. As we recall, listed in terms of their habitual motivational pattern from the least to the most unethical are the acquisitional Group I aberrants, the acquisitive Group III, and the malevolent Group II.

F. Desolates

That form of isolation known as desolation is commonly construed as being a more or less withering sadness due to being profoundly emotionally shut out via non-inclusion or shut off via exclusion from actual or potential intimates. So understood, desolation is predicable of significant types of loneliness (and aloneliness), especially the devastating type.

Any of the ten forms of loneliness above can be subjectively considered the most desolating since its sufferers typically feel that the sort they are presently experiencing is incomparably painful. Everything considered, social loneliness is the most desolate if only because it is the most fundamental kind and the one implicit in all the other nine species.

"Desolation," which stems from the Latin for abandonment more proximately and aloneness more remotely, is employed, therefore, to signify being woefully forsaken and otherwise maximally excluded (ibid., p. 49). These lonely feelings of rejection and desertion are especially predicable of Group III. As will be detailed in the next chapter, desolating loneliness is not restricted to mental trait disorders such as those of pathological personalities but is prevalent among mental state disturbances such as schizophrenia.

7. States of Aloneness and Personality Disorders: Amplification and Summation

I will now recapitulate and expand on how my three personality aberrant aggregates pertain to the kinds of aloneness, especially a lack of belonging. I re-stress that, unless otherwise stated, my interpretation of these pathologicals is almost entirely based on their *DSM* essential and associate diagnostic features, mainly from the perspective of the five FFM supertraits and their thirty traits.

As absolute *loners*, Group I do not suffer either from the loneliness of exclusion or non-inclusion. They, especially the schizoid, are also apathetically unresponsive to the indifference of others toward them. They are so since what they most prize is to be initially let and thereafter left alone in their social withdrawal. Group II are known as *lonerists* herein and may suffer from being excluded or non-included by specific others but not by others in general since they are either scornfully indifferent or actively hostile toward them. Group III are lonelies and suffer immensely from the isolation of exclusion, non-inclusion, and indifference.

A. Group I

Individuals in Group I are not lonelies, given their incapability or at least their lack of desire to be connected with others in general or with anyone in particular. As the *DSM* envisages them, schizoids seem to have been born without a need or have but a significantly reduced one in the case of the schizotypals. Nor do Group I seem to have any capability, desire or, at the very minimum, willingness for intimacy and love in particular (pp. 638–639, 641). To the extent that Group I are without such normal inclinations and requirements, they are not even potentially lonely, all of which is the first and foremost reason I consider the schizoid and schizotypal abnormal personalities.

Nor are Group I alonelies since they are not afraid to be alone in any sense of the word, unless, of course, they would feel that they are absolutely all by themselves in the external world. In which case, even the schizoid and schizotypal would be (a)lonelified by the prospect of such isolation. If these two aberrants actually believe they are literally all alone in the world, then they can be understood as merging with schizophrenics on the psychotic spectrum. Still, unlike some schizophrenics, Group I abnormals do not believe that they *are* the objective world. This conviction constitutes a blend of metaphysical and psychological solipsism, the view that only one's self exists, respectively, extramentally and mentally.

Group I are the consummate absolute social isolates since they try to elude all contact with others, save, according to the *DSM*, "possibly a first-degree relative" (pp. 638, 642). While they are total and permanent loners (lonists), the schizoid and schizotypal are not the kind referenced above as lonerists. They are not since Group I pathologicals are not disdainfully indifferent or hostile toward others either in general or in particular.

Group I may or may not be alonists since they may or may not wish to be domiciled with others. But if they reside with them, as social isolates, schizoids and schizotypals have little if any interaction with their co-residents since their overriding goal is to be separated from everyone, including other Group I types of personality. Not only social but physical separation from others would generally be welcomed by the schizoid and schizotypal since it would preclude any contact, not to mention any intimate sort, with their fellow human beings. Naturally, even for extraverts the desire for privacy is a normal inclination, but not the kind of extreme sequestration that marks the non-plus-ultra Group I introverts.

Nevertheless, these two pathologically odd personalities may, unlike absolute recluses, prefer physical proximity to others instead of extreme spatial isolation. However, as absolute loners, the schizoid and schizotypal would not favor a closeness that forces them into social situations wherein contact would become unavoidable.

Group I are not primary solitaries since their withdrawal from others is, for one thing, a matter of being constitutionally inclined if not completely compelled instead of being chosen. For another, the schizoid and schizotypal are not benevolently disposed toward others, as are primary solitaries. Instead, they are acquisitionally prone, which means that they are not motivated to act for others even in terms of fulfilling the requirements of justice.

However, the schizoid and schizotypal are not necessarily motivated to act contrary to these obligations. Group I are nonmoral isolates to the extent that they are acquisitionally motivated. Their self-centeredness is mitigated by the fact that the depth and range of their freedom are curtailed by genetic factors such that I refer to them as pre- or nonmoral instead of immoral isolates. In short, Group I are constitutionally *egocentric* but not malevolently *egoistical* as are Group II pathologicals.

Nor are Group I secondary solitaries, since they, especially the schizoid, are conspicuously bereft of any kind of genuine inventiveness. Nonetheless, the schizotypal has an FFM Openness to Experience that is necessary for creativity (see Costa and Widiger, 1994, p. 329; 2002, p. 461). Alas, this individual's kind of openness is far too chimerical and vaporous, perceptually and conceptually clouded and distorted, even quasi psychotic, and, in general, lower Dionysian to be genuinely inventive.

Though they are social isolates, Group I are not recluses since, for one thing, they are not automatically physical isolates. Nor are they secluses if only because their social and sometimes physical isolation is permanent, whereas seclusion is ordinarily understood as a temporary state no matter how long it lasts de facto. Group I are not positive seclusives who retreat from others, for instance, to mourn or bereave their absence. The schizoid and schizotypal have no connections to others let alone those whose loss would cause them bereavement-loneliness or other kinds of negative aloneness. On the other hand, they are not negative seclusives since they do not go into concealment, for instance, to scheme against others, behavior typical of Group II lonerists.

Nor are schizoids and schizotypals to be considered desolates in the sense that they have agonizing feelings of being excluded or unincluded such that they would experience searing (a)loneliness. Group I may be viewed as desolates in that they are cut off and divorced from others. In this sense, they are aliens, meaning individuals who are looked upon as foreigners and strangers coming from afar. This alienation especially characterizes schizotypals in terms of the nature of their consciousness, conduct, and often their appearance as displayed, for example, in their "unusual mannerisms" and "unkempt manner of dress" (p. 642).

B. Group II

Any loneliness to which Group II deviants might be subject is usually repressed, suppressed, or otherwise denied. As is the case with many individuals subject to trait and state mental illness, substance abuse and other types of addiction are used by Group II to medicate their (a)loneliness and the fear or dread thereof and other conditions of negative aloneness.

Group II can, therefore, be alonelies in that they are afraid to be alone for long periods since these hostile hyper-individualists still need others for protection and in general to do their bidding. Moreover, malevolent individuals, like sociopaths, paranoids, narcissists, and obsessionals typically have a profound apprehensiveness of being alone with themselves. One reason for this anxiety is that those who are malevolent and, a fortiori, maleficent to others often have a kind of self-hatred, which prevents them from wanting to be all by themselves. Still, Group II aberrants may lack any feelings of guilt about their negative aloneness. Or they may construe such comportment as being positive, all of which is especially the case with sociopaths followed by paranoids.

Group II may or may not be alonists since they may or may not want to reside with others. But if they do, they are fundamentally dis-related to them, given their selfish qualities and generalized animus. They may, however, dwell with fellow egomaniacs who mutually serve one another's interests. Or, more likely, they may live with those who are unwillingly or willingly their subservients, such as lackeys and other negatively dependent types.

As a rule, sociopaths, paranoids, narcissists, and obsessionals make for unequivocally miserable co-dwellers. Even a casual look at the list of their *DSM* diagnostic features will convince a person that they are not the kind of individuals desired as cohabiters in any sense of the term. While selfishness is their most common trait, it is manifested by each of the Group II pathologicals in a distinct but always repellent fashion.

Group II pathologicals are not absolute loners but are the relative partial sort of social isolates that I title lonerists, given their scornful indifference and animosity toward others in general. So understood, Group II as a totality rank especially low in gregariousness but even lower in warmth (Costa and Widiger, 1994, p. 329; 2002, p. 461).

Group II abnormals are not primary solitaries if only because their internal and external aloneness would be based on a habitual derisive uninterest in or antipathy toward their fellow human beings and their arrogant disdain for ethical self-improvement. Any desire on the part of the Group II obsessionals for moral self-betterment is principally contained in what they envisage as perfecting others by controlling them instead of themselves. Moreover, if they do engage in moral improvement, their notion of morality is the kind that fosters the fastidious, puritanical, and pusillanimous; in sum, it is a pseudo-ethics that is mean-spirited, small-souled, and cold-hearted.

Group II may be secondary solitaries in that they can be inventive types with respect to external products such as those of an artistic nature. Thus, the perfectionism of the obsessional may be used, for instance, in scholarship but even then it is often the kind of pedantry that reflects the lower Apollonian. The uppermost echelons of moral creativity belong to the higher Apollonian and above all the higher Dionysian, from which all those with personality disorders are precluded by definition due to their malevolent selfishness.

Group II are not, as a rule, recluses, especially the narcissist, since they do not seek a more or less permanent physical isolation from others in general. On the other hand, these four personality deviants are often negative secluses. Given, for instance, their abiding enviousness, vindictiveness, and overall misanthropy, the sociopath, paranoid, narcissist, and obsessional, and usually in that order, may seek seclusion to plot against others. They do so, especially concerning actual or potential enemies, who, for these supreme cynics, include all other human beings in principle.

Group II are not subject to desolation at least not that kind associated with extreme emotional isolation since they are not lonelies as such. Still, their aloneliness may bring forth feelings of being forsaken and other kinds of maximal exclusion. In any case, Group II are social and (im)moral isolates in that they are cut off from others due to their extreme egoism.

C. Group III

Group III have a strong need and desire for intimacy and usually respond to its absence by becoming more aware and demanding of connectedness. Regrettably, their longing for attachments is not matched by the traits necessary to bridge the gap between their wish for intimacy and its realization. As a result, they are highly subject to experiencing loneliness on a conscious and pathological level.

Group III are also hugely susceptible to the dread of aloneness in general and fear of loneliness in particular. The borderlines and dependents are of all the *DSM* ten sickly personalities the most at risk for both catastrophic loneliness and aloneliness. So much so are they that I am inclined to view these states as the defining elements of these two aberrants.

As to residing alone, Group III are the most unlikely aberrants to be alonists save for the avoidants. Unless they are guaranteed immunity from loneliness within a relationship, avoidants, as their name indicates, shun connectedness, all of which easily eventuates in their residing alone. Though avoidants may find their alonism frightful even abhorrent, it is preferable to the horror they feel at the prospect of being domiciled with others and then being demeaned and discarded by them.

Therefore, Group III, with the exception of the avoidants, tend not to be willing alonists, owing to their overriding need(iness) for intimates close at hand. When Group III reside with others, their interaction is most problematic. It is given their self-centeredness, which is exhibited in their "needing" (needy) and acquisitive kind of intimacy. Living with any of these four kinds of pathological personalities and pathologically lonely individuals means co-dwelling with extremely neurotic individuals. Neurotics almost always make for very difficult casual companions and all the more so ongoing co-habitants.

Warm types of personality, according to Paul T. Costa and Thomas A. Widiger, are "affectionate and friendly" individuals who are extremely interested in what these authors term "interpersonal intimacy." Consequently, they state that warm individuals "genuinely like people and easily form close attachments" none of which is true of Groups I and II individuals (2002, p. 464).

Of all ten of the disturbed personalities, solely the histrionic of Group III can be considered sociable in the sense of being both warm and gregarious. The borderline is gregarious but not warm (Costa and Widiger, 1994, p. 329; 2002, p. 461). Consequently, nine of the ten personality disorders, especially those of Group I, lack sociability, which is plainly evinced by their remiss relatedness to others. Unfortunately, the personality who possesses high sociability, the histrionic, has the sort that is predominantly self-serving and extremely neuroticized (ibid).

Both the histrionic and above all the borderline are outgoing not so much because they like or love others but mainly because they are terrified of feeling unliked and unloved. While, therefore, both these pathologicals are non-introverted personalities, their relatedness to others is qualitatively defective instead of being simply quantitatively deficient. The other eight abnormals fail in both categories.

Of course, being extroverted in itself is not necessarily a psycho-ethical positive. People can "go out to others" principally and even exclusively for self-centered reasons, as is the case with the absolutely extroverted histrionic and the relatively so borderline. Though Group III individuals greatly desire the shared warmth of intimacy, unfortunately, they tend to have a superfluity of personality traits that impede close relationships.

In my estimation, given that all individuals with personality disorders are essentially failures in terms of interpersonal relatedness due to their negative personality traits, their living with others poses serious and often insurmountable hurdles. These difficulties are not experienced to the quantitative degree or qualitative level by normals.

Consequently, we can generally expect that abnormal personalities will be more inclined or forced to be alonists than normals. Aberrants are also likely to have a much higher incidence of marital separation and divorce (which themselves frequently lead to alonism). These two conditions are often both causes and consequences of loneliness even as fear of being unmarried often stems from aloneliness and emotional isolation in particular.

Still, given that Group II are often alonelies and Group III are to the point of being pathologically afraid of being or feeling alone, these aberrants may want to reside with others. Only Group I tend to voluntarily live alone on a habitual basis, owing in the main to their desire not only to be socially but physically isolated from others since the second kind of aloneness assures the first.

Group III are not primary solitaries if only because they lack benevolence toward others. But they may be secondary solitaries and may even use their chronic (a)loneliness to increase their inventiveness. These abnormals are not recluses, although avoidants, given what the *DSM* titles their "pervasive pattern of social inhibition," are, along with the Group I, the most prone to seek both permanent social and physical isolation (p. 662). Their constant longing for and their general dependence on others keep the avoidants, like the other Group III deviants, from becoming recluses.

Owing to their extreme loneliness, all Group III may be secluses, but they are not as a rule the negative types. Therefore and unlike Group II, Group III do not furtively devise stratagems to deliberately hurt and harm others, the exception at times being the borderlines. Still, they are not fundamentally malevolent. Nonetheless, the lonely acquisitive kinds of personality may become malign when they feel threatened with maximal exclusion, especially via abandonment. Still, borderlines pose a greater danger to themselves than others, especially in the forms of self-injury and even suicide.

All the disturbed personalities are isolates in various fashions. Group I are extreme social isolates and often physical isolates as well. They are not emotional isolates, or lonelies, nor are they (im)moral isolates save in the manner acquisitionally motivated individuals are. Recall that Group I can be characterized as nonmoral isolates since they largely lack the condition of morality, namely the ability to freely function, insofar as they are thought to be genetically or quasi so necessitated.

Nonetheless, I believe that many ethicists would hold nearly all individuals with personality abnormalities responsible for their conduct, though in varying degrees, with the Group I being deemed the least and Group III the most. To the extent that personality aberrants or their traits are biologically dictated, to that measure they are not morally responsible for their conduct, though they may be legally so. Sometimes the reverse prevails, meaning pathologicals are held to be morally but not legally responsible (sometimes they are adjudged to be blamable on both counts).

Group I are immoral largely by default, that is, by omitting actions they should perform, although their lack of volitionality exonerates them in some measure. Group II are immoral especially by the commission of bad if not evil actions. Group III are a mixture: those who are inclined toward intentionally ignoring the well-being of others are so chiefly by commission (the borderline and, to a lesser degree, the histrionic). Those who tend to be ignorant, though culpably so, of others' welfare are immoral mainly by omission (the dependent and avoidant).

Group II are social isolates in terms of human beings in general, though not regarding a few chosen others. As an aggregate, they tend to be antigregarious and are very cold even bitterly so individuals. Group II are not necessarily physical isolates nor are they consciously emotional isolates, or lonelies. They are immoral isolates of the worst form in that they are malevolent if not maliciously maleficent, especially the paranoid but even more so the sociopath.

Group III are not as a whole social isolates since their pathological loneliness and their fear thereof drive them toward others, all of which makes them alonelies in addition to lonelies. Avoidants as partial social isolates are decidedly non-gregarious but only because they feel not wholeheartedly accepted. Group III are rarely physical isolates save for the avoidants who function apart from others unless they are assured of not being maximally excluded mainly via rejection. Group III are (im)moral isolates but their acquisitiveness arguably differs in kind from the selfish (im)moral isolationism of Group II deviates.

In my view, loneliness, especially pathological, is the most dystonic experience not only regarding other non-constructive kinds of aloneness but of all experiences. Considered as a unit, only Group III pathologicals suffer this species of desolation and only they do so to the point of frequent suicidal ideations and gestures, especially borderlines. Group II sociopaths may do so but usually only in the spur-of-the-moment to avoid, for example, being apprehended and punished.

Not all negative states of aloneness are dystonic, meaning painful to their possessors. Those that are felt as being intrinsically negative include loneliness, especially the pathological (for example, that experienced by Group III aberrants), aloneliness, some types of lonism (for instance, the relative species experienced by avoidants), seclusiveness (for example, that found in bereavement), and desolation. Those that are not felt as being intrinsically negative are alonism, voluntary or volitional absolute social isolation (for instance, that experienced by Group I), lonerism (for example, that ascribable to Group II), internal and external solitude, physical reclusion, and some kinds of seclusion. During this series, I wish to show how SCRAM has markedly increased negative aloneness and decreased its positive.

The states of aloneness, whether positive or negative, discussed in this chapter more or less explicitly concern the extramental—or what is usually titled the actual, concrete, or objective—existence of self and others. There are other types of aloneness, such as some species of solipsism, that—at least theoretically or for the sake of argumentation—do not assume the extramental existence of others except to doubt or deny them. Even more paradoxically and likely literally self-contradictorily, there are species of aloneness that do not even assume the objective reality of one's self save to question its extramental existence or to rule it out. These kinds of aloneness refer to solipsism, a subject that calls for a chapter all to itself.

Three

THE ALONENESS OF SOLIPSISM

1. Solipsism and Existence

The phenomenon of solipsism, in terms of its nature and species and as understood largely in the context of aloneness and mental illness, will be the principal focus of this chapter.

To examine solipsistic sorts of aloneness, existence itself must be further differentiated. It can signify that which is exclusively in the mind, solely outside it, both in and outside it, and, finally, neither in nor outside consciousness. In the last case, there is a total lack of extramental existence such that this absence is literally a nothing, to wit a no-thing, sometimes known as an absolute nil, nullity, or nihil.

Of course, the notion of no-thingness contains a meaning—and, accordingly, it has a mental existence—but it has no reference to any entity with an extramental, or objective, existence. As well, the term "nothing" when spoken or written has an external, or extramental, existence, as does its source, namely its originator.

Extramental existence is often termed real or at least more real than mental existence in the sense that the first, unlike the second, is viewed as existing independently of whether it is known by any subject qua mind. Still, it is the mind itself that discovers what exists in and outside itself and specifies what is real and its gradations in addition to its negation, meaning the non-real.

It merits notation that, in many cases, what exists mentally is more real in the sense of more important than what exists extramentally. Happiness is the ultimate quest of the self, yet it is formally a mental, or subjective, state. Nonetheless, felicity is generally considered to depend in part upon extramental entities, not the least of which are other subjects, especially those that are persons. The essence of well-being is widely held to entail relating well to other persons, especially intimates, such as those pertaining to companionate, friendship, and erotic types. The loss of such intimates can plunge the individual into feelings of non-being including that of an experiential kind of solipsism, in which the person feels completely alone in the world.

2. A Fivefold Division

Solipsism has at least five species that are especially germane to the concepts of aloneness, personality, and mental illness. They are the metaphysical, epistemological, and the methodological—all of which concentrate on more or less theoretical issues relative to the existence of the self—and the psychological and egological. These two types chiefly concern the self's existence vis-à-vis predominantly practical matters.

Metaphysical solipsism is the speculation that the only self that exists extramentally is one's own. Naturally, the very positing of extramental existence is a mental act of the self qua mind especially in terms of its knowledge. Accordingly, metaphysical solipsism necessarily involves the issue of the second sort of solipsism, namely epistemological, or cognitive.

Epistemic solipsism is the doctrine that holds that the mind can know—at least with any kind of clarity and certainty, two properties of cognition that are not necessarily mutually implicative—that only itself exists. Nonetheless, we may ask which kind of existence, mental or extramental, is in fact being postulated by such cognition?

To resolve these issues, René Descartes formulated a methodological species of solipsism by which he attempted to demonstrate that metaphysical and epistemological solipsism were untenable positions. The reader might recall the French philosopher's proclamation, "I think, therefore I am," in which the self, especially qua mind, in its acts of cogitation intentionally and systematically calls, into question its own objective reality. Descartes *thought* that this very doubt proves the self's extramental existence with absolute clarity and certainty.

In some quarters, including existential, phenomenological, and personalist, human consciousness is primordially relational and interpersonally so. In which case, the mind is originally ordered, and self-evidently so, to the objective existence of other selves (and qua persons) instead of one's own or at minimum is ordered to both others and oneself simultaneously.

Epistemic solipsism rests on the false (and arguably falsifiable) supposition that consciousness is initially (and irremediably) primarily directed to itself, as epistemic idealists (ideists), such as Johann Fichte, postulate. But even if others exist solely in the mind of the lone self, then their mental and extramental existence would be identical. And so, the relational and interpersonal schools argue that any debate as to others' reality would be both useless and unnecessary (vol. 1, pp. 54–59).

3. The Solipsistic Self

While the self qua mind might question the objective existence of others, it can be proposed that the self qua person would not. Individuals would not because they implicitly realize from the outset that the very notion of a person implies the extramental existence of other persons. Human beings do not extramentally exist in the sense of actually co-existing with other selves let alone other minds, but they do so with others qua persons (all of whom are embodied and manifestly so). In short, many metaphysical and epistemological solipsists mistakenly equate the human being with the self and the self with the mind, all of which arguably undercuts the foundation of their positions.

The very notion of a person, whether normal or anormal, ipso facto implies a duality and, in actual fact, a plurality of persons in radical relationship to one another in terms of their ontological structures. This means that it is the very being of human beings, especially qua persons, to exist together instead of there being but one single self, as metaphysical and specifically ontological monistic idealism (ideism) posits. (I say ideism lest this form of idealism be confused with moral idealism.) Personality is, therefore, innately constituted by the indelible sociality of interpersonality.

An abnormal personalty is essentially definable as functionally unrelated (Group I), dis-related (Group II), or seriously insufficiently related (Group III) to other persons. Consequently, I concur with Michael Stone when he writes that "*Personality* is fundamentally an aggregate of the ways in which [persons] habitually, predictably, and enduringly relate to other people" (2006, p. 2.).

This said, disordered personalities, including the antisocial (the sociopath) and the nonsocial (for example, the schizoid) aberrants, remain social beings, structurally considered. However, they functionally fail in terms of this interpersonal relatedness through lack of socialness (actualized sociality) and sociability (actualized socialness), for instance, in the form of incivilities.

The overriding problem for the person is, therefore, not that there are no other persons in the extramental world. Instead, it is that they are not in the individual's own world and vice versa in a suitable manner, namely a caring and otherwise humane fashion. Without other persons, the individual loses its intimacy and, therefore, the crux of its meaning and purpose. This absence is above all apparent in loneliness and no more so than it is among Group III pathologicals and, as will be discussed below, schizophrenics and some clinically depressed.

For human beings, at least those deemed normal, relationships are the chief wellsprings and mainstays of their wellness. In this vein, John Cacioppo and William Patrick document that, when queried as to what most contributes to happiness, the vast majority of people will rank love, social affiliation, and other variants of interpersonal relatedness over money, celebrity, and even corporeal health (2008, p. 5). However, they might not always uphold this ranking in practice until their relatedness, both temporary and ongoing, is deficient or, worse, non-existent, in which event, they re-cognize that other persons are the essence of their being and well-being.

A human being can question whether its self is alone in the world and do so in relative security and tranquility. It can do so only because it is already convinced that there other persons who actually exist not only in the extramental world as a whole, but in the individual's own sphere of reality. Even the very idea of aloneness implies a previous or at least a concomitant notion of togetherness with some other person or at least personation. Once human beings lack the presence, especially involitionally, of other persons they almost invariably create images of personifications and personalizations.

Once the individual starts to question in a non-theoretical manner as to whether there are other persons in the world, it may, by dint of its (a)loneliness, begin to seriously doubt its own extramental or even its mental reality. Loneliness is the foremost attestation to the reality of others but by way of their temporary or permanent absence. However, emotional isolation can also be the cause of the self's rendezvous with its feelings of non-existence. The self's existence may have begun owing to love but the latter may have begun due to loneliness: a "love child" and any other child are sometimes the results of loneliness on the part of one or both of their parents.

Human beings are so accustomed to being with other persons that they take their extramental existence entirely for granted. When people suddenly and unexpectedly find themselves all alone and fear that they will continue to be so, they sometimes actually die from (a)loneliness. Peter Suedfeld documents that a large proportion of castaways, even though they were not injured in the shipwreck, "may die within a few days." He essays that the likely causes of such deaths are due to "physical and mental shock and helplessness" which, in turn, are significantly owing to being all alone especially in a totally unforeseen fashion (1982, p. 58).

Were any metaphysical, epistemic, or methodological solipsist confronted with a comparable situation, their contemplating any state of total aloneness as possible not to mention desirable would likely soon stop. Not even individuals with a schizoid personality disorder doubt the extramentality of others, even though all such aberrants—whether voluntarily or volitionally—are usually lacking fellow human beings in their world. However, there is one kind of solipsist, namely the psychological, who experiences a fright of aloneness on a sustained basis to the point of fearing perishing from it and vanishing into nothingness (as if this no-thingness were actually some *thing*).

4. Psychological Solipsism

Unlike the theoretical solipsisms just outlined, the psychological species pertains to a person who actually believes and lives as if she or he were the only self in the world (every form of solipsism is psychic in that it inheres in a human psyche, or mind). People may wonder whether solipsism could possibly be true. Still, it is likely unanimously agreed even or perhaps especially among its theoreticians that no sane individual actually lives as if there were no others in the extramental world. It would not only be hellish to do so but completely contrary to what is utterly evident, even self-evident: the existence of other selves or, more precisely, other persons. Were persons to actually deny the truth of this most basic sort of evidentiality, their doing so would surely be a sign of mental abnormality.

Psychological solipsism refers to the kind of mental existence that is abnormal, especially in the sense of psychotic construed as schizophrenic herein. The psychotic is in a state of fundamental error such as that of illusion, delusion, and hallucination, in any case extreme confusion as to what is mentally or extramentally real. Psychosis, therefore, entails a mental derangement, in which there is defective or lost contact with reality, especially the extramental.

Solipsistic psychotics may not only hold that no others exist in any fashion but even that, wondrous to say, their own selves do not. They may think that their denying or at least doubting the reality of their selves is sufficient to demonstrate not only their non-extramental existence but their non-mental existence as well—if indeed they distinguish between the two states of being. All this may be construed as a kind of Cartesian methodological solipsism in reverse.

5. Psychotic Solipsism and Loneliness

Medical doctor and philosopher J. H. van den Berg proposes that the schizophrenic "stands apart from the rest of the world," with his or her own world being a hallucinatory construct in which "houses can sway forward" and "flowers can look dull and colorless." This medical doctor and philosopher contends that these cognitive aberrations in part stem from the schizophrenic's desolating "isolation," meaning the person's catastrophic loneliness (1972, p. 105).

Berg states that even a normal individual, when "subjected to harrowing isolation, hallucinates after a short while." He essays that eventually any gravely lonely person will invent "his own objects" (ibid., p. 107) (above all those that are other subjects). Human existence is unalterably programmed, so to speak, for co-existence, or interpersonality. When that kind of intersubjectivity fails, individuals may lose contact with the objective world and then manufacture their own and *people* it with their inventions.

Berg proposes that the objects or subjects concocted by the hallucinations of schizophrenics "are most definitely real" to them and, as a result, "are taken very seriously" by these unfortunates. Indeed, this phenomenologist insists that, for some abnormal and abnormally lonely individuals, the persons produced by their hallucinations exist in a way that is even more real for them than nonfictional extramental persons are for normals and non-gravely lonely normals. Berg appends that the extramental objects invented by significantly lonely but normal individuals are also often taken to be extramentally real, even though in actuality they are solely mental (ibid., pp. 106–110).

In accordance with the above line of logic, it may be conjectured that lonely schizophrenics' mental states drive them to assert even more firmly the extramental existence of what are in fact but fictitious others than the mental conditions of the nonlonely compel them to affirm the extramental existence of actual others. Nonlonely normals can and do take others' existence for granted even and sometimes especially when they are absent. It may be hypothesized that schizophrenics typically do not do so perhaps above all when they are under the aegis of dysfunctional (a)loneliness), all of which is arguably customarily the case with these types of psychotics.

Additionally, schizophrenics may be so lonely that they take others' physical absence as evident even when to normals these others are obviously spatially present. All this is reminiscent of R. D. Laing's notion of pathological loneliness as the felt conviction that every relationship is perceived as an absence (1967, p. 37).

Normals are so thoroughly social that they feel lost once all, some, or even one person, especially "the-one-and-only" sort, is envisaged as being interminably absent. In which case, their longing for those missing may cause normals to hallucinate such that they invent the presence of those absent and look upon them as present extramental entities. Their doing so may seem "crazy" to those who have never been seriously (a)lonely.

Bereaved normals, for example, may, in their loneliness, be completely certain that they hear, see, touch, or otherwise literally sense their "departed" intimates. In such instances, their longing, instead of signifying a clinical kind of psychosis on their part, may actually keep bereaved normals from temporarily undergoing insanity. If their grieving does become highly protracted, the bereaved may fall into a state of lonely clinical depression, which may involve recurrent even quasi-permanent psychotic features.

It is to be underlined that persons subject to pathological loneliness of the psychotic sort may yearn for sheer inanimate objects as intimates. They may do so given that they may have relinquished any hope for the presence of any extramental subject, indeed any living being, for companionate existence. Whereupon, they may long for the "company" of inanimates such as pillows or pills to assuage their isolation. They may hope that such objects might be or become subjects of intimacy however much at times they are terrified by the mere thought of any kind of closeness and all the more so from any actual contact.

That psychotics long for any sort of shared inwardness indicates that not only do they have some semblance of sanity but that this yearning prevents them from absolute despair and thus further descent into madness and melancholia. This latter mental state is definable as a condition characterized by extreme depression, loss of interest in activities, somatic symptoms, such as loss of sleep and appetite, and often hallucinations and delusions, especially when it involves manic-depressive (bipolar) disorder(s). Melancholia also refers to what is known as endogenous depression, namely the type devoid "of an apparent precipitating event" (Beers, 2003, p. 559). Endogenous depression also signifies the kind that stems from external sources in contrast to outer, or exogenous, ones. Among mental health disorders, those of depression are second only to those of anxiety in terms of prevalence (ibid.).

Many individuals still subscribe to animism understood as the doctrine that holds that all beings are living. Or they may believe in panpsychism, the notion that everything is mental in the sense of conscious. Such beliefs are not usually deemed insane, though in Western society, such convictions are often viewed as being prescientific. It is not unthinkable that some of those who adhere to animism and, a fortiori, to panpsychism, do so to keep (a)loneliness from coming to consciousness or at minimum keep it constrainable (vol. 1, pp. 72–79).

The pathologically (a)lonely may also believe that they have become unhinged due to their variegated isolation. A fictional example of cultural exclusion occurs when the character named Crooks in John Steinbeck's *Of Mice and Men* bemoans the fact that as a "nigger," he is an outcaste so much so that he "gets sick" and "goes nuts" (Dusenbury, 1967, p. 49).

Pathological loneliness is a, if not the, most painful of sicknesses, and those who are psychotic or depressed are routinely if not by definition most exposed to its often disabling suffering. According to a 1996 World Health Organization study, "the disability caused by active psychosis [is] equivalent to quadriplegia," while that "caused by major depression [is] equal to blindness and paraplegia" (*St. Mary's Hospital Foundation*, Montreal, autumn, 2004).

About 1 percent of people around the world will be subject to schizophrenia in their lifetime. One in ten schizophrenics commits suicide and, as will be documented below, loneliness is a most undesired accomplice of this devastating mental state disorder and of suicide in general. It is also reported, "the average age for the onset of schizophrenia is 18 for men and 25 for women" (Beers, 2003, p. 582). This period is almost the same shown generally in the literature as the loneliest age (15 to 25 years) for most Americans, save for the very elderly (80 and over).

Antonio Ferreira states that loneliness is most apparent in schizophrenics since their "enormously unsatisfied need for intimacy" is visible, he says, to anyone experienced in dealing with this type of patient. This psychiatrist proposes that the schizophrenic withdrawal is, in part, a self-imposed exile. It is a strategy adopted, Ferreira adds, to protect their vulnerability to loneliness, shattered self-esteem, and a crippled sense of identity, two phenomena which themselves are often both a cause and effect of emotional isolation (1962, p. 205).

Ferreira views the schizophrenics' decline into progressively deepening affective, social, and physical withdrawal mainly as a defense to circumvent the very contact they so desperately desire yet often dread. This predicament greatly accounts for the schizophrenic's devastating anxiety (ibid.). The psychotic's withdrawals are undertaken in part to elude or escape continued feelings of being deliberately excluded. This ostracism often occurs owing to the schizophrenics' extreme eccentricity. It can be witnessed in their often outlandish mental states, alien(ating) language and communication styles, bizarre bodily behavior, and lack of personal grooming and cleanliness.

These idiosyncracies strike both apprehension and revulsion in others and cause them to engage in rejection and avoidance of schizophrenics, all of which reinforces their multiple isolations. Nonetheless, in Ferreira's reckoning, schizophrenics find that however wretched their loneliness might be when others distance themselves from these unfortunates, such absence pales in comparison to the desolation schizophrenics experience in others' presence (ibid.).

Like many normals suffering from catastrophic, or debilitating, loneliness but only more so, schizophrenics may not allow themselves to acknowledge the tormenting isolation, which engulfs them, so terrified are they of their abiding and merciless adversary. Their refusal to recognize the sway (a)loneliness holds over their life and their failed attempts to immunize themselves against its painful feelings only attest to the fact that they rule the schizophrenics' very existence. Such wretched emotions persistently threaten these psychotics' being with nonbeing to which they are constantly subjectively and sometimes objectively exposed via suicide.

Ferreira states that the schizophrenic tries to make himself invulnerable to loneliness by retreating into his psyche so that in:

> his fantasies, undisturbed by others, he can become as powerful as "Napoleon," as handsome as "Valentino", as loved as "Christ." In his delusions and hallucinations, he may see himself as the best or perhaps the worst of human beings, but he does not [or want to] see himself as lonely. (Ibid.)

Eloise Clark relates how a schizophrenic patient embodied Ferreira's view that the psychotic's "feelings of loneliness are dissociated from self and then projected into his hallucinations." She recounts how the patient had given a nurse a torn slip of paper, which read as follows: "I am very sad and lonely. Ten." Thereupon, the following conversation occurred:

> Nurse: You want me to read this?
> Patient: Yes, the doctor told me to write down everything the voices say.
> Nurse: You hear voices say that they are sad and lonely?
> Patient: Yes.
> Nurse: What does the number ten mean?
> Patient: The voices repeated that ten times.
> Nurse: Do you feel sad and lonely?
> Patient: No, I don't feel that way. The voices feel that way. I'm a very happy boy. I've never been lonely. (Laughed a hollow laugh and walked on down the hall.) (1968, pp. 34–35)

Clark comments that the schizophrenic sought to share with the nurse his experiences, especially his loneliness-induced and loneliness-permeated hallucinations and delusions. However, Clark says that, when confronted with what "he seemed to want to communicate, his loneliness, he immediately used denial and moved away" (ibid., p. 35). It is as if the painful admission of his loneliness by the schizophrenic would lead to its unmanageable increase and thereby to his total undoing and eventually to his "unbeing."

Resultingly, this psychotic dissociated himself from his isolation but then implicitly re-associated it with "foreign" voices. This procedure is indicative not only of loneliness but alienation, a word still used to signify mental illness, while an alienist is a psychiatrist who treats it. No one is more alien in the senses of being both estranging and estranged than a schizophrenic for this individual is the epitome of the stranger from another but highly unparalleled universe.

Frieda Fromm-Reichmann maintains that individuals cannot endure what she calls "real" loneliness and other serious mental states, like panic, "for any length of time without becoming psychotic." The lonely (and alone-ly) are often in a state of panic predominantly because they feel frantic as a result of feeling displaced or replaced and, therefore, lost in maximal exclusion. Fromm-Reichmann notes that the directionality of such occurrences is usually the reverse such that loneliness is not the cause but the effect of a psychotic experience or state (1980, p. 345). This view would be more in harmony with most but not all current theories regarding both schizophrenia and loneliness etiologies.

Fromm-Reichmann essays that such painful isolation (and such isolating pain) seldom if ever can be even mentioned by its sufferers. She says that others do not want to hear anything about loneliness so "unpopular" is it, certainly in America, she annexes (ibid., p. 346).

David Riesman maintains that Americans are "supposed to be cheerful, competent, successful, and happy" and, as a result, they are not supposed to suffer from the "terrible pangs of loneliness." Hence, Riesman contends that its sufferers are inclined to look upon their affliction as "some sort of un-American inactivity" (Weiss, 1970, pp. xvii). SCRAM, which inculcates a worship of individualism and success in society at all costs, including unhappiness, causes people to feel especially guilty and embarrassed at being so unpatriotic as to be lonely, virulent chauvinism being another facet of this societal sickness.

Fromm-Reichmann further recounts how normals—who had been condemned to long periods in military concentration camps, in which they were solitarily confined—succumbed to insanity or at minimum teetered on its brink. She relates that when the prisoners were liberated they were afraid to speak, especially about their loneliness. They were because they feared people would think that their speech might suggest that they were in fact insane. The newly freed prisoners' resistance to disclose the extent and even the existence of their loneliness was due to many factors. However, often the foremost reason was that their isolation simply defied any conveyance that could be made halfway intelligible (ibid., p. 355).

Even normals who suffer from mild and transient experiences of loneliness may regard themselves as unable to communicate its nature and effects upon them. This conviction is all the more real and horrifying for those who are themselves mentally ill and who suffer from multiple forms of pathological loneliness such as schizophrenics generally do. It bears emphasizing that people can be relatively normal and yet experience pathological loneliness. They also can, like the schizoid, be abnormal and not experience any degree or any form of loneliness, save possibly existential—a possibility that I think is highly unlikely.

6. Schizophrenic Isolation

Kirson Weinberg has divided schizophrenics in terms of isolation into four interacting disengagements due to: first, a deficiency of social contacts above all intimate ones, owing, in turn, to social "inaccessibility"; second, tactics designed to protect self-esteem; third, the inability to create and continue social relations as such; and, fourth, "autistic, or emotionally withdrawn, behavior," a state of aloneness and detachment that will not be examined in the present study (1967, p. 33).

On the other hand, Weinberg stresses that isolation, in the form of solitude, "can be a creative and rehabilitative" kind of withdrawal, one which can counteract the influence of the negative sorts of isolation just listed (ibid.) Unfortunately, any lasting possibility for solitude, be it primary or secondary, is, in some quarters, by definition excluded from schizophrenic realization.

As to the first category, situational schizophrenic social isolation occurs, according to Weinberg, when social contacts are meager—and, a fortiori, if they are nonexistent—largely because of sheer physical inaccessibility. He states that extreme types of spatial isolation—which, for example, are experienced, especially unwillingly, in remote areas and institutions such as prisons—can produce the bizarre and "very disorganized, regressive, and hallucinatory behaviors which are consistent" (ibid.) with schizophrenia. Emotional isolation is undeniably a prominent risk factor in extreme, especially unwilled, mental, physical, and social species of isolation.

With reference to social isolation, more specifically, Weinberg alludes to studies that indicate that, for instance, urban areas with "indices of low sociability have higher rates of schizophrenia" than those that "have indices of [greater] sociability." Weinberg notes that, for example, those locales in Austin, Texas, that had the highest rates of schizophrenia were also those where people were largely anonymous and had fewer social contacts with one another chiefly due to physical inaccessibility (ibid.).

Weinberg stipulates that schizophrenics not seeking contacts, let alone intimate ones, may be attracted to the more socially isolated areas precisely because of their inaccessibility. Hence, he states that those predisposed to schizophrenia may seek relatively remote areas so they may be left alone "to escape the emotional demands of interpersonal relationships." It may also be the case, Weinberg adds, that the mentally ill residents of these areas "deteriorate as a consequence of their lack of contacts or their withdrawal from rejecting contacts" (p. 34).

Schizophrenics—whose personal identity is in jeopardy to begin with—may self-fragment due to living in a locale of social inhibition. Then, too, it may not be their mere quantitative lack of social contacts and relationships but more likely the shortage of qualitative ones, all of which is especially generative of schizophrenic emotional isolation. At any rate, the schizophrenic incarnates in textbook fashion what in this book are named species- and person-loneliness, or, respectively, an unmanageable dearth of human companionship in general and of the company of particular individuals.

Weinberg relates that situational isolation may be subjectively internalized, in which case individuals' indifference to and repudiation of others are due to their feeling that their surroundings are uninterested in or inhospitable to them. In such occurrences, the second type of social isolation arises: a defensive retreat to guard self-worth (ibid., pp. 36–37). The lack of self-value is prominent in all chronic loneliness but especially pathological, the kind habitually undergone by schizophrenics.

The third sort of schizophrenic isolation, described by Weinberg—in addition to the objective isolation and the subjective withdrawal due to real or perceived exclusion or non-inclusion and their felt assault on self-worth—is graver. It consists in the psychotic's increasing ineptness at making or sustaining relationships and signifies a social secession that becomes a way of life (ibid., p. 37). This inability decreases the schizophrenic's already minimal social skills and increases those personality traits, such as social anxiety and shyness, which often characterize chronic loneliness.

Weinberg proposes that the more schizophrenics desire the persons who reject them, the more devastating is "the impact as a precipitating experience on the schizophrenic onset" (ibid., pp. 38–39). This development means that the graver the loneliness, the more substantive is its effect on triggering this incapacitating mental illness.

According to Daniel Perlman and Letitia Peplau, lonely people tend to have parents who are perceived as being "remote, less trustworthy, and disagreeable," whereas the nonlonely have by comparison parents who are "warm, close, and helpful." As well, Perlman and Peplau maintain that the lonely come from families that in general impart less "emotional nurturance, guidance, or support" to one another and that concurrently spawn a climate that is "cold, violent, undisciplined, and irrational" (1984, p. 24).

These shortcomings are especially applicable to those schizophrenogenic families whose members fail to provide one another adequate acceptance, affirmation, availability, and other critical conditions of intimacy. These improvidences leave the family especially vulnerable to affiliative and affective deficiencies, like loneliness. While there is greater loneliness in schizophrenogenic families than in perhaps any other, this incidence does not mean that negative familial relationships initially caused the schizophrenia.

Schizophrenia can occur in individuals whose total family relationships may be relatively satisfactory and wherein intimacy levels may even be rather high. All this notwithstanding, inadequate familial connectedness can only foment those factors conducive to the inception or magnification of schizophrenia and deleterious species of physical, social, and emotional isolation. Poor parenting, psychotic or otherwise, is patently a, if not the, major source of childhood loneliness and may well be the origin of later pathological loneliness, including that routinely experienced by schizophrenics and Group III personalities.

David Rosenhan and Martin Seligman contend that "schizophrenic parents"—who, they say, are themselves likely to engage in poor parenting—are "capable of inducing schizophrenia in their children, regardless of their common gene pool" (1989, p. 388). Rosenhan and Seligman further claim that "faulty communications within the *family* may well promote the development of schizophrenia" (ibid., p. 407). This process can at least contribute to the onset or intensification of this singularly enfeebling illness. Inadequate and, a fortiori, nonexistent parental and sibling intimacy—not to mention those conditions that are directly contrary to closeness like abuse—can only corral and consolidate those factors that trigger schizophrenia and its variegated isolation.

Communicative shortcomings enkindle a sense of exclusion that results in greater schizophrenic withdrawal, all of which, in its wake, decreases the social exchanges required for enhancing desirable family and non-family relations in the first place. Hence, schizophrenics' mental isolation aggravates both their physical and social isolation and vice versa. Resultingly, these psychotics are likely to experience both trait and state loneliness in an ever-increasing negative dialectical fashion.

Even more than other unspeaking and unspeakably lonely people, schizophrenics are perfunctorily remiss with respect to social experience, social confirmation, social composure, social intelligence, and social skills (Riggio, 1986, pp. 649–660). Moreover, by definition, they lack not only the social techniques and traits requisite for being with others but for being with themselves in a constructive manner. Since the ability to profit from being in the self's own company via solitude often parallels that of being pleasurably together with others, their inability to be solitary hits schizophrenics with a double dose of wretchedness.

Hence, while schizophrenics may at times possess an underlying interest in being with others, they do not have the communicative or intimacy skills and personality features that are conducive to being with them. Yet these excruciatingly sad and lonely individuals cannot be content let alone truly happy by themselves in terms of a constructive aloneness. They cannot because they lack the requisite solitary aptitudes and talents to be so.

Consequently, schizophrenics are not only deficient in communicative capabilities but are also devoid of adequate self-contact and self-communication, proficiencies demanded for positive states of aloneness. Nonetheless, their rehabilitation often partially depends on creating and actualizing solitary skills. Regrettably, schizophrenic self-communications are frequently delusional in nature and their occurrence in stark aloneness risks making them more terrifying for that reason alone.

Schizophrenics display culturally inappropriate behavior, impaired speech, and thought disorders that are hardly amenable for intimate interactions and attachments. Alternatively, these shortcomings are instrumental in increasing negative types of isolation and detachment.

All this said, some schizophrenics may, nevertheless, achieve a state of limited positive detachment from others. Ellen Corin and Gilles Lauzon define "positive withdrawal" as "a position at a distance from social roles and relationships" but one that is "combined with various strategies for keeping more tenuous links with the social organization" (1992, pp. 266–267).

Corin and Lauzon report that the non-rehospitalized schizophrenic may, in this kind of private-cum-social-space-niche of positive withdrawal, achieve some semblance of a more viable self-coherence and integration with the world. Doing so, would thereby somewhat abate the effects of negative withdrawals, which eventuate in the schizophrenic's sundry infelicitating isolations (ibid., pp. 269–270).

All positive bonds must, in the end, be understood as attempts to garner or regenerate meaning/intimacy with the self, others, and the world in general or to make positive adjustments to their temporary or permanent loss. Lamentably, the schizophrenic lacks both the wherewithal for intimacy with others and self and, thereby, is left marooned in a most perilous and disconsolate state by these deficiencies.

Psychologists Robert Sangster and Craig Ellison point out that the schizophrenic, "to compensate for feelings of social isolation and lack of social recognition and status," might "entertain fantasies of being the focus of widespread interest and attention." According to Sangster and Ellison, the schizophrenic's delusions of grandeur and omnipotence may help the individual deal with a sustained sentience of "inferiority and inadequacy," again, typical traits of the lonely (1978, p. 286).

Sangster and Ellison append that schizophrenics may also deliberately use odd speech and thought to prevent interpersonal interactions that they deem dangerous (ibid.). However, the fortress they build is also their prison so that they "do time" in solitary (lone) confinement, "in the hole," as it is said, in the black hole of loneliness. Schizophrenics apparently believe that no one has the will or desire to find them. Or, even if they are found, these desolates remain convinced that others lack the key to unlock the door to their interiority and terminate their miserable and multiple types of dividedness from their fellow human beings.

Eithne Tabor, a recovering schizophrenic patient of German-American psychiatrist Fromm-Reichmann, versifies the feelings of barrenness in desolating loneliness in her poem the "Empty Lot":

No one comes near here
Morning or night

> The desolate grasses
> Grow out of sight.
> Only a wild hare
> Strays, then is gone.
> The landlord is silence.
> The tenant is dawn. (Fromm-Reichmann, 1980, p. 353)

Fromm-Reichmann suspects that omitting any explicit mention of loneliness is likely due to this patient's pathological fear of this desolation.

It is noteworthy that Fromm-Reichmann essays that such a harrowing affliction is the "common fate" of Americans, "be they mentally healthy or disturbed," like the non-plus-ultra desolately isolated schizophrenic (ibid.). Many Americans, it may be inserted, may be so divorced from one another that their social and cultural loneliness increases their division in terms, for instance, of ethnicity, race, economic class, and religion.

Erich Fromm essays that the complete loss of a sense of belonging and intimacy, above all love, can bring about insanity. He defines psychosis as "the illness characterized by total absence of the relatedness to the world outside" (1966, p. 241). Hopelessly split off from others and themselves, schizophrenics are lost in their own world yet are, nonetheless, terrified at being out of it. All this assumes, first, that these psychological solipsists believe that there is a world besides theirs, and second, that they could break out of their imprisoning world and enter any beyond it.

Catastrophic loneliness may not be the cause of schizophrenia, but it can readily contribute to—even trigger—its inception and assuredly its continuation and intensification. As with the other mental state disorders, such as depression, the linkage of loneliness to schizophrenia will rest to a significant degree upon the specific approach taken regarding the former.

It is notable that the approach to loneliness can be neurobiological, behavioral, cognitive, sociological, privacy, psychodynamic, phenomenological, existential, interactionist, integral, or interpersonal to mention but some of the more influential sorts (Perlman and Peplau, 1982, pp. 123–134). Much the same can be said relative to the perspective invoked concerning schizophrenia and personality disorders.

There continues to be mounting evidence that supports the position that schizophrenia is initially caused by brain abnormalities with pathologies of a structural, biochemical, and physiological complexion. Nevertheless, the precise nature and number of its causes remain debatable. Yet, even if it were conclusively verified that, for example, neurobiological elements were the exclusive cause of all the schizophrenias, the other perspectives may be required for diagnostic and therapeutic purposes. Martin Willick proposes:

> schizophrenia is most likely a group of disorders with different etiologies and modes of pathogenesis. Etiological concepts of schizophrenia are

> extraordinarily complex, and no single explanation is going to be adequate given the interaction among genetic, environmental, and psychological factors. (1993, pp. 1137–1138; see also Beers, 2003, pp. 582–583)

Schizophrenics' profound and ongoing lack of quantitative not to mention qualitative social contacts segregates them physically, emotionally, socially, and culturally from their fellow human beings. Unlike the *DSM* schizoids, the isolations and withdrawals of schizophrenics are extremely (ego)dystonic since many of them, perhaps even a majority, would welcome contact with others, all things considered.

The schizophrenic, in the view of Fromm-Reichmann, has both a huge capability and a deep desire for love and other sorts of intimacy—all of which is also utterly unlike the *DSM* version of the schizoid aberrant (1980, p. 350). Still, she says, this psychotic feels hopeless in attaining such connectedness or even imagining it at least in its genuine epiphanies (ibid., p. 345). In a poem entitled "The Disenchanted," by Tabor, the despairing concealment of the schizophrenic's wasted potential for intimacy is poignantly presented:

> The demented hold love
> In the palm of the hand,
> And let it fall
> And grind it in the sand.
> To bury it again,
> And hide it forever
> From the sight of men. (Ibid., p. 353)

Lawrence Gerstein, Harry Bates, and Morey Reindl report on studies indicating that loneliness "is central to the experience of schizophrenics" (1987, p. 246). Their findings reveal that these psychotics, unsurprisingly, suffer significantly more from social "isolation, agitation, and health-related stress" than do lonely normals not to mention nonlonely normals (ibid., p. 239).

Harry Guntrip states that the therapist, in order to treat psychotics, must realize that they suffer most from the "terror of their own isolation, their own ability to do anything about it, and their desperate hope" that the clinician will somehow understand their dilemma and be able to "get in touch with them" (1973, p. 275). Assuredly, few things relieve the diversified pain that is so ingrained into loneliness as being touched in any sense of the term, including the literal.

7. Schizophrenics and the Ten Types of Loneliness

Schizophrenics are liable to experience all the ten types of loneliness outlined herein and often simultaneously, all of which exponentially increases their negative impact on their sufferers. As to "eros" loneliness, schizophrenics have few if any romantic, sexual, or genital interactions and even less ones that involve ongoing attachments. Their multiple and abysmal lack of social and intimacy talents and their overall strangeness are not conducive to attract others in these spheres of *shared intimacy* that is common to all inwardness and to the intimate sharing most found in the erotic.

On the contrary, potential “erotics” are repelled by the eccentric demeanor, dress, speech, thought, and other eerily and bizarrely foreign features of schizophrenics (as they are of schizotypals who, according to some genetic studies of them, “may be a mild form of schizophrenia”— Beers, 2003, p. 583). Their being rejected here, as elsewhere, greatly exacerbates these psychotics’ agonizing loneliness and the loneliness of their overall agony. The suffering in loneliness is to be distinguished from the loneliness of the suffering itself, in this case, that found in schizophrenia.

Their superabundance of estranging peculiarities not only causes schizophrenics eros but “cultural” loneliness as well. Since they are usually un- or under-employable due to their multiple oddities, these outcastes feel inferior, useless, and inadequate. Such sentiments mightily contribute to their being convinced that they are cultural pariahs, which, in fact, they invariably are. For instance, Weinberg reports that “minority youth groups in a given area had a higher rate of schizophrenia than youths of the majority group in that area” (1967, p. 36).

People generally construe loneliness to be a social and personal failure, whereas they equate being liked, attractive, and popular with success and status, all of which schizophrenics most manifestly lack. Sangster and Ellison write that, for these misfits, their “loneliness produces diminished status and then diminished status produces more loneliness” (1978, p. 288). Due to their employability impairments, the economic situation of the schizophrenic is ordinarily desperately destitute. Poverty and, a fortiori, destitution is a fertile source of (state) loneliness in itself.

It bears mentioning here that around 45 million Americans, or about 15 percent, that is one in seven, subsist below the poverty line of $23,000 yearly (CBS, 13 September 2010). Even more scandalously and largely due to poverty, “925 million” people were undernourished worldwide in 2010 and in the same year “a child died every six seconds because of undernourishment problems” (*The Montreal Gazette*, 15 September 2010). Of course, poverty also plays a prominent part in all forms of disease. We can only wonder how much it is a factor in the onset and continuation of schizophrenia, depression, and Group III personality disorders—all illnesses subject to grave loneliness.

As Sangster and Ellison document, negative attitudes about schizophrenics abound, all of which causes them humiliation and, therefore, further withdrawal. These outlooks intensify both their illness and their cultural and other types of loneliness, an isolation that has become, for them, an illness in its own right.

While their circumstances have improved in recent decades, schizophrenics have long been considered and treated, according to Sangster and Ellison, as "unpredictable, dirty, worthless, and dangerous" (1978, p. 288.). All these factors make schizophrenics further candidates for different types of loneliness and alienation, especially social and cultural.

The more serious loneliness becomes, the more others blame them and its sufferers blame themselves for their malaise. Holding them responsible for their own predicament, people are not generally sympathetic to the lonely save perhaps at the outset. Even though schizophrenia is usually held to be caused by forces beyond a person's control, many people are inclined to be less than understanding toward these psychotics for reasons just indicated. This lack of commiseration and considerateness drives the schizophrenic into an even deeper catastrophically diversified segregation.

As Sangster and Ellison further report, people are more compassionate to those who appear to be making efforts to overcome their loneliness. Yet people also tend to believe—and to some extent rightly so—that schizophrenics have implicitly chosen to accept and even increase their social and physical retreat and, therefore, at least tacitly, are somewhat responsible for their continuing loneliness (ibid.).

I interject at this point that a person can have sympathy, which pertains to emotion, for another without having empathy, which is a kind of cognition. Still, sometimes empathy is deemed to be a blend of knowledge and affect. In which case, it is often affiliated, either as a cause or an effect, with sympathy, and above all the kind that emanates from love and its allegedly emotionally intuitive understanding à la Max Scheler.

It bears noting that people by means of empathy may try to enter the interior of others for negative reasons. These include the wish to control, a strong suspicion of which is found among schizophrenics, especially the paranoid type, and the paranoid personality, although, in my view, the first is more genetically based than the second.

Schizophrenics experience profound "metaphysical" loneliness in that they epitomize feeling singularly and irreversibly severed from extramental reality as a whole should, indeed, they acknowledge it as being entitatively different from their own mental state. They are also subject to metaphysical loneliness in a specifically ontological sense since, to recall, they feel that they have lost their *being* or are forever on the verge of doing so.

Schizophrenics are exceedingly vulnerable to devastating "cosmic" loneliness since they regard objective reality and often even their own subjective reality—should they make a separation or even a distinction between the two spheres—as unfriendly, indeed hostile. Schizophrenics—who account for 1 percent of the population worldwide and are the ninth leading cause of disability—are perceived as being intruders into the normal world, one that is concomitantly strange and estranging to them. They are literally the definitive version of "the odd-person-out" type of individual (the prevalence of this most harrowing illness appears to be equal among men and women—Beers, 2003, p. 582).

Theirs is a world, therefore, that segments schizophrenics not only from others but from themselves or the structural constituents thereof—be they those of the body, mind, or soul. Hence, it would belabor the evident to insist that schizophrenics are the quintessence of "intraself" loneliness and self-alienation. They are, according to Laing, the uppermost case of being divided from themselves and others (1965).

Concerning intraself loneliness, schizophrenics paradigmatically represent the feeling of being bereft of an interior and exterior compass. This anxiety can cause them to be what might be known as nomadic monads, meaning atomistic individuals who, often literally homeless, wander about the world detached from themselves and from every other human being.

Schizophrenics are like ghosts in that they are akin to the alleged apparition of spirits from some putative other world, usually a netherworld, meaning the world of the dead. As the nethermost, or most subterranean, region of the world, it is the darkest (most meaningless) and coldest (most intimacy-less). So stated, it is the land of loneliness, a fitting place for the schizophrenic who is locked into its deathly hell of frozen and pitch-black isolation, the kind Dante Alighieri describes in his *Inferno*.

Without other human beings—and nobody is more bereft of them than the schizophrenic—the self becomes lost within itself and at a loss as to how get out of it to access others. Yet, schizophrenics are terrified at this possibility because they are convinced that it is likely others, including their alien(ating) inner demons, who have committed them to this interior maze.

Intrapersonal loneliness is, therefore, an unwanted feeling of the division or divisibility of self-being, and no one epitomizes this scission more than the schizophrenic. On the other hand, such loneliness may be witnessed in the self's dissatisfaction with its present relationship with parts of its self. This disaffection has appeared in many (dis)guises throughout history. It is recurrently seen as the self's dismay at being trapped or entrapped by its supposedly inferior part. Thus, the soul and mind are held to be shackled by the body or whatever else is deemed the non-spiritual or non-conscious elements of the self. More rarely, it is the mind and soul that are believed to enchain the body (vol. 1, pp. 143–146).

Schizophrenics are at especial risk for "epistemological" loneliness, due to their profound perceptual difficulties, such as deficiencies in comprehending others' language, both verbal and nonverbal, their auditory and visual hallucinations, and their thought disorders both as to process, such as attentional deficits, and to content, such as delusions (Rosenhan and Seligman, 1989, pp. 367–379).

Schizophrenics are incredibly difficult to decipher in part because they send out either no messages or mixed messages, in any case, scrambled ones. They defiantly resist being known and may yet simultaneously tenaciously seek being understood even totally comprehended, an ambivalence largely derived from their anxiety concerning intimacy.

As to their "(in)communicative" type of loneliness, the schizophrenics' most curious ways of using language, again both verbal and nonverbal, are obvious sources of non- or misunderstanding, not to mention ridicule, revulsion, and rejection. Cordoned off from others, schizophrenics do not have, as Sangster and Ellison put the matter, the "social reality testing" that is needed to develop social skills and social intelligence, and the language befitting them (1978, p. 286). Schizophrenics are, undoubtedly, among the archetypes of ambivalence, given their desire to be both understood and not understood. They are also the foremost of ambiguity forgers as evinced, for example, by their "word salads and syllabic stews," as they have been called (Rosenhan and Seligman 1989, p. 381).

"Ethical loneliness" can be defined as the felt isolation experienced in the effort to become psychologically mature and morally authentic. In their own inimitable way, schizophrenics may be especially subject to these kinds of isolation. Still, for such paradigmatic isolates, how this vulnerability is the case is an extremely complex issue. In sum, it is contained in the struggle, for example, between their autonomous (independent) and homonomous (dependent) selves, their true and false selves, and their pretending to be one or the other not only to others but to themselves (Laing, 1965, pp. 160–177). This battle is constantly waged within these tragic and sometimes pathetic figures. The tragic may be defined as that which invokes sympathy; the pathetic as that which causes contemptuous pity. These two reactions commonly occur and often simultaneously concerning schizophrenics.

Like all human beings—save perhaps schizotypals but especially schizoids—schizophrenics are subject to "existential" loneliness. In any case, theirs is far more consciously excruciating and enduring than that which might possibly be experienced by these Group I abnormals. Their very illness makes these psychotics attuned to but unequipped to deal with the stresses of everyday existence. For these seemingly unreachable souls, life is an insuperable dissociation from mental and extramental reality.

Finally and as to "social" loneliness, if the schizophrenics need, for example, hospitalization, they are often cut off from family and all "normal" contact. While institutionalized, they may spend their days and nights all alone, prisoners of their own mind. At other times, they may be crammed together with other alienated, alienating, and sometimes violently so, inmates.

When not hospitalized, schizophrenics may witness how their family and others have intimacy in their lives and how they have none in theirs. They are also habitually subject to anti-intimate actions such as wholesale ridicule. All this exclusion and non-inclusion enlarge the gap between schizophrenics' desire and realization for intimacy and solidify their feelings of being outside society or at most on its outskirts reserved for other social and cultural lepers.

Schizophrenics are, therefore, mired in a morass of vicious circles such that their illness causes them unparalleled loneliness, which, in its wake, intensifies their sickness. Their apartheid is likely unrivalled because it comes in so many forms and in such devastating intensity. Each species of loneliness has a proclivity to increase the dystonic nature of the others so that the forms of this tribulation are extremely synergic but negatively so.

All illnesses of whatever nature—moral/spiritual, psychic, somatic, and psychosomatic (somatoform)—may split the self from others emotionally and often socially and physically as well. In some cases, these divorcements are the precipitators of a person's disorder, for example, emotional isolation with respect to lonely depression. We have seen that Berg, Fromm, and Fromm-Reichmann argue that loneliness can be the direct cause of mental illness, including schizophrenia. Alternatively, the ability and even the desire to unite with others, above all on a genuinely intimate basis, is a most rudimentary sign of normality and health in all its species.

As has been contended by many writers, human beings derive much of their sense of objective and subjective reality from other human beings. If they are absent in prolonged fashion, people begin to feel that reality, both mental and extramental, is highly tortuous and tenuous. Catastrophically lonely individuals, both normals but especially abnormals, like schizophrenics and borderlines, may be inclined to feel that they have actually ceased to exist, at least extramentally.

8. The Schizophrenic Spectrum

The schizoid and especially the schizotypal of Group I come closest to what I reference as psychological, meaning psychotic, solipsists with, in my view, the possible exception of the borderline (and, to a lesser extent, the paranoid). We recall that the schizotypal is, according to the *DSM*, subject to cognitive and perceptual distortions. When extreme, these defects may verge on the belief that others are not fully extramentally real. In which event, the schizotypal borders on being both a metaphysical and psychological solipsist, as is the case with the schizophrenic.

The strange mentalities and behaviors of the schizotypal and, to a lesser measure, the schizoid are the main reasons why they are sometimes held to be on the aforementioned psychotic spectrum, more commonly known as the schizophrenic spectrum. Paranoid personalities are frequently placed on this continuum, though, again, in my judgment, there is much less if any significant basis for their being located on it certainly less than either the schizoid or schizotypal.

According to David Bernstein and David Useda, the schizotypal disorder "from its inception, was conceptualized as a schizophrenia spectrum disorder," whereas today, they contend, as do I, that "the genetic connection between the paranoid PD and schizophrenia remains an open question" (2007, p. 46). I also agree with Bernstein and Useda when they maintain that there is even less evidence for holding that the schizoid belongs on the psychotic continuum than does the schizotypal and, a fortiori, in their judgment, the paranoid personality (ibid., p. 53). Of course, the paranoid mental trait disorder is to be differentiated from the paranoid schizophrenic mental state disorder, though precisely how different they are is much disputed.

Bernstein and Useda point out that the pathology of the schizoid and schizotypal appears to continue throughout life, whereas that of the paranoid need not (ibid., p. 73). I believe that one reason for their trait perdurance is that the Group I qualities are more genetically influenced, if not necessitated, than are those of the paranoid of Group II. The stronger the genetic basis for a particular personality disorder, the longer, in principle, it lasts.

Thus, I share the view of Bernstein and Useda who hold, "the paranoid is more a phenotypic personality than a genotypic personality, like the schizotypal" (ibid., p. 51), and, I would add, the schizoid. The paranoid is more a product of environment (and choice) than are the schizoid, schizotypal, and, a fortiori, the schizophrenic since all three appear to be more biologically and less environmentally based than the paranoid.

Bernstein and Useda propose, as do I, that the *DSM* criteria for the paranoid "appear to over-represent the cognitive traits of mistrust/suspiciousness" but "under-represent the prototypical behavioral, affective, and interpersonal expressions of paranoid personality traits" (ibid., p. 46). In my view, these under-represented qualities should place the paranoid in my Group II instead of Group I and out of the schizophrenic continuum.

For the *DSM*, the key to understanding the nature of the paranoid mentality is this pathological's universal distrust of others due to the first interpreting the actions of the second as being malevolently motivated. This cognitive trait of mistrust is both the cause and the effect of the paranoid behavioral, emotional, and interpersonal expressions of this aberrant's hyper-wariness.

Amazingly, while *The Manual* lengthily exemplifies how paranoids interpret the alleged malevolence on the part of others toward them, it fails to point out that this ill will is essentially an externalization of the paranoids' malevolence upon them (pp. 634–636). Yet it may well have been their numerous and variegated peculiarities that in their childhood caused others to be or at least be perceived as being malevolent toward the paranoids (ibid., p. 636). Such eccentricities appear to have been generated more by the paranoids' hostile reaction to those in their environment than by more or less purely genetic factors. In any case, it is the paranoids' negative interpersonality as, for instance, expressed in their bitter ill will that most allies them to the other Group II aberrants but differentiates them from Group I, especially the compliant and passive schizoid.

In my view, as well, the paranoid and especially the antisocial could be placed on a "morally psychotic" spectrum. To a lesser extent, so also could the other two Group II deviants, namely the narcissist and obsessional. All are frequently quasi ethically demented, despite or in part because of their all-around egoism as evidenced in their pretensions of moral superiority.

Antisocials would occupy first place on this spectrum because they are the sole personality pathologicals who cannot only be exceedingly immoral to the point of being viciously wicked but amoral and antimoral. The "immoral" can be understood as the violation of moral principles; the "amoral" as the ignorance, arguably culpable, not only of their nature but their very existence; and the "antimoral," their deliberate flaunting ethical precepts.

Consequently, while paranoids have an affinity with some psychological traits of the schizoid and schizotypal, the latter two have few if any of the formers' unethical traits, especially those that are of an inhumane nature. These qualities are the type paranoids share with sociopaths and, to a lesser extent, with narcissists and obsessionals of Group II (Costa and Widiger, 1994, p. 329; 2002, p. 461).

While the paranoid is an exceedingly immoral individual, the schizoid and schizotypal can perhaps be best described as nonmoral or even premoral. The reason is that these deviants do not typically violate moral codes by their actions but simply refrain from being engaged in them in large part due to their being absolute social isolates. Thus, their failures in morality are almost exclusively due to omission. Paranoids are relative social isolates (lonerists) and their moral shortcomings are often a result of choice and commission.

Though the schizotypal and especially the schizoid have a kind of eerie non-humanness about them, they are not malevolent and even less malicious inhumanists as the paranoid is. The schizoid and schizotypal are non-attached, or socially withdrawn, because they prefer to be alone but they, especially the schizoid, are not critical of others. Paranoids are detached because they are hypercritical of others, but extremely hypocritical of themselves. They furiously strive to protect themselves from imagined or real threats, which they themselves ordinarily provoke, behavior unlike that of the schizoid and schizotypal.

Bernstein and Useda propose, as do I, that the chief comorbidity of the schizoid is with the schizotypal and next with the avoidant instead of the paranoid (2007, p. 69). However, what mainly prevents the schizotypal and schizoid overlapping with the avoidant is that the former two aberrants, especially the schizoid, circumvent social connections because they supposedly have little or no need, capability, ability, desire, or willingness regarding relatedness whereas the avoidant does. It is their disposition to interpersonal relatedness that, in my judgment, most essentially differentiates all the personality disorders from one another and from normal personalities. Accordingly, such interpersonal association is, I believe, the best basis for aggregating pathological personalities.

9. The "Schizoidic" Condition

Laing discusses what he names the "schizoidic condition"—a state not to be confused with the *DSM* schizoid personality disorder—which he says generally precedes and often partakes of psychosis (1965, p. 137). What Laing has in mind by this condition seems to me to be a combination of, first, the *DSM* schizotypal, provided this disordered personality is interpreted as having some minimal interest in intimacy; second, the *DSM* avoidant; and, third, the psychotic viewed as the schizophrenic.

Laing says that the schizoid condition—henceforth the "schizoidic" lest it be confused with the schizoid(al) personality disorder—is characteristic of an individual who is singularly apprehensive concerning close relationships. This anxiety is due to the schizoidic being highly vulnerable to phenomena that the Scottish psychiatrist titles engulfment, implosion, and petrifaction.

With respect to engulfment, Laing maintains that schizoidics are terrified that they will be swallowed up in and by any intimate attachment. As a result, these individuals believe that they would forfeit whatever little identity and independence they have by such contact (ibid., p. 44).

Laing contends that schizoidics feel they must choose between being completely absorbed in what amounts to a negative homonomy, on the one hand, and being totally isolated, on the others, in which case, these isolates are condemned to a negative autonomy. According to Laing, since schizoidics most fear losing their independence, they opt to be severed from others. In doing so, they are subject to an irremediably mournful loneliness. Nonetheless, it is the kind that schizoidics figure to be less dolorous than the sort in which they feel forsaken inside an attachment, an attitude akin to the *DSM* avoidant's mind-set (ibid.).

Intimacy is the quintessential sort of positive union, in which case it entails a constructive kind of dependence. As is commonly conceded, only individuals who have a strong sense of self can merge with another and yet retain, indeed increase their autonomy, identity, and integrity. Schizophrenics, in particular, are woefully devoid of such attributes, in my view, ultimately because they have no interpersonal identity or one so (negatively) disintegrated and distorted as to be de facto missing. As a result, schizophrenics completely isolate themselves to protect their fragile and fragmented self-unity. Hence, they live in a state of negative autonomy in large part because they are afraid of being engulfed in any homonomy, or union, with others.

As to implosion, schizoidics, according to Laing, long for their loneliness to be eliminated and replaced by love, but they remain devoid of it and other forms of intimacy. The reason: they are afraid that if any such contact did penetrate their self it would blow it to bits, like a gas invading a vacuum, so empty is the schizoidic's being. Thus, Laing maintains that schizoidics feel that any concern for them would cause an inner explosion that would thereby obliterate their very being, the minuscule amount they have. This belief reinforces schizoidics' fear of staying or at least becoming a kind of non-being, to wit an ontological nullity (ibid., pp. 45–46).

In this fashion, Laing's schizoidics experience themselves as non-existent or at most as nothing more than a purely contingent and unnecessary entity, experiences typical of the cataclysmically lonely. Of course, any experience assumes the existence of the experiencer. But, then, the question becomes, once again, which existence, mental or extramental?

Schizoidics, in Laing's view, have persuaded themselves that others, especially intimates, will objectify them, like Medusa, who by its gaze turned people to stone and, accordingly, can be said to be the epitome of the "evil eye" phenomenon (ibid., p. 46). Schizoidics are also scared that others will steal their identity, subjectivity, their entire being.

In Laing's notion of schizoidics, they embody the horror of being violated, desecrated, and nihilized. Though they yearn for intimacy, these individuals are certain they will be destroyed by experiencing any inwardness, especially via its most powerful form, namely love. Thus, Laing maintains that if schizoidics believe in anything, it is in their own destructibility (ibid., p. 93).

Consequently, these desolates think they must avoid love if they and the possible objects of their affection are not to be ruined by such intimacies. They do so because these unfortunates are certain that such contacts are as annihilating as hate. Indeed, schizoidics, in the judgment of Laing, have come to hold that love is nothing else than hatred in disguise (ibid.).

Laing construes schizoidics' seeming indifference, aloofness, and overall lack of gregariousness as shields to conceal their cravings for closeness. In the end, these reluctant loners stay clear of contact with others because they are afraid of winding up with a wounded or shattered heart. Laing reminds his readers that the etymology of schizophrenia signifies a broken heart (1967, p. 130). (*Schiz* signifies split and *phrenos* means heart, though it can also signify the mind and soul.) A shattered heart implies a pulverizing of the person as a whole, a phenomenon predicable of the schizophrenic in model manner.

In Laing's view, schizoidics hide what they think is their true self, their intimate self. It is the one vulnerable to loneliness and to being absorbed in and "enstoned" by others in addition to exploding from within due to these isolates' cavernous affective vacuity. Consequently, schizoidics lead a life hounded by an inveterate and searing intrapersonal loneliness that breaks their heart, terrifies their mind, and tortures their soul. Laing proposes, therefore, that the schizoidic type of person in general "descends into a vortex of nonbeing [loneliness] in order to avoid being," which is preeminently intimacy (1965, p. 93).

Laing's notion of the schizoidic resembles Jean-Paul Sartre's idea of "being-for-others." In this phenomenon, people, in being known, become alienated and even robbed by others, frequently without their knowledge much less their consent. Thus, Sartre looks upon love as but a project to separate and thereupon capture the alleged beloved's freedom and independence, the fear of which is emblematic of Laing's schizoidic individual (Sartre, 1956, p. 375).

Group I abnormals and the paranoid of Group II can be candidates for psychological solipsism in that all three can, according to the *DSM*, precede "delusional disorder, schizophrenia, and mood disorder with psychotic features" (pp. 636, 640, 643). (From this perspective, paranoid pathologicals should be placed on the schizophrenic spectrum.) In any case, it is manifest that the combinations and permutations of psychotic solipsism and the loneliness, which so routinely suffuses it, are myriad.

In sum, psychological solipsists, construed above all as schizophrenics, are widely held to be quasi innately and non-plus-ultra lonely individuals (McGraw, 1999b, pp. 152–154). Contrarily, epistemic, metaphysical, and methodological solipsists are not reckoned as being necessarily lonely if only because the aloneness, which they contemplate is not one that pertains to emotional isolation, assuredly not in any direct manner. Naturally, if these kinds of solipsists actually habitually lived—that is thought, felt, and acted on a daily basis—as if they were extramentally all alone in the universe and would be forever, they would be desolately lonely and subject to becoming insanely so, to wit becoming psychological solipsists.

10. Egological Solipsism

If being loved is the greatest affirmation and confirmation of personal existence, then not being so is its foremost negation and disconfirmation. It is not only in not being loved that people can feel that their existence has "gone down the drain" and disappeared from among the living. In not loving others, they may also feel that they have made a beeline toward oblivion. Edward, a character in T. S. Eliot' play, *The Cocktail Party*, in realizing that he loves no one, feels that he has lost his life for all practical purposes (1950, p. 98).

Edward symbolizes the fifth type of solipsist: the egological, or egocentric. This species concedes that other persons exist extramentally but acts as if they were created solely to satisfy an individual's self-interest. Given their quasi-total egoism, those with a Group II abnormality are the most self-centered solipsists among the pathological if not all personalities, followed by Group III and then Group I.

Egoistic solipsists are partial immoral isolates and often are social isolates as well, as in the case of Group II individuals. They can be contrasted, for instance, with solitaries (primary) who are moral isolates in the sense that their volitional segregation is a means to ethical self-improvement and authenticity and a way to better the lives of others.

The Group II immoral isolates, above all the sociopaths, carry egocentricity to the absolute extreme in the form of egomania. Recall that sometimes sociopaths are labeled morally psychotic, or insane. They are not deemed to be strictly cognitively psychotic such that they experience schizophrenic irrationalities. Nevertheless, sociopaths are subject to delusions of grandeur, which explains their sense of impunity and immunity, and as such may be considered megalomaniacal.

The other Group II pathologicals may also be said to be subject to quasi-like delusions: of persecution (the paranoid); of grandiosity such as unlimited brilliance (the narcissist); and of being controlled by, for instance, schedules, a fixation that often parallels the compulsion to control others (the obsessional) (*DSM*, pp. 637–638, 649–650, 661, 672–673). It is apparent that such "thought disorders" of Group II are different in kind or at least in huge degree from those of the schizophrenic psychotic with his or her more or less complete failure in terms of "reality testing," a shortcoming that pertains to extramental and mental entities. I insert here that Paul T. Costa and and Thomas A. Widiger look upon paranoids as being but middling in terms of a lack of altruism, the most anti-egoistical of traits (2002, p. 466). Contrariwise, I rank them on the basis of their *DSM* depiction as being just behind sociopaths in terms of a generalized anti-altruism and anti-humaneness.

Costa and Widiger look upon Group III histrionics as being non-altruistic on the basis of their *DSM* portrayal (ibid.). Alternatively, I would argue that histrionics are not habitually malevolently motivated but acquisitively in that they tend to ignore others' needs and desires. However, they do not, as a rule, directly seek to contravene and in general undermine others' welfare as do the thoroughly ill-willed and selfish Group II pathologicals.

In short, Group II abnormals deliberately abuse the rights of others, whereas Group III and especially Group I are apt to neglect them. However, the borderlines of Group III are also guilty of intentionally violating the rights of others but do so largely out of a reactive anger in that they feel they have been maltreated. Group II mistreat others as a matter of principle and have, unlike borderlines, little or no shame or guilt in doing so, with the exception of the obsessionals.

The compulsives are the least bad of the psycho-ethically worst of the pathologicals, namely Group II, whereas the borderlines are the worst of the least psycho-ethically bad of the aberrants, namely Group III. From a strictly psychic point of view, Group I are the most disturbed of the ten abnormal personalities. I evaluate the degree or level of personality disturbance in terms of its proximity to egological solipsism, or self-centeredness, especially unethical instead of purely psychic.

11. Solipsism and the "Lone(ly) Thinker"

It is instructive that people speak of a "thinker" as someone who is lost in thought, especially that kind called cogitation, the kind that is highly deliberate and "deep." This characterization has been traditionally most applied to philosophers since they are given to pondering exceedingly abstruse complexities, not the least of which are the theoretic types of solipsism (I remember one philosopher defining philosophy as a most serious exercise in vehement abstraction). Being lost in thought is above all predicated of metaphysicians. Voltaire declares that these are the philosophers who continue to talk to those who do not understand them and wind up no longer understanding what they themselves are saying (1970, p. 471n45).

Such mental rumination is often said of the lone philosophical thinker, especially one who not only habitually reflects on reality but does so in social and physical isolation. This individual is often believed to be not only lost in solitary reflection but abandoned to the iciness of emotional isolation. John Keats asks, "do not all charms fly/At the mere cold touch of philosophy?" (1970, p. 470n14). Perhaps this supposedly frosty dispassionateness moved Georg Wilhelm Friedrich Hegel to declare that there is "no science in which one is as lonely as in philosophy" (Kaufmann, 1965, p. 342). For philosophers, such as Nietzsche, philosophy is a lonely calling in large part because its genuine practitioners are socially and culturally segregated due to professing unorthodox and unpopular ideas via "untimely meditations" (1991, pp. 182–194).

The above views about the loneliness of thinkers, especially philosophers are sometimes made about Edmund Husserl and his one-time student Sartre. It is pertinent that both strive to overcome metaphysical and epistemological solipsism by their method of philosophizing: Husserl by a phenomenology that is essentialist in composition; Sartre, by one that is existentialist.

Husserl proposes that in order to become a philosopher the individual must go "through loneliness" (Heinemann, 1965, p. 52). The person must do so if only because the German philosopher stresses that genuine philosophy must contain two types of lonelifying reductions, essentially meaning isolating separations. The first is the phenomenological separation of the self from the natural, extramental world as a whole, including other selves. The second is the transcendental severance of the self from its self, in which case, it becomes a pure, or disembodied, ego capable of contemplating pure essences.

This Husserlian philosophical bifurcation of the individual from the world and from its self had a counterpart in Husserl's personal life. He himself supposedly lived the phenomenological reduction in that he confessed having led a lonely (and solitary) life. Husserl did so because be held that philosophy itself demanded this apartheid: "Philosophy arises in the lonely responsible thought of the [individual] who is philosophizing" (ibid., pp. 52–53).

Husserl lived the second reduction in that he envisioned himself as being an ego separated from itself such that the philosopher claimed that he literally became "the transcendental Ego" (ibid., p. 53). Ben Mijuskovic considers Husserl's Ego to be not only "lonely" but "unremittingly lonesome" (1979, p. 79n9). These phenomena may be interpreted as Husserl's longing, respectively, for other egos and for the "natural" world as a whole instead of the abstract world of pure ideas, or essences.

F. H. Heinemann portrays Husserl's philosophy in the manner the philosopher himself describes his own person, namely as one "of the lonely transcendental Self." It is also a philosophy in which the ego is so lonelified and estranged from itself, the world, and others that Heinemann says "it is an autonomous consciousness which does not belong to anybody" (1965, p. 53).

Heinemann, who conversed at length with Husserl on several occasions, relates that the pioneering phenomenologist "did not talk as his natural Self, but as an anonymous transcendental Ego, as consciousness in general" (ibid.). Such professional divorcement, or estrangement, from extramental reality is, according to many non-philosophers, the typical mode of existence, for philosophers, phenomenological or otherwise.

The lonely do not feel that they belong to others or vice versa. But intrapersonal loneliness (and alienation) makes them feel, like Husserl's transcendental ego, that they do not even belong to themselves. This conviction is traceable to the fact that the lonely believe that their self is becoming more and more vacuous so much so that it is vanishing ontologically and psychologically. On the other hand, the more this disappearance pertains not to one's own ego but to the longed for others, the more the self is subject to metaphysical and epistemological solipsism and loneliness.

Heinemann goes on to depict Husserl as "a first-rate philosopher" but one so much lacking in "common sense" that, in his leaving the natural world via the phenomenological reduction so as to understand it better, he got utterly lost. And he did so in the world of the lone(ly) if not solipsistic transcendental ego with its ethereal idealities completely severed from earthly realities. In short, Heinemann says that Husserl was "enormously alive but alive as a mind and devoted to problems far removed from life" (ibid., pp. 51–52). Consequently, he epitomized the caricature of the philosopher as a thinker who is distracted via abstractions from the everyday world in order to ponder some other otherworldly existence, à la Plato, for instance.

In my judgment, Husserl lived a life of solitariness, meaning one of internal, or subjective, solitude combined with loneliness. But he was also a solitudinarian, meaning that his external, or objective, solitude bordered on reclusiveness. Husserl personifies philosophizing as a love of truth and knowledge but perhaps not wisdom—certainly not that of the heart and the kind devoted to the understanding of love rooted in the world at hand.

Such caring is arguably the phenomenon most concerned with the real world and real persons and whose study is found in the phenomenology of love and the very etymology of philosophy as a love of wisdom. It is one developed, for instance, by more existential and personalist phenomenologists such as Karl Jaspers and especially Max Scheler (and arguably even by Husserl in his later years).

Husserl's program is to describe the world in the consciousness of the single, or lone, ego via abstract essentialism, or pure ideation. Alternatively, Sartre's existentialist goal is ultimately to characterize consciousness—as it actually *ex-ists*. Accordingly, his project is to discover the world as it stands outside of sheer possibilities, including the conceptual. Still, the mind, for

Sartre, is not reducible to the world insofar as it is material. Nonetheless, he does not appear to hold that the mind is immaterial in the sense of being an immortal soul.

Both Husserl and Sartre consider consciousness as phenomenological, or intentional, meaning that it necessarily tends toward something other than itself, whereas the reflexive model claims the mind is originally focused on itself. Some may argue that the kind of consciousness posited by Husserl and Sartre does not succeed in escaping the self-isolating Cartesian inward turning of the mind upon itself, which is arguably the ultimate in conceiving it as a solitary process. Nor, according to some, does the phenomenological perspective escape loneliness since Husserl's transcendental ego is lonely alone, whereas Sartre's empirical ego is lonely amidst others.

Additionally, Sartre—who apparently once described himself as a lonely little shrimp—maintains that consciousness, considered in itself and as a kind of non-empirical ego, a sort of original solitude, meaning in this context a type of primordial ontological loneliness (1956, p. 456).

Sartre strives to bring consciousness into the extramental world, but he claims that lovelessness and conflict rule there, in which case, the self reflects a sort of egological solipsism (ibid., pp. 361–382). Husserl wants to bring the extramental world into consciousness and in doing so the self risks being subject to metaphysical and epistemological solipsism.

If philosophizing begins with an investigation of the ego, self, mind, or consciousness instead of the person as such, it may become mired, if not in epistemic and metaphysical theoretical solipsisms, then in psychological and egological types, the kind human beings actually experience. The concept of a person is necessarily allied to other persons in the extramental world and, accordingly, philosophy (and philosophizing) arguably warrants beginning and ending with notion of interpersonality and personalism as a whole.

Interpersonality suggests, in my view, that the human being is naturally benevolent or so disposed instead of being neutral and, a fortiori, hostile with respect to others. However, I am not proposing that a person or his or her consciousness is innately ordered to a behavior that is beneficent much less lovingly so and even less altruistically so, meaning universal in scope.

If, like Sartre, people do assume the extramental existence of others but solely the sort who are inherently not only non-loving but hateful or scornfully indifferent to one another, they also wind up in existential (a)loneliness and egological solipsism. This kind of isolated existence is typical of the Group II pathological lonerists.

Having sketched the notions of aloneness and their number, in the ensuing chapters I will relate them to a more systematic analysis of the nature and kinds of personality, especially that type designated as diseased.

Four

PERSONALITY: ITS NATURE AND NUMBER

1. Personality: Problem and Mystery

No entity is more problematic than personality—so much so that debates about its composition and classification are likely to continue indefinitely. Indeed, some questions about personality appear tantamount to being irresolvable in fact and perhaps in principle such that they are titled mysteries. (Personality as a natural mystery is distinguished from supernatural mysteries such as that posited by, for example, Christian theologians, who, though monotheists, believe that the godhead is a trinity of persons; see McGraw, 1992, pp. 320–321.)

Unquestionably, the subjects human beings find most problematic and puzzling—in addition to being intriguing and mysterious—are their own persons. Consequently, it is not surprising that over the millennia, there have been literally dozens even hundreds of definitions of personality.

The word "person" is ultimately derived from the Etruscan and Greek words for mask, originally meaning a covering used to conceal the face of an actor. This employment suggests that the true identity of the person inherently lies behind or is even purposely disguised by what appears outwardly.

Accordingly, a person is commonly considered to be that kind of individual that is singularly or at least exceedingly unfathomable and ineffable. It is notable that incomprehensibility and inexpressibility pertain, respectively, to epistemic and (in)communicative loneliness. If these types of isolation are envisioned as insuperably ingrained in all persons, they form part of that loneliness designated existential. Consequently, if the notion of personality involves the problematic—and all the more so the mysterious to the point of being a mystery—in the abstract, how much more so it is in reference to the actual individual who is this uniquely particularized and irreduplicable Tom, Dick, or Mary?

The copious conceptualizations of personality have prompted American psychologist Gordon Allport to propose that it "is one of the most abstract words" in human language and, as a result, can, he says, suffer "from excessive use." Allport contends that this over-usage of personality is owing, more precisely, to its "connotative" import being overly "broad" and its "denotative" significance being highly "negligible" in the sense of being remiss regarding depth and clarity of meaning (Millon with Roger Davis, 1996, p. 16).

2. The Person: The Most Special Individual

With respect to its being an individual, as distinguished from a class, species, or collection, a person is reckoned to be the most special sort of a singularized entity. Nonetheless, a person is intrinsically a communal kind of being such that its constitution is inherently and unalterably interpersonal in nature.

The word "individual" itself, especially as predicated of the concept of personhood and its distribution in diverse types of personality, has had a remarkably checkered career in that it has careened from one meaning to another, including even those that are opposites. Peter Abbs states that an individual initially signified the indivisible, which, in turn, meant "not to be parted" and as such could be ascribed, he says, to the Christian "Trinity" or to "a married couple" (Storr, 1988, p. 80). Abbs writes:

> The gradual inversion of meaning for the word *individual*—moving from the indivisible and collective to the divisible and distinctive, carries quietly within itself the historical development of self-consciousness—testifies to that complex dynamic of change which separated the person from his world making him self-conscious and self-aware, that change in the structure of feeling which during the Renaissance shifted from a sense of unconscious fusion with the world toward a state of conscious individuation. (Ibid.)

Similarly, Jacob Burckhardt essays that those who lived in medieval times were conscious of themselves not as individuals as such but solely as members "of a race, people, party, family, or corporation," that is "only through some general category." Burckhardt proposes that it was only after the Renaissance that people began to consider themselves as individuals in today's meanings of individuality, such as having personal distinctiveness and independence (Winter and Barenbaum, 1999, p. 4).

Robert Sayre contends that, during the Middle Ages:

> [the economy of feudalism] and the highly stratified, compartmentalized social system allow the individual to exist only within the group. The word *individual* in The Middle Ages means inseparable from a group or whole. Each group, in turn, has its place in a "great chain of being" which defines its relationship with other groups and its place in the universe. (1978, p. 30)

It may be true, as Sayre says, that medievals were envisioned as existing only within some group or subgroup. Yet, I submit that it is also verifiable that they did not view themselves as being simply literal parts of such units. Medievals were not, therefore, social "monists." Of course, even less were they social "atomists," whose extreme individualism prevented group consciousness and affiliation.

Medievals were, in my judgment, societal organicists and communalists and as such, stressed the priority of the common good over purely private concerns. Human beings as members of the all-embracing chain of being were invariably linked together. Still, each link had a distinctive identity in addition to its group identity within this universal catena.

In classical medieval times, each individual existed primarily to serve God and "his" "greater glory." Yet, everyone had his or her own particularity qua person as created "in the image and likeness" of God, customarily known as "the Person of persons." Hence, every individual had a unique place in the group and in the universe as a whole not via *a* but *the* single "great chain of being" since there was only one such universal entitative unification.

Ultimately, the person was held to be irreplaceable because of God's special love for each and every unique individual. This divine love precluded loneliness, or at any rate, reduced it. It was this kind of thinking that moved writers such as Ludwig Feuerbach and Jean-Paul Sartre to declare that God is but a fabrication on the part of human beings to deal with, respectively, their (a)loneliness, especially what I denominate metaphysical, epistemological, cosmic, and social. Indeed, for theists, including and perhaps especially Christians, God was reckoned to be the panacea of all ten forms of loneliness, as I have essayed elsewhere (McGraw, 1992).

The fear of being forever excluded from the global chain of being was the ultimate terror for the medieval Christian, since it meant being thrown into hell, which, in turn, signified an unending separation from God. Nevertheless, even hell was commonly conceived as constituting a kind of group, a negative one to be sure, since it was comprised of those who were everlastingly and literally condemned to its "fire and brimstone."

Later, hell, largely due to the influence of Dante Alighieri's *Inferno*, was regarded as a place wherein the individual was everlastingly separated from all other individuals; all the condemned were interred in frozen isolation, physical, social, and above all emotional. Since then, hell, instead of being viewed as an objective condition, has been increasingly envisioned as a subjective state wherein (a)loneliness rules supreme because absolute lovelessness and hatred (including self-hatred), the antipodes of intimacy, reign (vol. 1, pp. 97–100, sec. 13; pp. 373–374, sec. 10A; Sartre, 1955, pp. 5–6, 47).

Therefore, the original cause of the medieval all-inclusive concatenation of beings and its final cause was God in that the deity was pictured, respectively, as creating all the beings in the universe and as comprising their ultimate purpose for existing. God, while reckoned to be the source and summit of all beings, was also conceived as being ontologically separate from them. For Western religious medievals, if monistic types such as pantheists and some sorts of mystics believed otherwise, they were considered heretical. As a result, they were subject to the non-plus-ultra stigma of being maximally excluded from the chain of being via the anathematization of ex-communication.

When it became widely known that the earth was not the center of the universe and that the latter was not necessarily created by God—or at least that the divinity seemed increasingly unnecessary or simply indifferent to the universe's being or well-being—the ontological chain was greatly weakened if not shattered. It challenges even imagining how terrifying must have been the (a)loneliness, especially cosmic and existential, when the ordinary human being experienced the various disconnections resulting from the chain's disintegration. The same may be said of loneliness' siblings in the form of lonesomeness, homesickness, and homelessness in addition to its cousins of depression and alienation.

During medieval times, absolute monism was rejected to the point of incurring the aforesaid accursedness of hell insofar as it implied the heresy of pantheism. Moreover, it must not be forgotten that, while the contemporary conceptualization of individualism was largely a legacy of the Renaissance, it had its roots in the Middle Ages. They, in turn, were mainly offshoots of the Greek and Judaeo-Christian traditions in that they themselves contained highly individualist strains.

I note at this juncture that medieval thinkers customarily concurred with the definition of the person proposed by the Roman philosopher, Boethius, as being of a threefold nature. First, a person was an extramental, or actual, individual, in contrast to a mental, abstract, and general, if not universal, entity. Second, the person was construed as being a substance, the essence of which was to exist in itself instead of in another being and instead of being a quality whose existence might be totally transitory. Third, the person was visualized as having a rational versus a nonrational nature. However, medievalists also stressed the communitarian aspects of the person, which, in some interpretations of his notion of personality, Boethius had neglected.

Whatever its history, the personalist view of a human being is that, though the person is quintessentially interpersonal and communal in nature, it is a separate and *sui generis* individuated being. So conceived, individuality and community are reinforcing concepts. As ontologically divided from all other beings but undivided in itself à la Aristotle, the individual forms an indissoluble entitative whole. It is a completeness ascribed in unique fashion to the kind of individualization and individuation that the person is or, if you will, has.

3. Autonomy and Homonomy

John Macmurray proposes that a person is constituted by its relatedness to other persons such that "personal identity is not an original given fact." Instead, it is obtained, he affirms, by means of "the progressive differentiation of the original sort of [union] of the 'You and I'" (1991, p. 91).

So understood, the person is not at source an isolated autonomous entity and, a fortiori, not an atomistic one, but a being already in some sort of union, or homonomy, with other selves or, more exactly, other persons. Similarly, all theoretic considerations of whether the person is metaphysically solipsistic, meaning absolutely and objectively all alone in the universe, presuppose that the individual is already in the extramental world along with other persons and is, in principle, there for all to see and otherwise know.

Consequently, it would not occur to people that they were separate individuals unless they were not already cognizant of the extramental existence of some other person. Thus, a child first says "me" in contrast to another individual, for instance, its mother. The perception of "me-ness" and the discovery of the self of its extramental existence imply otherness and specifically other persons. Some distinguish between the awakening of the self to an awareness of being a human being and then to its being a singular person.

Harmonizing the needs for independence (autonomy) and dependence (homonomy) is a hard and sometimes Herculean undertaking such that it is a necessary and arguably a sufficient sign of maturity and authenticity. Federating these quasi-instinctive needs is also essential to preventing and coping with needless negative aloneness and togetherness. I say "needless" because experiencing the negative in these polarities, including the loneliness outside and inside a relationship, is usually required if individuals are to grow personally and interpersonally.

The abnormal personality, by definition, does not achieve a state of positive autonomy or positive homonomy and even less their synergistic merging. Even the statistically normal individual often does so only in a tenuous and frequently temporary fashion, whereas the supranormal does so on a sure and sustained basis (Maslow, 1970, pp. 161–162, 173–174, 199–200).

Space constrictions allow for only a couple examples of these autonomy-homonomy correlations. Before enlisting them, however, it deserves mention that positive autonomy is comparable, in my estimation, to what Lorna Smith Benjamin calls "friendly differentiation." Positive homonomy is similar to her "friendly enmeshment"; negative autonomy, to her "hostile differentiation"; and negative homonomy, to her "negative enmeshment" (1996, pp. 59–60).

Though Smith Benjamin's couplets are highly useful, I find it preferable to use the four concepts of positive and negative autonomy and homonomy. For one thing, the terms hostility and enmeshment already carry negative connotations, whereas autonomy and homonomy do not. For a second, to speak of "friendly enmeshment" seems not only somewhat nebulous but even contradictory since enmeshment usually signifies being unhappily caught or entangled in a physical or mental web, all of which suggests negativity.

For instance, entanglement can imply such mental non-desiderata as ensnarement in addition to perplexity, trouble, and complication. Thus, a person becomes enmeshed in a court case or, more to the point, embroiled or trapped in an unhappy relationship that generates loneliness such as occurs in an "empty shell" marriage. The term "friendly" suggests the positive—hence, the contradiction between what is constructive—the friendly—and the non-constructive, the enmeshment. Nonetheless, if the verb form of "enmeshment"—"to enmesh"—is used in the sense of to fit or work together properly, then it is an apt choice of words to ally with friendliness.

In any case, Smith Benjamin does distinguish between hostile and friendly "differentiation," a term suggestive of autonomy, one often proceeding from a homonomy, or the undifferentiated. She remarks as well that love and hate can stand in for, respectively, friendliness and hostility, though, in my view, the former two terms constitute the limit cases of the latter (ibid., p. 27).

For a third thing, autonomy (self-rule) and homonomy (joint, or shared, rule) can be appraised not only with reference to one another, but to heteronomy. This governance by someone over one or more others can also be negative or positive as, for instance, being ruled, respectively, by a malign dictator versus a benign monarch. Heteronomy, however, appears to have more negative than positive or neutral connotation, especially when applied to moral and political situations.

In any event, I am not aware of any similar distinction akin to heteronomy that Smith Benjamin makes with respect to her duo of positive and negative enmeshment and differentiation. Still, she might well think that none is necessary or desirable. (At any rate, I remain in substantial agreement with her interpersonal approach to personality and therapy; ibid.).

An example of negative homonomy comprised of negatively autonomous individuals occurs when sociopaths unite with other similar renegades to form criminal gangs. In doing so, these antisocials, the ultimate in negative and lower Dionysian autonomy, or independence, become even more deviant individuals when operating together than when they act unilaterally. Not all sociopaths band together, for many are aimless atomists such as when they become socially isolated "drifters." These nomadic monads, as it were, are bereft of permanent attachments and life plans, all of which is in keeping with their being extreme lonerist types of personality.

Likewise, when negatively dependent types—logically enough, the paradigm of which are those with dependent personality disorders—such as servile conformists unite with other submissives, their slavish mentality is exacerbated often exponentially. Friedrich Nietzsche is well-known for naming these negatively homonomous types, the herd-types, "*the sum of zeroes*," and other deprecatory—albeit, in his view, richly deserved—designations, such as unnecessary duplicates (1968, pp. 33n53; 19n27, 2).

In positive homonomy, the joining with others purifies and deepens a person's autonomy, such as occurs in any mature relationship. Thus, spousal independence and freedom increase precisely because of the partners' union and shared identity (homonomy). To illustrate, Charlotte Brontë's Jane Eyre exults that, in her marriage to Edward Rochester, their being together is "at once as free as in solitude" (1980, p. 506). As a result, the freedom they experience in their conjugal *dependency* upon one another is equal in strength to their *independence* experienced when each is constructively alone in internal (mental) and external (extramental) solitary fashion.

Correspondingly, Jane and Edward's augmented independence and liberty solidify and magnify the greatest source of their happiness: their *inter-independence* found in their functional oneness. This union occurs not only without the decrease of their respective identities but, contrariwise, with their enhancement of their singularities. In testimony to their felicitous fusion—functional instead of structural—Jane exclaims that she and Edward experience "no pulsation of the heart which beats in our separate bosoms" for it reverberates, she says, "*as* one" (ibid.). A wedding of positive dependence and positive independence can be called "inter-independence" instead of "interdependence," since the second could suggest a reciprocal parasitism. Inter-independence emphasizes the fact that the positive symbiosis (interdependence) of mutual caring for one another increases the partners' freedom and self-rule instead of lessening them as occurs in a negative symbiosis.

Such inter-independence and positive complementarity are states difficult to achieve and sustain if only because it takes but one of the partners to engage in hyper-independence or hyper-dependence to make the relationship falter. Correlatively, the happiness of the relationship manifestly demands that both partners simultaneously be independent and dependent in positive fashion, meaning, respectively, being friendly differentiated and friendly enmeshed, to use Smith Benjamin's terminology. It is not, therefore, the independence of the singleness of selfness that is sought in genuine intimacy but a two-in-oneness of interpersonality. Thus, Jane and Edward become more themselves, their better selves, when they form a positive union.

As thoroughly social beings, no human persons are absolutely complete in themselves since their existence is intrinsically bound to one another. A person can be interpreted as being relatively absolutely whole, or complete, and becomes more fully so vis-à-vis other persons through relatedness to them, providing this union, or homonomy, is positive, like that enjoyed by Jane and Edward.

It is undeniable that the Renaissance brought new meanings to, or least greater emphasis on, the notion of the uniqueness of the individual as predicable of the person and its identity. This concept, in short, began to move from group inseparability to individual separateness, culminating in the autonomous view of self-identity as it exists today foremostly in the West.

As well, there is little doubt that this increased individualism effected by the Renaissance generated the kind of autonomy that contained greater personal freedom than in previous periods. In which case, the person could become the distinct(ive) individual he or she wants to be, or at least could be, instead of what some authority decrees. This autonomy also brought greater horizontal mobility into society, since individuals could not only move up in their group but move to another aggregate instead of being restricted, for instance, to a particular occupation or profession.

4. Atomism and Monism

Individual independence had to await its greater fruition in the social and political revolutions that began in full swing during the nineteenth century and that continue to this day amidst struggles and setbacks to gain and maintain democratic rulers and rules (Tunisia and Egypt being prominent examples of such conflicts). Democracy ideally signifies a social-political-economic arrangement wherein all (homonomy) are for one (autonomy) and vice versa.

When autonomy (independence) came to be envisioned as being totally absolute instead of partially so, then the individual was construed atomistically, as has been the case in the United States insofar as it is under the sway of SCRAM. Social atomists claim that personal identity is solely intrinsic and independent of all other persons such that autonomy is totally absolute.

On the other hand, over-emphasis on the individual as having no identity or independence apart from the group, such as a church, clan, or country, has culminated in various kinds of modern monism, such as the political collectivism of present day North Korea or the former Soviet Union. Hence, social monists propose that there is no intrinsic personal identity save that derived from the group or its leaders, in which case homonomy is conceived as being totally absolute.

Social monism, therefore, is the ultimate instantiation of negative homonomy. It construes the person not as a whole unto itself but simply a literal part of some superordinate entity, like the tribe or nation, outside of which the self has no separate and independent personal identity. Social monism generates person-loneliness; social atomism, species-loneliness. Social monism is a species of metaphysical monism, sometimes known as Singularism. It views all beings as entitatively one and the same single reality or reducible thereto, a position advocated in classical fashion by Parmenides. On the other hand, metaphysical atomism considers all beings as irreducible, indivisible, imperceptible, and unrelated, a position expounded by Democritus.

Relatedness in general and interpersonality in particular are, in my judgment, the core constituents of personal identity. These associations are the lenses through which all other types of identity and identification are ultimately experienced. Thus, personal identity is always contextualized by connectedness to other beings, especially other persons and, to a lesser extent, other personations, namely personifications and personalizations.

Accordingly, personal identity is chiefly comprised of interpersonality, the foremost sort of homonomy. Hence, the very essence of a person is intrinsically a kind of co-existence with other persons, especially by means of shared inwardness, or intimacy. By the notion of "co-existence," or co-being, I do not mean mere toleration of others but, instead, a mutual affirmation that requires at minimum justice but ideally a fairness motivated by benevolence.

Insofar as personal identity is inherently a kind of interpersonality, the pluses and minuses that exist in the second are indicative of the assets and liabilities in the first and vice versa. Thus, we say that the kind of friends—and intimates in general—we have is revelatory of the kind of persons we are.

In contrast to the atomistic concept of identity, interpersonal identity signifies that the individual, though independent, is not absolutely autonomous but only relatively so. Individual identity necessarily occurs within a group or, more exactly, a community, such that true autonomy is always embedded in genuine homonomy (union and dependence). However, while relative to others in a kind of homonomy, the person's relativity is not absolute, as monism maintains, but relative. In contrast to the monistic view of identity, the interpersonal signifies that though personal independence is rooted in homonomy, the second is not absolute.

Personalism via communalism, therefore, avoids the social sicknesses of both atomitis and monitis. It emphasizes interpersonality, namely that a person is, by definition, intrinsically connected to and dependent upon other persons and that there is a common good that is jointly theirs. This benefit is not simply the sum of individual goods but a distinct good attainable only in and by the group but distributed to all the members according to needs and merits.

Since human beings are thoroughly social beings in both their basic needs and higher-level metaneeds, their autonomy must be subordinate to their merging with others and their common welfare in a functional instead of a structural manner. In this union, they are to be construed, therefore, as *sharing* but not literally *being* one soul, mind, or heart. Thus, persons can act as soul mates but they are not ontologically and numerically one and the same entity, in this case, the same soul.

Manifestly, this inter-independence of individuals and groups is increasingly taking place among peoples and countries as the world becomes more globally connected educationally, politically, socially, economically, and environmentally. This contemporary chain of beings must become more positively united if it is to prosper in a humane sense or perhaps even survive (Rifkin, 2004).

Unfortunately, the SCRAM mind-set endorses an incredibly antiquated and dangerous self-centered, privatistic, and atomistic isolationist philosophy as evinced, for example, in its anti-United Nations and anti-ecological policies and practices. SCRAM epitomizes a self-aggrandizing monadic mentality, by which each individual strives as much as possible to exist all by and for itself. By no means does SCRAM promote a philosophy of one for all others, whether all is construed as meaning for every other individual taken singly or as a totality of individuals taken together as a community.

Therefore, it is true, especially since the Renaissance, that the notion of person has come to imply the absolutely distinctive and unique individual as the self is viewed today. Nonetheless, it is also the case that this singularity is only achieved in communication and community with other persons. Even solitude, especially primary, is intrinsically social in nature. This constructive kind of aloneness is also used as a deterrent to excessive gregariousness.

Jim Swan states that the idea of the individual bore two related notions when it was initially part of Middle English (1100–1500), and that these two concepts became outdated during the second half of the seventeenth century. The first outmoded concept is that the individual was "one in substance," meaning "indivisible in essence"; the second, "inseparable" from others (1985, p. 159).

It is my view that neither of the above two ideas of individuality when applied to personality has become antiquated. I submit that still today, the individual qua person is ordinarily construed as inseparable from others in that a person is intrinsically and irreversibly social. Moreover, individuality remains commonly envisioned as that which is, à la Aristotle, ontologically and numerically undivided in itself in terms of its ultimate essence, or substance.

Hence, however much the individual qua person might be psychologically divided in terms of its mental functions—to wit its cognition, emotion, and cognition to be described momentarily—the person as a totality remains ontologically indivisible. It is similarly so with respect to the person's ultimate structural constituents, such as its mind and body, which remain ontologically inseparable irrespective of how disintegrated they are psychologically considered.

Thus, like other individuals, the human kind is ontologically independent from all other entities. Consequently, it is numerically and literally separate from them; in which case, Tom is not Dick and neither of them is Mary. Still, persons are inseparable from other persons in as much as they are social beings. Though personality is the non-plus-ultra sort of individuality, it is also the limit case in sociality. The greater is the singularity of human individuality, the more it reflects inter-independence and socialness in general.

A person is, therefore, the utmost type of singularity. Nonetheless, this uniqueness is developed only by being with and for other persons in a humane and caring twosome or other type of homonomy, such as a social support system or the wider community. Hence, it is highly questionable whether any kind of permanent solitude would be humanizing. I say, "would be" because in reality, there are and have never been any absolutely permanent and total solitaries, such as hermits. Were there such individuals they would have become dehumanized and depersonalized, if they survived at all.

"Individualization" can be looked upon as a process predicated of all human beings qua human, whereas "individuation" is ascribed to all human beings qua unique, or idiosyncratic, persons (the first is to the second as quantitative singleness is to qualitative singularity). Therefore, what is idiosyncratic can connote the positive such as heightened or deepened individuality or, more precisely, individuation.

On the other hand, the idiosyncratic can suggest the deficient, for instance, in terms of cognition, as when it refers to an ignorant, uneducated person, or one who is severely developmentally delayed. Excessively idiosyncratic individuals are considered most profoundly eccentric when they maintain a totally private and socially isolated existence in contrast to a connected and public one. However, some extremely idiosyncratic individuals are also highly public from a purely quantitative perspective, like the hyper-gregarious gadabout.

In sum, social atomism construes the individual as absolutely complete in itself, as if everyone were like Arnold's islet, initially unattached or eventually detached from everyone else. According to social atomism, only individuals have full extramental existence (and value) with the group having either no existence or the sort justified only as a vehicle to generate and guard the interests of the individual qua individual. Atomism's antithesis, social monism, conceives the individual as totally relative to the whole, which alone has absolute existence and value.

Social atomism produces its antithesis in the form of negatively homonomous groups in that negative autonomies, such as hyper-individualism, tend to generate their opposites, namely negative homonomies, such as hypo-individualism, and vice versa. Similarly, overly independent individuals, such as sociopaths, bring forth and prey upon overly dependent types, none more, of course, than the pathologically dependent personalities.

The personalist and communitarian critics of contemporary social atomism, as it exists paradigmatically in SCRAM, propose that this kind of hyper-individualism makes people forge their own absolute place in a privatizing, or privatistic, manner. Privatism, we recall, is the doctrine that holds that individuals should concern themselves exclusively with their own immediate interests.

The effect of this extreme autonomization is that the person becomes unconnected to or disconnected from anyone else except, as Aristotle might say, for matters of utility or pleasure (1941c, bk. 8, chap. 13). Ironically, the result of this atomism of convenience and comfort is self-defeating because each individual is viewed, in principle, as replaceable and discardable. Each is valued only as a means to other individuals' self-serving desires.

5. Personality: Changeless or Changing

To review, a person can, therefore, be defined as an ontological and unique wholeness that synergistically blends stable (Apollonian) and dynamic (Dionysian) factors. This organic unit is comprised of the structures of body, mind, and, by some beliefs, the soul which, in turn, have corresponding corporeal, mental, and spiritual powers in addition to properties, habits, and activities. Personality is the organizer—or the organization itself—of the physical, mental, and moral (spiritual) capabilities, abilities, attributes, and activities that a human being *has* or *is*. Which view prevails depends on whether persons are deemed distinct from these entities, all of which differentiates them from all other human beings.

Every individual possesses relative but not absolute distinctiveness, or uniqueness, sometimes known as unicity (God is said to possess absolute unicity). This singularity is relative since every person is a member of the human race and shares similar human features.

Aristotle, Thomas Aquinas, and René Descartes are among those who maintain that the qualities of the person are subject to change. Yet the person as a whole remains unchanged and unchangeable as to its ontological substrate, meaning its basic substance, or essential nature. These philosophers contend that persons are changeless as to their fundamental, or primary, composition but changeable according to secondary essences, such as personality traits. Thus, Tom, Harry, and Mary remain the same persons from birth (by some lights, conception) to death (and beyond if they are endowed with an immortal soul). However, they become different persons in terms of their qualities, such as their physical weight and mental knowledge.

So understood, the person *has* a metaphysical identity and, more specifically, an ontological permanent unity that continues throughout the lifespan, irrespective of any alterations it might experience regarding its aforementioned components. Those endorsing this view stress the Parmenidesian sameness, which forms the person's ongoing substance. Insofar as persons are changed by their qualities, it incorporates a Heraclitian dimension within itself.

Others, such as David Hume, Friedrich Nietzsche, and Jean-Paul Sartre, emphasize the transient metaphysical identity, which the self *is*. In this view, the person is literally constituted by its changes, in which event its present and continued unity, to wit its continuity, is totally fluid instead of fixed. Accordingly, these philosophers deny that there is any kind of substance, or permanent ontological substratum, which the person *has*. This second group stresses the Heraclitian dynamic diversity of *becoming* of the individual instead of the Parmenidesian static unity of *being*.

For Westerners in general, that a person could have no unchanging metaphysical identity is largely a confusing, even a contradictory notion. They wonder how, if the person is always in the process of changing, a person can literally be this or that *singular*, *individuated*, self with a unique and permanent identity.

In effect, some people take a kind of Kantian stance, in which the self qua mind is the organizer and unifier of its experiences and the entity behind all outward appearances (the "phenomena"). In this conception, the self can never be the object of direct knowledge but only its subject and, accordingly, it remains not only an unknown but unknowable entity (the "noumenon"). The Kantian position has an appeal to those who contend that, while the self cannot be shown to exist by theoretical means, it must be assumed to do so for practical purposes. In some quarters, the self and person are not the same entities such that, for example, the first pertains to the domain of problems, whereas the second pertains to the realm of mysteries. The relationship of phenomena to noumena can be analogized as problems are to mysteries.

These issues are not solely of philosophical import but psychological, including therapeutic, since, for example, they pertain to whether a person or its traits are changeable, directly or indirectly, and for the better or worse. As well, the viewpoint that there is no elemental constancy, or continuity, to the person—such that permutation is, so to speak, the only permanency—can directly lead to negative states of aloneness such as intraself loneliness (and alienation). In this case, the individual longs to have an abiding, unchanging dimension to itself for the sake of, among other things, intimate self-understanding. It is then put forth that if the person as a totality is in continuous flux, it would be unknown (if not unknowable) not only concerning its essence and properties but its very existence.

Westerners also propose that if the individual is forever entirely in a process of becoming, it is difficult to comprehend how its inwardness could be shared with others, who, correlatively, would have the same problem in sharing their endlessly fleeting selves. The inability to partake of interiorities would lead not only to intrapersonal (intraself) but interpersonal loneliness in some or even all of the nine other forms delineated above. The upshot of the matter is that, for most Westerners, an enduring self (person) is necessary, if they are to avoid metaphysical, epistemological, intraself, social, and other types of loneliness.

In the West, and in terms of intimacy, the distinction of the person from its qualities allows, for instance, Tom and Dick to be able to say that they love Mary "for herself," usually meaning for her person as such. Therefore, they love her for the unchanging person she is over and above her various changing personal corporeal, mental, and spiritual (moral) features, such as, respectively, her physical beauty, her intelligence, and character.

Hence, it may be asked if Mary's qualities are "hers" or "her" such that these traits are what she *has* or *is*. Additionally, does she *have* or *is she* her body, mind, and soul? Are these three structural entities themselves reducible to their properties or traits such that, for instance, the physical body has or is its color, weight, height, and the like? Or, à la Immanuel Kant, is the self unknown and unknowable in itself, although its existence must be postulated so as to account, for instance, the seeming unity and continuity of an individual through all its myriad variations?

I would also note here that the Parmenidesian is to the Apollonian as the Heraclitian is to the Dionysian. As well, the purely Parmenidesian is to the monistic as the purely Heraclitian is to the atomistic. With reference to personality disorders, some pathologicals are excessively Heraclitian and insufficiently Parmenidesian, for instance, the schizotypal, sociopathic, and histrionic. Others are the reverse, namely excessively Parmenidesian and insufficiently Heraclitian, such as the schizoid, obsessional, and avoidant.

6. Personality Structures: Body, Mind, and Soul

Depending upon an individual's metaphysics and epistemology, a person can be considered as either *having* or *being* its unique body, mind, and soul, along with their capabilities, attributes, and activities. Furthermore, these entities are, in some quarters, deemed as qualitatively different, irreducible components, which the person *has* or *is*. In other circles, they are envisaged as only quantitatively different and as reducible to one or the other.

To exemplify, wherever metaphysical materialism prevails, the soul, if it is even nominally recognized, is equated with or reduced to the mind that, in turn, is equated with or reduced to the body and in particular the brain. The reverse is the case wherever metaphysical immaterialism obtains.

The soul is sometimes construed as the person itself—such as saying Harry is a "good soul"—but more frequently, it is viewed as the animating and immaterial principle. As immaterial, the soul is considered the immortal element of the person. At times, it is denominated a spirit that, subsequently, is reckoned as giving life to that which is bodily. Recall that the spiritual can likewise be regarded as the highest realm of the mental, namely the moral, and it is largely in this manner that spiritual is used in the present study.

In the West, the human mind—or, as some prefer, consciousness, to emphasize, for instance, its non-substance and non-static nature—is generally adjudged as being necessarily embodied. For personalists, especially those influenced by philosophical existentialism and phenomenology, the body is a dimension of human subjectivity. In which case, I not only *have* a body but "I *am* my body" and, thus, "my body is me, me myself." Still, many Westerners envision their persons as essentially being their selves; their selves as quintessentially their minds; their minds as being their souls; and their souls as being their persons, or the essence thereof.

Some philosophers contend that there is a difference in kind between the mind and body such that they inhabit different ontological zones, in which case, the mind is commonly known as the soul. For others, the mind and body differ in kind but they still exist within the same ontological domain, namely that of the purely natural order.

Human beings, insofar as they are viewed as ensouled, are immaterial and immortal. As such, they are believed to be capable of existing unembodied and, in some philosophies and theologies, of being re-embodied after death has terminated the earthly living body. As embodied, a human person is contrasted with those types of beings who are defined as pure spirits, often meaning created persons (angels) or uncreated persons (gods, for polytheists or at least dualists, or God, for monotheists).

A pure spirit is ordinarily said to have (or be) a mind, meaning consciousness, but not an unconsciousness, the sort frequently but not always ascribed to human minds. Some philosophers, such as Sartre, appear to hold that the unconscious is but the least degree or level of the conscious. In which case, there is no such entity as an unconscious mind or a mind with an unconscious sphere unless it is conceived by consciousness itself as a kind of noumenal entity.

Souls, strictly speaking, are not usually predicated of pure spirits since the former are conceived as being necessarily and exclusively federated with bodies, which such spirits, often known as angels, by definition, do not possess. In some views, both angels and gods can have bodies or at least can assume, or become, them if they so wish. It is held to be so on the principle that the higher entity, in this case, the spiritual, can become or have the powers or virtualities, of the lower, to wit the material and corporeal.

In passing, it is to be underlined that the belief in angels is hardly extinct today. According to a 2007 national survey, two-thirds of Canadians, who as a group have a high educational rate and rating, believe in the existence of angels (*The Montreal Gazette*, 30 December 2007). To some ways of thinking, if a person is willing to believe in the existence of a totally uncreated purely spiritual being (the monotheistic kind of God), then the individual can surely believe in both created purely spiritual beings (angels) and embodied spirits construed as having immaterial, immortal souls (human beings).

7. Personality Functions: Cognitive, Emotive, and Conative

In addition to its structures, the person is looked upon as that kind of individual who is or has distinct(ive) functions. The most prominent are cognition, emotion, and conation, along with their capabilities (potentialities), properties, and qualities.

A. Cognition

In terms of its cognition, the person possesses internal types, such as those had by intellection, such as conceptualizing and reasoning, and, sensory sorts, such as those of taste and touch. In some quarters, internally and externally derived knowledge vary categorically (qualitatively); in others, they differ solely dimensionally (quantitatively).

The human mind is generally considered as being unique among earthly creatures in that it is able to be conscious of itself such that it is self-reflexive, and of its operations, such that it is self-reflective. Human consciousness can, therefore, ponder its own internal acts and external actions, in sum its activities, especially or perhaps only if the person or self qua mind is considered as distinct from its powers and products. The person via its mind also possesses the ability to perceive and reflect upon entities outside itself in the extramental world through "extrospection" in contrast to introspection upon itself and its states and qualities.

This singularity of human cognition is challenged by those who affirm that there is no qualitative difference between the minds of human beings and "the minds" of some non-human animals, such as apes. Jeremy Rifkin refers to "Koko, a 300-pound gorilla who was taught sign language and has mastered more than 1000 signs and understands more than 2000 English words" (2004, p. 348). Of course, we might ask what such mastery and understanding means. Does it signify, for instance, the ability to create or discover concepts (and words), especially abstract types such as those in metaphysics, mathematics, or symbolic logic? Probably not.

While non-human animals may supass human beings in sensory sorts of knowledge, such as the hearing ability of most dogs, there appears to be no clear or certain evidence that they do in intellectual types or even that they possess such cognition. As amazing as some non-human animals, such as chimpanzees, dolphins, and elephants, are in terms of cognitive functions, they are rather primitive compared to human beings. Still, our understanding of the consciousness of non-human animals (and even our own) appears to be in its early stages.

B. Emotion

The emotive realm of the person refers to the affective domain, with love and hate usually accorded primordiality among, respectively, the positive and negative affects. It has generally been proposed that human emotions—as do its purportedly reflective and reflexive sorts of intelligence and rationality—arguably differ not only in huge degree but in kind from those experienced by non-human animals.

For instance, universal love and hatred are predicated of human beings but not even of the highest of the other primates such as chimpanzees. Similarly, emotions such as envy and arrogance, though not jealousy and vanity, are usually ascribed only to human beings.

In the West, for the most part, non-human animals may be said to have souls in the sense of animating, or vitalizing, entities but not spiritual ones understood as immaterial, immortal types. Nor are they held to have spiritual processes like the kind of mental qualities that are formally moral. Thus, to speak of a mendacious monkey or a greedy giraffe would not be acceptable for the non-panpsychist Westerner because such ascriptions would imply anthropomorphism and the unwarranted attribution of human emotions to non-human beings.

C. Conation

The conative contains such entities as involuntary instincts, drives, impulses, inclinations, and desires in addition to the volitional and more or less conscious tendencies, such as those of intentionality (motivation), including benevolence, equalization, acquisition, acquisitiveness, malevolence, and their various species.

With reference to the volitive considered in itself, the mind—or, more precisely, the person by virtue of it—is held to have the power of self-determinism (freedom) as contrasted with determinism (necessitarianism) and indeterminism (acausality, or chance).

Generally, the cognitive, emotive, and conative functions are regarded as inhabiting distinctive but interacting spheres, or structures, of the self. Personality can be conceived as a human being's dynamic organization of these three processes. For perhaps most theorists of the mind, or consciousness, all spiritual and mental functions occur within the body and its behavior (of course, the majority view does not guarantee the truth of a judgment). In which case, the human person is an embodied mind, both as to its conscious and non-conscious components or, if you will, its less conscious elements.

The person is reckoned to be the principal, though not the sole, source of its goals and values as a whole; the active center of freedom; and inherently and irrevocably a social and communal being—or so the person has been construed by most who persistently and often professionally reflect on such issues, namely personologists, especially those who are philosophers and above all those who are personalists.

Regardless of other differences between them, most philosophical personologists agree that the higher the type of individual, the more unified it is within itself. The greater is its unification, the more the individual can include diversity within its personal and interpersonal identity. Alternatively, the lower the type of individual, the more its unity lacks diversification and vice versa. As the highest type of individual, the person is most able to harmonize even synergize unity and stability with, respectively, the diverse and dynamic. Abnormal persons are either unified at the expense of diversification (for example, schizoids), or the reverse (for example, schizotypals).

We recall that aloneliness means the fear or dread of any negative state of aloneness, including loneliness. Thus, an "alonely" is a person who is subject to constant trepidation concerning being and especially feeling alone—whether it pertains to social, physical, mental, or spiritual separateness or separation. For example, in terms of the customarily distinguished three mental processes, aloneliness can be cognitive such that individuals are afraid to think on their own; emotive, in that they are afraid of being affectively all by themselves, a consternation that attains its culmination in loneliness; or, conative and in particular volitional in that, for example, people are afraid to choose on their own.

8. Personality: Constitutional and Characterological Components

From an allied perspective, personality can be construed as an interacting mixture of necessitating or at least highly influencing—be they precipitating, on the one hand, or predisposing and maintaining on the other—of constitutional components, in addition to characterological ones. The second are frequently considered an ensemble of given and chosen qualities or at minimum qualities subsequently ratified by choice, be it in expressed or tacit fashion.

Erich Fromm defines personality as "the totality of acquired and inherited psychic qualities" that are typical of a particular individual and that provide the person her or his uniqueness. He proposes that the difference between such qualities is in general "synonymous with the difference between temperament" and the aggregate of "constitutionally given" attributes, "on the one hand, and character, on the other" (1968a, p. 59).

Fromm reminds us that Hippocrates initially devised what is now a traditional manner of classification of temperament, namely choleric, sanguine, melancholic, and phlegmatic types. Fromm states that temperament is essentially unalterable. He considers character as predominantly formed by experience especially that had early in life and, in contrast to temperament, is alterable, relatively speaking (ibid., p. 59–60). Fromm considers character as preeminently derived from the way an individual is "related to the world." This orientation is comprised of the assimilation of objects and socialization in terms of subjects, including oneself (ibid., p. 66).

Similar to Fromm, Theodore Millon, Roger Davis, and their associates Carrie Millon, Luis Escovar, and Sarah Meagher define personality as "the complex interaction of influences from both character and temperament." They consider temperament as "the sum total of inherited biological influences on personality which show continuity across the life span" (2000, p. 8). This totality is, in deterministic circles, held to be not only influencing and conditioning but necessitating.

The assemblage of inherited influences may be construed as contributing to the ontological unity of the self however much it might be disunited or disintegrated psychologically considered. Whereupon, despite its being highly fragmented from a mental perspective, the individual with, for instance, a schizotypal disorder has qua person an ongoing ontological identity. Those who emphasize a totally Heraclitian view of the person would take exception to this position since they argue that a person is totally and permanently in flux.

Temperament is further looked upon by Millon and George Everly as the "the biological materials from which personality will ultimately emerge." So understood, temperament includes, according to these personologists, "the neurological, endocrinological, and even biochemical substrates from which personality will begin to be shaped" (1985, p. 5). In some and perhaps most views, while the individual may emerge and take shape from such genetic substrates, its external (for example, social) milieus can to some extent (re)shape these initial and generally lower strata of personality.

Additionally, people's choices can modify their outer environments. Moreover, these decisions, which themselves are part of individuals' internal milieu, can somewhat alter the rest of their inner environment, including those more biological and heritable layers of personality, like temperament. Therefore, while people may inherit an extraverted temperament with its trait of gregariousness, they may to some measure change this quality and the outer milieu in which it functions.

Gordon Parker lists temperament as being among:

> the genetically-driven, constitutional components . . . which form a template at birth, ready for epigenetic development and environmental exposure. Temperament is the biogenetic hard wiring, significantly genetically driven, but with other prenatal biological influences. (1997, p. 346)

Parker states that genetic constitutionality evolves into personality, but the process, he says, is mediated by extrapsychic and psychic factors among which are the volitional, or chosen (ibid., p. 347). So envisaged, while freedom is part of the inner milieu, the first can alter the other aspects of the second.

Jeffrey Magnavita considers temperament to refer to the "innate or inborn biological dispositions such as affective reactivity," whereas character is "the behavioral manifestations of an individual's ego functions" (2000, p. 73). These functions, in my view, include those that are chosen in light of people's (meta)needs and values of which those of an ethical nature mainly comprise their character. Behavior may also be envisaged, while not formally characterological in nature, as the outer result of characterological plus constitutional factors.

Simone De La Rie, Inge Duijsens, and Robert Cloninger consider character as pertaining to "individual differences in concept-based goals and values and conscious expectations" (1998, pp. 4–12). So stated, character entails the normative and elective part of personality in a manner that makes it most differentiated from non-person types of individuals. In this regard, virtues—the more or less permanent positive ethical habits of personality—are the nucleus of character, with altruism, according to most ethicians, as being its crown and universal justice being its necessary condition, or platform. However, in some views, love need not be based on justice or any other virtue, such as the other traditional cardinal virtues of courage, temperance, and prudence.

In short, temperament is to character as nature and the innate are to nurture and the acquired, especially its moral and elected ingredients. Still, some personologists contend that character or lack of it is at minimum partially predisposed, as in the case of so-called good and bad seeds. Others go even further and support characterological determinism. It holds that the individual is virtuous, vicious, and everything in between due to internal or external necessitating, meaning absolutely compelling, factors.

Further to its axiological aspects, personality possesses what Kant reckons as an innate sacredness and dignity that demand an a priori kind of respect and deference (1964, pp. 127–130nn37–41). This natural entitlement—a recognition of a sort of inherent nobility on the part of persons—requires their being autonomous.

Still, even greater than those for autonomy, a person qua social being has a need for and right to joint, or shared, rule and dependence, to wit, homonomy in the form of community. The kind of autonomy that is especially detrimental to homonomy is, to say the least, the sort that is absolute in the sense of unrestrained egotism with its atomistic kind of aloneness and separateness.

Intimacy is the voluntary or volitional sharing of the person qua person and, while it involves individuals in their entireties, its chief focus is their inwardness. It is the most sacrosanct realm of their being, the one, therefore, most worthy of respect. This naturally sacred dimension of the self does not necessarily deserve esteem and admiration, for they are largely earned instead of being a matter of birthright, like respect.

In some quarters, is it held that there is a kind of respect that can be merited and thus increased and decreased and even lost by, for instance, forfeiting the grounds for such positive regard. Hence, two kinds of respect can be distinguished: one predicated of human beings qua human beings and that cannot be nullified, and the other predicated of them qua persons and that can be negated. Thus, Tom may respect Mary as a human being but not for the "kind of person" she is.

The part of personality that is somewhat alterable by people's experience and their values is itself partially chosen by individuals. However, according to self-determinists, it is also influenced though not necessitated by the social milieu, be it the family, neighborhood, society, or the world at large. Consequently, there are constitutional, axiological, and volitional elements along with other psychic and extrapsychic elements that figure into the formation and the unity and continuity of personality or its lack of the same.

9. Personality: Normality, Abnormality, and Supranormality

Personality can be divided into subnormal, normal, and supra or supernormal classifications, and done so from biological, psychological, ethical, volitional, or social perspectives. Defining personality normality has proven to be extremely problematic if only because it is comprised of so many variables, themselves viewable in multiple ways. Moreover, its definition, like that of the abnormal personality, is relative to how the supernormal or supranormal personality is defined.

If the superior personality is thought to differ absolutely in kind from the normal and, a fortiori, from the abnormal, then the supernormal nomenclature is more apt. If it is only a relative variation and a fortiori only in degree, then the supranormal is more fitting. For now, solely some of the more salient meanings of the notions of normal and anormal, especially in terms of personality and health, will be sketched.

It is widely advanced that a normal personality is principally constituted by being positively related to other persons as a whole. This relatedness, from a moral perspective, is founded on justice, especially one motivated by fulfillment not only of its letter but its spirit, all of which, in turn, implies goodwill. Benevolence is subsequently completed by beneficence and crowned in non-plus-ultra form by love and its *sui generis* heartfelt and committed caring. Pathological personalities fail in justice, benevolence, and, above all, love in terms of their intermittent interactions but especially their permanent attachments.

Hence, the gist of abnormal personalities is their being negatively disposed to others in that they are, as we recall, non-related to them (Group I), dis-related (Group II), or insufficiently related (Group III). Consequently, pathological personalities are chiefly characterized by an absence of positive affiliation with others, especially those that are of a meaning/intimacy sort, be they private, like friendship, public, like friendliness, or both as in the case of compassion.

Disturbed personalities' dearth of close connectedness is traceable to an extreme lack of an underlying need, radical potentiality, ability, desire, or willingness on the part of these aberrants to unite with others (Group I), a malevolently scornful indifference and antipathy to doing so (Group II), or a keen interest in fusing with them but one that is acquisitively needy in a largely neurotic sense of neediness (Group III).

All abnormals have personality traits that are exceedingly difficult to like and love. Indeed, these negativities, in my judgment, are the main reason pathological personalities are aberrant. On the other hand, some view personality as distinct from its traits such that the individual is considered normal or anormal quite apart from such attributes.

Regarding distinctions originally drawn by Daniel Offer and Melvin Sabshin, Stephen Strack and Maurice Lorr outline five concepts of normality and health that are presented here in an attenuated manner.

A. Normality as Health: Pathology as Illness

Strack and Lorr state that normality can be viewed as health and pathology as illness, in which event, "to be healthy is to be reasonably free of bothersome symptoms or disease," a construal which, they append, "includes most people" (1997, p. 109). This notion of health may be opposed, for instance, by those who contend that it is not so much being devoid of such negative symptoms of illness that signifies health but the ability to overcome them when they are present, a view I will sketch momentarily.

This first conception of well-being would also be challenged by those who regard health less in terms of its absence of minuses but more in terms of its presence of pluses and especially in the quality of the pluses. For instance and apropos of physical well-being in particular, if a person experiences health problems in several minor categories but is very fit a few major ones, then the second situation might be deemed more indicative of health than the first. Of course, the body is an interacting organic system such that a defect in one area ultimately affects some if not all others.

It bears inserting here that how physical and mental health and illness are related in terms of personality normality and anormality are themselves highly polemical issues. Generally, it appears that people continue to subscribe to the ancient adage that a sound mind and a healthy body condition and complement one another.

A minor weakness may lead to or be a sign of some underlying major infirmity if the body lacks sufficient strengths, or pluses, at least those of a higher order, to combat such lesser liabilities. Likewise, in terms of mental health, a defect in affect, such as persistent anger or anxiety, can negatively impact emotion as a whole. It can also negatively influence cognition, conation, and mental processes in their entirety. It may likewise directly weaken the body as a totality given that affects, like anger, are partially and, in some views, completely corporeal.

A comparable situation obtains with moral health. For instance, an individual who lacks many lesser virtues but who has the supra or super virtue, namely love especially when construed as altruism, is arguably the healthier type of personality. Therefore, love as a purely natural quality or set of qualities is sometimes construed as being independent of other virtues.

Thus, it has been variously stated that if people habitually love, they are not bound or fully so by the exigencies of other morally upright patterns, meaning virtues, of internal acts and external actions because in having its own criteria and laws, love transcends but need not incorporate these habitual moral ways of acting.

In this model of love and moral health, an individual, such as an alcoholic, who by definition lacks the virtue of temperance, could still be a highly loving person. In some quarters, no individual with a personality pathology is loving and lovable; every such aberrant is defective with respect to moral virtues, such as the cardinal sorts.

Love can be considered a super-virtue if it is envisioned as being absolutely independent of other desirable ethical habits, such as the traditional cardinal ones of justice, prudence (practical wisdom), courage, and temperance. This version of love and virtue in general is the kind especially prominent in religious and theological circles.

In this variant, love is envisaged as the super-virtue that is not only independent of other virtues but can exist alongside moral defects, including even some, though usually not all, vices. For example, love may be envisaged as existing without temperance or courage but not without justice.

Others view love as a purely natural supra-virtue that exceeds but must incorporate lesser virtues if it truly signifies moral excellence. In this model, alcoholics could not be loving persons because their failures in temperance would negatively, directly or indirectly, affect love and impact their commission or omission of other moral virtues, such as justice, and the acts and actions that constitute them.

In accordance with many ethicians such as Aristotle, it is held that failing by excess in such natural moral virtues is, generally speaking, less of a moral sickness than failing by deficiency. In this regard, the dependents of Group III are less sick than any of the other nine personality aberrants, especially those in Groups I and II, because in comparison to them dependents most strive to love. They largely fail in this effort because their motivational pattern is one of acquisitiveness. To the extent, that they are acquisitive, dependents lack benevolence, a sine qua non of love. Still, the persistent attempt to love, the greatest of virtues, may be ethically more commendable than success with reference to lesser positive qualities.

In any event, moral, mental, and physical health are interrelated. For this reason, clinicians, while they are formally engaged in judgments about mental health, are concomitantly involved in judgments concerning moral well-being. Clinicians whose patients are sick in terms of their personalities are dealing with individuals who, in my reckoning, are mentally/morally diseased.

B. Abnormality as Pathology; Health as Supranormality

Strack and Lorr propose that abnormality can be considered as pathological and health as some utopian, or supranormal, state, which, by definition, few if any persons ever attain (ibid.). Or, at least they do not forever remain in such an ideal personological niche in that they are periodically subject to some illness and eventually to death. In terms of mental health, it is said that everyone, including the normal human being, is neurotic to some degree, with the assumption being that Neuroticism is a negative state or at minimum less than one that is utopian.

It is notable that some personologists hold that there are higher and lower levels of neurosis, with the former being positive or at least potentially so. Existential angst occurs when a person feels threatened by the lack of meaning in the world or in her or his world. Such anxiety is considered by many normative personologists to be a higher and an even intrinsically constructive kind of neurosis than the kind involved in an individual's constantly worrying, for example, as to whether she or he is sufficiently thin or tall to be popular.

Existential anguish is frequently judged to signal a more elevated state of development than the absence of such apprehensiveness in the so-called normal person. This individual is considered average, statistically speaking, in a given cultural context, a notion of normality to be considered momentarily.

When researchers investigate health, perhaps especially its superior brand, they often do not precise what it is but only what it is not. For example, the *DSM* examines what is abnormal but says little about what is normal and even less about what is supranormal (it says nothing about what is supernormal). The World Health Organization (WHO) defines health as not only "the absence of infirmity" but a condition of "complete physical, mental, and social well-being," the last mentioned preeminently consists in good interpersonal relationships.

Health may envisaged on a scale of plus one to plus ten, the second figure representing the utopian, or ideal, to wit, the complete well-being stipulated by WHO. Illness may be regarded on a scale of minus one to minus ten, the second figure being symbolic of the dystopian. Again, to indicate what health is requires not only noting its lack of minus (unhealthy) gradients but its plus levels, especially those at the summit of the scale, the sphere of the supranormal. Supernormal health is "off the charts" such that it is in a realm beyond the plus ten ranking. Similarly, "subnormal" health is below a minus ten.

Abnormal and, a fortiori, subnormal health are known as illness, sickness, and disease—in a word, the pathological. This term can be predicated of the body, mind, and soul—including its spiritual meaning such as the moral—in addition to the person as distinct from these structures (and functions). Thus, we can say Mary has a pathological personality apart from her traits insofar as she is not reducible to them.

The scales of minus or plus one to ten, in being quantitative, refer to the numerical differences between the abnormal, normal, and supranormal and as such are one of degree, all of which would conform to the dimensional model of personality, the kind employed by the FFM. If the variations are understood as qualitative differences, or those of levels, then they would be in accordance with the categorical model, the type utilized by the *DSM.* The categorical, therefore, implies that the differences between the normal and abnormal are relatively but not necessarily absolutely absolute. Contrarily, the FFM implies that all such differences are relatively but not absolutely relative.

As for the supernormal in contrast to the supranormal person in terms of physical, mental, but especially moral health, this individual can be envisaged as varying from the normal and all the more so from the abnormal and above all the subnormal in absolutely absolute terms. This most exceptional person can consequently be thought of as being the most qualitatively, or categorically, diverse from other types of persons, including even the supranormal or the subnormal. (The diverse and the same are to the different and similar as the categorical is to the dimensional.)

Does being versed in the knowledge of the abnormal personality necessarily make make us understand what constitutes the normal and above all the supranormal? Like many others, I would answer "no." In general, it is easier to say what something is not, in this case the sub- or abnormal, than what it is and especially what it ought to be. However, we could say nothing about what is below or above the normal unless we had some notion of what the inferior and superior is.

I would add that those at the top of the psycho-ethical scale are better situated to understand those below them than the reverse, if only because they usually have been in some though not necessarily all lower stages themselves. I say usually since some supranormals and, a fortiori, supernormals may have been in such superior states since their youth, or even their infancy (Sorokin, 1950, pp. 125–205). Additionally, it seems to be the case that few supernormals were ever in the abnormal range and even less in the subnormal. For example, it seems that few saints—construed herein as moral, or characterological, paragons—have seldom if ever been psychopaths or sociopaths. Thus, the road to paradise is not always through purgative ways.

Researchers, therefore, generally pay less attention to the pluses as such and, as result, tend to exclude the supra- and all the more so the alleged supernormal persons and their kinds of health. One reason for this rarity in research is due to the paucity of subjects, since by definition, what is superior seldom occurs (as well, those superior are seldom available for such studies).

Another reason why researchers do not consider supra- or super- ideal health is that doing so necessarily involves its de jure domain(s). This realm, instead of being considered within the sphere of the psychological, is generally reckoned the province of the philosophical. In particular, it entails the axiological, especially the moral, and as such involves ethically utopian models of health (and happiness). Those who do study personality from the utopian perspective are frequently known as normative psychologists, such as Erich Fromm and Abraham Maslow.

The philosophical domains, for many scientific, especially scientistic and objectivistic researchers, are prohibited and, therefore, unknown territories, if not the reverse. For similar reasons, some researchers in addition to clinicians avoid even acknowledging the existence of the axiologically subnormal in the sense of the evil especially construed as maliciousness and other species of wickedness (Charny, 1996; Stone, 1993, pp. 453–486).

C. Normality as Statistically Average; Pathology as Sub-Average

The norm, therefore, can signify some ideal such as an ethical or cultural sort. Whichever the case, the norm entails a qualitative condition. It can also mean what is normal quantitatively considered. Thus, Strack and Lorr state that normality can be depicted as statistically average and pathology as deviant, ordinarily from a cultural perspective, such that abnormality is "applied to behavior outside this range" (1997, p. 109).

Throughout history, popular and professional verdicts have immensely varied as to what is implied by statistical, or quantitative, normality. It might be held that normal persons qua average are healthy if they register at least a plus one on the scale of minus ten to plus ten. If normals are regarded as being, for example, a minus five, they may be described as being more normal and healthier than persons who are minus seven. Nevertheless, in fact they are only less sick if health is construed as plus one or above.

In this fashion, the notion of the psychopathology of the normal, meaning statistically average, individual comes to the fore. If some norms are taken to mean cross-cultural, then some cultures are, at least statistically speaking, more normal than others.

It is a common outlook that most differences vis-à-vis normality and anormality are somewhat culturally conditioned, including those concerning personality as such. Personologists Theodore Millon, Roger Davis, Carrie Millon, Luis Escovar, and Sarah Meagher essay, "all such distinctions, including the diagnostic categories of the *DSM-IV*, are social constructions and cultural artifacts." They maintain that placing individuals into groups according to explicit diagnostic criteria provides these classifications "the respectability of science." However, they contend that such segregating categorizations are "uniquely social" and "ultimately value laden and circular" (2000, p. 11).

I concur with the view that all judgments concerning what are normal and anormal in terms of personality are culturally conditioned. But I do not agree that they are totally so such that these appraisals would be absolutely relative (and circular) instead of being only relatively relatively so, the perspective I endorse.

As well, what is culturally conditioned must be distinguished from what is ethically conditioned, though they often occur together. Some ethical values (for instance, strict, or quid pro quo, justice) and disvalues (for instance, incest, rape, infanticide) are recognized as such across all societies, certainly among all civilized cultures.

It may be advanced that a culture and its society are civilized to the extent that their judgments concerning what is relative and absolute and their combinations are humane. As such, they are transcultural and universal, or quasi so, in the sense of ubiquitous (sometimes known as human universals in contrast to those of an a priori nature, such as obtains in pure mathematics).

As being value-imbued, *DSM* categories, including those referring to personality disorders, at least implicitly involve ethical aspects, a position to which I adhere and one used in my grouping of these ten personality aberrations. Hence, I denominate them as psycho-ethical disturbances.

In these matters, I am partial to Jerome Wakefield's views, namely, first, that personality-disorder judgments involve both the de jure axiological elements, including the moral and cultural, in addition to de facto psychological components. Second, "that cultural values are neither the lone essence of such judgments nor extraneous to them" (2006, p. 162).

My division of the personality disorders, especially in its ethical as distinct from its psychological component, is mainly based on the motivational differences of acquisition (Group I), acquisitiveness (Group III), and malevolent selfishness (Group II) in terms of interpersonal relatedness. These distinctions refer to varying levels of self-centeredness—itself a notion that is both psychological and ethical in composition—which are absolute or at minimum, relatively absolute in terms of one another.

As well, I hold that, for example, the acquirantly motivated Group I schizoid, the malevolently intentioned Group II sociopath, and the acquisitively motivated Group III borderline would be considered at least relatively ethically abnormal in any civilized culture.

In my view, anything that is below a motivation of simple equalization, meaning justice in terms of its *letter*, signifies psycho-ethical illness and abnormality of personality. Correlatively, every motivation above it signifies ascending mental-moral health and ultimately supranormality of personality. I maintain that the different levels of motivation from benevolence to its full realization in altruistic beneficence to malevolence and its total actualization in maleficence are at least relatively absolute and cross-cultural.

Assuredly, other factors beyond the motivational enter into the notions of normality and anormality, including those mentioned by the *DSM* in its general and specific definitions of personality disorders. However, the motivational are indispensable in adjudicating what is an abnormal or anormal personality.

It is patently true that powerful social and cultural institutions, like those of SCRAM, can blind individuals and groups to their absolute axiological, or value, order and even reverse them. Selfishness has become something good (Ivan Boesky), even a virtue (Ayn Rand).

Millon and colleagues essay that "American writers" are highly inclined to view functioning autonomously as the gauge of normality (2000, p. 11). Hyper-independence, or social atomism, is considered by SCRAM's proponents as not only indicative of normality but of supranormality (and of morality and supramorality). Success, especially in the form of fame and fortune, is considered the chief goal of hyper-autonomy.

For instance, material success is sometimes interpreted by "SCRAMites," meaning, obviously, those afflicted by the mental/moral disease of SCRAM, as a sign of having been predestined for eternal salvation à la Calvinism. Alternatively, functioning homonomously and dependently is judged by SCRAM as being far less normal—not to mention supra or supernormal—even abnormal. Accordingly, SCRAM tolerates, and in some cases, encourages values and social conditions that foster the malevolence, selfishness, and hyper-independence of Group II, especially the sociopathic and narcissistic. Thus, SCRAMites under the aegis of Atomitis and Successitis, still retain not only a fascination for the kind of corporate czar who is morally perverse and a criminal to boot but a veneration of this individual as a social-cultural icon. The same may be said of the puerile adulation of self-obsessed celebrities.

Consequently, SCRAM as a philosophy of life is guilty of converting what is in se abnormal into being perceived as normal and even supranormal. Accordingly, this social sickness represents a reversal of authentic values and, therefore, a decline in the health of the American personality.

Of course, most Americans decry SCRAM's "transvaluation" of what are usually construed as genuine values. However, confusion, hopelessness, and lethargy in addition to pseudo-patriotism, negative nationalism, and misguided religiosity often prevent Americans from changing "the system." It is an arrangement that is increasingly making such diseased personalities as the sociopath and narcissist to be considered statistically and even ideally normal.

D. Normality as the Ability to Adapt and Respond Effectively to the Environment

Strack and Lorr state that normality and pathology can be construed as "transactional systems." In this event, these conditions are evaluated according to a person's ability or inability "to adapt and respond effectively to ongoing internal (biological, psychological) and external (social) demands" (1997, p. 109). Healthy persons are also able, in some measure, to alter these exigencies in light of their needs and values. As well, this fourth paradigm of health would include the notion of being not only reasonably free from illness but being able to control it when present and then advance toward a more desirable state of well-being.

Nietzsche considers the ability to overcome abnormality to perhaps be the surest sign of potential good and even "great health," namely supranormality seen in what he terms "overmen," or "supermen" (1989b, p. 298n2). The philosopher is (in)famous for many seeming outrageous proclamations, not the least of which is his assertion that "What does not destroy me, makes me stronger" or at least it can potentially do so (1965b, p. 467n8).

What is often unknown or perhaps forgotten is that Nietzsche stipulates that the individual has to be fundamentally healthy to convert illness—physical, mental, or spiritual (moral)—into health not to mention superior health (1989b, p. 224n2). Thus, while sickness may strengthen the already basically strong, or healthy, nature, the iconoclastic philosopher avows that it is a poison by which "weaker natures perish" (1974, p. 92n19).

Hence, Nietzsche proposes that sickness can "become an energetic *stimulus* for life, for living *more*" (1989b, p. 224n2). This greater living, which he titles the "Joyous Wisdom," his philosophy of the affirmation and love of life, requires, then, undergoing and overcoming variegated illnesses.

Because these Nietzschean mental/moral paragons are totally natural instead of supernatural in composition, such aristocrats might better be known as "supramen" instead of supermen lest they appear to be superior by dint of some supernaturally, in the sense of divinely, endowed ability. Nonetheless, since Nietzsche sometimes argues as if these models exceed all others in an absolute sense, they would then be beyond the plus ten on our scale. Accordingly, "supermen" would be a more fitting title, provided the preceding caveat is kept in mind.

It is notable that what Nietzsche denominates personality pertains only to the exceptionally healthy individual who has established a kind of "creative sovereignty over himself" (1991, p. 137n3). Indeed, he contends that nothing is more excellent and, therefore, more rare than this self-mastering kind of personality or what it is designated above as the higher Dionysian individual (1968, p.

472n886a). Consequently, Nietzsche asserts that "most" individuals are not and do not become personalities at all. However, he says, some are in the sense of having "*several*" personalities, meaning an anarchic "rendezvous" of inferior Dionysians who themselves are characterized by mental/moral chaos (ibid., n886b).

With the above considerations in tow, it might be said that an individual whose persistent ranking is very high on our health chart can have it plunge temporarily to even a minus level and still be reckoned essentially healthy (plus ten can be deemed suprahealth with ten plus being superhealth). This assessment is owing to the individual's powerful resilience and overall robustness that enable the self to bounce back to a plus eight or higher.

This appraisal is less applicable to mental and moral health than physical because gaining and regaining the first and second are usually far more difficult than the third. A person can have, for example, a physiologically damaged heart surgically repaired or even replaced. On the other hand, a heart impaired by the likes of habitual bitterness and envy is quite another matter.

Few would disagree with the position that changing personality, especially the subnormal, is a more formidable feat than changing anything else external. Thus, to transform the self is a far more formidable challenge than changing anything in the outside world. Accordingly, Descartes urges people "to conquer" themselves instead of the universe (Sartre, 1948, p. 39). Nietzsche praises those who via "self-overcoming" master and command themselves instead of others (1965a, pp. 225–227).

The ability to defeat illness and negative states in general may be a greater sign of health and normality than their sheer absence. Some individuals, including those in Group III, may have a deeper need for intimacy than the statistically normal individuals with their psychopathology of the average. Thus, so-called normal individuals may seldom be subject to persistent and intense loneliness since they have but a middling requirement for or interest in interpersonality as a state of being. Hence, these normals are less affected by its unwanted absence than, for example, the neurotic dependent and other Group III individuals whose existence is riveted on shared inwardness.

Consequently, the dependents' coping with what is often cataclysmic loneliness (and aloneliness) may demand more psychological health than doing so with merely a mild and periodic loneliness—or some other affliction, especially a cognate, such as depression—experienced by the average person. Still, their sheer capability to suffer from loneliness with its absence of intimacy by and in itself is not sufficient to make Group III abnormals, such as the dependent, as healthy as or less sick than the so-called average personality. There are other constituents of disturbed personalities than the lack of intimate sociality, though I am persuaded that it is the most telling feature regarding them and their groupings.

Normals can live in loneliness and they can live through it without the tribulation living them, so to speak, as it does in the case of the pathologically lonely individuals of Group III. They have become (a)loneliness in its various forms in that it has taken over their lives and is now tantamount to being the nucleus of their personalities. If anyone can be dubbed a lonely personality, it is one of the four Group III pathologicals, especially the borderline and dependent who are also the most alonely of all the aberrant personalities.

Furthermore, some persons, including the aberrated, are more vulnerable to particular types of loneliness than to others. Though all the forms of emotional isolation manifest a presence of pain and absence of pleasure, they all do not do so equally or certainly not for a given normal or abnormal personality. For instance, erotic loneliness appears, at least on the surface, to be more troubling for the histrionic than it is for the avoidant, whereas social loneliness appears to be just the reverse.

E. Normality and Pathology as Pragmatically and Consensually Determined by Health Professionals

Fifth and finally, Strack and Lorr state that normality and pathology can be envisioned pragmatically and consensually such that mental disorders are those conditions so troublesome that they are brought to clinicians for treatment. These professionals decide what is normal or anormal in terms of personality health and illness (1997, p. 109).

Naturally, such experts do not rule upon such matters out of thin air but may rely, for instance, on any of the other four models of health or combinations thereof insofar as they are compatible with one another. As well, they are experts precisely due to the art, science, and philosophy of personality that they have acquired through training, reflection, research, experience, intuition, moral qualities, such as caring and compassion, and other sources of professional proficiency.

Strack and Lorr note, "in many cases the [five] perspectives are not mutually exclusive and can be complementary" (ibid.). Though the viewpoints may be consonant with or even supportive of one another, still they by no means remove all the difficulties as to what constitutes the normal and abnormal, and, perhaps, above all, the supra and supernormal personality. Consequently, it is not surprising to find Allen Frances, Thomas A. Widiger, and Melvin Sabshin propose that these five paradigms have "proven problematic and inadequate" (1991, p. 13) in differentiating normality and health from abnormality and illness.

The supra or supernormal types refer to the ideal, or utopian, model of health. In this paradigm, it is not only a question of an individual's lacking pathology—certainly one that is insuperable—that characterizes the model personality. Instead, it is also an individual being more or less completely healthy or what Carl Rogers titles "the fully functioning" person; Abraham Maslow, "the self-actualizing"; and Kazimierz Dabrowski, "the secondarily integrated," or highest level, personality.

Additionally, the supranormal and, to a lesser extent, the normal personality are able to withstand negative milieus and sometimes to change them to conform to their own ideals, presuming the latter are of some objectively absolute ideality. Hence, along with Dabrowski (1972, pp. 299, 301), I hold that positive (developmental, critical) and negative (nondevelopmental, uncritical) kinds of alienation and adaptation, or adjustment, must be distinguished relative to both internal and external milieus. Also, positive and negative types of maladjustment and self-maladjustment should be differentiated, depending upon whether they are in conformity with the individual's ideal self, or personality paradigm.

It needs amplification here that the utopian models of normality require consideration of other persons and their notions of their authentic and ideal selves. The concept of ideality is not, therefore, purely subjective in the sense of being utterly idiosyncratic, private, relative, and autonomous. Personal ideality must be in accord with universal or at least ubiquitous values and civilized cross-cultural standards of personal psycho-ethical excellence. Obsessionals have personality ideals but they are egocentric, sanctimonious, pusillanimous, and successively obstinate and obsequious.

If, therefore, we examine what civilized societies consider ideal selves, they have much in common. What especially stands out about these exemplars is a reflection of a commitment to universal empathy, sympathy, kindness, justice, and integrity, the last can be construed as a combination of courage, sincerity, and devotedness. These traits pertain to the essence of humanism from an ethical perspective and for this reason alone are universal or at minimum ubiquitous in scope.

Clearly, not every culture or every individual within a humanistic culture practices humanistic values in general. Anti-humane and even wickedly abnormal and immoral regimes and individuals are found around the globe. Moreover, even normal people(s) can become morally remiss even malevolent at times. Correspondingly, if we consult positive cultures' views of the anti-ideal individual, we find that they agree, at least in theory, that it is the psychopathic personality. These often malicious even sadistic individuals have no ideal selves, although they may at times mindlessly fancy themselves as the epitomization of the exemplary (male sociopaths outnumber their females counterpart about three to one (p. 648). Hence, an individual's desired self may be immoral in composition such that it is subjectively revered but is objectively reprehensible.

Being true to the desired self is, therefore, not necessarily being authentic unless this self is morally desirable and essentially in accord with others, especially those recognized as supranormals, and their ethically objectively desirable selves.

10. The Interface between the Normal and Abnormal Personality

Besides what Strack designates as the above five "broad, philosophical perspectives" regarding health versus sickness or a healthy versus a disordered person, he contends that the majority of clinicians and researchers adhere to one of four positions as to the interface between normal and abnormal personality. The first is the categorical paradigm that stipulates that the two personalities are qualitatively distinct. They are so due to objective criteria that are "ultimately biological or genetic" in composition (2006b, p. xxiv).

The second is the dimensional, in which Strack stipulates that the normal and abnormal personalities "exist on the same plane and merge at some point on one or more sets of trait dimensions," for instance, those of the FFM (ibid.).

The third perspective combines the dimensional and categorical such that quantitative trait variations can generate, Strack says, "qualitatively different normal and abnormal personality types." Thus, he maintains that particular combinations of FFM dimensions, such as Extraversion and Neuroticism, "can lead to habitual patterns of behavior that are so pervasive and distinct that they can be defined as particular normal and abnormal personality styles," for example, the paranoid or compulsive (ibid., p. xxv).

Strack relates that the fourth position signifies that the normal personality is founded on dimensional, or quantitative, traits. He maintains, "the abnormal personality results from biological processes or genetic elements that interact with these traits to produce categorically distinct disorders." For instance, Strack argues, "the presence of a genetic marker for schizophrenia in an otherwise normal introvert might [terminate] in disturbed thinking, a predisposition to psychotic breakdowns, and a schizotypal PD" (ibid.).

Strack remarks that it is a frequent fault of researchers to:

> ignore the conceptual differences between different models of psychopathology [for example, the categorical and dimensional], and to erroneously conclude that one study supports or does not support a particular model when the research does not actually address the model in question. This is akin to comparing apples and oranges and should be avoided. (2006c, p. 195)

Strack essays that there is no generally agreed notion and certainly no:

> "gold standard" . . . of what makes one person "normal" and another "abnormal." The most widely accepted definition of personality disorder is the one offered by the *DSM* . . . but [it] is widely criticized because the diagnostic criteria are sometimes confusing and arbitrary. . . . Curiously, there is no counterpart to the *DSM* in the realm of normality . . . . In current research, normality is usually *assumed* among persons who (a) do not meet *DSM* criteria for a personality or other mental disorder, (b) have no history of psychiatric problems, and (c) are not currently seeking help for mental health reasons [of course, normals may seek such help to become more normal or even supranormal in idealistic terms]. (Ibid.)

According to the WHO, "mental illness will be the number two cause of death and disability by 2020" (*The Montreal Gazette*, 27 February 2010). For example, one in every five Canadians will have a mental health problem at some point in life (ibid.). Of course, this occurrence does not ipso facto mean that people are becoming more mentally ill for it may be a case, for instance, of less reluctance to admit such illness in addition to better means of detecting and dealing with disease.

As for moral health, it is not so much the omission of bad or evil actions but the commission of good and great ones that matters more. Still, it is likely that the so-called average person fails more often by default than by actual immoral deeds, and does so owing to apathy, timidity, or being overly tied up in the demands of making a living.

Human beings may be malevolent at times but, arguably, they rarely translate such hostile wishes into actually willing others something negative and even less carry out such ill will. In short, if people are to be faulted morally, it is because they are more neglectors than abusers, though the first, if habitual, often leads to the second and the second almost invariably leads to the first.

As to physical health, it is also more important what persons do than what they do not do. Thus, not gasping for breath while slowly walking a short distance on a level surface is hardly a sufficient sign of good physical health. However, breathing effortlessly while running up a long, steep hill may well be a strong indication of sound health.

Mental health from a cognitive perspective involves, for example, not so much merely the absence of ignorance but the presence of insight into self, others, and the world in general.

From an affective point of view, mental health is not only the absence of negative emotionality, such as FFM Neuroticism, but the presence of positive emotions such as love, joy, serenity, and optimism.

With reference to a conative and specifically motivational vantage point, mental health, in my estimation, involves at minimum habitual equalizational intentionality, meaning a more or less continuous striving to fulfill the exigencies of justice, including social and economic.

Though psychology and ethics are distinct disciplines, any rigid separation of the descriptive traits of the psychic from those that are prescriptive qualities of the ethical, or characterological, is more an abstract, theoretical dichotomization instead of one that is faithful to concrete experience.

Therefore, while mental and moral health are distinguishable, they are not totally separable in the actual person, including the abnormal sort. For example, sociopaths and paranoids are not only psychologically ill, they are morally diseased; this holds true also of the other eight personality disturbances. They all substantially lack moral health in various significant degrees if not in kind.

Human beings are quintessentially ideal-forming social mammals; this idealism is first and foremost ethical in nature. It is one that entails the private and individual in addition to the public and communal spheres. If their personalities are ill, it is because in some measure, human beings are defective not only vis-à-vis private ideals but species-wide ones.

The most sick personality in terms of the totality of psychical and ethical personality traits is, without question, the sociopath, the utmost egological solipsist and immoral isolate.

As detailed in Volume I (pp. 410–413), the linkage of the ideal and ethical with the actual and psychic goes against some, albeit a waning of, current academic American and British psychology. This unacceptable association is especially true insofar as these *psychologies* are still influenced and, a fortiori, governed by the *philosophies* of positivism, objectivism, and scientism in general.

The non-negotiable bifurcation between the descriptive and the evaluative, especially the ethical, can impede both conceptual and curative processes. Erich Fromm states that his own experience:

> as a practicing psychoanalyst has confirmed [his] conviction that problems of ethics cannot be omitted from the study of personality, either theoretically or therapeutically. The value judgments we make [influence] our actions and upon their validity rests our health and happiness. (1968, p. v; see Livesley, 1998, p. 144)

11. Personality: Health and Happiness

Unfortunately, the notion of health in all its forms, psychic, somatopsychic/psychosomatic—today more commonly known as somatoform—and moral (spiritual), is seldom related to happiness. It is the goal of all human beings and is arguably the most significant subject of philosophy and ethics in particular, surely as they are applied to the person both in terms of its individuality and sociality.

Psychologists Carol Ryff and Burton Singer illustrate how, through their investigation of philosophical notions of happiness:

> the key goods in life central to positive human health are, primarily, having purpose in life and quality connections to others; and, secondarily, possessing self-regard [self-worth] and mastery . . . . in the life course unfolding of well-being it is an individual's sense of purposefulness and deep connection to others which likely builds and maintains positive self-regard, sense of self-realization, personal growth, and mastery, with the latter serving to enhance the pursuit of life goals and quality relations with others. (1998, pp. 3, 10)

It is routinely proffered that purpose in life is quintessentially due to the special significance that only intimacy—above all its love-species—can provide. Correlatively, the unwanted absence of meaningful intimacy and intimate meaningfulness, to wit loneliness, is arguably the chief source of infelicity and aimlessness, especially when it is mixed with its cousins depression, alienation, and boredom. This isolating malaise is also a cause or major contributor to various sorts of illness, including mental, clearly many cases of clinical depression, possibly some instances of schizophrenia, and most probably some personality disorders, especially Group III.

Ryff and Singer write that "passion in life purpose," or love of life, contributes not only to happiness but "to positive human health." They propose that love of life, which is principally comprised of a life of loving and being loved, is not only the basic factor in well-being but likely "the most powerful preventive medicine there is" (ibid., p. 11). Hence, people who are not loving and, therefore, not loved—are extremely likely to believe that there is little if any value to their existence and perhaps existence as a whole. Consequently, they may feel that there is no point in taking care of their all-around health. The loveless may even deliberately set out to ruin it or simply give up via depression or ultimately suicide.

Aberrated individuals are highly unloving individuals at least in an authentic, or benevolently, based manner. As a result, their traits are unlovable. Still, they may be loved for the persons they are if, be they abnormal or not, persons are not held to be totally comprised by their qualities.

To be sure, some diseased personalities, namely Group II, are also hateful even ruthless sorts of individuals. This cruelty is the calling card of sadistic sociopaths, individuals who are evil and sometimes diabolically so. So defined, they gleefully inflict pain on others—most of all on the innocent and helpless—and exerting power over them as if they were animated toys.

Not all such unloving persons, even the callous sociopaths, are necessarily unhappy since their personality traits need not cause them pain. While they may not be unhappy individuals, their qualities do not bring them happiness in the form of genuine contentment and peace of heart. Nor does it bring them joy, the emotion that is the essence of happiness.

However, Group II pathologicals are prone to a sort of perverse joy that inheres in *Schadenfreude*, which is pernicious gloating over the misfortunes of others, especially perceived enemies. Such savoring of the sorrows of others is typical of those who are persistently envious, like Group II aberrants. These individuals are liable to habitually regard their fellow human beings as potential if not actual adversaries, especially if they are deemed superior by these individuals who tend to be people of *ressentiment* with its enviousness and vindictiveness (vol. 1, p. 225).

As a philosophy, SCRAM does not bring serenity and gladness. Among other things, its successism, rivalism, and materialism are riddled with envy, enmity, and greed, traits especially typical of Group II pathologicals. These vices are especially inimical to happiness, above all its most elevated echelons of equanimity and ecstasy. Not being unhappy is not the same as being happy just as not being unhealthy is not identical to being healthy since the absence of the negative is not equal to the presence of the positive.

Generally speaking, all abnormal personalities have an extremely infelicitous and unhealthy impact on others: Group I, customarily unwittingly and involuntarily; Group III, ordinarily knowingly and often at least partially volitionally; and Group II, most consciously and deliberately. It is noteworthy that those pathological personalities, who are themselves most subject to feelings of unhappiness—including that effected by loneliness, depression, and lonely depression, namely Group III—, are less psycho-ethically sick than those less subject to such woes, namely Groups I and II.

In observations that reflect a classification of individuals into abnormals, normals, and supranormals relative to life-enjoyment, Cloninger hypothesizes that the population as a whole can be approximately divided into thirds in terms of their level of well-being: one third are immature and at least moderately vulnerable to psychopathology; one third are average and getting by without much disability [psychological] or happiness; and one third are flourishing with high frequency of positive emotions, low frequency of negative emotions, and satisfaction with their life. The extremes (upper and lower 10 percent) of personality disorder and of well-being represent the extremes of the human capability to spiral down into misery or up into happiness, wisdom, and virtue. (2006, p. 78)

In my view, as long as SCRAM dominates a society's way (philosophy) of life, whether on a conscious or non-conscious level, it will continue to elicit and exacerbate conditions instrumental in increasing unhappiness and the lack of character and virtue that are essential ingredients of all-around well-being. SCRAM's hegemony will also continue to sustain a culture that is propitious for contributing to the initiation and magnification of personality aberrations, especially those of Group II, above all, the sociopathic and narcissistic.

In general, SCRAM remains injurious to interpersonal relatedness. Since such connectedness is the mortar of society, SCRAM's five institutions will persist in prolonging the kind of social situations that hinder the development of positive personality traits but help those that are negative. In short, SCRAM will increase the number of those vulnerable to abnormality but decrease the number who are normal and potentially supranormal.

12. Personality and Mental-Moral Health: Par, Subpar, and Suprapar

As the adage goes, it only takes one bad apple to ruin the bushel. A single vicious sociopath can have a devastating effect on numerous normal individuals. Alternatively, a supranormal can have an extremely uplifting effect on others. Still, all the best apples combined can rarely make an exceptionally bad apple, like the vicious sociopath, good.

As well, there are arguably more subnormals and submorals, such as sadistic antisocials, than supranormals and supramorals, which is patently a ground for pessimism. Nevertheless, there is reason to believe that there are far more psycho-ethical normals—the majority of human beings lying in this range—than mental/moral abnormals, all of which is a basis for optimism. Admittedly, however, generalizations and, all the more so, universalizations in these matters are especially risky however desirable and even necessary they may be at times.

As is commonly conceded, the injection of the normative and specifically the ethical into the clinical setting can be highly problematic. Doing so may degenerate, for example, into a kind of judgmentalism or moralism that is detrimental to therapeutic objectivity and thereby to overall clinical effectiveness. Nonetheless, it is arguably more dangerous to systematically exclude moral matters from the clinical context of pathological personalities—and from the theoretical research realm—than to include them, issues which will be addressed in the final chapter.

One most conspicuous intermingling of the psychological and ethical pertains to the division of motivation into benevolence, equalization (acquirement), acquisition, acquisitiveness, and malevolence and their different species, such as pure and mixed benevolence and violent and non-violent malevolence. The notions of motivation, or intentionality, and its classification are, in my view, crucial to the comprehension of the nature and taxonomy of personality and its therapy. All these motivations entail ethical aspects such that, in my judgment, any theory of personality that omits them and other such relevant axiological aspects from its analysis will be to that extent not only generally deficient but specifically defective.

People, including personologists and therapists, are forever rendering judgments, whether explicitly or implicitly, about the mental cum moral status of human beings as a whole. Surely psychiatrists and psychologists should render such judgments, according to Cloninger, since they profess to be students of the psyche and, hence, the spirit(ual) (ibid., p. 66). These appraisals necessarily include types that concern the purely malevolent and maleficent versus the purely benevolent and beneficent and every intentional pattern in between.

Such verdicts are often embedded in lay persons' language: evil, bad, average, good, excellent, and saintly, or whether they vary, if you will, from grades F- or even below (the submoral) to A+ (the supramoral). This said, it might be asked where the normal, abnormal, and supranormal personality, as understood in reference to the five paradigms of moral health and sickness sketched above, be placed vis-à-vis the motivational patterns considered from a moral perspective.

With respect to the statistical model of health and sickness in terms of ethical motivation, the supranormal person might be located at the level of universal beneficence in the sense of altruistic philanthropy. Correlatively, the most psycho-ethically abnormal personality would be found at the level of universal maleficence as in sadistic misanthropy.

The proper place of the statistically normal person within this motivational framework is, patently, far more debatable. To some, human nature is a psychological and ethical tabula rasa, such that the person is neutral in these respects, meaning neither good nor bad mentally/morally. To others, this average person is intrinsically psycho-ethically good or bad or has or at minimum a genetic predisposition to being so. For still others, it is not nature or its proclivities that solely decree or even dispose a person to being or becoming good or bad nor his or her environment but instead the individual's unique personality with its freedom of choice.

The answers to these and a host of related questions are pivotal in a person's attitude toward others and self in terms of, for example, cynicism, pessimism, optimism, and everything in between, such as peiorism and meliorism, which are, respectively, the doctrines that life is or can be getting worse or better due to human intervention. Hence, becoming habitually worse can involve going from persistent acquisitiveness to malevolence and selfishness; becoming better, the reverse, or a transition, for instance, from the equalization of justice unmotivated by benevolence to one that is.

My views about these matters are that, first, human beings are generally benevolent, or at minimum inclined to being so, or at the very minimum are disposed to being just not only as to the letter but the spirit of the law, a spirit that implies benevolence. On the other hand, I am open to the position that human nature is largely neutral vis-à-vis its motivations such that it is almost entirely influenced by its social environment, especially its early familial milieu, and its later choices.

Second, I hold that the aforesaid motivations differ in kind such that there are absolute boundaries between them or at least ones that are quasi so. For this reason, personality evolution, in my judgment, seldom if ever leaps or skips over motivational grades and patterns. For instance, rarely does this change go from malevolence to equalization and even less from malevolence to benevolence, without first going through the stages of acquisitiveness and acquisition.

For these reasons alone, it is very difficult to change the psycho-ethical structure of any personality, especially the disordered sort since the lower the type, the more resistant, in most views, including mine, it is to change. Moreover, the lower the pathological personality and its particular grouping, the more the aberrant personality is reluctant to being changed by others.

From a purely psychological perspective, the schizoid or schizotypal of Group I is the most difficult to alter and the dependent or avoidant—contingent upon the *DSM* diagnostic traits stressed—of Group III are the least. However, overall, the *DSM* sociopath, meaning the criminal antisocial, offers the most resistance to change, especially that of self-therapy. In general, the more the pathological personality is open to therapeutic intervention, the less sick is the individual. As well, the more the sociopath is a psychopath in the sense that the sickness is due to genetic or biological factors, the less is the individual a candidate for positive change.

This said, I would not preclude the real possibility that if people habitually perceive themselves to be unconditionally loved (or hated), then they can far more easily go from one level to the next (and possibly even skip one). Unconditional love is generally viewed as the greatest force for psycho-ethical improvement provided such love is able to call upon a conditional sort of love, one that entails the ability for loving criticism that, in turn, requires a benevolently motivated concern for justice.

Hence, by being loved and generally affirmed and validated, individuals can proceed, for instance, from non-sadistic malevolence to simple ill will. Doing so is difficult in part because their malevolence is often syntonic, meaning in keeping with their basic desires and self-image and, accordingly, such a transition seldom transpires.

Remaining at a psycho-ethically healthier level without falling back to a lower one is perhaps even more toilsome than arriving there. As a rule, the lower the level of psycho-ethical health, the easier it is to sink to an even lower stage. On the other hand, the higher the state of such health, the easier it is to go on to a higher state. Virtue is hard to acquire but its practice becomes easier through its very practice. However, practice never makes perfect in moral matters since even supermorals will falter or fail at times unless they are actually superhuman (to my knowledge, the only one who is believed to be so is Jesus Christ).

Still, people can and do get beyond their lower levels of motivation. Nonetheless, they rarely do so without the insightful and persistent care of others. Unfortunately, such unloving persons, like the pathological, typically lack such solicitous individuals in their lives and lacked them and their unconditional love in formative years. On the contrary, they often suffered from unconditional hatred and indifference.

The paradigm of the supranormal personality from an ethical perspective is the saint, construed herein as the moral model, or paragon. Sanctity reflects a singular superiority of spirituality. This moral excellence is essentially comprised of universal love (altruism), the sort that entails universal empathy and sympathy, in addition to justice, including its social and economic species. This eminence has nothing intrinsically to do with religion, belief in God, and the supernatural order. Atheists and agnostics can, therefore, be saintly and spiritual and thereby exemplify the pinnacles of virtue, while theists, pantheists, and deists can embody the dregs of vice.

The saint and the sociopath represent the polarities of mental/moral health and illness, not only from a statistical point of view but from the utopic or dystopic perspective. There appear to be many more sociopaths than saints, clearly more than those officially recognized. This lends more plausibility to the views of pessimism or cynicism about human nature as a whole. Yet the statistically average person may be closer to altruistic sanctity than to sadistic depravity, all of which argues for a more optimistic or at least a melioristic view of human nature.

It is unlikely that we will ever know with any certainty or even any high degree of probability where personality normalcy lies in the scheme of things. There are simply too many complex variables to take into consideration to ascertain where human beings as a totality fall on any psycho-ethical gradation. Moreover, attaining a sufficient study sample regarding human beings around the world in these matters seems improbable. Still, it is well documented that optimism and pessimism and everything in between tend to be self-fulfilling prophecies.

One reason for adopting a more positive interpretation of human beings' basic nature in these areas is that they apparently tend to believe themselves and others to be fairly humane. Humaneness would rank high on our scale and perhaps by comparison to justice motivated by benevolence in terms of motivational gradients. Valerie May reports that the largest Internet survey of its kind found that, of the 80,012 participants in 178 countries and territories, "more than 80% . . . believe that people 'are kind,'" a chief ingredient of humaneness (1999, p. 130).

Received wisdom has it that we treat others as we expect to be treated by them such that acting beneficently, maleficently, and every way in between are sorts of self-fulfilling prophecies. Thus, normals, considered as average, arguably expect kindness from their own kind. Moreover, normals increasingly anticipate their conspecifics to be solicitous toward non-human types of beings and the environment. Many ethicians argue that how adults treat other human beings and non-human beings run in parallel fashion.

Kindness is the antithesis of hard-hearted self-centeredness and selfishness typical of Group II aberrants. According to a German study, greedy individuals not only want to gain as much as possible for themselves but to do so at others' expense, all of which epitomizes the unkind person (*The Montreal Gazette*, 24 November 2007). "Greedies" hugely enjoy seeing others fail, which is characteristic of SCRAM's rivalism's shortage of kindness and caring but typical of its abundance of the enviousness that culminates in *Schadenfreude*.

Goleman reports on research that indicates that what most attracts women toward men and vice versa is not success or even sex but human goodness such as kindness (2006, p. 199). He further maintains that the human brain has been biologically "preset for kindness," a humaneness, he says, that stems from people's innate tendency for empathy (ibid., p. 60). To substantiate his stance, Goleman contends that human beings naturally, or instinctively:

> go to the aid of a child who is screaming in terror; we automatically want to hug a smiling baby. Such emotional impulses are "prepotent"; they elicit reactions in us that are unpremeditated and instantaneous. That this flow from empathy to action occurs with such rapid automaticity hints at circuitry dedicated to this very sequence. To feel distress stirs an urge to help. (Ibid.)

Thus, empathy can lead to benevolence, although the second can also be construed as a condition of the first. Goodwill, in its wake, may lead to actual assistance to those in distress or need. It may be argued, therefore, that such goodwill is normal not only in a utopian but in a statistical sense. Average persons commit very few bad acts in a day but many good ones, though they omit perhaps even more, including some of which they are obligated to perform. To be sure, all these tendencies hugely depend on societal conditions.

Empathy seems to be a quasi-innate trait. Together with benevolence and justice, including the respect owed every human being, these form the foundation of civilization.

SCRAM creates a non-just and non-empathic society in part because it fosters a self-absorbed individualism instead of a mentality that tries to understand the mind of someone else, be it a stranger or non-stranger. Consequently, it is understandable why Barack H. Obama has said that America is suffering from an "empathy deficit" (Albert Nerenberg, *The Montreal Gazette*, 5 July 2008).

Sustained empathy requires, as a precondition to understanding another human being, that the empathizer be present to the individual, at least in spirit. It is typical of SCRAM's adherents to be "off in their own worlds," "doing their own thing" and "going it alone." These mentalities are largely due to social isolation and the quest for success, especially in the form of fame and wealth. Studies indicate that those more actively social are inclined to be more empathic (the reverse is also likely the case) (ibid.).

In chasing the national dream, the SCRAM supporter tends to be too busy, too much in a hurry, to be empathic. Such a person is often overworked and overstressed, all of which, according to Arthur Ciaramicoli, makes this individual lack "the physiology to empathize." The reason, he says, is that the haste-driven individual is "somewhere else" instead of being present to and concerned about the other, as empathy requires (ibid).

Richard Schwartz and Jacqueline Olds relate that, in talking with Americans, people will discover that the one thing about which they constantly complain is how tremendously busy they feel. Yet, these authors note that Americans "are proud of their busyness" since it "is a badge of toughness, success, and importance," (1997, p. 14) all values endorsed by SCRAM and arguably its supreme "virtue." As well, America is, by any standard, a very violent society, and violence, with its desensitizing powers, is both a cause and an effect of anti-empathy and antipathy.

Pathological personalities profoundly lack empathy and benevolence not to mention applied and efficacious goodwill, meaning beneficence, above all the sort that is love. Some pathologicals, to wit Group II, are more or less anti-altruistic and misanthropic. It is these and the other non-benevolent types of personalities, which now warrant a more methodical examination.

Five

PERSONALITY: ITS DISORDERS

1. Personality: Intimacy, Loneliness, and Health

With the preceding chapter concerning the nature of personality and the various models of health and illness serving as a background, it is now time to focus on the pathological personality especially in the context of loneliness and other negative states of aloneness.

Nikolai Berdyaev asserts that loneliness is the underlying plight of human beings such that its understanding can illuminate their entire existence (Cowburn, 1967, p. 102n5). Shedding light on the person's whole being via loneliness, which is chiefly the unwanted absence of love, is ironically partially a lack of self-being, especially through feelings of emptiness and self-worthlessness. In this regard, a character in the popular television series M*A*S*H asks, "without love, what are we worth? 89 cents—89 cents worth of chemicals walking around lonely."

Consequently, the lonely bewail their feeling like "nobodies" or non-persons"; for instance, they believe that their presence is not noticed and their absence is not missed. In terms of its temporal modes, this felt absence of self-being takes place in the privation of yearning and the deprivations of missing, mourning, and bereaving so much that the self may pine away in sorrow and hopelessness.

As argued above, ongoing intimate relatedness to fellow human beings, both those near and far, is a necessary condition of basic mental health, while the absence of such connectedness seriously impairs it. The research of Elaine Hatfield and Richard Rapson has led them to conclude, "intimacy problems are linked to many mental health disorders . . . intimacy and psychological health seem to go hand-in-hand" (1993, p. 145).

John Cacioppo and William Patrick maintain that all types of health are allied to sociality such that "human connections, mental health, physiological health, and emotional well-being are all inextricably linked" (2008, p. 131). They posit, "unwanted isolation in any of its forms," whether "physical, emotional, spiritual, is deeply disruptive to an organism designed by nature to function in a social setting" (ibid., p. 143). They continue, "so much of modern thought celebrates"—in my view, especially that germane to SCRAM—human beings as "'existential cowboys,'" meaning "various kinds of isolates" (ibid., p. 131).

Intimacy difficulties are the heart of interpersonal problems, which, in turn, are absolutely central to those mental health and, more specifically, mental trait disorders known as personality aberrations. Daniel Leising, Doreen Sporberg, and Diana Rehbein state, "interpersonal behavior is a crucial element in descriptions of personality disorders"—in my view, it is *the* crucial component—and "all ten *DSM-IV* personality disorder categories relate to interpersonal behavior in one way or another," (2006, p. 319) a position I have stressed throughout this study.

Apropos of loneliness and mental illness in general, J. H. van den Berg, among many others, proposes that emotional isolation is itself "the central core" of the psychiatric patient's illness, irrespective, he says, of what that illness is (1972, p. 105). He even calls a chapter of his work "Psychopathology: Science of Loneliness" (ibid., p. 103). Indeed, Berg insists that were this affliction non-existent, it would be reasonable to conclude, "psychiatric illnesses could not occur either." They would not, he appends, save for "the [relatively] few disturbances caused by anatomical or physiological disorders of the brain" (ibid., pp. 105–106).

2. Personality Disorders: Self-Centeredness and the Lack of Intimacy

Max Hammer claims that loneliness is the "central problem" of therapy. He argues that this affliction "undergirds all pathological symptoms." However, he contends that what underlies loneliness is egocentricity, the self-absorption that prevents people from being genuinely related to one another (1972, p. 24).

I have distinguished three increasing levels of self-centeredness—the acquisitional, acquisitive, and the malevolently selfish—that govern the motivational molds of, respectively, the Group I, III, and II personality disorders.

In terms of intimacy, Group I are non-intimates; Group II are anti-intimates; and Group III are pro-intimacy but too neurotically self-centered to achieve its genuine types.

Hence, it is my position that protracted problems with intimacy and interpersonal relatedness pertain to the gist of personality aberrations. Or, if not to their core constitution, then at minimum they refer to their being predisposing, precipitating, and aggravating factors in addition to their being customary properties and consequences of personality disturbances. I further hold that having no need, potential, capability, desire, or willingness for intimacy, or shared inwardness, on a persistent basis signals a disordered personality. Correspondingly, I contend that the nucleus of normal and, a fortiori, supranormal personalities is marked by the prolonged presence of their positive relatedness to others, both in general and in particular.

Serious difficulties in secondary relationships, such as those at the workplace, are less intrinsic to deviant personalities than those in primary relationships. Yet, these aberrants also frequently experience ongoing problems in the less intimate realms of their lives if only because they are individuals whom merely tolerating can be tremendously trying. Seldom if ever does an individual with a serious mental disorder, especially one with a disorder of personality, make for even a temporary pleasurable affiliate, let alone a constant one such as is often required in the workplace.

Jeffrey Magnavita submits that once a diagnosis about the type of personality disorder is decided, then decisions must be forthcoming as to the following therapeutic areas: first, "treatment format—long-term, intermittent, intensive, short-term, supportive"; second, "type/model—cognitive, behavioral, interpersonal, psychodynamic, integrative, pharmacological"; third, "modalities—group, individual, family, couples, mixed, sequential"; and, fourth, "setting—hospital, outpatient, partial, residential" (2004a, p. 4).

Magnavita's first, third, and fourth therapeutic spheres are for the most part beyond the parameters of this study. It will continue to concentrate on the second area especially concerning these aberrants' diagnostic features, typologies, and their models, principally the integrative and interpersonal. As for the therapeutic paradigms and the disorders, they will be mostly addressed in Chapter Ten.

It is imperative at this point to consider, at least in preliminary fashion, the interpersonal model, which I consider the most fitting perspective for understanding pathological personalities, their attributes, classification, and professional treatment (see Pincus, 2005). The overriding reason for my judgment that the interpersonal is the most suitable way to assess these aberrants is that they themselves are essentially failures in terms of interpersonality. Hence, they can be notionalized and categorized both from the philosophical and psychological interpersonal perspective, as can the various states of aloneness in which these pathological personalities are being contextualized.

Even though it may seem obvious, still it is useful to emphasize that an individual with a major *personality problem* is abnormal precisely with respect to being a *personality* as such. Why label such a disturbance one of personality if it does not first and foremost pertain to being a person qua person? As I shall continue to stress throughout this study, human beings are denominated persons quintessentially in view of their relatedness to other persons, in a word, their interpersonality. In sum, a person is preeminently an embodied inwardness who longs to intimately (re)connect with another human interiority. A personality who is not so disposed is, in my judgment, abnormal qua personality for that reason alone.

3. Personality and Interpersonality

There is a tendency to overlook the fact that human beings are in substance their relationships, in part because such connections are simply taken for granted as being the essence, or heart, of their existence. As stipulated earlier, even the profoundly unrelated Group I and dis-related Group II abnormals, if they were to think that they would be without the possibility of simply seeing any other human being in the proximate future, not to mention ever, would immediately feel terrifyingly (a)lonely. By definition, nothing more (a)lonelifies a person than the feeling of being all alone in the world, a fact brought to its culmination in Group III aberrants, especially the borderline and dependent.

Correlatively, nothing more personalizes an individual than feeling inwardly connected to other human beings both generally and specifically. Group I aberrants are not connected to anyone. Group II are not connected to others in general but only to those specific others who serve their selfishness. Group III seek connectedness to all or most others but do so acquisitively and neurotically. However, the self-centeredness of disturbed personalities keeps them from genuine relatedness since people generally want to be liked and loved for themselves instead of being used primarily or exclusively as instruments of the aberrants' pursuit of their own interests and their eluding or escaping (a)loneliness.

Because of their perceived endless isolation, all normal human beings would more or less immediately realize that they *are* irremediably their relatedness, not only in reference to their depths, or basic needs, but heights, or metaneeds. They would (re)acknowledge that these intimate ties are not only the foundation but the fabric of their being and well-being. However, even their periodic and transient interactions pertain to their life-blood. Consequently, if human beings were unable to have any contact with casual acquaintances, they would become diminished human beings. Most assuredly, they would be indescribably lonely ones, even if, perchance, they were "zombie"—like schizoids.

Consequently, the human world is strictly an interpersonal one. If students went to a classroom expecting to see their teacher and classmates, but owing to a cancellation, they were absent, the students' perception of the room would change and so would the students. If the other students and the teacher were there, the classroom would have a meaning, even its own kind of subjectivity and personality. This meaning(fulness) would be given to the classroom by the personalization projection by the human beings who shared the room and made it a lived-in place instead of a dead space.

Emptied of its human occupants, the classroom now has a kind of eeriness to it perhaps even one that is dehumanizing and depersonalizing for the returning student. It is now felt as an alienating and (a)lonelifying locus in that it is bereft of the feelings of, respectively, familiarity and warmth. The now uninhabited classroom may be filled with various objects, such as desks and chairs. Yet however physically close they are to one another, without the presence of the other students and teacher, these objects now seem remote from and even foreign to each other.

As sheer objects, or things, the furniture and the like of the classroom form no world even less a co-world, as is the case when the teacher and other students were present. The objects had formed part of the intimate ambience, which contributed to the closeness of the now missing subjects. Of course, alienation and (a)loneliness can occur in the room even when the teacher and students are present, but emotionally absent to one another, through frigid indifference or heatedly hostility. Or, the rooms themselves can be physically ugly and uncomfortable, all of which is further conducive to estrangement and (a)loneliness.

Consequently, without adequate intimacy, a person's sense of reality eventually dissolves and degenerates into varying degrees or levels of emotional segregation. This isolation can lead to feelings of absurdity, or a generalized meaninglessness, whereas loneliness is specifically a lack of meaning-intimacy and intimacy-meaning. Loneliness can also be a cause and consequence of alienation with its negative feelings and thoughts, such as those of bewilderment, displacement, outsidedness, normlessness, and powerlessness.

It is instructive that the English word "world" is derived from the Old English "woruld." It signifies both human existence and this world, or earth, and is akin to the Old English "wer," meaning man, and "eald," meaning old. So understood, a world is a distinctly human creation. Unlike subjects, objects do not ex-ist, that is, they do not emerge, stand out, and stand forth in relationships since they are confined to themselves. Therefore, they have no world even less a shared world of togetherness, above all one that is intimate.

Bereft of emotions and their unique kind of connectedness, objects are intimacy-less. If we human beings are confined to the realm of things, we feel dissociated, especially if we expected our ambience to be a human, or interpersonal, world, that is, one of intimate meaningfulness and, above all, meaningful intimacy. If we remain in such a non- or de-interpersonalized and de-intersubjectified setting such as the now empty classroom, we will feel not only lonely and alienated but bored and depressed.

While people may be said to have relationships, even more so they *are* them, meaning that they are primarily constituted by their bonds or by their very absence insofar as, paradoxically, attachment-(de)privations can comprise the being of an individual by way of non-being. If the self is composed of its nexus of relationships, as, for example, George Herbert Mead and Antoine St. Éxupéry propose, then the unwanted absence of its intimacy matrix could be said to ipso facto "ontologize" loneliness into the person (McGraw, 1992, p. 326).

Those who subscribe to the interpersonal view of a human being emphasize that individuals receive their original and ongoing experience of selfness (selfhood) from their relatedness to other persons. Correlatively, without them, human beings are afraid, and rightly so, of not remaining persons so much so that they fear for their sanity and possibly their very life. Accordingly, if people are principally nothing other than their relatedness, then to the extent that they are gravely lonely, their sense of being a human being and a distinct person wanes. For all practical purposes, it may vanish, as occurs in the cases of lonely borderlines and schizophrenics who routinely feel that their being is on the edge of nonbeing or already engulfed in nothingness.

Resultingly, the lonely are prone to think of themselves as non-entities for at least two substantive reasons. The first is the ontological and the felt lack of self-being. Thus, the lonely are haunted by a sentience of emptiness. This feeling of being a void is allied to feelings of contingency, in which the lonely feel unnecessary to anyone. Consequently, they feel un-anchored, in which case they may be subject to "existential vertigo." In this feeling of being ungrounded, the lonely experience the world as whirling about them, causing them an anguishing dizziness. In its wake, this bewildering state puts the lonely on the precipice of non-existence or as having already plummeted and disappeared into it.

The second reason, which is often both a cause and an effect of the first, is the psychological, in that the lonely suffer from extremely low self-worth such that they feel themselves to be failed human beings and persons. Without the requisite intimacy, especially love, the lonely feel as if they are nobodies. Thus, the truth of the words of a popular song, to wit:

> when all is said and done, ...You're nobody 'til somebody loves you, you're nobody 'til somebody cares. . . . so find yourself somebody to love. (Morgan, Stock, and Cavanaugh, 1944).

This advice is often timely for the lonely provided it is the genuine kind that stems from benevolence, respect, and empathy. Alas, such prerequisites are missing the more loneliness is of the pathological brand suffered by some aberrant personalities, namely Group III. Group II abnormals may so abhor loneliness that they block its awareness, at which point it may go underground and thereby infest their unconscious. Then it may resurface in anti-intimacy, such as aggressive and violent behavior. On the other hand, the inability to experience loneliness at any level save perhaps the existential marks Group I abnormals.

Whereupon individuals qua persons, instead of being plumbers or clerks, professors or cooks, are principally their relationships, above all, their primary, or intimate, ones such as friendships. Again, it is received wisdom that our choice of friends is a reliable indicator of the kind of person we are. Emmanuel Mounier states that personhood is mostly "an eagerness for friendship" (1970, p. 24) and, more generally, for companionship. Friendship not only contributes to health but it helps restore it when it is missing. To paraphrase Karl Menninger, genuine friendship is but another name for therapy.

Without our intimates, we feel and, indeed, we are truncated or even non-persons, all of which explains why the lonely are prone to say that they feel like sheer non-entities or "zeroes." These self-ascriptions are especially the case with respect to Group III and highly representative of their and other lonelies' abysmal sense of self-worth. Nothing causes less self-regard even to the point of heartbreak and actual heart illnesses than not being cared for and needed by others.

It is, then, intimacy and above all love that are the most deep and durable sources of self-validation and often of a healthy heart in every sense of the word. Correlatively, the absence of such intimacy can be the source of an unhealthy, shattered heart. Carin Rubenstein and Phillip Shaver record how one person describes her absence of intimacy and the resulting loneliness as:

> [a] pain in the chest—almost literally a broken heart. The problem is I need to be needed. That's what I'm missing. . . . Nobody needs me, nobody. I have friends at work and people I can call, but they really don't *need* me. (1982, p. 8)

People can want to be needed by others and to need others for both self- and other-serving reasons.

Therefore, intimacy can be envisaged as the heartwood of intersubjectivity. Sometimes, according to Daniel Goleman, the intersubjective is used for empathy and the desire to be attuned to the "inner reality" of another person. Psychoanalysts, in particular, employ the notion of the intersubjective as "the meshing of two people's inner worlds" (2006, p. 107), which Goleman appears to consider to be an I-Thou connection à la Martin Buber.

Stephen Strack and Maruice Lorr relate that interpersonal models have been taken to task for allegedly being too narrow in scope since they consist of but two spheres. The first is that of dominance/submissiveness or something comparable (I prefer the notions of autonomy and homonomy for reasons spelled out in previous and subsequent chapters). The second sphere is love/hate (I favor the intimacy/non-intimacy and intimacy/anti-intimacy couplets if only because the love/hate unit is, in my view, too proscribed in its parameters) (1997, p. 113).

Strack and Lorr concede that it remains debatable whether interpersonal models can embrace the total range of the disordered personalities. Nevertheless, they are of the mind that these perspectives furnish significant "features not found in other models." For instance, they claim that the interpersonal approaches appear to be mandatory "for understanding and predicting interpersonal behavior in normals and psychiatric patients" (ibid.), observations that, I think, at minimum, intuitively make sense.

Judith Jordan goes so far as to recommend that "the construct" of personality aberration be replaced by affiliation disconnection as developed in the Relational-Cultural Theory (RCT), a perspective that can be considered a species of the interpersonal model. Jordan argues that the objective of therapy "is to bring people out of chronic disconnection and back into growth and movement of mutual relationship" (2004, p. 121), or interpersonality. Group I abnormals are completely non-connected to others. Group II are almost totally disconnected. Group III are connected but inadequately so, save for the avoidants who, like Group I abnormals, are completely unattached, but the first, unlike the second, crave connectedness.

4. The *DSM*: Personality Disorders and Interpersonality

Because it focuses on the abnormal personality, this volume avails itself of the definitions of personality disorders as formulated by the *DSM*. I re-stress that it is crucial to realize that my discussion of these deviants is essentially carried out in light of their primary and associate diagnostic criteria as set forth in the *Manual*. My position, unlike that of the *DSM*, is that, for an individual to be considered a disordered personality, the individual not only possibly can, but necessarily must manifest deviancy in terms of interpersonal functioning, though not everyone who does has such an anomaly.

The *DSM* has stated in its general definition of the personality disorders that interpersonal functioning is but one of four possibilities of these aberrants' personality patterns. Nonetheless, an examination of each definition of the ten disturbed personalities reveals that the *Manual* has notionalized at least implicitly all the aberrations, save the compulsive, in terms of relational difficulties and, more precisely, interpersonal ones.

Still, when it comes to detailing what it means by the compulsive's fixations, the *DSM* specifically mentions "interpersonal control" and difficulties in expressing "affection" in general and "tender feelings" in particular (pp. 669, 671). Thus, its profile indicates that the obsessive has serious problems with intimate relatedness and interpersonal functioning as a whole.

The *DSM* even explicitly defines three of the aberrants as having major issues regarding interpersonal—meaning intimate, or close—relationships as such. The schizoid and schizotypal have difficulties by default, namely by unattachment to others due to an incapability (the schizoid) or at least a restricted capability (the schizotypal) for affective contact. Finally, the *Manual* maintains that the borderline has unstable relationships traceable to personality shortcomings, such as irrational emotional volatility.

Consequently, it can be proposed that the *DSM* itself holds, at minimum tacitly, that all ten disorders manifest serious distress or impairment in terms of interpersonal relatedness. Nevertheless and notwithstanding what the actual outlook of the *DSM* may be vis-à-vis the abnormal personalities in these matters, it is my position that they necessarily involve significantly deficient interpersonal functioning either by quantitative deficit (Group I), by both quantitative and especially qualitative defectiveness on a rather unconscious basis (Group II), or on an extremely conscious one (Group III).

Nonetheless, the psycho-ethical traits of the deviated personality, though all hinder normal interpersonal relatedness, do not always cause every disturbed individual clinically significant stress in terms of dystonicity and impairment. They do in the cases of the borderline, histrionic, dependent, and avoidant of Group III; much less vis-à-vis the sociopath, paranoid, narcissist, and obsessional of Group II; and none whatsoever concerning the schizoid, although they do to some extent to the schizotypal of Group I, mainly insofar as the latter is in a situation wherein this aberrant cannot escape contact with others.

Loneliness—or the inability to experience it—is not the only problem in interpersonal functioning not even that involved in a lack of meaning/intimacy. A great deal of the difficulties in such relatedness is owing, for example, to aloneliness. Still, loneliness is the interpersonal problem that is the most painful in addition to being the most prevalent and evident. Although loneliness is a highly rampant problem, it is not necessarily evident for at least two reasons. First, its sufferers often intentionally conceal it. Second, they frequently—unintentionally and sometimes even intentionally—confuse it with other phenomena. To exemplify, people, especially males, will admit to being lonesome but less so to being lonely since they consider the first as less embarrassing than the second. As well, men are more likely to acknowledge *being* than *feeling* lonely since confessing to the second is felt to be more humiliatingly unmanly than confessing to the first—both by themselves and others, especially other males. Such thinking stems in part from men's belief that loneliness is essentially a weakness and one befitting women, the "weaker sex." As will be detailed in Chapter Seven, males are predominant in the nonlonely Groups I and II; females, in the lonely Group III.

The *Manual* gives scant attention to loneliness as part of personality pathology, mentioning it only twice: once each in the cases of the borderline and avoidant (pp. 653, 664). Why it is so silent with respect to this affliction in terms of the disturbed personalities and yet frequently implies its being so widespread among them is addressed in later chapters. For now, it warrants interpolating here that sometimes the *Manual* does employ terms that implicitly suggest loneliness, such as its usage of the word "emptiness" with reference to the borderline (p. 651).

Still, unless the emptiness concerns the void in the heart due to the absence of a wanted personation, it can signify distresses and stressors other than loneliness, such as boredom. Monotony can be viewed as boredom in terms of the meaningfulness of an individual's activities and interests. Ennui is boredom vis-à-vis life's meaning as a whole. When such dissatisfaction becomes a kind of world-weariness, it can lead to alienation and depression. Loneliness is a lack of meaning concerning a person's connectedness, or intimate relatedness, to personations, especially persons.

Absurdism can be understood as the view that the universe is not only unintelligible but irrational and that any search for meaning in it is misguided or, in any case, futile. Nihilism can be defined as the doctrine that holds that the universe is innately and unalterably meaningless, or senseless, especially regarding values, above all those pertaining to truth and goodness.

We have taken note that the *DSM* differentiates personality disorders from simple personality traits and personality types. Personologists Theodore Millon, Roger Davis, and their assistants Carrie Millon, Luis Escovar, and Sarah Meagher additionally distinguish "personality style," which, they say, "expresses a way of functioning in the world," and "personality structure." They state that this structure "refers to the actual substrates which undergird functioning" and supports such processes, "thus forming the architecture of the mind" (2000, p. 343). They maintain that personality style, which is potentially positive, is distinguishable from the disordered personality, which is manifestly a negative condition. For example, they contend that the dependent aberrant is afraid of being unable to cope with aloneness, which makes this individual an alonely in my terminology. However, these authors maintain that individuals with a dependent style, though they favor being in others' company, can "enjoy occasional solitude" (ibid., p. 209), an aloneness that those with a dependent personality disorder cannot tolerate.

Furthermore, Millon and associates propose that, in the case of the dependent aberrant, the termination of an attachment triggers a desperate search for and merging with a "new partner." On the other hand, they state that the dependent style, though it is "nostalgic [and lonely] about lost intimacy," does not immediately seek fusion with a replacement. As well, they stipulate that, whereas dependents with a full-blown personality disorder fear "being left alone to fend on [their] own," those with the dependent style are "not terrified of abandonment" (ibid.)

All this said, an individual's personality style can be indicative of or at least lead to a personality disorder. Millon and colleagues state, "personality styles shade gently into personality disorders," with the first occurring in the normal range and the second in the abnormal. They append that both personality styles and disorders are "higher-order constructs composed of personality traits." They further claim that these constructs "integrate the part-functions of personality," while personality traits themselves "are simple behavioral consistencies within the various personality domains or perspectives" (ibid., p. 97).

Not every personologist would agree that personality traits are necessarily translated into external behavior, certainly none that are perceptible. In fact, many of thirty FFM traits, including those of fantasy, feelings, and ideas of the supertrait of Openness to Experience, do not at all refer to behavioral activities in the sense of their being externalized via bodily comportment.

Millon and colleagues emphasize, "[personality] traits refer to long-standing personality characteristics which endure over time and situations," while "[personality] states refer to potentially short-lived conditions, usually emotional in nature" (ibid., p. 80). Here the usage of trait and state regarding longevity pertains to their being internal phenomena. This employment should not be confused with that concerning their origin vis-à-vis mental conditions since in these usages trait refers to that which is internally (endogenously) caused and state to that which is externally (exogenously) brought about.

Millon and Seth Grossman propose that the pathological personalities are most correctly considered variations "of personality prototypes." This description, they annex, "communicates their relatively unique clinical 'complexion,' without conveying the erroneous connotation" of these personality styles or disorders as being totally "distinct diseases" (2004, p. 31).

My treatment of personality disorders, including their taxonomy, is based on their being pure types, or archetypes, such that the narcissist, for example, is analyzed in terms of the person's possessing all nine *DSM* diagnostic features. Had I attempted to treat these disorders as prototypes and subtypes this book would have been substantially longer than it already is.

At least some 7 billion people live on the planet, and we have seen that it is estimated that anywhere from 10 to 20 percent, if not more, of them have one or more personality disorders (these figures are not inclusive of the PDNOS). Consequently, there are some 700 million to 1.4 billion people who have at minimum one such abnormality—a worrisome number given that aberrated persons are so troublesome to others and, as in the case of Group III, to themselves. Also, given the individual variations that exist among such mammoth multitudes, organizing them into ten specific categories would entail massive streamlining to say the least (The *Manual's* first edition in 1952 distinguished no less than twenty-seven personality deviancies).

Thus, fitting personalities and personality disorders into a classification of prototypes and, a fortiori, ideal types (archetypes), involves a process of cognitive extrapolations, constructs, and compartimentalizations. They contour and codify what in extramentality pertains to quasi endlessly varying individuals from a psycho-ethical perspective. Thus, however similar identical twins might be, they are not exactly the same regardless if they remained in the same environment.

Lord Chesterfield states, "few [people] are of one plain, decided color." Those rarest of individuals who are may be said to represent the categorical and more absolute models of personality. But "most men," Chesterfield claims, "are mixed, shaded, and blended" (1970, p. 466n680). This hybrid view of personality would be commensurate with the dimensional and more relative paradigms.

Personality traits, as conceived by the *Manual*, are to be diagnosed as signaling a personality disorder only when they contain the properties of inflexibility, maladaptiveness, and pervasiveness, and cause major impairment or personal distress. Both adjustment and maladjustment can, in my view and in concert with Kazimierz Dabrowski (1972, p. 299), be reckoned to be positive or negative with respect to both normal and abnormal personalities and societies. For instance, to be well-adjusted to a negative, or inhumane, society is itself negative; to be maladjusted to a negative society is itself positive. Correspondingly, to be well-adjusted to a positive, or humane, society is positive; to be maladjusted to a positive society is negative.

Thus, some deviants, such as antisocials, are, as their name suggests, negatively maladjusted to a positive society and to normal and above all supranormal persons. On the other hand, full-blown sociopaths or at least highly dyssocial types, such as many of the Nazis, were well-adjusted to their own negative, or inhumane, society but were in effect negatively maladjusted to any kind of positive, or humane, sort and to normals as a whole.

Additionally, personalities, for Dabrowski, Andrew Kawczak, and Michael Piechowski, can be positively or negatively adjusted or maladjusted to their own ideal selves (1970, pp. 162–163). These selves can themselves be positive or negative, depending in part on their conformity or nonconformity to the model selves of others and to constructive cultural and social environments as a whole. All the disturbed personalities are, in one way or another, negatively maladjusted or negatively adjusted to others but only Group III—plus and to a lesser extent the obsessional of Group II—are negatively adjusted to themselves and their ideal self-images. Group I schizoids do not have an ideal self; schizotypals may at times have one but it is completely fragmented and often illusory and magical. Group II may have a desired self but it is essentially egoistic and inhumane insofar as it becomes actualized.

All these views are in accordance with the position that mental and moral health are not relative only to the culture in which they occur. Extreme inhumaneness, such as sadistic sociopathy, is indicative of a personality disorder in any civilized culture. As well, we see some cross-cultural differences, for instance, schizoids might be deemed less negative in the traditionally more introvertive Japanese culture than in the more extrovertive American culture. Conversely, the extremely extrovertive histrionics would likely be deemed less disturbed in the American than in the Japanese culture.

On the other hand, in most, if not all cultures, even uncivilized ones, the sociopath is negatively adjusted to others. Regrettably, sociopathic types, if not full-blown antisocial personalities, tend to wield power—including economic, political, police, military, and even clerical or ecclesiastic—in societies, including civilized ones. As a result, these non plus ultra pathologicals strive to make everyone else adjust to their intrinsically maladjusted personalities.

5. Two Taxonomies of Personality Disorders

At this point, it behooves us to briefly compare and contrast the two taxonomies, the *DSM*'s and mine. Further juxtaposition of the two divisions will be carried out in Chapter Seven.

As stipulated, the *DSM* has divided the ten specific personality disorders into three clusters. Cluster A is comprised of the paranoid, schizoid, and schizotypal personalities, all of whom, "often appear odd or eccentric." Cluster B contains the antisocial, borderline, histrionic, and narcissist, all of whom, "often appear dramatic, emotional, or erratic." Cluster C entails the avoidant, dependent, and obsessional, all of whom "often appear anxious or fearful" (pp. 629–630).

Consequently, the *DSM* has at least three, likely five, and possibly as many as seven foundations for its aggregates—namely odd, eccentric, dramatic, emotional, erratic, anxious, and fearful—depending on how these words are understood. Before continuing, it is instructive that the *DSM* itself concedes that its clustering procedure "has not been consistently validated" and "individuals frequently present" comorbidity, meaning "co-occurring personality disorders from different clusters" (p. 630). A less strict meaning of comorbidity is the co-occurrence of aberrants from any cluster, including even the same, such as the sociopath and paranoid of Group II.

Many personologists, perhaps especially those who support the dimensionalist model of personality, would agree with Timothy Trull and Christine Durrett who state that the *DSM* "cluster organization is designed to make the personality disorders easier to remember by [aggregating] those with similar features." However, they argue, as do most personologists, that the *DSM* clustering procedure "is not based on theory or empirical evidence" (2005, p. 357) .

As indicated earlier, I have likewise relegated the ten specific personality anomalies into three clusters, which I name groups (aggregates, sets, or units). They essentially vary from the clusters of the *DSM* in that mine have but a single basis for their differentiation, namely a lack of interpersonal connectedness. I submit that this sole rationale for the classification of these personality anomalies lends greater clarity and cohesion to it than does that of the *Manual* with its three or possibly sevenfold foundation. In addition to this rationale for my three sets, I will submit, in due course, many other reasons why I depart from the *Manual*'s clustering system.

I propose, therefore, that whatever else the abnormal personality is, it is essentially constituted by a significant deviation from interpersonal normality. In my judgment, this non- or dysfunctioning vis-à-vis interpersonality is not just one of the possible four components of personality aberration, as the *DSM* holds in its general definition of the personality disturbances, but is intrinsic to all ten of them.

Space does not allow for elaboration on how each of the five senses of normality—the utopian, reasonable absence from bothersome symptoms or disease, statistical, environmentally adaptive, and consensual—can be discussed with respect to interpersonal relatedness.

As to the specific abnormalities in terms of my three aggregates, those of Group I are basically unrelated to others, especially in terms of intimacy, due to their incapability, uninterest, and unwillingness regarding it. Whereupon they display a non-attachment and non-disdainful indifference concerning others, especially with respect to any connectedness with them, let alone one which is close, or intimate.

Group II are dis-related and scornfully detached regarding others, owing to their anti-intimacy mentality. Nonetheless, their opposition does not prevent them from engaging in intimate activities. For instance, the sociopath and narcissist may make negative sexuality a way of life.

Group III, though they keenly desire intimacy with others, are inadequately related largely due to their acquisitive and neurotic traits. All FFM Neuroticism is ultimately self-centered, but the reverse is not necessarily the case since, for example, the schizoid of Group I is extremely self-centered, though not egotistically so. However, this aberrant is highly non-neurotic.

The schizotypal is also highly self-focused but is extremely neurotic (Costa and Widiger, 2002, p. 461).

Group I abnormals lack any desire for intimacy such that they are more or less non-hearted due to their impoverished emotionality. Thus, they display, according to the *DSM*, "emotional coldness, detachment, or flattened affectivity" (the schizoid) and "constricted affect" (the schizotypal) (pp. 641, 645).

Group II lack intimacy in that they are cold-hearted in the sense of being hard-hearted. They may be said to be heartless in that they are unkind, antipathetic, unforgiving, and often callous. Their hearts are icy but they possess the burning quality of dry ice. In which case, Group II, especially the sociopath, scorch those in their presence because they are hostile and cruel-hearted.

Group III tend to be warm-hearted, which makes them the best candidates for interpersonality. Still, they are too acquisitively self-centered for genuine connectedness, above all on a sustained basis. The mercurial borderlines of Group III can be also be stony-hearted, like those of Group II. In these respects, as in many others, borderlines are well-named because they *border* Group II and their hard-heartedness and the soft(weak)-heartedness of the other Group III aberrants. In their depths, borderlines are less hard-hearted, and, therefore, are far more interested in intimacy than are Group II.

Consequently, tender-heartedness and strong-heartedness are not to be confused, respectively, with soft-heartedness and hard-heartedness. Tender-heartedness is sometimes understood as signifying a negative kind of sweet-heartedness in the sense of a syrupy, maudlin sort of emotional makeup. But what is sweet-hearted can also mean a charming, amiable, joyous, kindly, and loving heart. All these are traits of genuine sweethearts, in the sense of trueloves, which they attribute to one another and which they envisage as anything but sugary in the sense of schmaltzy, qualities that most typify the dependent personality disorder. Similarly, tough-heartedness can deteriorate into what is hard-bitten and bitter, all of which is most representative of the sociopathic personality disorder.

At this point, it is necessary to consider the three groups of pathological personalities in greater depth in terms of their relatedness, or lack thereof, to others. The groups and the personality pathologicals in each of the three aggregates are considered in the order of their overall psycho-ethical shortcomings and their lack of amenability to therapy.

A. Group I

Perhaps with the exception of extremely autistic individuals and those with Asperger's Disorder, no personalities are more devoid of relatedness than the absolute loners but nonlonely, non-neurotic schizoid and the nonlonely but neurotic schizotypal (p. 640). The *DSM* states that schizoids appear "to lack a desire for intimacy" (p. 638). Yet, it then says only two pages later that these abnormals have, in comparison to avoidants, a "more limited desire for social intimacy" (p. 640). Having a limited desire for intimacy is plainly a very different thing than having none whatsoever. Perhaps, but doubtfully, the *DSM* is distinguishing social intimacy from intimacy in general or, alternatively, is implying that all intimacy is social in nature, two views with which I am in complete accord.

Additionally, the *DSM* maintains that, unlike, for example, obsessionals, schizoids have no "underlying capability for intimacy" (ibid.). It is not clear whether this means that the schizoid has no potentiality for intimacy or the lack of an ability to actualize it. It warrants underlining that the *DSM* does not state that the schizoid has no need for intimacy. Someone can have the need for something but not have the potential let alone the ability to actualize it. Sometimes a capability signifies the aptitude to fulfill a need; less frequently, it refers to the need itself.

As well, if a person has absolutely no need for something, it is not evident how the individual could have a desire for it. Clearly, someone can have a need for something but not desire it in the sense that the person does not act upon the need. But having a desire for something without any need whatsoever for it is quite another matter. In any case, if schizoids do have a need for closeness, then their motivation to fulfill it is so feeble and fleeting that it virtually nullifies the existence of any such exigency on their part.

It might be objected that people can acquire a need for something even though they do not have any innate capability or requirement with respect to it, but the *Manual* engages in no such distinctions apropos of these issues. Finally, individuals could have a desire for something but lack the willingness to get it.

Consequently, it is arguable from the *DSM* description of schizoids that they seem to have little if any need, capability, ability, interest, or willingness concerning intimae. Even if these absolute loners choose to interact with others, they profoundly lack, according to the *Manual*, the communication and other skills to relate to them (p. 639).

The *DSM*, at the very least, implies that, for whatever reasons, schizoids are so constituted that they are unable to take much if any pleasure in intimacy and, in actuality, they find it painful to do so (p. 638). This displeasure is one of the rare cases in which schizoids appear to depart from what the *DSM* references as their "restricted range of emotions in interpersonal settings," their apparent indifference "to the praise or criticism" by others, and their generalized "emotional coldness, detachment, or flattened affectivity" (p. 641).

Given their customary pathological non-dystonicity and non-syntonicity, meaning their lack of either pleasure or pain with respect to their traits, it is most unlikely that schizoids would acquire an interest or willingness concerning intimate attachments of any sort. What is probably the truth in these matters is that schizoid connections, if they exist at all, come under the categories of paradigmatic superficiality and evanescence.

If individuals never desire and, a fortiori, never need intimacy, they manifestly contradict a, if not the most, universal and deepest demand of human beings qua persons. Though they are obviously human beings, schizoids evince a kind of non-sociality that renders them rather eerily non-human and non-persons (and potentially inhumane and depersonalized should they, for instance, be co-morbids of the sociopathic sort). It is as if these consummate loners hail from some hinterland, an iceland, largely due to their affect-iciness and subsequent detachment (more exactly, their unattachment). Schizotypals would also be perceived as aliens but in an even more literally outlandish fashion given, as the *DSM* says, their bizarre behavior, their "odd beliefs and magical thinking," and their "unusual perceptual experiences, including bodily illusions" (p. 645).

What lends strength to the position that schizoids have little or no need, capability, ability, desire, and willingness for intimacy is that, of all the disordered personalities, they along with the schizotypals, score the lowest in the FFM dimension of Extraversion, especially in terms of its traits of warmth and gregariousness. Only the avoidants of Group III rival these Group I abnormals for being the most introverted, but the social withdrawal of the first is not as radical as that of the second two aberrants (Costa and Widiger, 2002, p. 461). Moreover, the social isolation of the avoidants is not due to a lack of warmth or interest in intimacy. On the contrary, the avoidants' crave such togetherness. Their social segregation is an outgrowth of their fear of being found wanting in terms of personal qualities and then being reproved and ultimately rejected for such supposed defects (p. 644).

Thus, unlike schizoids and schizotypals, avoidants very much desire intimacy and, due to their lacking it, experience deep loneliness, as the *DSM* has expressed the matter (p. 662). All three aberrants have deficient communicative aptitudes. These drawbacks are demonstrated in that, for example, avoidants lack relational skills traceable to their social anxiety that subsequently results from their hypersensitivity to criticism. We can also argue, albeit to a lesser extent, that the source of the avoidants' social anxiousness is their lack of communicative abilities (pp. 662–664).

Schizoids, according to the *DSM*, seem "oblivious to the normal subtleties of social interaction and often do not respond appropriately to social cues" so much so that they are "socially inept" (p. 638). With reference to schizotypals, their communicative competence is compromised by, among other things, their cognitive distortions, paranoid ideation, and, more directly, their strange manner of discourse and, at least indirectly, their unconventional appearance (one that is frequently both alien and alienating) (p. 645).

Consequently, Group I lack the means to communicate with others in a fashion, which would satisfy any need or interest they might have in reaching them, especially in terms of intimate contact. If perchance, they actually did have a strong need and desire for intimacy, then, without the necessary skills to convey them, Group I would suffer serious communicative loneliness by definition and other forms as well, at minimum, social.

Throughout it all, the *DSM* remains noticeably cautious about pronouncing with any kind of finality that schizoids are utterly incapable of or lack desire for intimacy. Hence, it frequently prefaces its judgments in these matters by stating that schizoids "seemingly" or "apparently" have no need, capability, desire, interest, or willingness as to personal relationships or by saying that all of them are "limited" or "reduced" in nature. The *DSM* notes that neither schizoids nor schizotypals have any close contact with others—such as friends or confidants—" except possibly a first-degree relative" (pp. 638, 642).

By employing a more guarded and less absolute wording, the *DSM*, in effect, leaves the door open for schizoids to have both a capability and perhaps even a desire for intimacy, although they are both, in its reckoning, at best clearly weak in urgency and intensity. The *DSM*'s hesitation to declare outright that schizoids have absolutely no need, potentiality, or wish for intimacy is understandable. Without them, especially the need, schizoids would be so utterly non-human that they would be tantamount to being androids or robots, conditions that the *DSM* does not ascribe to these aberrants. In any case, the schizoid, in being completely unattached to others, especially in terms of intimacy, acts like a kind of non-person akin to an automaton.

What lends credence to the limited capability and desire interpretations of individuals with the schizoid personality divergence in the *DSM* account is that it says that these abnormals have "few friendships" instead of none—which it just previously stated was the case—and "date infrequently and often do not marry" (p. 639) instead of never.

Schizoids could have friends, date, and marry for reasons other than intimacy but the *Manual* does not raise these possibilities. At any rate, all normals or even abnormals who desire but a most superficial relationship with a schizoid are destined for disappointment because, should such a wish be realized, it would likely prove disastrous for all parties.

The *DSM* states that schizotypals display an "acute discomfort with and reduced capability for close relationships." Yet, according to the *Manual*, schizotypals exhibit not only a reduced capability but "a decreased desire" for intimacy (p. 642). As just cited, it maintains that schizoids have no capability for closeness and either no desire or but a limited desire or somehow simultaneously both.

It could be proposed that the schizoid and, above all, the schizotypal eschew close attachments or even casual interactions, not because they lack the need, capability, ability, desire, or willingness for intimacy, but because they are afraid of any affiliation whatsoever. Thus, these two Group I aberrants may fear any close encounters, as it were, with their own kind but, nonetheless, want them—an apprehensiveness that would render them akin to avoidants, who, according to the *DSM*, refrain from connections with others simply because they are afraid of "being exposed, ridiculed, or shamed" (p. 662).

The *Manual* states that schizotypals are highly uneasy in the presence of others, both familiars and perhaps even more so non-familiars, because they mistrust their motives. We are not precisely informed why these individuals are suspicious of others' motivations (ibid.). Perhaps schizotypals are apprehensive because, as the *DSM* stipulates, they do not feel that they fit in because of their eccentricities (and, in fact, they do not fit in at all). This lack of belonging would make schizotypals subject to the unhappiness of cultural loneliness and cultural alienation if, indeed, they actually sought inclusion instead of social and often physical isolation.

The *Manual* further states that, though schizotypals "may express unhappiness about their lack of relationships, their behavior suggests a decreased desire for intimate contacts" (ibid.) Consequently, we are back at square one: what is the exact meaning of a "reduced" wish for intimacy on the part of schizotypals in terms of the *DSM* account of them?

For their part, schizoids seem unconcerned about others' views of them, be they approving or disapproving, so much so that they appear invariably indifferent to the praise or criticism of others. The *DSM* states that schizoids seem to have little if any interiority, especially affective (re)activity and diversity (all of which distinguishes them from avoidants). Nevertheless, it concedes that in those exceedingly rare occasions when the schizoids do reveal themselves, they "may acknowledge having painful feelings, [especially relevant] to social interactions" (p. 638).

Given that schizoids have no or at most a limited desire for intimacy, it is presumed that these feelings are painful not because these pathologicals "want in" regarding social interactions but are "kept in." Presumably, the pain is owing to the fact that schizoids "want out" of social interactions but are kept in them due to some obligation, such as a job that requires their association with others. In passing, this is the rare if not the only occasion on which the *DSM* views the schizoid as having dystonic traits. Otherwise, they are portrayed as displaying a lack of not only painful but pleasurable qualities.

Schizoids and schizotypals are, then, eccentric in the etymological sense of the word, in that both stand outside the center of human beings' sociality and its actualization via socialness and sociability and the interpersonal sort of relatedness that primarily comprise them. Still, these two deviants do not exist outside the circle of human beings in an absolute sense. Irrespective of their pathological withdrawal and oddness, they remain social beings. However, the schizoid is incredibly passively and quietly eccentric, whereas the schizotypal is actively and often agitatedly so.

Therefore, while Group I are extreme introverts, they hardly live beyond society as if they were beasts or gods, as Aristotle famously declares of social isolates (1941c, 1253a25). Despite their radical withdrawal and unattachment concerning others, Group I are extraverts in that their being is, in the most fundamental sense of the term, directed toward other human beings. All human beings, even the most socially remote, like Group I abnormals, are extrovertive precisely in that their consciousness is necessarily ordered to the world of their conspecifics.

As Robert R. McCrae and Paul T. Costa remark, "relatively speaking, we all *are* extraverts—we all live in social groups" (1990, p. 148). Even hermits are extraverts for, though they may dwell alone, they do not *ex-ist* alone. They depend on others for both basic needs and metaneeds. As well, it is highly doubtful that any human being has ever lived years on end—not to mention a lifetime—absolutely all alone, as argued in the first volume (pp. 31–32).

Schizoids have the least personological consciousness, assuredly among the disturbed personalities and arguably among all human beings. Yet, they remain irreversibly directed in their consciousness to their fellow human beings. To re-invoke Aristotle, those who would live outside human society are inferior or superior to human beings but the plain truth of the matter, according to the philosopher, is that no person is sheer animality let alone divinity.

Schizoids and schizotypals may live on the outskirts of society in terms of interactions and attachments, but these environs, by definition, remain within society. As well, Group I are not necessarily alonists, or those who physically reside alone, much less need they be recluses who seek physical isolation in every sense of the word.

It is sometimes held that the propensity for unattachment to or detachment from relationships begins for the schizoid and schizotypal possibly as late as adolescence. Hence, there may have been a time when these personality anomalies had both some need and a desire for intimate attachments but the willingness to pursue them may have later vanished due to various internal or external factors.

This disappearance could also have resulted from their need for intimacy becoming non-functional or dormant. In the right circumstances, it might have been re-activated and begun to operate once again. The more usual view is that of the *DSM*, namely that the schizotypal and especially the schizoid seem to have been born without much if any need, potentiality, ability to fulfill the potential, desire, or willingness for intimacy perhaps beyond parental nurturance and an occasional or superficial contact with but one blood relative.

If Group I abnormals have an unsatisfied need for intimacy, they would represent the social needs model of loneliness. If, contrarily, they have an unmet desire for it, they would represent the cognitive discrepancy model of affective isolation. If schizoids have a limited desire, then we would have to conclude that what the *DSM* implies by its description of them is that they might possibly experience mild and periodic loneliness at most. The very possibility of chronic loneliness would be ruled out, if we adhere to the definition and diagnostic features of the schizoids as laid out by the *DSM*.

Schizoids and schizotypals are, therefore, among the least lonely and alonely of individuals, if they are so at all. Indeed, the schizotypal and especially the schizoid do not experience loneliness except perhaps existential insofar as this species of emotional isolation is predicated of all human beings, normal and anormal alike. However, schizotypals have neurotic traits like FFM depression and self-consciousness that make them possible candidates for other sorts of loneliness, chiefly cosmic, cultural, epistemic, communicative, and intraself.

Group I are loners par excellence but they, especially the schizoids, are not the kind of introvertive individuals who are much given to introspection about themselves and their inward states. This kind of self-consciousness, above all when it is brooding and anxious, is typical of the lonely Group III, perhaps principally the avoidant. Even less are the schizotypal and especially the schizoid likely to engage in the kind of introspection characteristic of the solitary.

According to Millon and colleagues, while the basic schizoid is best portrayed as being "cognitively vacant," the depersonalized" subtype is "cognitively absent" (2000, p. 317). Consequently, they maintain that of all the deficiencies the schizoid has, "perhaps the most tragic is a failure to develop an intimate relationship with the self" (ibid., p. 327). They further contend, "the more isolated schizoids become, the more they become devoid of any genuine self." It is a self, therefore, incapable of any "deep feelings of attachment, intimacy, or community" (ibid., p. 328), if they have any such feelings whatsoever. It is perhaps even more the case that the less they have any contact with others, the less capable are the schizoids of developing any sense of self—not to mention a person—especially an authentic one. Hence, the schizoid's self is not so much vacant or absent as it is simply non-existent or, at most, paradigmatically minimalist.

Not only are the schizoid and schizotypal unattached to others, but they seem unattached, or unrelated, to their actual selves and, a fortiori, to any ideal sort of self. They do not have any profound interest in their own persons, in part because they seem to have little if any interiority, surely not the sort that seeks union with another inwardness. Admittedly, the schizotypal generally has a fertile cognitive life but one that is pathologically febrile and distorted (typical of the lower Dionysian, which this pathological paradigmatically is) (p. 645). Hence, these disordered personalities, above all the schizoid, come across as having but a small or slight instead of a substantive self, or what Henri-Louis Bergson designates the superficial instead of the profound self.

In sum, the schizoids of Group I are socially but not emotionally isolated in the sense of feeling lonely. The schizotypals are also socially isolated but occasionally may suffer some degree of feeling emotionally isolated as well. The avoidants of Group III are socially isolated, like Group I, but they are also highly emotionally isolated in the sense of feeling lonely due to their unfulfilled strong capability and desire for emotional contact.

In reference to the schizoid and schizotypal, Jonathan Dowson and Adrian Grounds posit that persons with "reduced capability and desire for close relationships may," nonetheless, "feel the 'need' for positive feelings and concern for others in the context of a rather immature dependency" (1995, p. 53). I might agree with this assessment provided the schizoid and schizotypal have, in fact, some need for closeness but—and especially in the case of the schizoid—it is not at all manifest that they do in terms of their *DSM* characterizations.

B. Group II

Group II are dis-related to others in that they are derisively indifferent or antipathetic toward people in general, especially to any close relatedness with them, at least the kind that does not serve their selfish interests. Their malevolently contemptuous uninterest or intense animus vis-à-vis others as a whole make Group II the sort of partial relative loners that I have titled lonerists.

In their dis-relatedness to others, Group II aberrants manifest a multitude of undesirable traits. As the *DSM* portrays them, these pathologicals display such psycho-ethical drawbacks as mendacity, gross insensitivity and injustice, aggressiveness, aggression, and, in some cases, violence, in addition to irresponsibility, shamelessness, and remorselessness (the sociopath); inveterate suspiciousness, jealousy, possessiveness, and unforgivingness (the paranoid); grandiosity, exploitativeness, compassionlessness, and imperiousness (the narcissist); and pharisaical perfectionism, pettiness, parsimony, intolerance, and rigid control of others (the obsessional) (pp. 636–637, 649–650, 660, 672).

i. Sociopaths (Antisocials)

The sociopath, in being antagonistically dis-related to others, above all in terms of intimacy, acts like a kind of anti-person akin to a subhuman being in contrast to the non-human-like schizoid. Thus, the appropriateness of the sociopath's being referenced as an antisocial, or dyssocial.

Sociopathy, at least according to the *DSM* version, emphasizes highly socially deviant if not criminal behavior and its external wellsprings. To be diagnosed as a sociopath, the *Manual* requires:

> the individual must be at least 18 years and have had a history of some symptoms of a Conduct Disorder before age 15. [It] involves a repetitive and persistent pattern of behavior in which the basic rights of others or major age-appropriateness societal norms of rules are violated. The specific behaviors characteristic of Conduct Disorder fall into one of four categories: aggression to people and animals; destruction of property; deceitfulness or theft; or serious violation of rules. (p. 646)

It is evident that the first three categories explicitly involve not only psychological traits but ethical ones. More specifically, they all contain infringements of justice in that they concern trespasses of the rights of others. Failures in justice preclude any positive relationships to others, both intimate and non-intimate, such as those of business or commercial nature.

A fortiori, these shortcomings bar any true bonding since benevolence, a necessary condition for intimate attachments, itself demands the wish to be just. Hence, for most ethicists, people cannot be good-willed let alone loving toward others unless they first give them what is owed, including the justice inherent in human respect.

Most ethicians would also add to the list of requirements for true ties to others, the trait of empathy, a quality gravely missing in all Group II aberrants, especially antisocials. On the other hand, some would claim we owe our fellow human beings goodwill and, in some cases, even love, as, for example, spouses are obliged to give one another and their children.

The sociopath, the aberrant who epitomizes FFM inhumaneness, is, to repeat, sometimes known as a psychopath, a term that does not necessarily imply, unlike the *DSM* sociopath, being guilty of "Conduct Disorder" with its serious violation of rules. Psychopaths are ordinarily viewed as contravening rudimentary prescriptions of morality but not necessarily those of legality. In any case, all antisocials, be they sociopaths or psychopaths, act contrary to or simply ignore the feelings and wishes of others and are "callous, cynical, and contemptuous" regarding them (pp. 646–647).

Psychopathy stresses internal factors as being the genesis of this personality sickness, whereas sociopathy underlines the external, especially the social, including the familial, sources. (Of course, etymologically considered, like sociopathy, antisociality also stresses the social nature and origins of this personality disorder). There is good reason to believe that there are genetically based bio-psychic causes, which the notion and the name of psychopathy imply, that may be equally or even more important to the onset and prolongation of antisociality than social factors themselves (ibid., pp. 649–650).

Psychopaths often have one, usually a father, or both parents who also are antisocials. Still, this parental linkage to psychopathy could itself be argued as environmentally instead of genetically induced, if not perhaps necessitated. Largely, however, the notion of psychopathy stresses the internal origins of negative conduct.

Be they sociopaths or psychopaths, antisocials fail to observe the most elementary demands of ethics by being, to reiterate, immoral, amoral, and antimoral individuals. They are at minimum maleficent, often maliciously and even sadistically so such that they deserve, if any individuals do, the designation "moral monsters."

Given their over-abundance of repugnant characterological features, antisocials are the most negatively detached of all pathological personalities. But for all that, they are subject to little if any conscious loneliness. Like other Group II alonelies, antisocials use intimacy not to relate or be related to others in terms of shared inwardness but predominantly to ward off or escape from the anxiety of being and feeling alone. Moreover, they use their associates to protect themselves against their countless real or imagined enemies, as befits their ingrained "me-versus-the-world" mentality.

Therefore, antisocials might use the company of others to assuage their fright of aloneness. It may be felt as prefiguring, for instance, dying and death, the fear or dread of which is regarded herein as a species of existential aloneliness (McGraw, 1992, pp. 334–335).

In this regard, antisocials' anxiety arises not because they are primarily afraid of losing the company or companionship of others. Instead, they seek others' presence only or mostly to allay their apprehensiveness at the prospect of their life ending and the variegated negative types of aloneness they imagine that might come their way during their dying or after their demise. Yet, antisocials are exceedingly reckless and often die at a relatively young age, and occasionally by their own hand, if, for instance, they think that they will be caught and incarcerated for their illegal behavior (ibid., p. 646). Perhaps the real punishment for such conduct is that the antisocial must live alone with the hatred and malice that are lodged within this people-predator's diseased heart. The antisocial is the most perverse of not only of all pathologicals but of all human beings.

ii. Paranoids

We recall that paranoids are the personality pathologicals who, according to the *DSM,* manifest habitual "distrust and suspiciousness such that others' motives are interpreted as malevolent" (p. 629). This mentality makes paranoids along with sociopaths the foremost instantiations of cynicism that, in turn, greatly accounts for their antagonistic attitude and domineering behavior toward others. This obnoxious mentality and conduct, in their wake, tend to elicit hostile reactions to the paranoids who then retaliate with mistrust, animosity, and aggressiveness that is even more pronounced. Thus, in terms of interpersonality, a vicious circle is perpetuated and exacerbated by the paranoid's array of psycho-ethical shortcomings.

The cynically structured paranoid suspects that all intimacy is but an effect of hostility in the way that love is sometimes envisioned as being formed by a reaction to hatred à la Sigmund Freud. (It is more commonly and accurately claimed that hatred arises toward someone who is perceived as endangering what a person, in some sense, likes or loves.)

Like all Group II individuals, paranoids fear intimacy if only because it requires a positive acceptance and togetherness (homonomy) that intrude upon these aberrants' aspirations for complete autonomy. In these respects, the *DSM* states that paranoids want to keep total "control of intimate relationships," and they do so "to avoid being betrayed." Accordingly, the *Manual* maintains that paranoids "may constantly question and challenge the whereabouts, actions, intentions, and fidelity of their spouse or partner" (p. 635).

If paranoids do have intimates, the second are likely to bear the brunt of the distrust, jealousy, and conceitedness of the first who often fancy themselves as members of an ethical elite. Like other Group II abnormals, paranoids may display loyalty to a coterie of those they count among their confidants. But once these pathologicals suspect their being perfidious, others become members of the ever expanding throng of supposed treacherous conspirators who are then the paranoids' sworn enemies.

Clinton McLemore and David Brokaw locate the origins of the paranoid personality in having being subjected to "early, repeated experiences of rejection, coldness, and humiliation from significant others." These experiences furnished the foundation for the paranoid's view, according to McLemore and Brokaw, that "all relationships are hostile or threatening." As a result, the paranoid underwent extreme social, if not emotional, isolation. McLemore and Brokaw conclude that this ever-wary personality then developed mistrust and enmity toward others as a defense mechanism to protect itself against further rejection (1987, p. 278).

As they age, paranoids increasingly resort to suppressing or repressing their need for intimacy and the isolation that stems from its absence, namely loneliness. These denials are consonant with the other Group II abnormals, though not with Group I, especially the schizoids.

Paranoid personalities, then, typically arise from a climate of non- and anti-intimacy, including forms of lonelifying maximal exclusion. As a result, they became accustomed to expect ill-will from specific others and eventually others in general. Thereupon, paranoids became habituated to interpreting the actions of their fellow human beings, including any overture or inkling of intimacy on their part, as masking malevolence and animosity, two attitudes which are the bases of the paranoids' own mentality. All this would account for the paranoids being, along with sociopaths, the paramount misanthropes.

How the absence of intimacy and the presence of its antithesis in loneliness affect given individuals varies. It does so in great degree relative to the biological rigidity or elasticity of their personality traits. Patently, the more the traits are genetic givens and drivens, or at least powerful inclinations, the less a person can alter them through choice and the less social and other environmental factors can modify them.

I view paranoids as being more "made" than "born," all of which is the reverse of schizoids and schizotypals. This difference is a major factor for my not aggregating, as the *DSM* does in its Cluster A, these Group II conniving lonerists with the rather naive loners of Group I.

Hence, I have submitted that the nonhumanness and other attributes of the schizoid and schizotypal are more a matter of biological determinants or at least potent influences than are the inhumaneness and other detestable qualities of the paranoid. These traits include the paranoid's extreme contentiousness, smugness, and a generalized offensive negativism as witnessed in this lower-level Apollonian personality's hyper-critical and contemptuous attitudes toward others in general. Despite their pretensions to moral superiority and in part because of it, paranoids are moral reprobates.

After antisocials, paranoids are easily the most inhumane of the personality disorders. They are essentially bad and sometimes evil individuals, especially if they are blended with sociopathic types, a famous case of this comorbidity being Joseph Stalin. It may be, as Michael Stone suggests, that psychotherapy, in the state in which it presently exists, "can make the good better," which may be said of "normals." However, he adds that it cannot make "the bad, good," a judgment which may be said of pure types of abnormals, especially the sociopath and, in my view, the paranoid (2002, p. 415).

Because paranoids are immersed not only in jealousy but envy and enmity, they are leading examples of those vices that inhabit the venomously sickened soul of the person in which *ressentiment* reigns. We have seen that this moral malady is an exceedingly intense and inveterate combination of not only enviousness and hatred, but also spite, revenge, vindictiveness, and all-around malice further marked by feelings of spiritual powerlessness and inferiority that, in turn, so often underlie the paranoid's pretensions of superiority. I have proposed that paranoids psycho-ethically, especially ethically, little resemble the *DSM* cluster A aberrants. I have in mind pure types or at least prototypes instead of comorbids, such as the withdrawn, antipathetic, schizoid-like sociopaths some of whom have been serial killers (see Stone, 1993, p. 172).

iii. Narcissists

Narcissists are disrelated to others largely because their extreme arrogance, owing to their grossly inflated sense of self-importance, severs them from their fellow human beings save for the few they deem worthy of their self-imputed superiority. Their grandiosity is coupled with their downplaying or ignoring the abilities and accomplishments of others whom they often envy and, like paranoids, erroneously believe are envious of them (p. 661).

Possibly even more than paranoids, narcissists epitomize the moral disease of *ressentiment*, the previously mentioned mixture of poisonous and loathsome attributes ruinous to genuine relatedness. SCRAM is especially adept at bringing forth and cultivating this moral malady above all via its Rivalitis and Successitis, all of which have so immensely contributed to the United States being characterized as a culture wherein narcissism reigns.

All individuals with personality disturbances are, to repeat, self-centered, an affliction that undercuts and attacks intimacy with others at its heart. However, narcissists are the most self-absorbed of the ten aberrant personalities. No one so preoccupied with self, so full of self, has much interest in anyone except those who cater to these lower-level Dionysians' craving for veneration and entitlement.

Thus, no one who has so fallen in love with his or her self has any room for being and remaining in love with others except those who unfortunately have fallen for this sometimes charming but paradigmatically pompous and often duplicitous individual (ibid). If narcissists dream of what the *DSM* labels "ideal love" it is only the kind that is that they deem is directed exclusively to them (ibid.).

Of course, no one so obsessed with being loved cannot boast, as these pathologicals are habitually prone to do, of having the kind of love of self that stems from self-worth. Indeed, the *DSM* characterizes narcissists as having an "almost invariably fragile self-esteem" (p. 658). As a result, these abnormals frequently fall in love not with their actual selves which they little respect or esteem so much as with their idolized selves, which, objectively speaking, are nothing more than worshipped fabrications.

Those who have the misfortune of being intimate with these empathyless individuals will find them, according to the *Manual*, to typically display "emotional coldness" and a contemptuous non-interest in others' interests and needs (p. 659). It is no wonder that non-intimates readily and eventually intimates immensely dislike and distrust these extremely mean individuals—mean both in the sense of unkind and stingy.

Contrastingly, narcissists are so generous toward themselves that they go to any expense to satisfy their desires and in doing so routinely squander their talents, which sometimes are considerable. Since narcissists tend to be extremely self-indulgent and undisciplined, they are not likely to want the gratification of their urges concerning any form of intimacy to be postponed and, as a result, they habitually misuse others and their goodwill.

iv. Obsessionals

While the *DSM* states that schizoids have no "underlying capability for intimacy," it holds that obsessionals do. It stipulates that the "social detachment" of these Group II abnormals is owing to their "devotion to work and discomfort with emotions" (p. 640). These two statements when conjoined make it appear that the *DSM* has confused simple social disengagement, or detachment, with the unwanted emotional disengagement and non-engagement that pertain to a lack of intimacy.

I would also comment that, first, this basic potentiality, albeit relatively minimal, of obsessionals for intimacy is a main reason why I place them as the least aberrant of Group II, since sociopaths, paranoids, and narcissists have even less capability for genuine closeness than compulsives.

Second, whatever capability obsessionals do have for close connections, they do not display much desire for or interest in expressing them in part due to their discomfort with emotions. Nonetheless, the obsessionals' shortcomings in these areas go much deeper, in my judgment, than their being merely ill at ease, affectively considered. Like their fellow Group II pathologicals, obsessionals do not like or love others so much so that they are disdainful and dismissive of them and, accordingly, seek social and emotional detachment.

Obsessionals are also pusillanimous individuals and, therefore, lack both the generosity—as do the other Group II pathologicals, especially narcissists—and courage that genuine attachment requires (ibid., p. 670).

Third, whatever the potentiality and the desire for relatedness to people obsessionals possess, they view them as being objects to be perfected. They do so to mirror their etherealized model for actual human beings whom they typically dislike even despise. Any seeming concern with reference to actual others obsessionals might have is fashioned out of their tendency toward funereal, cadaverous, moralistic, pharisaical, cynical dutism. Hence, their attention to others does not stem from the kind of solicitude that comes from benevolence not to mention the warmth of love and its caring for imperfect but real human beings.

This said, the obessionals' fixation on the perfect is not so much for itself. Instead, their scorn for the imperfect motivates them. They loathe whatever is messy, untidy, unfinished, un- or disorganized. Obsessionals are, as it were, messed up, that is disordered, personalities, in part because they cannot, as the saying goes, mess around. They are unable to enjoy themselves or others and, accordingly, dislike and mistrust intimacy and the variegated leisure it requires (ibid., p. 669).

C. Group III

Group III have considerable capability and an even greater desire for relatedness. Sadly, their extreme inability to realize their potentiality for connectedness, owing predominantly to their neurotic emotional fragility, insecurity, instability, and to their acquisitiveness, hugely contributes to their pathological emotional isolation.

The histrionic and especially the borderline tend to be habitually motivated by the kind of acquisitiveness that entails deliberately ignoring others' welfare unless their own needs are fulfilled first.

The avoidant and above all the dependent exhibit an intentionality pattern mainly marked by ignorance of others' needs. Avoidants are unaware of them because they isolate themselves from others socially and often physically as well. Dependents may give immediate heed to others' requirements but in fact, the first will eventually overlook or be oblivious to the needs of the second out of their morbid preoccupation with the satisfaction of their own neurotic "neediness."

Group III's disparity between their extreme desire and willingness for intimacy versus their extreme inability to gain it on a consistent basis leads them to experience incredibly intense and extended loneliness on a highly conscious level. In my view, these abnormals, above all the borderline and dependent, become psycho-ethically ill, in no small part, precisely because they suffer from such catastrophic loneliness and aloneliness.

i. Borderlines

The *Manual* portrays borderlines as having a pattern of unstable and intense relationships, as evidenced by their instantaneously divinizing others and then just as quickly demonizing them. This transition, in significant part, is due to the borderlines' fear, like that of the dependent, of being maximally excluded via abandonment (p. 650).

Thus, the *DSM* states that borderlines "may idealize potential caregivers and lovers at the first or second meeting, demand to spend a lot of time together, and share the most intimate details early in a relationship," and then shift from deification to denunciation (pp. 650–651). This behavior attests to the borderlines desperate yearning for connectedness but even more their horror at being forsaken and forlorn. However, they then may—often in a fit of fury—discard these same intimates, typically doing so out fear of or actual retaliation for being ditched themselves.

The *DSM* relates that borderlines have a capability for empathizing with and nurturing others but actualize it only on condition that the second are available to satisfy the firsts' "needs on demand." This proclivity is patently indicative of the borderlines' acquisitive motivational pattern. If their needs are not immediately met, they routinely resort to "extreme sarcasm, enduring bitterness, or verbal outbursts." This borderline behavior, according to the *DSM,* is often accompanied by rage, especially if the "caregiver or lover is seen as neglectful, withholding, uncaring, or abandoning," in short as displaying actions involving maximal noninclusion or exclusion (p. 651).

Rollo May writes that people basically "feel empty or anxious" when lonely—or what I term "alonely"—because he claims:

> [a] human being gets his original experience of being a self out of his relatedness to other persons, and when he is alone . . . he is afraid he will lose this experience of being a self. (1953, p. 28)

Correlatively, the more human beings feel intimately related to other human beings, the more they feel like a self and above all a person. Consequently, even the unrelated (Group I) and dis-related (Group II) pathological personalities would be horrified at the prospect of losing their sense of being a self, and more exactly, a person, if they always felt, respectively, unassociated or dissociated, regarding all other persons. The unrelating and unrelatable schizoid and especially the schizotypal are, of all the personality deviants, the two closest to being psychotic and to lacking the experience of being a self and person.

The felt absence of being a person is also the case of borderlines insofar as they are subject, according to the *DSM,* to "severe dissociative symptoms" such as depersonalization itself (p. 650). This malaise makes its sufferers feel severed from or uncertain of their personal identity.

Consequently, a persuasive case could be made for placing borderlines alongside the schizotypal since the *DSM* maintains that the first shares with the second "psychotic-like symptoms," including "Paranoid ideas or illusions" (pp. 652–653). (Indeed, it is often said that borderlines were so named because they were considered midway between psychosis and neurosis in terms of mental illness.)

However, unlike Group I schizotypals, borderlines are keenly interested in intimacy but are largely failures in getting and keeping it. Thus, borderlines "exhibit a pattern of instability in interpersonal relationships," whereas schizotypals "display a pattern of acute discomfort in close relationships" (p. 639).

As well, the Group III borderlines could be assigned to Group II since both aggregates manifest extreme hostility toward others. Still, unlike, for example, sociopaths, borderlines' antipathy is directed mainly to themselves instead of others. Borderlines are aggregated with the Group III abnormals predominantly because all four of these pathologically lonely disordered personalities have an enduring need, desire, and willingness for close connections, all of which is relatively uncharacteristic of Group II and absolutely untypical of Group I.

The *DSM* states that borderlines' "chronic feelings of emptiness" may be so powerful that they may believe their existence is not real (p. 651). These feelings of non-realness, of literal nonbeing, are once more indicative of this pathological personality sometimes teetering on the border of psychosis at least one that is episodic and transient in nature. Grave loneliness can drive people to feel they are losing their self-being and, thereby, on the edge of extinction, a conviction highly predicable of the pathologically lonely borderline.

Like other emotional isolates, including the other Group III abnormals, borderlines have a self-image mired in self-worthlessness. However, their self-abasement is carried to the most extreme point wherein they deem themselves, according to the *DSM*, to be "bad or evil" (ibid.). This conviction clearly further adds to their propensity to constantly agonize about the threat of being forsaken.

The *Manual* appends that borderlines' "abandonment fears" are associated with their "intolerance of being alone and a need to have other people with [them]" (ibid.). So understood, their pathological loneliness is rooted in an equally aberrated aloneliness. It is instructive that American children were and, in many instances, still are punished for being "bad" by being sent to their rooms or other places where they are sentenced to being all by themselves until they are ready to be "good" again. Consequently, they may grow up having a distaste for solitude, both primary and secondary, and, as a result, find it difficult to meditate, study, research, and engage in other creative ventures.

ii. Histrionics

The *Manual* states that histrionics, like borderlines and especially dependents, seek the kind of intimacy entailed in various sorts of nurturance (p. 657). This affinity is another basic reason for my placing these deviants into one and the same unit. The *DSM* holds that the histrionics' lack of realizing such care and other sorts of closeness incite them to frequently engage in "flights into romantic fancy," all of which, in my view, reveals their characteristic erotic loneliness. This deficiency also inclines histrionics to pronounce their relationships to be "more intimate than they actually are" (p. 655). This conduct is highly typical of the lonely individual, especially but not only the erotically isolated type.

The *DSM* records that histrionics have "difficulty in achieving emotional intimacy in romantic and sexual relationships." It posits that this problem is a factor in their "flirtatiousness" and their adopting "inappropriately sexually provocative or seductive" behavior (ibid.). This conduct is once again suggestive of serious eros loneliness and other forms of unwanted detachment. I look upon histrionics as flitting from one interaction or relationship to another such that they vacillate between feeling lonely (and alonely) both inside but especially outside such connections.

The *DSM* underscores histrionics' neglecting "longer-term relationships" to "make way for the excitement of new" bonds (p. 656). This comportment, it says, is a customary consequence of histrionics' tendency to engage in "rapidly shifting and shallow expressions of emotion" (p. 658). This fluctuating and superficial affectivity may, in my judgment, be indicative of a person suffering from profoundly lonely sentiments instead of an individual who is devoid of deep and abiding affect and incapable of permanent ties to others.

Hence, histrionics' continuous need for affection and attention may largely be deemed as being compensatory for a lack of a constant connection(s). Their frenzied search for the spotlight may be interpreted as a sign of the histrionics' craving for a more substantive and sustained relatedness that would generate a deeper affectivity and linkage to one or more select others.

Thus, histrionic behavior may reflect individuals who are extremely sad and anxious regarding their relationships instead of those who are bereft of profound and prolonged emotions and incapable of or at least uninterested in penetrating and lasting ties to others. Astonishingly, the *DSM* never mentions that the histrionic (or the dependent) may be lonely or may be an individual driven by the desire to elude or escape emotional isolation.

The histrionic in the clinical population has a greater prevalence among women than men, a comparable male type is referenced as the "macho" man (p. 656). Women tend to prevail in Group III, whereas men do in Groups I and II, another reason for my aggregating these disorders of (inter)personality in the manner I do.

iii. Dependents

The *DSM* states that dependents' fondest desire is for intimacy that consists in being taken care of. These abnormals subserviently fasten themselves to others out of fear of being separated from their nurturance and protection. So terrified are dependents of functioning all by themselves, that, according to the *DSM*, they will go along with others despite their not being interested in and even opposed to what these other may do (p. 665). Of course, fear of separation on the part of dependents, the ultimate conformists, signifies aloneliness.

The *Manual* stipulates that dependents will make "extraordinary self-sacrifices" to keep a relationship from ending. In the process, they may undergo "verbal, physical, or sexual abuse." Hence, they may engage in masochistic conduct to evade being isolated. Moreover, once a tie has been terminated, such as in the case of an erotic breakup or the death of their guardians, dependents will "quickly and indiscriminately" attach themselves to someone else. They do so lest they are "left alone to care for" themselves, all of which again testifies to dependents' extreme (a)loneliness (p. 666).

The *DSM* proposes that dependents' all-consuming need for being supported and safeguarded and their concomitant horror at the prospect of being abandoned leads them to remain in "imbalanced and distorted relationships" (ibid.). In such instances, dependents experience (a)loneliness inside their attachments, which, nonetheless, they will tolerate far more than when they are subject to these feelings of isolation outside them. All this is especially so if the severance involves a state of maximal exclusion and in particular abandonment. This greater tolerance of negative aloneness within instead of without a relationship renders dependents like histrionics but unlike avoidants who are lonely more within a relationship than outside one.

Similar to all seriously lonely people who are conscious of their loneliness, especially their fellow Group III, dependents are mired in passivity, self-worthlessness, and pessimism. They are also ordinarily devoid of adequate social networks in part because their clinging complex annoys and alienates others. Still, all the aberrants have, at least objectively considered, deficient social support systems. From a subjective perspective, Group II aberrants do not feel they need a large social matrix and Group I feel they do not need any support system.

This lack of a connection grid is predominantly traceable to the fact that these abnormals tend to be relatively unliked and unloved (Group I). Or, it is attributable to their being absolutely disliked and usually loathed if not immediately then eventually such that being loved is out of the question (Group II). Or, these pathologicals are relatively disliked and unloved, although from their own perspective, they feel that they are absolutely unlovable (Group III).

No one with a clinically disturbed personality is benevolent, certainly not habitually. Consequently, none is capable of a genuinely intimate relationship on a long-term basis. The aberrants who come closest to any such goodwill, especially its universal species of altruism, are the dependents (Costa and Widiger, 2002, p. 461). From this perspective, dependents are the least abnormal of the aberrants. Still, theirs is not a true solicitude for others. It is an outgrowth of dependents principally viewing people as actual or possible sources of being nurtured.

This consequence is especially the case should dependents believe they will suffer neglect via, for instance, being overlooked or consciously excluded or, on the other hand, being maximally discarded through abandonment. Hence, these pathologically homonomous individuals barnacle themselves onto or burrow into others lest they be exposed to being and feeling alone.

Dependents principally pursue relatedness to avoid aloneness and the dangers that might accrue to being separate(d) from others. This endeavor makes dependents' loneliness embedded in chronic aloneliness. Still, it bears recollection that throughout these discussions, we are discussing habitual motivations. People, such as the dependents, who are persistently acquisitive, may, in a given instance or period, act benevolently toward others and thereby possess a necessary condition for experiencing genuine intimacy.

The dependent personality disorder usually manifests an indefatigable interest in love and other intimacies. Nevertheless, this individual feels forever unloved, even unlovable in principle. Karen Horney has described this type of person as a "self-effacing" neurotic (1991, pp. 214–258). For those with a dependent deviancy, the ultimate motivation of their "love" invariably concerns their being loved instead of loving others. Eventually, people are apt to see through such "loving" as a not very subtle advertisement to be loved, primarily, if not exclusively.

Dependents want to be loved totally and forever, despite and sometimes even because of their unloving and unlovable qualities, to quell their fear of being alone and uncared for. The most neurotic of the aberrants, borderlines, also seek being loved unconditionally to foreclose the possibility of being forsaken. However, their fear of such maximal exclusion is principally due to being alone qua alone instead of being alone and, thereby, bereft of nurturing, as is the case with dependents.

The positive kind of unconditional love for the person as such is to be distinguished from the negative sort of unconditional love for a person's traits even if these qualities themselves are unloving and, therefore, unlovable. Sometimes when it is said that people want to be loved "for themselves," it can signify an egoistic desire on their part. At other times, it can mean the benevolent wish to be loved to gain the confidence to love others. Being loved unconditionally can also initiate or increase non-egoistic self-love, which is generally considered a necessary condition for loving others. The lonely and the neurotic are customarily extremely remiss with reference to such an empowering self-love.

Dependents are by far the least inhumane of the *DSM* pathological personalities in that they come closest to being trusting, sincere, altruistic, cooperative, humble, and tender-hearted. Indeed, dependents score higher in Humaneness than all the other nine kinds of pathologicals combined (Costa and Widiger, 2002, p. 461). They err by excess regarding these six traits predominantly because they are so desperate in their attempts to get others to take care of them. Dependents do so lest they be ostracized and thus without protection and other forms of being looked after. Mature individuals "grow up," in that they shed their negative dependence. On other hand, they do not grow into the negative independence, which characterizes Group II aberrants and SCRAMites as a whole.

Consequently, dependents' trust is all too often based on wanting to believe others are benevolent out of fear that they might not only be non-benevolent but malevolent toward them. Their sincerity stems from naïveté. Their altruism emerges from the need to please and placate everyone. Their compliance arises from spinelessness and slavishness. Their humility and modesty hail from self-deprecation. Finally, their tender-heartedness is an effect of maudlin sentimentality and soft (weak)-heartedness. In passing, it is notable that all these qualities both those positive and negative are more ascribed to women than men. As will be detailed in Chapter Seven, this gender differentiation plays a part in my classifying the pathological personalities in the manner I do.

Nevertheless, it is ethically if not psychically better to fail by excess in such humane qualities than by deficiency. It is more morally laudable to be overly humane as is the case with the Group III dependent than non-humane (Group I) or anti-humane (Group II).

iv. Avoidants

The *DSM* records that avoidants are described by others as "shy" and "timid" in addition to "isolated" and "lonely" (with the first two traits often causing the second two). Avoidants want relationships but, due to their overpowering fear of rejection, they do not gain and even less sustain them. Because of this lack of intimacy-fulfillment, avoidants "feel their loneliness deeply" (p. 664).

Along with that of the borderline's experiencing "chronic feelings of deep emptiness and loneliness," the above two references are the only times the *DSM* mentions any Group III—or any other personality aberrant for that matter—as explicitly undergoing emotional isolation (p. 653). It does so despite its frequent allusion to these four abnormals exceeding lack of connectedness.

The *Manual* also stipulates that, though avoidants can "establish intimate relationships," they will not do so unless assured of being accepted uncritically. Thus, these pathologicals refrain from affiliating with others until, according to the *DSM*, they can be guaranteed "generous offers of support and nurturance." For example, it says that avoidants will circumvent "making new friends" unless they are certain that they themselves will be unequivocally accepted. Therefore, they will, the *DSM* adds, "withhold intimate feelings for fear of being exposed, ridiculed, or shamed" (ibid.).

Like the other abnormals in Group III—and lonely people in general—avoidants are portrayed by the *DSM* as being bereft of self-worth. It states that this lack is manifested in the avoidants' conviction that they are "socially inept, personally unappealing, or inferior to others." All this greatly accounts for what the *DSM* says is their "restricted social support networks," especially that component named above as centrality (p. 662). All these liabilities go far in explaining why avoidants are subject to profound social and affective isolation and often physical as well.

Consequently, and like the borderline, histrionic, and dependent, the avoidant will, in the view of the *DSM*, "fantasize about idealized relationships with others" (p. 663). Such reveries are seldom realized by these deviants, a deficiency that causes them grave loneliness, all of which principally prompts me to aggregate these four aberrants together. In sum, the *DSM* considers Group III as being subject to what in effect is loneliness. Still, only in the instances of the avoidant and borderline does it explicitly say so.

6. Intrapersonal and Interpersonal Loneliness

The avoidant and the other Group III pathologicals are also highly subject to intraself loneliness in that they painfully long for connection to their ideal self. This sort of self, which for them, as for any normals, is frequently envisioned as consisting in and attainable only through intimacy, especially relationships of eros and friendship. This longing might be better portrayed as intrapersonal instead of intraself loneliness since ultimately—and often proximately as well—it stems from the absence of positive interpersonal relationships or the presence of negative ones.

Group I, especially schizoids, do not posit any ideal self. Group II, above all the sociopaths, paranoids, and narcissists have little or no gap between their actual and desired selves. In their case, they are "so full of self" that it leads them to find no discrepancy between their empirical and any desired selves. Accordingly, they manifest what Alfred Adler titles a "superiority" instead of an inferiority complex. Group II obsessionals may at times experience considerable dissatisfaction between who they are and who they aspire to be. This dismay can also characterize narcissists especially when it springs forth from their wounded and exorbitant pride.

Jordan—who appears to have in mind what I reference Group III aberrants, primarily dependents—claims that in bad relationships, such as abusive ones, people start to "disconnect" from themselves. They begin to keep their ideal and more genuine selves out of the relationship to remain in them, all of which engenders what I refer to as intrapersonal loneliness. Jordan maintains that these self-disconnected individuals no longer pursue realizing their authentic selves (2004, p. 122). They give up doing so because it would prevent them from having any kind of attachments whatsoever. For many of these lonelies and alonelies, negative relationships are perceived as better than none. Many but not all since some, like the avoidants, opt for being lonely outside instead of inside relationships.

Consequently, Jordan essays that to keep "alive psychologically and sometimes physically" these isolates create what Relational Cultural Theory (RCT) terms "strategies of disconnection." That is to say, they "disconnect from their own real affective-cognitive experiences." They then "begin to twist themselves to be acceptable to literally stay alive" and connected in their often abusive but desperately needed relationships. As a result, these pathologically dependent individuals are prone to ignore or misunderstand their own true feelings and genuine ideals (ibid.). Hence, to (re)connect with others, these typically dependent personalities—those I designate Group III since they are all excessively homonomous personalities—disconnect from themselves and their desired selves. They then proceed to invent what are variously termed "false," "idolized," or "inauthentic" selves. This lack of connectedness leaves the individual in a condition of intrapersonal loneliness, one that will eventually lead to or reinforce interpersonal loneliness, as the case may be.

Jordan mentions how abusive relationships can alter the biochemistry, for example, of isolated children in manners that render:

> them more vulnerable to affective instability and traumatic disconnections. Thus, a small hurt may lead to a big chemical and behavioral reaction as the over-reactive amygdala short-circuits the cortical mediation of pain. The relational images of, "If I register my hurt or anger, I am shunned, abandoned, or endangered" [all of which typifies Group III but not Groups I and II] begin to generalize to all other relationships, and slowly children learn to bring only partial aspects of themselves into relationship. Their vulnerability in particular is not safe. . . . In the case of abuse, they also experience the more alarming symptoms of Post-Traumatic Stress Disorder (PTSD), characterized by hyper-arousal, panic, nightmare, self-destructive behavior, flashbacks, and intrusive thoughts, which further isolate and confuse them. It could be argued that some of the more painful consequences of these symptoms (the startle response, affective lability, inauthenticity, lack of trust, self-harm, substance abuse, and eating disorders) are the deepening sense of isolation, shame, and helplessness [all common Group III problems and traits]. These symptoms make the possibility of reparative connection even more elusive. (Ibid., pp. 122–123)

It bears underlining that Jordan maintains that the RCT model regards "isolation as the greatest source of suffering for individuals" (ibid., p. 121). Though she does not explicitly say so, I interpret the use of the term "isolation" as signifying all forms of negative aloneness, above all those of loneliness, and their fear of them, namely aloneliness. If the absence of the wanted intimate is the supreme suffering especially insofar as it pertains to lonely depression, then it may be put forth that the presence of this most needed and desired intimate constitutes the utmost pleasure and joy.

Intimate union with others is the model of the social being that is the human being. It is that which is most emblematic of mental/moral health as a whole. Therefore, isolation, especially that of loneliness, is the affliction most opposed to human sociality. It is also most emblematic of psycho-spiritual illness, primarily the kind ascribable to the pathological personality, most predominantly the Group III type. Even more indicative of such sickness is the incapability of a person to be subject to loneliness because such an individual is either pathologically nonsocial and unrelated (Group I) or more or less dyssocial and dis-related (Group II with the sociopath obviously being the ultimate dyssocial). On the other hand, supranormal individuals may also experience serious loneliness, but its effect on them only increases their psycho-ethical health and assists them in realizing their ideal selves.

Many factors account for the commencement and continuation of aberrant personalities, but all of them, in my view, are found, either directly or indirectly, in a lack of intimacy in the broad sense of the term. At this juncture, it is imperative to consider systematically and in detail why personality disorders can be construed as essentially failures in intimate relatedness, a chief consequence of which is loneliness consciously or otherwise experienced.

Six

PERSONALITY PATHOLOGIES: FAILURES IN INTIMATE RELATEDNESS

1. The Pathological Personality: A Failure at Interpersonality

Different conceptualizations of the disturbed personality abound, but space allows only a couple to be invoked here. One propounded by John Livesley:

> explicitly concerns interpersonal relationships and the failure to function adaptively, as indicated by the failure to develop the capability for intimacy, to function adaptively as an attachment figure, and to establish affiliative relationships. (1998, p. 142)

I concur with the above assessment since I have already proposed that the defining dimension of all pathological personalities is their failure vis-à-vis intimate relatedness. However, it is not only that these aberrants fail "to develop the capability" for relatedness in terms of attachments but some of them have little if any capability and no desire for any bonding to begin with (Group I).

While some of these pathologicals may have some potential for close connections with a few chosen others, they are disdainfully indifferent or overtly antagonistic toward human beings in general. In any case, these individuals are too selfish and malevolent to obtain and especially maintain genuine affiliations (Group II).

Others of these aberrants may eagerly seek intimacy with people but are too habitually acquisitively and neurotically self-involved to be agents or recipients of lasting genuine bonds with them (Group III).

Livesley further claims that, if we peruse:

> [the relevant] literature in an attempt to understand the way clinicians conceptualize personality disorder, it is apparent that [they] emphasize two features: chronic interpersonal difficulties and problems with a sense of self or self-identity. . . . Thus, there appears to be a general acceptance that chronically dysfunctional interpersonal behavior is an essential element of personality disorder. (Ibid., p. 140)

I concur with Livesley's view that clinicians conceive habitual interpersonal problems to be a defining hallmark of a personality pathology. Still, I posit that such chronic difficulties are not *just* but *the* essential feature of the abnormal personality. Accordingly, I have proposed that the principal therapeutic method regarding the aberrated personality should be interpersonal in nature.

I endorse the view that people's sense of self and self-identity, if only on a nonconscious level, is chiefly comprised of their intimate identifications with others, or interpersonality. Because, therefore, individuals with deviant personalities have a pathological lack of genuine affiliation with other persons, they have grave problems with an adequate sense of self and self-identity (and vice versa).

As the main effect of abnormals' deficient and defective connections with others, their self-identity is or has become essentially negatively integrated (for example, the schizoid) or negatively disintegrated (for example, the schizotypal). As I will discuss in the next chapter, we can distinguish, following Kazimierz Dabrowski, both positive and negative personality disintegrations.

In any case, the pathological personality can be envisaged as a failure qua interpersonality, which, in turn, constitutes the essence of personality. Of these failed personalities, only Group III actually feel that they are. Notably, gravely lonely individuals, owing to their abysmal sense of self and self-worth, feel they are failures qua persons and Group III personalities tend to be pathologically lonely.

I have proposed that inadequacies apropos of intimacy can lead to negative sorts of aloneness, which themselves can predispose, precipitate, maintain and, in some cases, cause personality aberrations (for example, the dependent) or some of the subspecies these disorders assume. Correspondingly, personality disturbances can inaugurate or exacerbate negative types of aloneness and the fear of them, such as the borderline's aloneliness. This individual experiences terror at the thought of being abandoned, especially to catastrophic loneliness.

Livesley maintains that the *DSM* general criteria for a diseased personality have no "rationale . . . based on an understanding of the functions of normal personality" and, thus, he says, they "are merely a catalogue of descriptive features" (ibid.). Likewise, Lee Clark, Lively, and Leslie Morey contend that "*DSM* criterion sets" relative to the pathological personalities are nothing more than "a hodgepodge of clinical experiences" (1997, p. 210) . I endorse these views and hold that they represent in part the reasons for what I believe is the *DSM*'s lack of a clear and congruent ground for its personality disorder taxonomy.

2. Personality Disorders: Insufficient, Off the Mark, and Toxic

Unlike that of the *DSM*, my three-unit taxonomy of the abnormal personalities is based on the single foundation of the absence of intimate connections, which can be considered in light of the following views of Allan Frances:

> The essence of being a mammal (and, most essentially, we are mammals) is the need for and the ability to participate in interpersonal relationships. . . . Virtually all of the most important events in life are

> interpersonal in nature and most of what we call personality is interpersonal in expression. Indeed, psychotherapy can be defined as a specialized interaction designed to support or change someone whose ambient interpersonal behaviors and relationships have been insufficient, off the mark, or toxic. (Smith Benjamin, 1996, p. v)

I have the following animadversions concerning Frances' views cited here. First, not all mammals are social animals; for instance, badgers and tigers are not, though buffalo and lions are. Second, only human mammals participate in interpersonal relationships, since only they are persons, at least according to the customary criteria used to decide which individuals qualify for being a person. Third, indisputably, human beings are mammals. Nonetheless, being mammalian is hardly the defining ingredient of human beings. Instead, their rationality, freedom, creativity, morality, and other mental and spiritual traits constitute the critical, distinctive core of their being. Still, all human mentalness and spiritualness is arguably embodied, and that embodiment is mammalian.

On the other hand, I completely second Frances' division of personality abnormality into off the mark, toxic, and insufficient since it perfectly reflects my classification of them. My reading of the *DSM* schizoid and schizotypal of Group I is that these eccentrics exhibit Frances' off the mark interpersonal relationships to the extreme, for they have no attachments whatsoever. Nevertheless, given that their behavior is highly—and, by some personologists, totally—biologically necessitated, the schizoid and schizotypal are not ordinarily fully (if at all) morally faulted for their failures, though they may be legally.

It merits emphasizing that all the pathological personalities—and not only Group I—are radically off the mark in that they are eccentric—off center—as to interpersonality because of their ego-centricity. This self-centeredness deepens as these deviants vary from the acquisitional sort (Group I) to the acquisitive (Group III), and, finally, to the malevolent and selfish type (Group II) types.

Furthermore, the first aberrant listed in each of the three units—respectively, the schizoid, sociopath, and borderline—is the most egocentric; the last mentioned is the least self-centered, that is, respectively, the schizotypal, obsessional, and avoidant. Still, a case can be made for dependents instead of avoidants being the least egocentric of all the abnormals, not only of Group III. This ranking especially holds up if avoidants are pictured—as they sometimes are, though not by myself—as being more like Group I, above all the schizotypals, than the other Group III deviants.

In terms of interpersonal bonds, Frances' toxicity is most manifest in Group II, since they have traits that are thoroughly venomous owing to their extreme lack of FFM Humaneness. For instance, antipathy toward others is habitually overtly expressed by the sociopath and paranoid, but alternatingly expressed and repressed by the narcissist and obsessional. The enmity—often coupled with jealousy and envy most especially on the part, respectively, of the paranoid and narcissist—is the logical outcome of these four Group II aberrants' completely centripetal "me-only" and malevolent "me-versus-them" motivational styles.

I note that Paul T. Costa and Thomas A. Widiger inexplicably omit mention of the fact that the *DSM* at least implicitly considers the paranoid to be anti-altruistic (2002, p. 461). It states that this aberrant's essential feature consists in interpreting others' motives as being malevolent, an offshoot of this individual's cynicism, a trait manifestly opposed to altruism.

As well, to some extent, we have seen that the *DSM* views paranoids as pathologically jealous, grandiosely delusional, especially concerning their own status and power, argumentative, stubborn, dogmatic, fanatical, hostile, merciless, begrudging, sarcastic, and vindictive (pp. 634–638). All this makes these pathologicals, among other things, exceedingly bad-willed and (ob)noxiously so. This pathological who, as just indicated by the *DSM*, is a veritable study not only in the lack of virtues but in a plethora of vices (not being bad, especially viciously so, does not make a person good but being good, or virtuous, makes a person "unbad")

The pathologicals of Group III display Frances' *insufficient* intersubjectivity due to their self-centered and acquisitive motivational pattern. The borderline and histrionic tend to deliberately ignore the needs of others; the dependent and avoidant are more inclined to be ignorant of them, although usually culpably so, especially the dependent. Their acquisitiveness is a result of this quartet of abnormals being pre-occupied with satisfying their own largely neurotic neediness, above all that relevant to relationships.

The borderline, dependent, and, to a lesser yet significant measure, the avoidant can sometimes be overly solicitous regarding the needs of others. They do so to placate others in an effort to elude abandonment or rejection. If this trio of Group III deviants is unduly concerned about others, it, nonetheless, remains traceable, albeit disguised by their attention to others, to their underlying "me-first" mentality.

If, therefore, we view the *DSM* clusters in terms of Frances' off the mark, toxic, and insufficient interpersonal behaviors and relationships, its Cluster A federates the extremely non-toxic schizoid and schizotypal with the incredibly toxic paranoid. In Cluster B, it allies the even more pestilential sociopath and the usually less menacing but still very harmful narcissist with the rather harmless histrionic and the sometimes rancorous borderline. However, the "fangs" of borderlines are out mainly due to an enraged reaction to their fears of being forsaken instead of being caused by sheer malice as is the case with sociopaths or intense malevolence as is the case with narcissists. As well, unlike these Group II deviants, borderlines are envenomed more by anger and hatred toward themselves than others. Finally, the *DSM* admixes in Cluster C the vituperative obsessionals with the largely spiteless and spleenless dependents and avoidants.

As I will elucidate in the final chapter, I agree with Frances' position that psychotherapy is essentially a specialized interaction dealing with problems in interpersonal relationships, of which, intimacy is the defining characteristic.

Similarly, Drew Westen and Jonathan Shedler maintain that regardless of theoretical orientation, therapists appraise "personality pathology" in essentially two manners. The first is by listening to the "narratives" the patients tell the clinicians concerning "their lives and significant relationships." The second, is by "observing the way patients relate to [clinicians] in the consulting room" (2000, p. 112). This venue is itself a setting for what can be a kind of intimate affiliation: the therapeutic alliance, the essence of which consists in interpersonality.

If the clinical ambience is, for example, non-welcoming, it will likely undermine the objectives of the alliance. The notion of a partnership between clinician and client also implies a kind of shared inwardness that requires veracity, loyalty, empathy, and sympathy, traits, which are psycho-ethical in nature.

Given that human beings are social mammals; that almost all significant events are interpersonal; and that personality is interpersonal in nature, Frances says he finds it amazing that until recently there has been rather little "systematic theory and research on the ways in which people interact with one another in life and in psychotherapy" (Smith Benjamin, 1996, p. v). He reasons that the main factor for the failure to heed the interpersonal is likely because it "is the prose we speak" without our awareness of its being so. Therefore, he contends that the language bespeaking interpersonality "tends to be lost in the shuffle of more abstract model building or research" (ibid.).

From my perspective, the best manner of theory construction about personality and its disorders appears to be that of Frances and Livesley, which is via an analysis of interpersonal relatedness. Loneliness is the principal problem relevant to the deficiency of shared inwardness. Yet, this tribulation may also be not only ignored in model construction and research but often in clinical settings because it is frequently not the presenting or any subsequently acknowledged symptom.

This oversight occurs, among other reasons, because of the nature of loneliness in question, the nature of the therapy used, and the kind of persons the patient and therapist are. Loneliness is often lost in the shuffle, because it is often (con)fused with its cognate phenomena.

Loneliness may be deemed unsuitable for any curative process for many reasons. One is because both the patient and the therapist may think that little if anything significant can be done about this problem since it often requires a considerable change in the mentality and behavior of the individual. Thus, they may think that it is futile to even bring it to one another's attention.

Loneliness is unlike most other difficulties in that it explicitly and directly requires others for its amelioration and all the more for its permanent resolution. This exigency is routinely difficult to fulfill due to the very nature of this isolation.

Lonely individuals' traits such as anxiety, shame, and pain—brought about or bolstered by loneliness—may make them reticent to reveal them. Clinicians may look upon loneliness as so anxiety provoking for themselves that they sidestep it, consciously or otherwise, even resisting mention of it by name (vol. 1, pp. 401–410).

3. Personality Disturbances as Mental Trait Disorders

Personality aberrations are classified as mental trait disorders since they are deviations constituted by negative personality qualities. In my view, they are classified so primarily because of their interpersonal non-functioning (Group I) and more or less complete (Group II) or partial (Group III) dysfunctioning.

As I envisage them, these abnormalities might be best known as psycho-ethical interpersonal disorders since they entail negative mental and moral qualities that impact their relationship in un-constructive even destructive fashion. Manifestly, all ethical traits are psychic in the sense of formally inhering in the human psyche. Still, not all mental qualities—for instance, the trait of fantasy in the FFM's supertrait of Openness to Experience—are moral.

Some mentally ill individuals are pathological precisely so because their very personalities *are* pathological, such is the case with those with a *DSM* personality disturbance. Thus, they are mentally/morally unbalanced because their traits are abnormal or their very persons are if human beings are considered as distinct from their attributes. Robert Cloninger proposes that all abnormal personalities "can be defined as extreme configurations of normal personality traits" (2007, p. xii). This view envisions such qualities as differing in degree instead of kind.

Contrastingly, there are individuals who are mentally ill because they have what is known as a "mental state" sickness, such as depression, psychosis, or an anxiety disorder. It is widely, though far from universally, held that what individuals *are* in terms of mental illness, especially if they are disordered qua personality, is less subject to change than what people *have*, such as depression.

By definition, personality traits are relatively stable throughout the life span, whereas mental illness, such as depression, is usually, if not by definition, far less permanent. Still, and as David Bernstein and David Useda claim, even those with extremely pathological personalities can "grow out of" them, either because they obtain professional help or, more typically, due to "ameliorative life experiences" (2007, p. 51).

Bernstein and Useda further precise that a pathological personality may go for months "without presenting serious manifestations of the disorder" (ibid.). On the other hand, mental state disorders can last for years without improvement and without their most significant symptoms necessarily being evident. Indeed, some mental state disturbances, such as depression, can even last a lifetime, a fact that leads some to think that this illness should also be classified as a personality disorder (the depressed personality). It is noteworthy that Costa and Widiger list depression as a trait of Neuroticism (2002, p. 463). I refer to this trait as depressiveness or despondence to avoid confusion of the mental trait disorder with the mental state disorder of depression.

Not only mental trait disorders but also mental state disturbances, such as schizophrenia and depression, feature personal qualities that are pathological in dimensional degree à la the FFM or in categorical kind à la the *DSM*. Yet, the focus of mental state abnormalities is not formally on their personal traits however much these attributes are involved in these diseases.

Recall that philosophers are divided whether, metaphysically (ontologically) considered, the person *is* its qualities or *has* them. Similarly, with respect to the disordered personalities, their mental illness either *is*, or is *in*, their very personality instead of something they *have*, or contract. Hence, in some quarters, it is more exact to say that it is the personality that is pathological not its traits; in others, it is the reverse; and, in still others, both the personality and traits are considered diseased, mentally or mentally/morally.

If people are simply the sum of their traits, in changing one of them, they are themselves changed at least partially. If people are not their traits as such, then a change in one or even all their qualities leaves them unchanged as to the primary essence of their personhood.

Arguably, a change in a trait alters the person as a whole not directly but indirectly, for example, by affecting the individual's mind, body, or soul that contain(s) such attributes. This transformation would then raise the further question whether individuals are distinct from their bodies, minds, or souls. It would also raise the question whether these three entities, in turn, are distinct from their features such as, respectively, size, intelligence, and immateriality.

The *DSM* multi-axial system tries to address "the whole person." Axis I refers broadly to the principal disorder that needs immediate attention; for example, a major depressive episode, an exacerbation of schizophrenia, or a flare-up of panic disorder. The Axis I disorder is usually, but not always, the presenting condition. Axis II includes personality disorders as well as any developmental disorders that may be predisposing the person to the Axis I problem. Axis III lists any relevant medical or neurological problems. Axis IV codes the major psychosocial stressors the individual has faced recently, and Axis V codes the "level of function."

Widiger writes that innate and unique to the personality disorders of Axis II "is that they concern a person's sense of self and identity" (2003, p. 90). Accordingly, such disturbances may be envisaged as *being* the person itself or distinct from it, whereas the person may be interpreted as *having* instead of *being* Axis I disorders. In any case, it is my judgment that people's sense of self and self-identity are essentially derived from their interpersonal, or intimate, relationships, and, in general, others' conveyed view of them. Even the extremely socially isolated schizoids are impacted by others' view of them.

Widiger relates the customary position that personality disorders:

> have an early onset, characterize everyday functioning, and relate closely to personality functioning evident within the general population; Axis I disorders, in contrast, have an onset throughout adult life, are episodic, and are readily distinguishable from normal personality functioning. (Ibid.)

This said, personality disturbances may also be readily distinguishable from everyday, or normal, functioning, precisely because they involve non-, mal-, or inadequate functioning that is ascribable, respectively, to Groups I, II, and III abnormals. Nevertheless, these serious shortcomings concerning ordinary functioning may not always be manifest. Such is especially the case if the abnormal individual is conceived as differing only in degree from the normal, as dimensional models, like the FFM, interpret personality, in contrast to categorical paradigms, like the *DSM.*

In terms of the relationship of the two Axes, Frances reports "evidence that the quality and quantity of pre-existing" aberrants of Axis II can "influence the predisposition, manifestation, course, and response to treatment of various Axis I conditions" (Widiger, 2003, p. 92) .

Robert Krueger and Jennifer Tackett allude to four paradigms of the link between Axis I and Axis II disorders, which, they say, appear to "have gained consensus within the field as plausible explanations for this relationship." These models are, first, the "predisposition/vulnerability" perspective, in which case "the presence of an existing disorder increases the probability of developing a second disorder" (2003, p. 110). For example, the maladaptive traits of borderlines of Axis II dispose them to develop a specific Axis I disorder such as major depression.

The second perspective is "the complication/scar," in which case "the direction" of the conditioning or causal factor "is reversed" (ibid.). For example, a preexisting depression disorder may induce changes in personality such as the FFM Neuroticism of the borderline. Still, this supertrait of Neuroticism contains the trait of depression (depressiveness or despondence) such that Axis I clinical depression can be envisaged as being intrinsically related to this FFM personality trait.

The third model is "the pathoplasty/exacerbation," in which "there is an assumption that the co-occurring Axis I and Axis II disorders may have independent etiology and onset." However, Kreuger and Tackett note that an Axis II illness can "influence the course or manifestation of an Axis I disorder" (for example, the dependent personality disorder in relation to clinical depression). They add that this influence may be "due to either a synergistic effect," in which event the Axis II personality disorder "negatively impacts the course or prognosis of the Axis I disorder (exacerbation)." Or it may be due to "a modifying effect," in which case the Axis II personality disorder influences, they say, "the way the Axis I disorder is expressed, for example, the specific symptom profile (pathoplasty)" (ibid., pp. 110–111).

The fourth approach involves "the spectrum model," in which instance the Axis I and Axis II disorders are perceived as proceeding "from the same constitutional" source. The aberrations exist on a "continuum ranging from subclinical traits to full-blown psychopathology" (ibid., p. 111). This model is frequently used vis-à-vis the schizophrenics of Axis I and the paranoids, schizoids, and schizotypals of Axis II. As stated above, it is my position that the paranoid personality does not belong on this schizophrenic spectrum, though and by definition, the paranoid schizophrenic does.

According to the *DSM*, an individual is to be diagnosed as having a personality disorder only when there is a lasting "pattern of inner experience and behavior that deviates markedly from the expectations of the individual's culture." Arguably, all experience is inner, or mental, while its objects can be mental or extramental.

As well, all behavior is necessarily embodied and, therefore, invariably external(ized). However, not all that is internal is held to be necessarily embodied or arguably embodiable (for instance, the entities of pure mathematics or symbolic logic), depending upon the theory of the mind (epistemology) utilized. Nonetheless, all embodiment is part of people's subjectivity. Of course, individuals may be so self-alienated that they perceive their bodies as not belonging to themselves but to someone else or even to no one else, as can occur in schizophrenic self-estrangement.

In some quarters, individuals can have or be disordered personalities regardless of whether their traits and behavior depart from cultural expectations. This outlook is apparently not shared by the *DSM* since it holds that an essential feature of a personality aberrant is that it substantively differs from cultural expectations.

With the possible exceptions of schizoids and schizotypals, psychopaths and especially *DSM* defined sociopaths are more likely than any other deviants to be deemed pathological regardless of the society in which they are found—at least from a combination of psychic and ethical features. Any society with a high prevalence of antisocials in positions of political, military, or police power, as they did, for instance, in Nazi Germany is, by some estimates, a sine qua non of an uncivilized society. Of course, a society where antisocials are extremely numerous even among the rank and file would be judged to be even more uncivilized.

It is generally held that the more aberrated personality traits are biologically based, the more they are pathological in deterministic fashion and, therefore, less subject, if at all, to personal alteration and influences such as the cultural and social. So understood, those in Group I are more likely to be looked upon as the most disturbed, especially from a purely psychic perspective.

Yet, being the most mentally disordered within themselves does not necessarily mean being the most disturbing and injurious to others. Though Group

I are the most sick from a purely mental perspective, among the ten specific pathologicals, they are the least detrimental to others or to themselves.

The *DSM* maintains that a person can be abnormal without being so in terms of its relationships since to qualify as a disturbed personality, the individual need only be aberrated in two of the following four areas: cognition, emotion, impulse control, and interpersonal functioning (p. 633). Perhaps, in theory, it is possible to have serious intrapersonal abnormalities that do not affect interpersonal relationships, but in practice, it is in all likelihood otherwise.

Aberrant personalities contain not only negative internal traits but display either maladaptive behavior, as is most prominently observable in the Conduct Disorder of the sociopath, or overly adaptive comportment, such as the dependent's sycophantic submissiveness. All this assumes that the maladaptiveness and adaptiveness in question are themselves negative in nature.

My position in these matters follows from my views that, first, all personality disorders are primordially aberrations in interpersonal relatedness and that, second, problems in other realms, like work, are often offshoots of these abnormals' non-existent relatedness (Group I), dis-relatedness (Group II), or inadequate relatedness (Group III).

For instance, the Group II obsessional's preoccupation with orderliness is, for the *DSM*, an intrapersonal mental trait being converted into interpersonal and, therefore, extramental, or external, compulsiveness. An equal if not stronger argument can be made for the reverse being the case in that an interpersonal quality is the origin of an intrapersonal attribute.

Thus, the obsessional's craze for orderliness about such things as cutlery being perfectly in order in the drawer originates in this individual's mania concerning orderliness about subjects. The compulsives' fixation arises from its pathological propensity to order and order about those subjects that are persons. In short, while obsessionals attempt to impose their subjectivity on objects, this drive is rooted in a more basic desire to foist their rule on person-subjects by objectifying them.

The obsessive-compulsive's constant effort to monitor others to the point of rendering them quasi-lifeless objects is typical of this aberrant's morbid fondness for death-like abstractions and other etherealized formulae. In any event, its internal obsessions and external compulsions reinforce one another.

Obviously, the obsessional actually fears subjectivity. Since intimacy is the ultimate in subjectivity, above all insofar as it is affective in nature, this individual is pathologically afraid of experiencing and expressing such inwardness. In parallel fashion, the compulsive is uncomfortable with and intolerable of such closeness expressed by others toward itself (ibid., p. 671).

Like the other Group II lonerists, obsessionals are scornful of intimacy because they dread it in general and fear specific instances of it such as simple affection. Intimacy bespeaks union and homonomy, a togetherness that alarms these individuals bereft of warmth and feelings (Costa and Widiger, 2002, p. 461). Correspondingly, compulsives crave distance and unlimited autonomy.

Still, these aberrants may also subserviently seek a negative homonomy by force of their fixation on fulfilling the demands of duty however irrational and immoral such obligations may be in themselves. Hence, the obsessional manifestly embodies the axiom that negative autonomy and negative homonomy are parallel, just as positive autonomy and positive homonomy are isomorphic.

In their unconscious depths, obsessionals are often out-of-control. So stated, they are at base unruly lower-level Dionysians instead of rigid lower-level Apollonians. This means that obsessionals must be(come), for instance, highly assertive, disciplined, or deliberate individuals to despotically control their chaotic Dionysian traits, which govern them on an unconscious psychic level. Thus, in the smaller world in which they consciously live, obsessionals are in control; in the larger, they are out of control, disorganized, and lost. The problem in therapy for these pathologicals involves how they can learn to control their mania for control.

4. Personality Disorders: Abnormalities in Relatedness

From my perspective abnormals first and foremost exhibit a major deviation in interpersonal functioning either by omission (Group I) or by commission due to personality qualities not conducive to closeness or contact with others (Groups III but especially Group II). Group II manifest psycho-ethical traits, mainly inhumaneness and selfishness, that powerfully and overtly militate against relatedness to others. Group III display attributes, especially those of FFM Neuroticism and acquisitiveness, which oppose interpersonality but do so less potently and less overtly than malevolent selfishness.

These abnormals' intersubjective makeup is greatly responsible for their difficulties in the objective realm, such as with occupation. Nonetheless, the objective domain may be the proximate source of their problems. The emotional isolation experienced in the unwanted lack of primary relationships can be designated primordial, or primal; that of secondary, subordinate, or subsidiary.

As I see it, personality is chiefly comprised of relatedness, or the deficiency thereof, to other persons. In which case (intra)personal abnormalities are induced or aggravated by abnormal interpersonal disturbances. Why title such mental trait disorders as being pathologies of personality if, one, they are not a matter of personality as such and if, two, personality is not quintessentially a matter of interpersonality or lack thereof?

Given their negative psycho-ethical qualities, all ten aberrants have pronounced problems in making and maintaining interpersonal bonds especially in making and preserving primary attachments. Nevertheless, abnormals often display problems concerning non-intimate, or secondary, ties as well, such as those at the workplace.

In my judgment, serious troubles in relating to others in all situations are typically the first complications to habitually occur in these abnormals' life.

They are also the last to be mitigated and, a fortiori, to be overcome if they ever are at all.

My outlook on the disturbed personality matches that of Erlene Rosowsky. She contends that problems in interpersonality are "distinctively" characteristic of such an aberration and are, in fact, its very nucleus (1999, p. 154). Group I and II pathologies are, respectively, owing to the non-relatedness in their being extreme loners and to the anti-relatedness in their being extreme lonerists. Contrariwise, Group III's abnormality lies in their defective kind of relatedness, especially in terms of their being extreme lonelies. Though loneliness is hardly the only predicament of Group III, I propose that, along with aloneliness, it is among if not the most drastic of them.

Loneliness, therefore, may follow from personality pathology, as most patently occurs in the case of the Group III avoidant. It may predispose and even precipitate personality sickness as arguably occurs in the borderline and dependent. Or, it may both precede and result from personality pathology, as occurs in the histrionic (see Millon with Davis, 1996, pp. 81–82). At the very least, loneliness accompanies all Group III deviants in functionally impairing fashion. In addition, it is extremely distressing, or dystonic (dystonicity may cause or increase non- or dys-functionality and vice versa).

When predicated of relationships, the terms "interpersonal" and "intimate" are usually construed as interchangeable. The word "intimate" makes the relationship more explicitly warm and heartfelt than does interpersonal. Thus, when people say they are in a relationship, it is usually understood as signifying an intimate attachment, and ordinarily, if not always, one that is or includes the erotic.

Costa and Widiger characterize warmth as that FFM trait of Extraversion most pertinent to "interpersonal intimacy" and nearest to Humaneness in terms of "interpersonal space." They note that warmth, however, has "a cordiality and heartiness" that Humaneness and its traits do not possess (2002, p. 464). (The reader may recall that *cor*diality is derived from the Latin for heart.) Thus, a person can have the Humaneness attributes of cooperativeness or even altruism, such as the philanthropic type, and not necessarily be warmhearted.

As to pathological personalities, Group I are persistently cold toward others but ordinarily in an apathetic and non-hostile fashion, whereas Group II are habitually cold but in a scornfully indifferent or oppugnant manner. Only Group III pathologicals are, as rule, warm toward others, with the histrionics being the most; the borderlines, the least; and the avoidants being warm or cold, depending on whether they are, respectively, accepted or rejected by their fellow human beings (ibid., p, 461; 1994, p. 329).

The *DSM* itself appears to concur with some of my pivotal positions vis-à-vis the usage of the terms "social," "intimacy," "interpersonal," and "close relationship." First, it explicitly alludes to there being a kind of "social intimacy" (p. 640), what I reference as a publicly shared inwardness.

Second, the *DSM* posits the reality of an "interpersonal intimacy" (p. 662). In so doing, it appears to suggest that there is also a kind of intrapersonal intimacy, a usage I employ as well, though I construe it as being essentially derived from the interpersonal.

Third, the *DSM* distinguishes social relationships in general from interpersonal ones in particular (pp. 641, 665). Whereupon, it appears to hold that social relationships pertain more specifically to non-interpersonal attachments instead of what I title secondary attachments. I denominate interpersonal ties primary attachments.

In a broad sense, all social relationships, such as that between lawyer and client, are interpersonal, but their foci are not necessarily on intimacy whether in content or in form. All social relationships should contain public intimacies, such as friendliness, if they are to merit being termed interpersonal. Given that I am of the mind that all personality disorders are fundamentally disturbances concerning intimacy, taken in a broad sense of the term, all relations between clinician and patient are, therefore, basically interpersonal.

Fourth, the *DSM* equates intimacy with close relationships, as it does regarding the schizoid and schizotypal, but in their lack of them (pp. 638, 641), a usage I adopt as well. The *Manual* states that histrionics are exceedingly concerned about their relationships to the point of considering them more intimate than they actually are. Its omission of the word "close" before the word "relationships" suggests that these attachments are all more or less intimate. The *DSM* employs this wording not only concerning the histrionic but the avoidant (pp. 644, 664).

The *Manual* appears to presuppose, therefore, that its readers will assume that a relationship without a modifier means an interpersonal type and that the latter signifies an intimate, or close, connection. The *DSM* contrasts these more personal and private relationships with the less personal or, if you will, the more impersonal, and with the more public, or social, relationships in general (p. 644; see pp. 641, 645, 654, 665, 669).

These *DSM* conventions are central to my contention that aberrations of personality are, in one way or another, preeminently intrinsic failures in terms of "intimate" interpersonality, more explicitly inward, private, complete, and heartfelt. Thus, individuals with a personality disturbance *have* their disorder or, more exactly, *are disordered* primordially due to intimacy deficiencies—quantitative deficits but above all qualitative defects—in terms of their relatedness, or lack thereof, to other human beings, both qua human beings and qua persons.

All connections are obviously not only close but actually contactual, meaning joined, above all affectively, especially from within, in that they are intimate, or inward. Physical contact is part of a person's inwardness expressed outwardly. For this reason alone, sexual and genital intimacies are often felt as the utmost fusion of the interiority and exteriority of the person.

Assuredly, individuals with abnormal personalities customarily come up short regarding social relatedness as a whole. They do so especially insofar as this connectedness involves public intimacy, deficiencies in altruism being the most notable of such shortcomings. Nevertheless, people can more easily fake public intimacies, including that kind of philanthropy viewed as altruism, than they can private because the private, by its very nature, divulges inwardness far more directly and accurately than does the public.

Patently, inadequacies in relatedness can, in their wake, cause their possessors other substantive problems, including those in the areas of work, school, and leisure. In turn, difficulties in these spheres can cause intimacy liabilities, not the least of which is loneliness. Especially is this the case concerning leisure since it is the domain most proper for the realization of shared inwardness.

It merits interjecting here that, in comparison to people in most other industrialized societies, especially relatively rich ones, such as France, Germany, and the Netherlands, Americans overwork and often give up their leisure time to "get ahead" due in part to SCRAM's Successitis, Rivalitis, and Materialitis. Cutting down on leisure often means cutting out intimacy and, therefore, bringing in loneliness, among other malaises. Diminishing intimacy also causes maladies for, as documented throughout this study, loneliness is a contributor and often a cause of physical ailments, not the least of which are those hurtful and harmful to the heart and other organs (Lynch, 1977, 2000; Lynch and Convey, 1979).

Intimacy is felt as the fullness of being—and if it is the intimacy of love, as its overabundance. It is so largely because the intimate immensely adds to the individual's felt sense of being, for such is the nature of interpersonality's "two-in-oneness." Correspondingly, loneliness, as a failure regarding intimacy, disastrously subtracts from a sense of self-being in that the potential intimate is actually absent in the case of yearning, or the intimate is perceived to be so in the cases of missing, mourning, and, above all, bereaving.

Intimacy is an ongoing requirement for normals and supranormals. Those who have their need for it met are usually best able to go on to other concerns, whether desired or necessary. Those who do not possess such shared inwardness often have their consciousness riveted on the pain that presents itself in loneliness, as occurs in the case of Group III. The need for emotional contact and indwelling may be repressed or supressed, as in the case of Group II.

Nonetheless, any truce with the awareness of the negative feelings that loneliness effects can only be temporary. Eventually, people experience "the return of the repressed" or otherwise denied awareness, often in even more upsetting epiphanies of this isolation by engaging in negative behavior, such as aggression and addiction.

Loneliness may be sublimated through, for example, work and, to a lesser extent, leisure. I say "lesser extent" because leisure time, more easily than work, can, as a rule, provide the occasion for the lonely to refocus on their plight. Hence, sometimes the lonely are advised to "keep busy" in order to close their consciousness to their adversary. This counsel generally seems only to postpone dealing with the affliction and often worsens it.

Consequently, if all our relatedness is removed—that which is extremely close and even that which is casual—what remains of the person? Nothing but a very dwarfed and sometimes demented personality, one who feels completely lonely, possibly bored, likely alienated, and most probably clinically depressed as well (McGraw, 1999b, pp. 152–156). Not even the paradigmatically non-gregarious, introverted, emotionally frigid, and habitually nonlonely schizoid could tolerate an existence completely bereft of any sort of relatedness.

Hence, I am in accord with Myrna Weissman when she states that mental state disorders such as depression can be diagnosed according to an individual's intrapersonal, or intraself, symptoms. Alternatively, she emphasizes that personality disorders, which are trait abnormalities, should be "diagnosed in an interpersonal context" (1993, p. 45). Naturally, with greater consensus about the notions of personality and its anomalies, including their diagnoses and taxonomies, greater consensus could be reached as to which therapies should be utilized in their treatment.

Weissman and Gerald Klerman, in concurrence with John Bowlby, contend that "many mental state [Axis I] disorders"—and, hence, not only those of personality and mental trait Axis II disorders—"may be the result of an inability to make and keep affectional bonds" (1986, p. 432). One of if not the most prominent causes and effects of this inability to start and sustain attachments is loneliness. For instance, the Axis I mental state disorder of depression is frequently induced by emotional isolation, most often by its temporal modalities of mourning and bereavement but also by yearning and missing.

5. Personality Disturbances as Interaction Disorders

Jan Derksen points out, "the majority of the criteria which form the foundation for the *DSM*[-IV] personality disorders relate to interpersonal behavior." He proposes that, given this reality, "a patient with a *DSM* [personality disorder] diagnosis has disrupted interpersonal relationships" to such an extent that the personality "disorder is in the relationship" (1995, p. 15). Therefore, a disordered person, in Derksen's reckoning, should be construed not as *having* a personal disorder in the sense of a purely intrapersonal, or individual, disturbance but instead as *being* an interpersonal aberration.

To bolster the intelligibility and merit of his claim, Derksen mentions, "of the 101 criteria from the *Options Book* for the *DSM*, well over 60% fall under the relational style section" (ibid., p. 14)—meaning the part that chiefly concerns interpersonal relationships. This preponderance gives more support to the view that the *DSM* frequently identifies personality deviations with problems of relatedness but does so in implicit and unsystematic fashion.

Derksen notes that the rest of the criteria for the *Options Book* rank in the following order: "behavioral phenomena, mood and affect, cognitive style, and outward presentation" (ibid.). In my judgment, all these factors, along with conational elements, such as the voluntary and volitional, inevitably show up in a person's relationships.

In concert with many other personologists, Derksen spotlights the fact that a disorder of personality ordinarily attracts the clinician's explicit attention only after difficulties with relations in the individual's interpersonal milieu have surfaced. To offset this tendency, he has proposed that the *DSM-5* should designate personality disturbances as "interaction disorders." Consistent with his thought, therefore, Derksen recommends that Axis II of the forthcoming *DSM-5* (likely in 2013) be known as "the axis of disorders in relationships" (ibid., p. 310).

Seeking clinical attention by individuals with serious relational problems or other difficulties experienced by those with personality aberrations does not ipso facto mean that loneliness is one of them. Some *DSM* delineated personality aberrations, namely Group I, do not suffer from loneliness, apparently not even on an unconscious level.

I endorse Derksen's views that the personality pathologies primarily involve anomalies with respect to interpersonal relations such that they are in the relationships and that they would be better known as interaction disorders.

However, I would prefer to call the personality disturbances "interpersonal relationship disorders" or either "interpersonal" or relationship disorders," because these aberrations may not always exist or be apparent in simple, episodic interactions. Anomalies of personality invariably become manifest in the complex and assorted demands of ongoing interpersonal relationships and are among the central causes of why such bonds deteriorate or break up.

Even antisocials, the most anti-intimate and anti-person(al) of individuals, can at times be charming, even quasi gallant, in social interactions. Yet, theirs is but a momentary, superficial magnetism that masks an underlying habitual treacherousness. This perfidiousness may suddenly explode in aggression and violence, even torture (pp. 646–647). Eventually, in any relationship with these exceedingly inhumane dyssocials, their negative personality traits manifest themselves and so much the worse for everyone near and often even far from them should they gain the requisite power, be it military, police, political, economic, cultural, social, educational, psychological, even ecclesiastical.

If the Latin proverb, "*corruptio optimi pessima*" ("corruption of the best is the worst") is true, then the psychopaths who are religious and clerical individuals are the worst of personality scoundrels. Fortunately, such occurrences are relatively rare, but likely not as much as the public thinks or is led to believe.

Derksen further maintains, "the conceptualization of interactions is less abstract and requires less theory" than the notion of personality as such because relations between individuals "can be better established descriptively than someone's personality." The reason is, he says, because personality involves increasing layer after layer of depth and, therefore, greater inscrutability (1995, p. 310).

As stated, personality is easily the most intricate and inward of problems (or mysteries) and depicting it directly may be more difficult than doing so vis-à-vis its behavior in terms of relatedness to others. Still, any description of a relationship eventually entails the interiority of those who comprise the attachment. Normals are essentially inwardnesses in search of other interiorities. They are not solely or even predominantly their externalities. Otherwise they would be but things and objects instead of the utmost of inmost subjects.

I insert here that psychology is a study of the mind as well as of behavior. The human mind and behavior—contrary to metaphysical as distinct from methodological behaviorism—are not the same or reducible to one another. Thus, the mind makes the distinction between itself and its behavior instead of the reverse being the case.

Derksen writes that his interaction disorders could be "registered on the basis of criteria which would form steps on a dimension of severity" such that "the more criteria applicable, the more serious the situation of the person in question." For Derksen, a dimensional (quantitative) perspective is preferable to a qualitative (categorical) because in the first, unlike the second, "the number of criteria is," by definition, "indicated with a figure." Derksen proposes that this quantification facilitates a greater grasp and treating of interaction disorders. In addition, he states that it gives a more rational basis for their classification than does a qualitative paradigm such as that utilized by the *Manual* (ibid.).

Finally, Derksen states that, akin to the personality disorders of the *DSM*, "interaction disorders must be stable and observed over a longer period of time" (ibid.). These requirements would appear to argue for their being titled relationship, or interpersonality, disorders instead of interaction disorders because the first, unlike the second, have a continuity and longevity, which make them more likely to be observed by others.

What, then, is at issue, Derksen insists, is "the interaction patterns of the person in question." In which event, he argues, "it is not the personality which is diagnosed, but instead [the individual's] interactions which remain constant and observable in various situations" (ibid., p. 311).

In my view, it is still the case that it is the personality that is being appraised in the various circumstances, since it is essentially comprised of its interactions and relationships. If Derksen means to say that the whole personality is ever changing because it is but the totality of an individual's situations, then his position is more clear but not necessarily more tenable.

Consequently, Derksen argues that it would be better "to limit criteria regarding personality disorders to interpersonal style and to cease speaking of personality disorders." Nonetheless, he admits that doing so would be "incompatible with the entire *DSM* enterprise" and, as a result, it is most unlikely that these changes would be countenanced by the *Manual* (ibid., p. 310).

In my estimation, a if not the main reason for this improbability is that the *DSM* views personality disturbances, like all other mental disorders, as occurring predominantly if not exclusively within individuals instead of or at least in addition to a relatedness between or among them. Thus, the *Manual* states:

> each of the mental disorders is conceptualized as a clinically significant behavioral or psychological syndrome or pattern which occurs in an individual. . . . Whatever its original cause it must currently be considered a manifestation of a behavioral, psychological, or biological dysfunction in the individual. (pp. xxi–xxii)

Assuredly, only individual persons exist extramentally but a crucial, and arguably the commanding, element of their existence is comprised of their relatedness (or non- or dis-relatedness) to other individuals. Unlike Axis II personality disorders, Axis I illnesses are, as a rule, more or less individual, or intrapersonal. Still, the original source of such mental state disorders may be extra or non-personal and, therefore, need not require interpersonal therapies as, in my view, Axis II mental trait disorders, at least those of personality, do.

My preference in these matters is to retain the *DSM* personality disorders' nomenclature. However, I would accentuate much more the role of interpersonality and its styles within each of the ten *DSM* pathological personality profiles in terms of their primary and secondary diagnostic hallmarks.

I would reference these aberrations as interpersonality or relationship disorders with the explicit understanding that they are psycho-ethical instead of simply psychic (or behavioral) abnormalities. Were the *Manual* to adopt this revision, it would, among other things, require transforming its clustering system possibly more along the lines that I have suggested in my groupings for reasons stated above but mostly in the next chapter.

If all this were done, the role, for instance, of various sorts of aloneness—such as that found in lonelies, alonelies, loners, like the lonerists—among the aberrated personalities would also come more to the fore. I believe this amendment should be adopted given that the absence of interpersonal relatedness is so much a part an individual whose very personality is pathological.

6. Personality Disorders as Originating in the Family

In outlooks similar to those of Derksen and mine, Jeffrey Magnavita maintains that individuals with deviated personalities invariably have problems with interpersonal attachments such that they "are a defining feature of personality pathology" (2000, p. 9). He further proposes that personality is shaped and reinforced from "the earliest interpersonal experience and attachments." He states that there is ample "research and clinical evidence" indicating "the roots of personality are in the earliest maternal-infant bond," unarguably the most enduring of all intimacy attachments. He insists that if there is "disruption" in such primordial connections, it "can cause lifelong personality disturbance." Thus, he contends that it is commonly held that all individual pathology has its beginnings "in primary relationships" (ibid.).

While I posit that all the personality disorders have their temporal onset in deficient primary bonds, I do not hold that all of them are necessarily initially caused by such inadequacies. The schizotypal but especially the schizoid are aberrants who, while they may be strongly influenced by negative familial experiences, are more or less predetermined, in the sense of pre-necessitated, by genetic factors. Magnavita does not appear to explicitly distinguish between those factors that are conditioning and influencing, on the one hand, and those that are necessitating and strictly determining, on the other.

Magnavita essays, "personality is organized and shaped by the relationships in the interpersonal matrix which is unique to each family system" (ibid., p. 10). This is a tack I also largely but not entirely take, since there are attachments beyond the familial that frame and contour personality. Nonetheless, the family represents the first and often the most powerful and protracted convergence of the forces of nature and nurture.

Still, freedom can somewhat alter the impact of the biopsychosocial and in particular the home factors, which so greatly influence the evolution, stagnation, or involution of personality. As people mature, their choices, at least tacitly considered, of friends and other members of their social support network shape their personalities. Still, while the influence of the family may ebb as the individual grows up, it is rarely if ever fully extinguished for better or worse. As is commonly conceded, those whom we first love (or hate) tend to imprint a lasting albeit not always a conscious effect on later relationships and on our life as a whole.

Magnavita states that an individual with a dysfunctional personality has inevitably been subject to destructive family patterns, which have been exaggerated from the biopsychosocial matrix [specific] temperamental predispositions, styles, and reactions (ibid., p. 50). This position, in my judgment, somewhat clarifies if not corrects his first animadversion. Accordingly, he posits that the family is:

> the crucible for personality development, and intimacy is the transformative element which shapes the biopsychosocial ingredients. The intimate attachments the individual experiences in childhood provide the crucible for both "healthy" and "disordered" personality development. The dysfunctional family system frustrates or substitutes . . . the craving for intimacy. To some degree, all the dysfunctional [family] systems . . . disrupt or prevent the development of close relationships with significant figures. Either there is too much—fusion [an unwanted kind of ho-

> monomy]—or too little—abandonment [an unwanted kind of autonomy]. (Ibid., p. 25)

So understood, the lack of intimacy—or its specious versions—is the foundation for the emergence of aberrated personalities. In my judgment, this lack is not necessarily their cause since, for instance, Group I aberrants appear to have been born pathologically predisposed or even necessitated. Therefore, in terms of loneliness, the dysfunctional family leaves its members isolated, for example, by either creating pseudo-intimacy through hyper-dependence (negative homonomy) or by eliminating any intimacy whatsoever through hyper-independence (negative autonomy) which it does, for example, via neglect.

Aaron Pincus and Michael Gurtman cite Abigail Bakan, who claims that agency and communion are the "fundamental modalities" of human existence and that a proper balance between them is mandatory for well-being (2006, p. 98). They envisage agency as entailing the synthesis of self-focus and separation (positive autonomy) and other-focus and communion (positive homonomy) as being "optimal" for well-being (ibid., p. 99). I concur with their position except that I emphasize that genuine autonomy occurs within genuine homonomy such that true individualism takes place inside sociality, especially when the latter bespeaks community.

Pincus and Gurtman note that agency and communion are, respectively, "closely tied to traditional conceptions of psychological masculinity and femininity" (ibid.). As discussed throughout this series, the mentally healthiest type of personality is arguably the androgynous. This orientation combines positive autonomy (agency) and high masculinity with positive homonomy (communion) with high femininity. A loving family provides, by the power of its positive homonomy, the grounds for its children's positive autonomy, which, in turn, furnishes the basis for the intimacy of adult homonomy.

Jacques Martin points out recent surveys that indicate people—and he specifically has in mind the English—are less happy today than in times past because there obtains "a malaise at the heart of the modern notion of progress," that includes today's selfish individualism and the commercialism of everything (all of which characterizes SCRAM). Martin maintains that the essential source of this malaise is that our sense of well-being is derived mainly from "our closest, most intimate relationships, above all the family," whose ties, he argues, are becoming moribund (*Guardian Weekly*, pp. 24–30 September 2004)

The effect of this lack of family relatedness often results in extreme childhood loneliness. One psychiatrist remarked regarding serial rapist, murderer, and cannibal, Jeffrey Dammer, "anyone who is subject to abject loneliness as a child will likely have serious problems when older" (History TV, 15 May 2010).

In support of his stance, Martin essays that the British family—and much the same if not more so can be said of the American—has:

> become a weaker institution . . . extended families are increasingly marginal, nuclear families are getting smaller [atomized] and more short-lived, almost half of all marriages end in divorce, and most parents spend less time with their preschool children. The central site of intimacy is the family, as expressed in the relationship between partners, and between parents and children. . . . It is the deterioration in the parent-child relationship, though, which should detain us most. This, after all, is the cradle of all else, where we learn our sense of security, our identity, our ability to love and care, to speak and listen, to be human. The parent-child, especially the mother-child, relationship stands in the sharpest contrast of all to the laws of the market. It is utterly unequal, yet there is no expectation that the sacrifice entails or requires reciprocation. On the contrary, the only way children can reciprocate is though the love and the sacrifice they make for their own children. (Ibid.)

Magnavita argues that individuals with personality abnormalities "consistently demonstrate disturbances in the relational matrix" which, he says, "are the most obvious manifestations" of such aberrations. He proposes that these anomalies "are made apparent through repetitive maladaptive patterns in various areas such as work, home, and community" (2000, p. 10), outlooks I also essentially endorse.

Yet, while such departures in the relational— interpersonal—realm are likely the most apparent aspects of their abnormality and are so to clinicians as a whole, they are not so evident to everyone, such as authors of the *DSM*, since they conceive personality disorders chiefly if not entirely in terms of strictly individual and intraself deviations instead of interpersonal ones, even though their formulation of all of these disturbances is explicitly or at least implicitly interpersonal. With Daniel Leising, Doreen Sporberg, and Diana Rehbein, I argue, "interpersonal behavior is a crucial element in descriptions of personality disorders. . . . all ten *DSM-IV* personality disorder categories relate to interpersonal behavior in one way or another." (2006, p. 319)

Magnavita states that each kind of personality abnormality has a unique "style of managing and regulating intimacy levels when they become too threatening." He says, "the histrionic makes a scene, the obsessive-compulsive gets lost in the details, and so on," and "each style has its own characteristic relational and defensive responses." Magnavita proposes, "the various substitutes for true intimacy" engineered by the aberrant individuals "only serve to further derail" their efforts "in an endless attempt to overcorrect the deficits" (2000, p. 25).

I have nothing to add to what I believe are Magnavita's accurate interpretations of pathological personalities in these regards save to say that the presence of intimacy most threatens Groups I and II, whereas its absence does Group III.

Magnavita writes that abnormals have developed defenses "to protect themselves from early painful, disturbed, or non-gratifying relationships" and "to prevent others from hurting or neglecting them again." He specifies that these unbalanced individuals develop powerful preventive measures "against intimacy" that thwart the healing possibilities of human relatedness and contends that the result of this interference is that diseased personalities "avoid intimate connections with the people in their daily life" (ibid., p. 10). His position here I second in reference to Group II and especially Group I but not Group III. The borderline, histrionic, and dependent constantly seek intimacy, while the avoidant eschews it not in and of itself, but because this abnormally anxious person is afraid of losing connectedness due to being jettisoned.

Magnavita's proposal that "the pathological aspects of an individual's personality often tie the person to the relational field in an attempt to gain lost love and intimacy" is wholly predicable of Group III but only in a very restricted sense of Group II (ibid., p. 21). The pathologies of these four abnormals lie in their attempt not to gain but circumvent intimacy unless it can serve their egocentric goals. Group II aberrants predominantly seek success via power, prestige, popularity, and possessions, which may be considered compensations, albeit gravely inadequate ones, for their missing connections.

As well, I believe Magnavita's ascription is even less warranted in the case of Group I, at least insofar as they are characterized by the *DSM*, because schizoids and schizotypals are likely absolutely non-transformable loners who never appear to have had any capability for or interest in intimae. Therefore, they are, in my judgment, pathological personalities precisely for those reasons.

For Magnavita, "intimacy is the currency of all healthy, close interpersonal relationships and the realm in which corrective therapeutics occur." I am totally in tune with these two judgments since it is my view that disturbed personalities are failures in intimacy to begin with. They are fundamentally treatable only by interpersonal therapies, though ordinarily in conjunction with other appropriate interventions. Magnavita then cites Cheryl L. Brandt's definition of intimacy, namely that it "involves a caring relationship," one which is "a giving and receiving," or what can be described as a reciprocal efficacious beneficence (ibid., p. 25).

Caring individuals, above all the kind of caring that involves love, are often believed to be endowed with intuitive faculties. They are imputed with the ability to immediately reach into the recesses of the persons for whom they care. Accordingly, such caring can be understood as being exceptionally empathic and sympathetic.

Magnavita writes, "one of the main assumptions of an integrative model," the paradigm he advocates, "is that all people seek intimacy" (ibid.). I would interject that all *normal* people search for emotional connectedness. I also propose that abnormality is predominantly a matter of not having a need or at most a highly limited one for connectedness (Group I), denying this need due to derisive uninterest or animosity concerning others (Group II), or seeking it in an especially neurotically self-centered and repetitious self-defeating manner (Group III).

Magnavita posits, "intimacy in the integrative relational model, in fact, is a primary drive," while "in the classic psychodynamic model, sexual and aggressive drives are primary" (ibid.). Arguably, genuine intimacy—defined as the radical requirement to share inwardness in a benevolent fashion—is the fundamental drive of human beings sometimes even more compelling than the needs for sustenance and security.

As discussed in Volume I, the erotic is a kind of basic intimacy and, in some ways, its paradigm instantiation. Aggressive drives are less basic than non-aggressive types if benevolence is more fundamental than malevolence and love more than hatred. Furthermore, if by "drive" is meant a necessitating kind of urgent physiological instinct, it is highly disputable whether there are such deterministic aggressive personality conditions save perhaps in the case of "bad seed" psychopaths.

Another approach with which I am in essential agreement is Relational-Cultural theory (RCT). Judith Jordan proposes that RCT "challenges many of the traditional psychological theories of personality in terms of their emphasis," for instance, on the development of the overly autonomous separate self. She regards this kind of self as not being mentally healthy but sickly (2004, p. 120). This sickliness is, I submit, typical of Group II abnormals and the sort of personality especially promoted by SCRAM.

Jordan argues that RCT maintains, "people grow through and toward connection," or homonomy, and they do so throughout the life span. Hence, she proposes that "the ideal of *separation*" and independence—the atomistic kind of absolutely absolute autonomy advocated by SCRAM—are adjudged by RCT as being erroneous and self-defeating. They are, Jordan insists, because "the human condition is inevitably one of ongoing interdependence" and union (homonomy) (ibid., pp. 120–121). I favor the term "inter-independence" to signify that genuine homonomy, or "interness," not only creates a shared autonomy but that independence remains embedded in mutual dependence and does so both with reference to basic needs and metaneeds.

In the words of Jordan, RCT considers personality growth "as involving increasing elaboration and differentiation of relational patterns and capabilities" (ibid., p. 121). So stated, her position reflects the notion that true autonomy and diversification are based on the homonomy and the unification effected by genuine relatedness. Healthy personalities display a rich diversity within a strong but flexible unity. Unhealthy ones can be said to exhibit an undiversified and rigid unity (for example, the schizoid), an extreme diversification but little or no integration (for example, the sociopath), or an oscillation between the two deficiencies (for instance, the borderline).

Jordan essays that the RCT personality model indicates "that human beings seek engagement in relationships in which both people are receiving and giving." To be genuine, such mutuality must, in my view, stem from mixed benevolence or at minimum from a benevolently based justice. We can get and give for non-benevolent reasons in which case our ties neither are nor can be truly intimate. Jordan remarks that the RCT recognizes that in personality growth "there is movement toward relational authenticity, mutual empathy, and mutual empowerment" (ibid., p. 125). All such positives require an elemental goodwill that is lacking in the disordered personality.

Jordan locates the aberrated personality in the absence of authentic connections to others and to societal units as a whole instead of being due to what are traditionally considered as an individual's more or less permanent personality traits as such. As a result, she maintains that most diagnoses of such deviants are remiss in understanding "the importance of context beyond the traditional nuclear family and often beyond the influence of the early mother-infant relationship" (ibid.).

Whereupon, Jordan argues, "the social conditions and the relational failures" emanating from factors such as "physical and sexual abuse" that "result from a massive misuse of power and violation of trust" are seldom examined as origins of personality problems. Consequently, she exhorts people to look "into chronic disconnection" as the ultimate source of personality aberrations instead of locating their origins solely in the personality of the individual (ibid.).

Therefore, like Derksen, Magnivita, and myself, Jordan maintains that problems in interpersonality are the premier wellsprings of abnormals instead of intrapersonal difficulties of individuals qua individuals. Still, all such disturbances occur within individuals and there are no relationships without individuals. Nor is there any supra-individual, which has an extramental existence beyond the individuals who comprise the interpersonal relationship. Nonetheless, there are solid grounds to argue that relationships or the lack thereof are the most crucial factors in an individual's mental/moral makeup.

Wayne Denton calls attention to the incongruity of interest in an aberrant personality diagnosis being riveted almost entirely on disorders of individuals but that relationship-distress, including that within families, is the most frequent difficulty presented by those seeking therapy (1996, p. 35).

Denton states that concern for "the diagnosis of relational problems is relatively recent and has come from different directions." Some researchers, who once were mainly interested in individual disorders, have now turned toward an investigation of attachments if only to better comprehend individual disturbances. Alternatively, other researchers whose principal interest had been in relationships have now attempted "to demonstrate the importance of relational functioning to individual health" (ibid.).

According to Denton, while "it might be convenient if individual mental disorders could be tied to specific relational disorders," it is clear "the interaction of relational and individual functioning is not so simple" (ibid., p. 39) because, "relational disorders impact upon individuals and vice versa." However, he says, "it is unlikely that we will find simple, 'linear' linkages between what goes on *within* and *between* people" (ibid., p. 42), a conclusion I share.

Social atomists avow that only what occurs within individuals alone is real or at minimum really matters. Social monists assert that only what is trans-individual is true or at least truly counts. For personalists, all that happens is within individuals but that the most crucial part of what constitutes their being and well-being is their relatedness to one another. This trans-individuality is interpersonality, the nucleus of which is intimacy, be it private or public.

Consequently, I believe most personalists would endorse Stone's view:

> *Personality* is fundamentally an aggregate of the ways in which we habitually, predictably, and enduringly relate to other people. These "ways," taken one by one, are the individual *traits* of personality. (2006, p. 2)

Joel Paris proposes that any future paradigm of personality disorders "should be consistent with a scientific hierarchy" that goes from "a bottom-up classification of traits and disorders, linking molecular genetics, neurobiological markers, and temperamental variations" (2000, p. 127). Alternatively, Jordan argues for a top-down classification, meaning a model that first looks to social and cultural factors in explaining the genesis of these disorders.

A bottom-up approach is, in my judgment, most appropriate for Group I, the most biologically influenced if not necessitated of these aberrations. However, a top-down procedure is, I think, more appropriate for Group II and above all Group III, which is generally the least genetically influenced or necessitated aggregate, in my estimation. Whereas further discussion regarding these issues will ensue in Chapter Nine, my concern in this volume is not so much the general and specific etiology of these abnormals but their nature and diagnostic features, especially in terms of their taxonomical implications.

7. The Pervasiveness of Loneliness and Personality Disorders

I now turn to the matter of the pervasiveness of both loneliness and personality aberrations among the general population. I do so before returning to the question of why the *DSM* has so little explicitly to say about this rampant tribulation among those with mental disorders in general and personality disorders in particular.

As to loneliness, Richard Schwartz and Jacqueline Olds cite a Gallup poll that found "36% of its respondents" admitted feeling recently lonely (1997, p. 94). Carin Rubenstein and Phillip Shaver relate that, of the 30,000 respondents to their national survey, 15 percent acknowledged feeling lonely "most or all of the time" (1982, p. 4). These two statistics reflect both the size and duration of loneliness in the United States.

Keith Karren, Brent Hafen, N. Lee Smith, and Kathryn Frandsen report that as much as a tenth of Americans are subject to "overwhelming loneliness at least once a week" (2002, p. 346). Perhaps even more telling—and disturbingly so—is the study by Rosalie Bradley, which found that, in any given fortnight, approximately 25 percent of Americans were believed to be "very lonely" (McGraw, 1991, pp. 136–137). Baukje Miedema and Sue Tatemichi relay that an estimated one quarter of the United States population "experiences episodes of loneliness on a regular basis" with the degree varying "from 20% to 60%" (2003, p. 95). These three findings indicate not only the high extensiveness and quantity of loneliness but its intensiveness and quality as well.

According to Valerian Derlega and Stephen Margulis, the longer loneliness lasts, the more its sufferer is persuaded that an "appropriate" intimate will remain unforthcoming (1982, p. 155). The longer it continues, the more despairing and depressive it becomes. The more taciturn and passive its sufferers becomes, the more probable is loneliness not to be reported or at minimum under-reported.

The longer loneliness persists, the more those burdened by it tend to blame themselves not only for its continuation but its beginning. According to John Cacioppo and William Patrick, the greater a person's loneliness, the more likely is the individual "to attribute failure to something about herself and success to something about the situation" (2008, p. 174).

These self-assessments are often accurate since peoples' traits are largely responsible for at least the perpetuation of their loneliness, and the traits of others or objective circumstances that relieve their isolation either directly or indirectly. Changing these perceptions is difficult because attribute-alteration is itself a most arduous undertaking.

This transformation is problematic since, by definition, personal qualities are quasi-indelible, as the seriously lonely are themselves especially prone to believe. They are especially indelible if such traits are considered as constituting what the person is instead of what the person has.

Significant loneliness is essentially an emotional (heart), problem. In being envisioned as the center of affects and the locus of the most personal (intimate) values, the heart is often used as a symbol for both the organizing process and the organization itself of the entire personality. Recall that personality pathologies can be understood as being rooted in non-heartedness (Group I), hard-heartedness (Group II), or soft-, or weak-, heartedness (Group III).

It may be asked, therefore, what is more challenging than radically revamping the heart, meaning reconfiguring personality. A change of heart can occur in principle about almost anything, but a change in the heart itself is quite another matter. Love is the greatest transformer of the heart in terms of the emotion and of the person as a totality. Lamentably, for the lonely and for those with a personality disorder, it is love which is most missing in their hearts (and in those they believe cause them such misery).

As many savants in these matters have essayed, altering the outer world is far easier than reconstructing the inner world of personality and its traits. It is assuming, once again, that, first, these qualities are distinct from one another and, second, that a person is somewhat at liberty to reconstitute them.

The nucleus of a personality disorder consists in shortcomings in relationships engendered by negative personality traits, some of which result from negative sorts of affiliation. Moreover, trying to reconstruct personality even by dedicated self-resolve is difficult. Consequently, reshaping or revamping the personality qualities of disordered individuals, including those that dispose them to pathological loneliness, is difficult even in the best of circumstances. When severe loneliness is part of the picture, things are very far from being the best. Often these very situations are what trigger or intensify trait loneliness.

Though loneliness is not a mental trait or a mental state disorder, it can be pathological in nature. However grave this affliction may be, it dwells only within the individual subject. Yet, it is, strictly speaking, an intersubjective and interpersonal phenomenon and, accordingly, may be predicated of both individuals and groups. Loneliness could not occur without the absence of other persons, personifications, or personalizations insofar as personality, subjectivity, and interpersonality can be predicated of non-person personations.

I view lack of relatedness as being the chief social stressor in the origin and magnification of pathological personalities. Still, this absence is often and, in some instances solely, the consequence instead of its being a contributor to or the cause of it. The shortage of connections is more an effect of personality aberration in Group I than a source, whereas in Group III it is the reverse. As for Group II, the lack of relatedness is a blend of both with its being more of a consequence than a precipitating influence with respect to the psychopath and paranoid and its being the opposite in the cases of the narcissist and obsessional.

I am reluctant to hypothesize that any of these pathologies is directly not to mention exclusively caused by lack of intimate connection, but if any are, I would venture to say it would be Group III and, to a lesser extent, Group II. As for Group I, it is my take on the research regarding them that they are almost solely caused by genetic instead of social factors, including relational types.

The inception and prolongation of these personality deviations are due to multiple and complex considerations. As will be further amplified below, I agree in general with the position put forward by Paris, namely that "the overall risk for PDs involves interactions between temperamental vulnerability, psychological risks, and social factors," with the social being, in my view, most prominently the absence of relatedness, or connectedness (1996, p. 90).

With respect to the incidence of individuals with personality anomalies, Linda Coker and Widiger report, "it is estimated that 10% to 15% of the general population would meet criteria for one or more of the *DSM* PDs" (2005, p. 202). Katherine Fowler, William O'Donohue, and Scott Lilienfeld took "averaged data across a number of epidemiological studies" and found that "in community samples, 13% of individuals had at least one personality disorder" (2007, p. 5).

Concerning the prevalence of individuals with personality disorders in therapeutic venues, Coker and Widiger estimate it "to be above 50%." They add that perhaps "60% of inpatients within some clinical settings" are borderlines and that antisocials may make "up to 50% of inmates within a correctional setting" (2005, p. 201).

The *DSM* states that the schizoid is clinically uncommon and that the dependent is among the most commonly reported of the aberrants (pp. 639, 667). Taking these and other germane considerations into account and the actual numbers it provides for the other eight aberrants, the *DSM* implies that at least 20% of the general population has some sort of personality aberration (pp. 636, 643, 648, 652, 656, 660, 663, 667, 671).

The *Manual* does not speculate as to the prevalence of the Personality Disorder not Otherwise Specified (PDNOS) either within the clinical population or as to the populace in general. Lee Clark, John Livesley, and Leslie Morey report that in a national sample of clinical patients, 22 percent were best described as PDNOS—also known as mixed or atypical personality disorders. Clark and colleagues also refer to a survey of more than 18,000 personality deviant patients, of which 30 percent were diagnosed as mixed, a figure that hardly suggests their being numerically "atypical" (1997, pp. 211–212).

In reckoning the pervasiveness of personality disorders, the *DSM* does not take into account that many aberrated individuals have comorbidity of personality disturbance. Especially dimensional critics of the *DSM* contend that overlap among the pathological personalities is indicative of the *Manual*'s lack of construct validity due to its use of the categorical model for these aberrants.

By compiling the *DSM* estimates vis-à-vis Group III into one, I think it is reasonable to speculate that this aggregate comprises almost half of the individuals with disturbances of personality (pp. 652, 656, 663, 667). Consequently, given that all Group III suffer from pathological loneliness or are, at the very least, extremely vulnerable to it, it appears that nearly half of the individuals with abnormal personalities are subject to this malaise in its most harrowing manifestations. The other six deviants are pathological in prominent part because of their inability to experience loneliness (Group I) or their unwillingness to risk it (Group II) except in the rather restricted senses specified earlier.

If at least 20 percent of the general population of the United States has a specific personality disorder, and half of the individuals with this aberration suffer from serious loneliness, then at minimum, 10 percent of the overall populace experiences serious emotional isolation based solely on its incidence vis-à-vis abnormal personalities. Again, this figure does not take into tally those individuals who have a PDNOS or who exhibit comorbidity.

Neither do any of these numbers include individuals who have other mental disorders, such as Axis I schizophrenia and depression, illnesses that render their sufferers extremely susceptible to debilitating emotional isolation. According to Magnavita, at least a 40 percent comorbidity rate obtains between Axis I mental state disorders and Axis II mental trait disorders (1997, p. 4). This figure would lend further support for the view that loneliness permeates those who are mentally ill.

The clinically depressed and even more so the schizophrenics of Axis II are often additionally subject to highly undesirable sorts of social and physical isolation. Though they do not cause loneliness as such, these states are frequently instrumental in predisposing, triggering, intensifying, and prolonging it.

Unlike possibly more than half of the personality disturbances of Axis II, the disorders of Axis I are almost all more or less dystonic. Loneliness is both an exceedingly painful condition and likely a major element in many even most of those mental state aberrations. These illnesses, like schizophrenia, are highly incapacitating if only because they are so frequently subject to grave emotional isolation not to mention unwanted physical and social segregation.

Additionally, people with severe mental problems are generally prone to a number of forms of loneliness concomitantly. My research suggests that a significant segment of schizophrenics appears to suffer most and possibly all ten forms of loneliness not only successively but simultaneously and do so intensely. The lonely depressed and Group III deviants also routinely experience several types of this painfulness concomitantly, especially social, erotic, metaphysical, cosmic, epistemic, and communicative.

Taking into consideration all those with major mental disorders, it is reasonable to conjecture that perhaps a quarter to a third of them are liable to suffer consuming yet enduring emotional isolation. Many, perhaps most, of the severely mentally disordered are vulnerable to multiple kinds of loneliness (in some quarters, all mental disorders are deemed to be "major"; otherwise they would not be known as disorders).

Mental illness, as does physical, tends to segregate people socially and often physically, conditions themselves that are highly instrumental in initiating and intensifying emotional isolation. In all such discussions, the following caveat merits mention: there are preciously few statistics on the mentally ill in terms of loneliness in general, let alone its specific forms, and even less about mental trait disturbances in particular.

8. The *DSM* and Interpersonal Connections

As to why the *DSM* has not dedicated a section to aberrations of interpersonal attachment—in which case the question of loneliness and other states of aloneness would be more prominent in the *DSM*—we can refer to Widiger, who wonders why it has:

> sections devoted to disorders of mood, anxiety, impulse control, eating, somatization, sleep, substance use, cognition, sex, learning, and communication but, surprisingly, no section devoted to disorders of interpersonal relatedness. A new section devoted to [them] would represent a significant expansion. . . . interpersonal relatedness is a fundamental component of healthy and unhealthy psychological functioning that is as important to well-being as existing sections. . . . A new section devoted to disorders of interpersonal relatedness would also go far in providing marital and family clinicians with a section. . . . that is more compatible with the focus of their clinical interventions. . . . [They] treat relational disorders which are now not currently represented well by existing diagnostic categories. . . . A section devoted to disorders of interpersonal relatedness would still be organismic (intrapersonal) instead of relational, but disorders of interpersonal relatedness would have more potential for representing relational disorders than the existing mood, anxiety, or, impulse dyscontrol disorders. (2003, p. 98)

What Widiger advocates makes eminent sense from my perspective. Yet, it is not clear, in my estimation, as to how disorders of interpersonal relatedness would remain intrapersonal instead of relational were the *DSM* to add a specific segment on the interpersonality of the abnormal personalities. There is a sense in which any disorder is and must inhere within the person qua individual and is, consequently, intrapersonal. All mental disorders, including those of personality, are located in individuals since only they exist extramentally, all of which Widiger may have in mind.

While it can be a disturbing, even crippling, affective condition, loneliness is not classified by the *DSM* as a mental disorder. If emotional isolation is so rampant among the mentally ill and has such deleterious effects upon them, why then does the *DSM* have so little to say about this personal and public malaise, as Widiger implies? Its reticence may be owing to the belief that this problem is so plebian that it can be considered statistically normal, as it often is, at least in its mild and episodic manifestations.

Hence, drawing attention to loneliness in terms of personality abnormalities might have been reckoned unnecessary, if not inappropriate, by the *DSM.* After all, it is a guidebook that deals specifically with mental disorders instead of mental normalities, such as loneliness, problematic and even significantly so though it may be or become, especially among Axis II Group III and, for example, Axis I schizophrenics and the depressed.

The *DSM*'s silence on the matter may also be traceable to the tendency of many researchers and clinicians to equate this malaise to mood disorders, as will be detailed in Chapter Eight. Like most loneliness investigators, I maintain that all grave loneliness is necessarily depressive. Yet, it is not despondent to the same extent as is clinical depression. In this illness, people's whole world may fall apart and not only their interpersonal relations, even though the latter is the core of their universe.

Recall that we can distinguish a species of depression induced by loneliness and that both depression and loneliness can be caused by either endogenous or exogenous factors. As well, loneliness, like depression, can, in its own right, be pathological and dysfunctional, although the second, unlike the first, is so by its very nature. It then may be asked whether a person who has a pathological complex of negative affects and self-attributes, as obtains in dysfunctional loneliness, is pathological qua person? Insofar as loneliness itself is not considered a mental illness in itself, it is likely that the response to the question would be no.

For whatever reason, that the *DSM* has all but completely omitted mention of loneliness is rather puzzling given that human relationships, especially primary, play such a prominent part in its pathological personality diagnostic criteria, including those that are not only associate features but those that are primary.

9. Possible Locations of Loneliness in the *DSM* Divisions of Mental Disorders and Mental Problems

Before concluding this chapter, it is important to speculate where loneliness might fit within the *DSM*'s divisions of mental disorders and mental problems. It might well be located under Axis IV "for reporting psychosocial and environmental problems" that "may affect the diagnosis, treatment, and prognosis of mental disorders (Axes I and II)" (p. 29).

First, we have taken note that loneliness is a psychosocial problem par excellence. It is so because emotional isolation is a psychic condition that pertains to the gist of human sociality. It is a problem insofar as this affliction entails an involitional lack of intimacy or, more precisely, the temporary or permanent absence of an intimate personation, preeminently a person.

Second, we have also witnessed that loneliness, in terms of its locus, is formally a subjective difficulty, which can affect mental disorders though it is not one itself. For example, loneliness impinges upon the Axis I disorder of depression and Axis II personality disorders, especially Group III, and can often be detected doing so due to the signs and symptoms of these illnesses.

The *DSM* states that beyond their role in the "exacerbation of a mental disorder, psychosocial problems may also develop as a consequence of a person's psychopathology" (p. 629). Emotional isolation as an effect of a mental disorder appears to be the case in the *Manual*'s diagnoses of, for instance, borderlines and avoidants whom, as noted above, it portrays as being deeply troubled by loneliness. Hence, though loneliness itself is not deemed to be a mental aberration by the *DSM*, it could readily follow from such a disturbance, according to the *Manual*'s own guidelines.

Furthermore, the *DSM* states that a psychosocial or environmental difficulty might include "problems with primary support groups." They involve troubles related to family members' death, separation, divorce, estrangement, or remarriage, all of which obviously may instigate loneliness, especially its social, erotic, and existential forms. The *DSM* also mentions removal from home, sexual or physical abuse, child neglect, and child discord with siblings as part of primary support group problems (p. 29). All these ordeals are manifestly potent sources of loneliness, especially of the erotic and social types. It is notable that all these difficulties readily contribute to both lonely and non-lonely clinical depression if, in fact, there is such illness as a depression not affected or even effected by (a)loneliness.

The *DSM* identifies problems related to the social environment in terms of their origin as those due to the death or loss of a friend, inadequate social support, living alone, acculturation, discrimination, and "adjustment to life-cycle transition [such as retirement]" (p. 675). Such difficulties are intrinsically germane to loneliness: the known permanent absence of the friend to lonely bereavement and to a specific sort of social loneliness; inadequate social support to social loneliness in general; living alone to all forms of loneliness but perhaps especially erotic, social, and communicative; acculturation and discrimination to cultural; and life-cycle transition to existential.

Other psychosocial and environmental difficulties include those relevant to education, housing, economic status, and health care. When such concerns involve loneliness, they would be instances of state loneliness (for example, impoverished economic status) instead of trait loneliness, or that caused by mental/moral qualities.

Generally, trait loneliness has a greater impact on state loneliness than the reverse. For example, shy people who are usually lonely and vice versa have trouble gaining and keeping employment, all of which may lead to impoverishment. This state is highly conducive to loneliness, since it powerfully promotes a variegated isolation and even desolation, especially when penury becomes sheer destitution. When people are financially "down on their luck," they are quite vulnerable to the sadness, hopelessness, and anxiousness of emotional isolation.

On the other hand, poverty does not have the same wherewithal to make a person shy, though this consideration greatly depends on to what extent small group anxiety and poverty are regarded negatively in any given culture. In the United States, for example, given that extraversion and affluence are so highly esteemed—whereas in Denmark, for instance, they are not—shyness and poverty are likely to be symbols even code words for a shameful loneliness.

The *DSM* might most logically locate loneliness under "Relational Problems." It states that these difficulties may reflect predicaments in the affiliative patterns of those, for example, of a family in which is found:

> clinically significant impairment in functioning or symptoms among one or more members of the relational unit, or impairment in the functioning of the relational unit itself. (p. 680)

Emotional isolation, above all when pathological, may induce or increase clinically significant disablement in the various individual members of the family or the family as a whole. It is notable that the *DSM* acknowledges that there are communal difficulties as such, in this case familial ones, beyond those of the individuals who comprise a given relational unit.

The *Manual* states that it includes relational problems in its compendium because they are often "a focus of clinical attention among individuals seen by health professionals" (ibid.). It further states that relational difficulties may, first, "exacerbate or complicate the management of a mental disorder or general medical condition in one or more members of the relational unit." Second, they "may be a result of a mental disorder or a general medical condition." Third, they "may be independent of other conditions which are present." Fourth, relational problems "can occur in the absence of any other condition" (ibid.). I contend that loneliness can easily assume any one of these four positions with respect to a mental disorder and specifically the mental trait disorder of the aberrated personality.

It appears that the *DSM* does not hold that relational difficulties, such as loneliness, can cause mental disorders. In my view, loneliness can, at minimum, predispose and precipitate mental aberrations, such as schizophrenia, depression, and Group III deviants (McGraw, 1999b, pp. 152–156). My research also inclines me to maintain that continuous pathological loneliness can instigate some mental disorders such as those of the lonely depressed and dependent personalities.

Nonetheless, it is far from clear or certain to me whether this initiation is actually a matter of simple correlation or of direct causation. Though distinct from them, precising the place of loneliness in starting, sustaining, or aggravating mental disorders, whether of Axis I or II, is extremely challenging. It is now apropos to consider in a more orderly fashion my reasons for proposing a personality disturbance taxonomy that differs from the *DSM* categorization.

Seven

PERSONALITY DISORDER DIVISIONS

1. Multiple versus Single Foundations for Aggregating Personality Disorders

This chapter will advance reasons why I propose personality disorder aggregates different from those in the *DSM.* My arguments sometimes take exception to what it says or omits saying about its personality disorder typology. At other times, I state rationales for devising my division without necessarily intending them as criticism of the *DSM* classification.

The *Manual* concedes that its clustering system, while "useful in some research and educational situations, has serious limitations and has not been consistently validated" (p. 630).

My classification of personality disorders is predominantly based on their threefold disposition concerning interpersonality. Such pathological individuals display an unrelatedness to other persons (Group I loners), a disrelatedness (Group II lonerists), or insufficient relatedness (Group III lonelies). Hence, my typology is a triadic variation based on one theme, namely a wanted or unwanted absence of meaning/intimacy connections. For reasons of simplicity, consistency, and coherency, a unitary foundation for classifying phenomena is generally preferable to a non-unitary substratum.

Recall that the *DSM* arranges the pathological personalities into three clusters. Cluster A pertains to those aberrants who, "often appear odd or eccentric": the paranoid, schizoid, and schizotypal. Cluster B concerns those who "often appear dramatic, emotional, or erratic": the antisocial, borderline, histrionic, and narcissist. Cluster C refers to those who "often appear anxious or fearful": the avoidant, dependent, and obsessive.

It might be proposed that Cluster A has two bases, namely oddness and eccentricity, since the *DSM* appears to imply that these terms are not synonymous. The same can be said of Cluster C, where anxiety and fear appear not to be used as equivalents. In Cluster B, it is evident that the dramatic, emotional, and erratic are not considered to be equivalents, although it could be contended that, grammatically speaking, the *DSM* renders them to be synonyms.

With respect to Cluster A, the first dictionary definition of "odd" means without a corresponding mate. This meaning well fits the schizoid and schizotypal (but not the paranoid) since, in their cases, companionship is usually out of the question. While schizotypals have been known to marry, which appears to presume that they have some willingness for intimate relatedness, those who do and remain so are proportionally very few in number (p. 641).

"Odd" can also signify peculiar or strange, meaning what deviates from the usual or accepted, in which case it mirrors the first meaning of eccentric. Eccentricity, signifying standing outside of the ordinary, is highly characteristic of the schizoid and schizotypal, who do so pathologically in terms of mental and behavioral normality.

Still, what is especially atypical with regard to these two abnormals, according to the *DSM*, is their complete "detachment from social relationships" (the schizoid) and "acute discomfort in close relationships" (the schizotypal) (p. 629). I prefer to use the term "unattachment" instead of detachment of these aberrants, especially the schizoid, since this absolute social isolate, or loner, is highly unlikely to enter into relationships with others and, therefore, is seldom detached from them but remains unattached.

The paranoid is a relative social isolate of the lonerist type and, as such, wants to remain unattached to others in general but is negatively attached to a select few. Unlike the schizoid and schizotypal, the paranoid's unattachment or detachment are owing to derisive indifference or overt animosity toward others. All this is a major reason why, unlike the *DSM*, I do not assign these three pathologicals to the same aggregate.

For the sake of argument, let us grant that "odd" and "eccentric" are equivalent. Nevertheless, it may be reasonably asserted that, for instance, the exaggerated emotional expressiveness and extreme extraversion of the *DSM's* Cluster B histrionic are just as outlandishly eccentric, or odd, as, for example, are the emotional coldness and extreme introversion of its Cluster A schizoid.

Equally peculiar is the *DSM* Cluster C obsessional's preoccupation with minutiae that controls its consciousness. Nonetheless, it might be proposed that the oddness of the schizoid and schizotypal is both more conspicuous and profound than that exhibited by the other eight aberrants, including the histrionic and obsessional.

We must not overlook the reality that all individuals with personality disorders have the unenviable distinction of being "ec-centric," meaning all are deviations from the center—that is the norm, both what is ideally considered and normal statistically construed. Thus, all individuals with personality disorders are ec-centric in that they are pathologically egocentric, with Group I being the least ethically so but the most psychologically so. Hence, I look upon the schizoid and schizotypal as egocentric and "egotistic" but not "egoistic,"in the sense of being conceited. Accordingly, I have titled them as "acquisitional non-morals" instead of acquisitive (Group III) or selfishly malevolent (Group II) "immorals." Group II are the most unethical, or egoistical, and the second most psychologically self-centered. Group III are the second most unethical and the least psychologically self-centered.

I consider immorality as essentially based on egoism in the sense of greed, or selfishness, regardless whether physical, mental, or spiritual. I construe selfishness as the antithesis of spirituality, meaning morality in this context instead of the spiritual as signifying the soul or soul-like.

It appears reasonable to propose that the mental—especially emotional—distance or closeness in terms of intimate relatedness is a far more important consideration for establishing a division of personalities and their disorders than, for example, those based on oddness of appearance. Thus, schizotypals' often bizarrely atypical physical demeanor and dress are far less crucial components of their illness than is their pattern of social unattachment. I submit that their behavior and apparel are more consequences of their social and cultural isolation than causes.

What, then, is most peculiar about schizotypals is not their idiosyncracies in clothing or even their comportment and cognitive distortions but their "unease" vis-à-vis intimate interactions and above all ongoing attachments. What, therefore, accounts for their mental "dis-ease" is, first, their persistent lack of a capability, need for, interest in, and willingness to engage in matters interpersonal and, second, their resulting corresponding more or less complete immunity to emotional isolation in the form of loneliness, save perhaps existential.

Nevertheless, it must be admitted that schizotypals' ideas of reference, magical thought, unusual perceptual experiences, and paranoid ideation are eccentric in a very relevant and significant sense in terms of their pathological lonism, or social isolation. These idiosyncracies would likely be considered weirdly off center in any contemporary culture and by any normal human being (p. 645).

Yet, all schizotypals' irregular cognitive, emotive, and conative attributes are not as constitutive of their mental makeup as their lack of an ability and desire for "close encounters with their own kind." Nor do they have closeness even with other kinds of personations such as pets unless used as means to insure being left alone instead of being together with other human beings.

2. Lack of Clarity and Coherence in the *DSM* Clustering System

My second reason for differing with the *DSM*'s division is that it is not always transparent why a specific personality disturbance belongs in a given cluster. In some cases, the assignment is, in my view, simply mistaken. For example, for reasons adduced earlier, I argue that the paranoid does not belong to the same cluster, namely A, as do the schizoid and schizotypal.

Additionally, the obsessional, the avoidant, and the dependent are consigned to Cluster C, the unit for those individuals characterized by fear and anxiety. Yet, according to the *Manual*'s description of them, the obsessionals do not seem to be especially fearful or anxious individuals, certainly not to the extent dependents and avoidants clearly are. Or, if obsessionals are subject to extreme apprehensiveness, their focus is very different from that of dependents and avoidants. I will propose below that the object of the emotion not the emotion itself should more determine its cluster or group location.

Dependents' and avoidants' anxiety primarily refers to subjects and the absence of relationships, while, according to the *DSM*, obsessionals' primordially pertains to objects. I have proposed that compulsives principally externalize their dis-relatedness to subjects upon objects instead of the reverse, though these aberrants are by definition fixated upon controlling both people and things. Thus, obsessional fear is about failing to adhere to their obsessions.

I group dependents and avoidants, along with the borderlines and histrionics, together in my classification because their worries predominantly revolve about being excluded, unincluded, or being the recipients of indifference regarding relationships. None of these concerns is ascribable to the obsessionals, who, contrarily, are (di)stressed about being included in attachments. These hyper-cold lonerists mistrust intimates and scorn intimacy as a whole, especially actual contact with others. If obsessionals do deign to soil their bodies and souls in intimae, they do so reluctantly, grimly, rigidly, and possessively. Their excessive engrossment in work and their repudiation of leisure, recalcitrance, miserliness, and determination to subordinate others hugely contribute to disorders in their interpersonal relatedness. Therefore, it would be better, in my estimation, to place the obsessionals in a unit along with those who are also anti-intimacy: the antisocials, paranoids, and narcissists of my Group II.

Interestingly, the Five Factor Model of Personality (FFM) dimensional paradigm used almost exclusively in the present study lists as anxious the dependent and the avoidant of Cluster C, but not its obsessional (Costa and Widiger, 2002, p. 461). Consequently, this particular FFM view of the *DSM*, based on the latter's own diagnostic criteria regarding the obsessional, is in effect that it does not belong to Cluster C because the obsessional does not manifest any great anxiety. Furthermore, according to this FFM exegesis and mine, the *DSM* does not restrict anxiety to Cluster C but disperses it to Clusters A and B as well (ibid.).

It could be reasonably set forth that all the aberrants are characterized by disquietude concerning something or other (or nothing in particular, as is often predicated of existential dread). For instance, even the emotionless Cluster A schizoids fear losing their social cocoon and all the *DSM* Cluster C pathologicals fear intimacy itself either as to its absence (the dependent), both its absence and presence (the avoidant), or solely its presence (the obsessional).

The *DSM*'s Cluster B has indisputably a manifold and specifically, a threefold basis, since it differentiates dramatic, emotional, and erratic features. I would argue that none of these characteristics can be construed as exact synonyms for one another, albeit their meanings may at times somewhat overlap.

The *DSM* Cluster C contains the abnormals who display fear and anxiety (in some quarters, fear and dread are considered types of anxiety). The *Manual*'s taxonomy might be better served if it were it to drop the emotional component from Cluster B because all the personality disorders are intensely emotional in one fashion or another, save schizoids. Still, these non-plus-ultra social isolates, are exceedingly "emotional" about being initially or habitually left alone whenever possible despite their obligation to work amidst and even in collaboration with others to make a living.

Curiously, the *DSM* says its Cluster B members appear "emotional" as if being so were itself a component or consequence of abnormality. From my perspective, lack of emotionality in general and emotional intelligence in particular are greater signs of abnormality than, for instance, a shortage of cognition in general and intellectual intelligence specifically. As well, hypo-emotionality is frequently more indicative of a serious personality problem than hyper-, but then, it much depends on what the emotion or the complex of affects concerns. For instance, lack of emotionality apropos of making friends is plainly a far more serious personality deficiency than the absence of passion for making money—though those given to successism and materialism act otherwise.

Additionally, positive emotions can be considered the most telling signs of normality and supranormality. Sheer intellectual—in contrast to emotional, conative, and social—intelligence is not the best indicator of mental health; the first kind of acumen can be found in individuals with any of the ten deviants but not the last three or if so only in remiss respects.

Recall that in its general diagnostic criteria for a personality disorder, the *Manual* stipulates that affective shortcomings are but one of four areas in which a person may deviate from normalcy. Yet, the *DSM* proceeds to explicitly depict every abnormal personality as being significantly flawed in terms of emotionality, not just those of Cluster B. It would appear, therefore, that such deficient affect is perhaps a necessary instead of a merely possible condition for being a *DSM* abnormal.

Furthermore, distinguishing one personality disorder as not being emotional at all and another as being excessively and yet insufficiently emotional, and then placing both in the same cluster, as the *DSM* does with respect to the schizoid and schizotypal, does not seem especially logical. Schizoids are deficient in emotionality in that they display "emotional coldness, detachment, or flattened affectivity" (p. 641). While schizoids are non- or under-emotional, the *DSM* lists schizotypals as both under- and over-emotional since they manifest, respectively, "constricted affect" and "paranoid fears" (p. 645).

As just stressed, being hypo-emotional is generally a more serious defect than being hyper-emotional. Pushed to its limit, lack of emotionality is deathly, like the lower Apollonian in its extreme forms—for example, extreme obsessionals. Excess of affect, as in the lower Dionysian, may be undesirable, but it remains, considered in itself, a kind of affirmation of life, even if recklessly squandered.

Again, all the personality disorders described by the *Manual* are extremely emotional at least in some instances, save the robot-like schizoid. Lack of emotion is a defining reason why this individual is, in my estimation, the most psychologically sick of the ten deviants. If personality disorders and their aggregates are to be based on emotions or lack thereof, it might be advisable to do so on the most primary passions, namely the contraries of love and hate or their contradictories via indifference. Love, albeit the "needy" and neurotic sorts, characterizes Group III. Hatred (and dislike) of others typifies Group II. Dislike and even hatred of self characterize Group III, save the borderline, who fluctuates between hatred of others and self but is especially given to self-contempt. Apathetic indifference to others marks Group I, while derisory uninterest toward them, mainly stemming from hatred, stamps Group II.

In stating that Cluster B individuals often appear as being not only emotional but dramatic and erratic, the *Manual* is apparently forming a triple foundation for this one cluster, all of which diminishes the transparency and consistency of its typology. True, emotions can be both simultaneously dramatic and erratic. If this co-incidence is what the *DSM* wishes to convey, then it should not, I think, state that Cluster B deviants "are dramatic, emotional, *or* erratic." So stated, the *Manual*'s wording might imply that these three entities are all different phenomena instead of the dramatic and erratic being species of the emotional. Additionally, in some quarters, the erratic applies more to external behavior than to the internal emotionality that causes such lower Dionysian conduct.

The dramatic can suggest the positive emotions, such as excitement or thrill, all higher Dionysian entities, at least potentially so. Yet, the dramatic can also imply the negative, such as the melodramatic or sensational, all lower Dionysian qualities and ones in model manner predicated of the histrionic.

Contrastingly, the erratic, unlike the dramatic, is never higher Dionysian but always lower; it is capricious, inconsistent, fitful, volatile, impulsive, wayward, and unreliable. These affects also are highly ascribable to the histrionic. If these emotions become aggressive, violent, and sadistic, they are especially commonplaces among sociopaths.

The *DSM* federates the sociopath and borderline in its Cluster B because they are both extremely emotional. According to the *Manual*, the sociopath's affective cravings pertain to "profit, power, or some other material gratification" (p. 649). Of course, power need not concern only the material realm but the non-material, including the spiritual. (This mentality makes the antisocial a prototypical illustration of a SCRAM sort of personality.) Contrarily, the emotions of the borderline refer primarily to intersubjectivity and the fear of aloneness, especially that involving maximal exclusion (p. 650). Hence, the points of concern of their intense desires are exceedingly different for these two abnormals. Those of sociopaths refer to objects or the objectification of subjects via, for instance, their manipulation and exploitation of them for purposes of gaining success via power over them. The goals of the borderlines pertain to subjects to gain relationships with them.

Cluster B refers to the "erratic," but this word can suggest what is eccentric, odd, and peculiar. So interpreted, the erratic would characterize not only Cluster B but A and even C, as in the case of avoidants, who can suddenly turn from warm intimates to cold isolates, depending on whether they feel accepted or rejected.

The erratic can also signify the deviant and abnormal. This is applicable to all three of the *DSM* clusters and all ten of their personalities, since a pathological personality is a departure from the norm in any one of the five senses sketched in Chapter Four.

If the erratic is construed not so much as volatile but impulsive, then it applies to the Cluster B sociopath and borderline, since both are given to recklessly acting out their problems. However, the erratic does not as much (if at all) apply to the Cluster B narcissist and histrionic, both of which are more dramatic than erratic in their behavior.

If the erratic is understood as volatile and impulsive, then sociopaths and borderlines are markedly different as to their objects. Strictly speaking, volatility more formally pertains to the domain of emotion; impulsiveness, more to that of conation that includes impulse monitoring and conduct control.

The sociopaths' explosiveness and unpredictability arise from their extreme irritability, meaning low frustration toleration, and their lust for power, materialistic goods, and hedonistic pleasure (p. 645). Borderlines may also be involved in a power struggle with others. If they are, it is predominantly to create or continue ties with them. Still, they habitually fail in such efforts, and their attachments remain vulnerable to affective and conative instability. This trait is typical of all neurotics, such as those of Group III. The borderlines are the most neurotic of the aberrant personalities. Among all the pathologicals save Group I, borderlines are also most at risk for psychoticism.

All Group III pathologicals experience power struggles concerning intimate relationships, whereas normals generally desire to share power in relationships and usually employ peaceful means to achieve these ends. The borderlines' emotional volcanism emerges especially from their deep need and desire for intimacy, including that of nurturance and being cared for in general lest they be left alone in forsakenness and other states of maximal exclusion (p. 654). Consequently, although both the sociopath and the borderline have intense and often mercurial and evanescent emotions in addition to impulsivities, these affects, conations, and their externalizations in behavior are very dissimilar in terms of their focuses.

Sociopaths consider others stupid, naive, and bad or evil and themselves as smart, savvy, and good, or at least better than most if not all others, although some antisocials revel in their iniquity and its admission. Borderlines envision others or the same individual as all-good or split between good and evil, but themselves—not only their conduct—as largely evil. These appraisals are obvious factors why sociopaths and borderlines have disastrous relationships, including those with therapists (the first pathologicals run away from clinicians and the second run to them, although both are highly manipulative of therapists). Nonetheless, the different reasons these two deviants have such attachments warrant, in my estimation, putting them in different aggregates.

"Volatile" can signify an inclination to erupt into violence; that of sociopaths has others for its object but rarely themselves. Borderlines' violence is almost always turned toward themselves, such as in acts of self-injury or suicide. Theirs is usually more a matter of emotional aggressiveness toward others than the physical aggression and often brutal, even sadistic, violence that so often characterizes sociopathic conduct.

We have seen that dyssocials may suddenly and unexpectedly commit suicide, but their rashness is ordinarily to escape apprehension and punishment. Group III Borderlines' self-harm even suicide, is often predictable in the sense that it is a relatively frequent occurrence with these aberrants due to clinical depression.

Rebekah Bradley, Carolyn Zittel Conkline, and Drew Westen report, "between 70% and 75% of borderline PD patients have a history of at least one self-injurious act." They also inform us "that of the 6 million individuals currently estimated" to be borderlines "in the United States alone, 540,000 will [eventually] die by suicide" (2007, p. 168). In sum, sociopaths are seldom physically violent toward themselves but frequently toward others; borderlines represent the reverse.

Assigning sociopaths and borderlines to the same cluster because they are both highly emotional, regardless of their having significantly different affect-foci, does not seem to be an especially sound rationale for classifying these pathologicals, since all but the schizoid, are extremely emotional.

3. Personality Disorders as Psycho-Ethical Failures

My distinguishing the ten aberrants and their three aggregates explicitly in both mental and moral terms marks a third major departure from the *DSM*. While the *DSM* is a medical guidebook dealing with mental disorders, it is suffused with moral concepts and language, especially concerning disordered personalities. This suffusion is understandable since, though they are distinguishable as to what is deemed psychologically normal and ethically normative, these spheres are ultimately inseparable. In the end, any theory and therapy that understands the actual personality must deal with the whole person, although it may be the kind that is split, as in the case of schizoids, or the kind that splits others and themselves into good and evil, as in the case of borderlines (p. 651).

John Sadler and Bill Fulford state, "in the clinical setting, normal and normative usually refer to prescriptions about [mental] health." They append, "in mental health, normal and normative may also imply prescriptions" (2006, pp. 172–173) concerning ethics. Insofar as the psychological is understood as embracing all that occurs in the mind, the moral is also a psychic phenomenon. For example, the mendacity of the sociopath is a mental quality, but one specifically immoral in composition.

On the other hand, all that is psychic is not moral. The shyness of the avoidant is not formally a moral but solely a mental trait, although it can become an ethical quality. Thus, shyness may cause the avoidant to shy away from duties to self or others.

Of course, the *DSM* is not in the business of rendering formal moral judgments about psychologically disordered individuals lest it disintegrate into a kind of judgmental posture. Hence, my third variation from the *DSM* should not be construed as a criticism of its clustering system for being purely a classification of psychic phenomena.

The *DSM* makes no apparent attempt to list its three clusters in terms of their psychopathological gravity, especially the moral aspect of it, or as to the specific aberrants within any of the units. I speculate that one reason why it could not do so even if it so wished is that the *Manual* has so many foundations among and arguably within its clusters. Contrastingly, my groupings are listed among and within themselves according to their psycho-ethical deficiencies, principally with respect to one basis: interpersonal shortcomings.

Accordingly, and almost exclusively in light of the *DSM*'s own diagnostic criteria, Group I are the most disturbed followed by those of Groups II and III and within each grouping the first mentioned is the most aberrated taken as a combination of mental and moral traits. Thus, in Group I, the schizoid is a more disturbed personality than the schizotypal since, among other things, the first's seeming incapability for intimacy is even more profound than the second's. Yet, insofar as the schizoid is reckoned to be further from psychosis than the schizotypal, the first may be envisioned as being less purely psychologically ill than the second, not only from the vantage point of a mental trait, but from a mental state one.

As to Group II, the sociopath is the most disturbed psychologically and ethically followed by the paranoid, narcissist, and obsessional. The sociopaths are the most ill of all ten personality deviants from a purely ethical perspective in that they are the most inhumane of them, often viciously so. The next most morally aberrant are the paranoids, though they are more psychologically diseased than the sociopath, especially if the first are placed on the schizophrenic spectrum. If we are to create an immorality spectrum for all the mentally disordered, both trait and state, then inarguably antisocials would lead the list.

All told, psychologically and ethically, sociopaths are, therefore, the most pathological of personalities, including the paranoid. Dyssocials are the most ill in prominent part because they are the greatest threat to the well-being and often to the very being of other persons. Therefore, sociopaths are the most anti-(inter)personality of the deviates. In terms of an abnormal mental/moral tandem, I have, therefore, relegated the sociopaths to first place and the paranoids to second, among not only Group II but all the pathological personalities and, therefore, all individuals.

In preceding chapters, the ethical shortcomings of not only the sociopath and paranoid but the narcissist and obsessional of Group II were discussed. Less attention was given to the Group I moral failures because, in my view, the schizoid and schizotypal are essentially nonmoral instead of immoral personalities, in great part because they are highly genetically influenced and possibly necessitated; consequently, they have at most minimal freedom, arguably a necessary condition for (im)morality.

Additionally, the schizoid and schizotypal are the ultimate loners, which means that they do not interact, or rarely so, socially. Therefore, these abnormals do not directly and volitionally commit acts against justice and other predominantly social virtues. Still, insofar as Group I aberrants are compelled to be amidst others for purposes of gaining a livelihood, they may be obliged to interact and doing so raises questions concerning what is owed them. Moreover, these pathologicals cannot be counted on, especially for acts of justice or other positive social behavior that contribute to the common good. As a result, schizoids and schizotypals may be guilty of injustice above all via omission.

All the traditional cardinal virtues, to wit justice, courage, temperance, and prudence and their contraries, or vices, are at least indirectly social in nature since all (in)actions at minimum obliquely affect others. Also, each vice and virtue affect every other virtue and vice at least indirectly; for instance, lack of courage affects justice and vice versa. Thus, habitual drug abuse is often regarded as a purely private vice opposed to temperance. Nonetheless, this addiction, like most if not all others, has vast negative repercussions not only for the abuser but the addict's family, friends, associates, and society as a whole.

Social atomists by definition like to think and act as if each person were a totally separate and complete world unto itself. The truth of the matter is that the world of the individual person is embedded in a co-personal social and moral world even if the individual is a recluse or hermit.

With reference to Group III, especially in terms of some of their more salient moral deficiencies, the borderline is the most disordered ethically (and psychologically) of them followed by the histrionic and either the dependent or avoidant. (Notwithstanding this claim, I would argue that the histrionic is the least mentally ill of all the pathologicals, if indeed this personality should be considered gravely aberrant at all, although it is morally disturbed, yet perhaps least so of the all abnormals save Group I abnormals.)

Concerning the borderlines' specific ethical shortcomings, their tendency to believe that they are bad even evil is opposed to the kind of love of self that human beings owe themselves in terms, for instance, of natural self-worth in contrast to acquired.

Lack of proper self-regard is also antithetical to the virtue of temperance and specifically humility, the characterological trait that avoids both excessive and deficient self-value. Also, borderlines' inappropriate anger, often of the enraged sort, is contrary to temperance and may lead to aggression, such as physical fighting and verbal abuse, conduct indicative of a lack justice and prudence (pp. 650–651). Borderlines' self-destructive behavior, such as reckless spending or sex, and their propensities toward self-injury bespeak failures in all four of the primary virtues (ibid., p. 650).

Like the other nine disordered personalities, borderlines most significantly lack the supra-virtue of love. However, they revere and repudiate love quasi simultaneously both with respect to a general affective mentality and as directed to the same individual (p. 654).

Histrionics also display shortcomings in the four central components of moral rectitude. Like borderlines and their fellow Group III deviants, histrionics exhibit insufficient self-worth as evidenced in their habitual demands for reassurance, praise, and other kinds of acceptance and attention. Their inappropriate and alleged superficial and ephemeral emotionality in addition to their penchant for phony communications suggest a lack of truthfulness, a virtue that is a species of justice. Their seductiveness and fixation on physical and sexual attractiveness manifest a lack of temperance. Their inability to withstand frustration and delayed satisfaction in the sense of gratification displays a deficiency of temperance and courage, especially in terms of patience (pp. 655–656).

Like the borderline, the histrionic demonstrates the kind of extreme self-centeredness characteristic of the sort of acquisitive motivational pattern that perpetually ignores the welfare of others. Such egotism represents drawbacks in temperance—specifically humility's moderation of self-worth—justice, and the practical wisdom of prudence if only because such inordinate self-interest causes others to react negatively to the histrionic who desperately craves their attention.

Dependents by definition fail in taking control of their lives. Their lack of responsibility and mindless and spineless conformity to others, largely out of fear of being alone and specifically lonely, implies a gross shortage of courage (pp. 665–666). Dependents, as their name suggests, and Group III pathologicals as a whole are liable to engage in acts contrary to temperance such as those involved in addictions.

Avoidants fail in fortitude because these paradigmatically shy and socially anxious individuals cannot adequately cope with being criticized by others so much so that they remain alone and separate in a pseudo-autonomy (pp. 662–663). Therefore, both the dependent and avoidant lack the moral mettle to take even reasonable risks regarding relatedness to others either by, respectively, not leaving or not staying with them when it is ethically responsible to do so. Both aberrants also fail vis-à-vis prudence since dependents indiscriminately attach themselves to others due to fear of losing their nurturers. Avoidants indiscriminately detach themselves from others due to their largely unfounded, at least initially, irrational fears of being rebuked and ultimately forsaken.

Dependents and avoidants do not deliberately ignore the needs of others, as do the borderline and histrionic. Still, they are so neurotically wrapped up in their need to be loved and other forms of intimacy that they tend to be culpably unmindful of others' welfare. All Group III personalities are consumed by the desire to be loved especially in an idolized fashion. This craving renders them extremely vulnerable to loneliness, and one of the pathological brand, but it also makes them less psycho-ethical than the non-loving Group I and anti-loving Group II abnormals.

In sum, all the deviants err by excess or defect relative to the above core virtues not to mention their more or less purely psychological failures. In addition to being remiss with reference to the supra-virtue of love of others, they lack a proper love of themselves. They do so by under-loving (Group III), overly (Group II), or by neither loving nor disloving themselves such that they appear to be lethargically indifferent to their own well-being, if such is possible (Group I).

Still, all human beings, even abnormals such as schizoids and schizotypals, have a kind of innate, or natural, love for themselves in that they wish for themselves what they perceive as being to their benefit, not the least of which is their own survival, obviously the indispensable condition for being further benefitted at all. Nevertheless, abnormals lack an acquired kind of genuine love of self, as exhibited in that achieved through a kind of virtuous self-worth.

In general, Group I neither like nor dislike themselves or others, though to some extent they, especially schizotypals, fear their fellow human beings. Being afraid of others can be an effect or cause of dislike of them.

Group II dislike and even hate others but tend to exorbitantly to like and love themselves in that they are all extremely egoistic. Only narcissists can be said to fall in love with themselves. Yet self-disapproval may temporarily cause them to fall out of such specious self-love but only with their actual but not idolized selves. Rather paradoxically, of these four pathologically self-absorbed Group II abnormals, only narcissists have a penchant for both inordinately approving and disapproving themselves on a conscious level.

Group III are ambivalent, especially the borderlines, regarding others in terms of liking/loving and disliking/hating them. Concerning themselves, they are highly prone to dislike and even hate themselves.

Consequently, the aberrated personalities are failures at interpersonality whose heart is intimacy, of which love is its "heart of hearts." Hence, pathologicals are sick in the heart, a disease that is both psychological and ethical in nature. Accordingly, these pathologicals are non-hearted, or largely affectless (Group I); heartless in the sense of hard- (bitter-)hearted (Group II); and soft- (weak-)hearted and "sick at" or "in the heart," especially in the sense of being "lonely hearts" and lovelorn (Group III).

So understood, the more undisposed (Group I), anti-disposed (Group II), and pro-disposed but inadequately due largely to neurotic features (Group III) is the person with respect to heartfelt connections, the more disordered the individual is.

The pathological personalities come up seriously short relative to the FFM supertrait of Humaneness and its six traits. These aberrants are remiss in these traits with reference to the traditional cardinal virtues of justice, such as straightforwardness in the form of truthfulness and sincerity (for example, the sociopath by defect) in addition to cooperativeness (for example, the paranoid by defect and the schizoid by excess); its courage such as achievement striving (for example, the narcissist by excess and the dependent by defect); and temperance, such as humility (for instance, all Group II by excess and all Group III by defect). The pathological also fail in terms of prudence, such as by the supertrait of Conscientiousness in terms of its trait of deliberation (for example, the obsessional by excess and the borderline by defect) (Costa and Widiger, 1994, p. 329; 2002, pp. 461–467).

Group I are morally remiss by not performing good actions but mainly by not acting at all due to their extreme social isolation such that I have variously referenced them as being non-social, non-humane, and non-moral. At minimum, the schizoid and schizotypal are profoundly devoid of not only love but justice, the two greatest types of moral excellence.

Group II fail ethically by commission of actions directly opposed to Humaneness such that they are grossly inhumane, including being the most antipathetic, anti-altruistic, conceited, and callous of the abnormals. They are also highly inclined to enmity and envy, vices that are directly inimical to both love and justice. Consequently, their shortcomings in Humaneness render the sociopath, paranoid, narcissist, and obsessional not only bitter-hearted but mean and small-hearted. Thus, instead of being magnanimous and great-hearted, virtues that include courage and generosity, they are pusillanimous. This mini-soulness is evidenced, for instance, in the obsessional's pettiness, fastidious scrupulosity, niggardliness, and indecisiveness.

Group III often fail by commission, though not as grievously as do Group II, for the first are not habitually malevolent like the second. Group III are also highly deficient characterologically by omission, as noted in the case of the avoidant. Still, these abnormals, especially the dependent, strive to love, though it is the kind based on a preceding and dominant desire to be loved.

For all their ethical drawbacks, Group III may be said at least to "have a heart" and one that is in the right place in that it concerns a strong wish to be intimate with others. As well, they all manifest some degree of both tender- and big-heartedness, especially the dependent. Their neurotic and needy kind of love may not "cover a multitude" of sins—meaning their bad and sometimes evil (in)actions—but Group III are, as an aggregate, far less ethically sick than the apathetic and non-loving Group I and the antipathetic (uncompassionate), unempathic, and anti-loving Group II abnormals.

4. Personality Disorders and Gender

A fourth reason for my diverging from the *DSM* taxonomy is that, unlike it, mine reflects consistent gender uniformities, ones based on the very figures published in the *DSM.* These numbers indicate that Groups I and II are more male dominated and Group III more female (pp. 631–632, 636, 639, 643, 647–648, 652, 656, 660, 663, 667, 671). Though the *Manual*'s numerical variations in terms of gender are sometimes slight, nonetheless, the differences are significant vis-à-vis the gravity of their disturbances and the grounds for classifying the aberrants in the fashion I do.

The *Manual* makes no mention of gender as being a factor in its rationale for its taxonomical system. Nevertheless, it notes that some personality aberrations are more of one gender than the other. The *DSM* does issue a caution concerning over or under-diagnosing personality disorders due to "social stereotypes about typical gender roles and behaviors" (pp. 631–632).

It is hardly news that the non-attached and detached independent personality styles have traditionally been more associated with men and that the attached and dependent ones have been more ascribed to women. Consequently, it will not be startling to learn that women have a higher incidence in the aggregate that emphasizes dependence (homonomy), namely Group III, and that men more frequently populate those units that stress independence (autonomy), namely Groups I and II.

In other words, males are more common among those abnormals characterized by social and often physical but not emotional isolation, namely the total social isolates (loners) of Group I, and the partial social isolates, the intimacy-scorning lonerists of Group II. Alternatively, females are far more prevalent in the intimacy-starved lonelies of Group III. Correspondingly, they are less found in the non-intimacy and anti-intimacy of, respectively, Groups I and II.

As detailed in Volume One, women appear to be more interested in interpersonal relationships than men and, therefore, are more negatively affected by the absence of such connections. Consequently, it is often claimed that women are more lonely than men, at least on a conscious level, but that they are more able to deal with this affliction and its effects than men.

As just recorded, women are more prevalent among Group III, the aggregate in which consciousness of intimacy and its absence in loneliness abounds. Men are slightly more rampant among Group I wherein loneliness is virtually nonexistent, save possibly existential. They are far more common than women among Group II wherein loneliness less occurs or at least is more apt to be denied via mechanisms such as suppression and repression.

To illustrate these gender differences, we can refer to the schizoids, who are "diagnosed slightly more often in males and may cause more impairment in them" than in females (p. 639). The schizoids of Group I are, as absolute loners, exceedingly withdrawn and unattached individuals.

Group II are customarily anti-intimacy and routinely demonstrate extreme detachment from others, though not to the extent that the Group I manifest unattachment. Group II, as a rule, have had multiple connections. Yet, theirs ordinarily end in disrelationships typically traceable to their hostility, uncooperativeness, and general incompatibility.

Note that my term "anti-intimacy" does not mean refraining from engaging in intimate behavior. Instead, it signifies that, while anti-intimates may participate in close affiliations, they do not possess the requisite qualities necessary for genuine intimacy, such as benevolence, respect, and empathy. These traits can exist—perhaps solely theoretically independently of one another—in terms of simple interactions but not, as a rule, with reference to ongoing relationships. For example, sociopaths are inclined to be highly hedonistic and promiscuous. Accordingly, they have a propensity to indulge themselves in numerous erotic liaisons often simultaneously and do so impulsively or schemingly. But in whichever case, doing so hardly indicates that sociopaths are intimately related to others in a positive sense but only that they seek sexual and genital pleasure solely for selfish motives.

When women are unrelated or dis-related to intimacy, as is, respectively, the situation with the individuals of Groups I and II, it is thought to be a more abnormal departure for them than it is for men apparently regardless of the culture in question. Intimacy, taken in its entirety, is ordinarily judged more ascribable to women than men and is deemed to be so by both genders. Undoubtedly, this ascription is greatly tied to the reality of motherhood, which, in many respects, is the most elemental and enduring of all intimate unions.

Women are also more prone to experience not only loneliness on a conscious basis than men, but lonely depression as well. Likewise and in conformity with the numbers given by the *DSM*, the pathologicals of Group III, the unit in which women predominate, are more likely to be subject to clinical depression than are Groups I and II, the aggregates in which men are more prevalent. These gender variations with respect to loneliness and lonely depression are, then, further grounds for my grouping the aberrant personalities as I do.

Those pathologicals most at risk regarding serious loneliness, namely Group III, especially the borderline, are also those most susceptible to bulimia and anorexia, two disorders that are highly associated with emotional isolation and depression. William Reid and Michael Wise report that at least 90 percent of those afflicted by these food disorders are women (1995, pp. 247–248).

The overweight and especially the obese are highly subject to exclusion and non-inclusion and to many forms of loneliness, especially, erotic, cultural, and social. The poor—who, because of their socio-economic plight, tend to be more lonely than other such groups—also tend to suffer more than other such aggregates from weight and overall health problems, all of which makes them highly susceptible to emotional isolation.

Theodore Millon, Roger Davis, Carrie Millon, Luis Escovar, and Sarah Meagher report that these four disturbed personalities—what are in fact my Group III aberrants—all have depressive and other negative qualities. These attributes typify serious loneliness which, in my view, is a defining facet in the personality structure and style of Group III. These researchers also contend that, as a general rule, "any personality pattern which [excessively] makes others the center of life," meaning one with a dependent personality style or structure, is vulnerable to developing a borderline personality (ibid.). I have stressed that all Group III aberrants are basically negatively dependent types and, therefore, not only the dependent disordered personality as such.

Millon and colleagues state that the wish to "magically fuse with others who will support you emotionally and meet your every need"—all of which epitomizes the negatively homonomous Group III aberrants and not only the borderline—"is evidence both of ego weakness and identity disturbance." They append that identity problems generate, for the *DSM* borderline, "instability in interpersonal relationships and feelings of emptiness and desperation" (ibid.). We have seen that such feelings are characteristic of loneliness which, in turn, typifies the borderline and the other Group III pathologicals who, as just noted, tend to be more female in number than male.

In positions that implicitly support my rationale for classifying the abnormals, at least as to Group III, Millon and colleagues maintain that, first, "most subjects diagnosed as borderline are female by a ratio of 2 to 1 or even higher." Second, the borderline shares features with the histrionic, dependent, and avoidant, the very aberrants who comprise my Group III (2000, p. 417).

Millon and colleagues state that a borderline kind of diagnosis is less common among males and the sadistic types—who, among the pathological personalities, are, in my view, sociopaths—paranoids, "some narcissistic personalities," and compulsives, all of whom belong to my Group II and tend to be men (ibid., pp. 417–418). These authors can be understood as implicitly supporting my taxonomy regarding the eight Group II and III aberrants and at least by default and implication the Group I schizoid and schizotypal.

In my estimation, SCRAM is especially adept at promoting and proliferating those personality disturbances wherein men have a greater prevalence, above all Group II. The negative independence of Group II also generates its antithesis in the negative dependence of Group III wherein women are more rampant. Unfortunately, Group III, with their desperate and often indiscriminate longing for fusion with others, can be rather easily victimized by Group II, especially by the psychopath and narcissist. These two people-predators are forever on the lookout for just those individuals easily coerced or manipulatively coaxed to serve as means to attain their selfish ends.

This is not the place to discuss the question of the possibility of the preeminence of one gender over the other in terms of autonomy and homonomy. However, I think it is useful to state now that what is ordinarily advised is for women and men to help one another bring out the best in themselves in terms of their unique person central to which is their gender. Men generally concede that women outrank them in terms of sustaining positive attachments, such as the parental and other forms of shared inwardness, in addition to inward sharing, as in the erotic with its romantic, sexual, and genital intimacy.

Even friendship love, which traditionally has been adjudged by men as their special bastion of bonding, is now often reckoned to be more predominant among women than men in the United States. Female friendships, as documented in the first volume, are presently considered longer, stronger, and more numerous than those of males such that even adult men's best friends are often women while theirs are usually other women.

The gender question is allied to personality orientations, of which the androgynous type is usually held to be the most (supra)normal from a psychoethical ideal. According to Carole Rayburn, this orientation displays both high masculinity and high femininity. She stipulates that the purely male orientation exhibits high masculinity and low femininity; the purely female, high femininity and low masculinity; and the undifferentiated type evinces low masculinity and low femininity (1986, p. 33).

Arguably, high femininity insofar as it accentuates positive homonomy (constructive dependence) is more in accord with the social nature of human beings than is high masculinity with its positive autonomy (constructive independence). In any case, the androgynous individual blends superior individuality with superior socialness in the sense of communality.

The undifferentiated type of personality orientation is especially characteristic of Group I, above all the schizoid. The purely male sort typifies Group II, preeminently the male sociopath. The purely female reflects Group III, predominantly the female dependent. In actuality, there are no pure types of personality but only hybrids. Regarding personality-disordered pure types, Michael Stone defines them as those who, for instance, display "only the traits described in each of the ten *DSM*" categories of abnormals (2006, p. 79).

Since it bespeaks supranormality, no abnormal personality is close to attaining the androgynous personality orientation, although, everything considered, those of Group III are the least far and Group I the most from doing so. None of these personality orientation issues figures, at least not in any discernably explicit fashion, into the *DSM*'s rationale for its clustering system.

5. Personality Disorders: Syntonicity and Dystonicity

My fifth reason for dividing the personality pathologies as I do and for departing from their *DSM* typology is that, unlike it, mine explicitly takes into account one of the *Manual*'s own general criteria for a personality disorder, namely distress with respect to personality traits. This agitation and dissatisfaction with reference to such qualities involve syntonicity and non-syntonicity plus dystonicity and non-dystonicity.

Non-syntonic and non-dystonic traits can be construed as being, respectively, neither pleasurable nor painful and, hence, are neither wanted nor unwanted. A painless trait is not ipso facto pleasurable nor is a pleasureless one automatically painful such that the absence of one would necessitate the presence of the other. Since non-syntonic and non-dystonic qualities are neutral in nature, their possessors may likely be unaware of them or even if they are, the individuals may be largely and possibly solely indifferent to altering them.

Contrariwise, syntonic traits cause their possessors pleasure, whereupon they are disinclined to alter them. Dystonic qualities are painful and, accordingly, their possessors would like to change them unless, for instance, doing so would cause even more painfulness. It bears stressing that syntonicity does not mean that such subjectively pleasurable traits necessarily cause or are to be equated with putatively objective standards of pleasure let alone the joy of happiness. Frequently, pain is predicated of the corporeal and suffering of the mental (and spiritual). Herein they have been used synonymously and will remain so.

No human being with a personality abnormality—even if its traits are syntonic—is a truly happy individual, meaning joyous and serene, traits that paradigmatically stem from love. All individuals with personality disturbances evince variations in lovelessness, meaning they are unloving and, therefore, unlovable by others in general. Yet, they in fact may be loved in some relationships, perhaps especially those that are biologically based. For example, sociopaths are loveless individuals but their family members may, nevertheless, love them and clearly do so unconditionally. On the other hand, the lack of sibling and above all parental love may contribute to, trigger, and, according to some researchers and clinicians, even cause sociopathy.

Whereas all the abnormals represent various gradations of egocentricity, love requires being altero-centered. Other-centeredness parallels having a valued center to the self, meaning a genuine love of self. Pathological personalities have no such proper self-worth since they have virtually no self-regard (Group I), excessive (Group II), or deficient (Group III).

A strong though not a sure sign of the presence of a personality problem is the inability to alter these qualities, due, for instance, to the absence of self-insight or the unwillingness of people to perceive their having negative traits. Aberrated personality attributes ordinarily meet stiff internal opposition to being transformed. They do so because they are consistent with people's abstract self-concept or concrete self-image and their overall sense of self-identity however unreflexive or prereflexive it might be, all of which is especially the case with Group I. Normals also have difficulty changing qualities they find dystonic or impairing but they have greater ability and facility in altering them. Moreover, their qualities are by definition less onerous and painful than those of abnormals.

As to their syntonicity or lack thereof, I have grouped the abnormals according to the *DSM*'s own diagnostic criteria vis-à-vis the pleasure and pain caused them by reason of their traits and, accordingly, the interest and willingness of these individuals to change them. Group I are non-syntonic and non-dystonic (the schizoid) in addition to at times being highly dystonic (the schizotypal); Group II traits are syntonic; and Group III are dystonic.

More specifically, Group I schizoids, in that their traits are not felt as especially pleasurable or displeasurable, can be characterized as being neutral in quality due mainly to what the *DSM* references as their emotional coldness and flattened affect. As well, since they are loners, schizoids do not need to or, in any case, feel like altering their qualities to meet the desires of others.

The *DSM* holds that schizotypals primary diagnostic feature is acute discomfort with close relationships, in which case their most basic attribute is dystonic. Their anxiety is apparently not connected with being lonely in the presence or absence of others but with their inability to be alone and safe from criticism and other forms of intrusion. The *Manual* further stipulates that schizotypals often seek treatment not so much for their personality disorder features per se but for "associated symptoms of anxiety, depression, or other dysphoric affects" (p. 642).

The *DSM* says that schizotypals are characterized by restricted affect. This statement could be taken to mean a kind of affective neutrality on the part of these aberrants. Yet, the *Manual* further claims, "from 30% to 50%" of those diagnosed as being schizotypals "have a concurrent diagnosis of Major Depressive Disorder [MDD] when admitted to a clinical setting" (ibid.).

As an extremely debilitating mood disorder, the MDD entails unrestricted negative affect in the sense that it is both emotionally widespread in its sufferer and affectively piercing instead of blunt. Nonetheless, an individual with this mental state disorder may at times experience total emotional apathy and aridity.

What the *DSM* appears to mean by "being restricted" with respect to the schizotypal is that this aberrant is "usually not able to negotiate the full range of affects and interpersonal cuing required for successful relationships." Whereupon, the *Manual* states that the schizotypal "often appears to interact with others in an inappropriate, stiff, or constricted fashion" (ibid.). Thus, the *Manual* is apparently claiming not so much that the schizotypal has a restricted range of emotions but that this individual's manner of expressing them is constrained and often rigidly so.

The above issues are further complicated by the fact it is unclear whether the *DSM* contends that the schizotypal has but "a decreased desire for intimate contacts," or has no desire whatsoever since this aberrant may have no capability or felt need for such contacts to begin with (ibid.).

If the Group I schizotypal has a desire, decreased or not, for relatedness, and it goes unsatisfied, then it is dystonic. No desire at all would be a matter of non-dsytonicity. In saying "reduced desire," it is not evident with whom the *DSM* is comparing the schizotypal's desire. Is the comparison with normals or other abnormals and specifically the schizoid? At any rate, unlike the schizotypal, the schizoid can be reckoned as having little if any dystonic diagnostic attributes.

The schizotypal essentially has dystonic qualities, but much depends on how this individual is to be construed in terms of its need, capability, ability to actualize this potentiality, desire, and willingness for intimacy. If this individual's traits are deemed extremely painful, then the schizotypal is like the Group III deviants, especially the avoidant. If they are reckoned non-painful, the schizotypal more resembles Group II abnormals. Still, the schizotypal is most of all like the schizoid in that both their traits result in behavior that is abnormal in a prescriptive (qualitative and ideal) and descriptive (quantitative and statistical) sense, above all with reference to interpersonal relatedness.

The *Manual* groups in Cluster A the paranoid (whose traits are syntonic), the schizoid (whose traits are neither syntonic nor dystonic), and the schizotypal (whose features are also essentially non-dystonic and non-syntonic but often dystonic, depending on how this aberrant's traits are construed in terms of intimate relatedness). Arguably, when schizotypals are by themselves, their attributes are non-syntonic and non-dystonic. When they are with others, especially when involuntarily so, their qualities are dystonic.

Unlike the apathetic schizoids, who appear to neither approve nor disapprove of their traits, paranoids' affirmation of their attributes is arrogant. Correspondingly, they are convinced, at least on a conscious level, that they have no negative qualities. This conceit is a trait paranoids have in common with sociopaths and, to a lesser yet still significant extent, narcissists and obsessionals. All four of these aberrants experience their qualities as syntonic in various degrees.

The mistrustful schizotypals may suspect others' motives but they do not find it pleasurable, much less maliciously so, to think in this fashion. Contrariwise, the exceedingly suspicious and ill-willed paranoids actually revel in doing so at some level. The reason for this extreme satisfaction is owing to their conceited but erroneous conviction that others are centering their consciousness on them. They act in this manner because they erroneously believe that they are so singularly important that others are envious or jealous of them and, as a result, are bent on attacking them in some fashion. The truth of the matter is otherwise: paranoids are highly jealous and envious individuals. People, including other abnormal personalities, dislike such qualities and, hence, avoid paranoids and try to give little thought to them.

Naturally, being so consumed with self-importance and yet so afraid of its being challenged, implies, on the part of paranoids, a lack of trust in themselves and their own stature. This status can be objectively high given their FFM Conscientiousness in terms of the trait of competence. Moreover, paranoids sometimes display aggressiveness beyond mere assertiveness and, in any event, ambitiousness beyond the reasonable wish for recognition of accomplishment (Costa and Widiger, 1994, p. 329). All these negative qualities make paranoids a firm fit for SCRAM's roster of personality types that it more or less directly brings forth and cultivates, namely those of Group II.

Some subtypes of the narcissist and obsessional personalities can be negatively critical of themselves but they generally approve of their traits however reluctantly at times. Correspondingly, Group II disapprove of others' traits, unless but often even if they somehow serve the formers' selfish interests. Yet, compulsives can act as if they approve of those individuals whom they judge as being relatively superior to them. Consequently, these deviants behave slavishly submissively and obsequiously toward their perceived betters, whereas those whom they reckon inferior, they treat with disdain.

Additionally, in Cluster B, the *DSM* unites the sociopath and narcissist, whose traits are syntonic, with the borderline and histrionic, whose traits are dystonic. As to Cluster C, it links the obsessional, whose traits are largely syntonic, with the avoidant and dependent, whose traits are dystonic. In being syntonic, the Axis II mental trait obsessive-compulsive personality disorder is not to be confused with the Axis I mental state disorder of obsessive-compulsiveness. In the second case, these individuals feel their traits as extremely dystonic. Most and, in some views, all Axis I disorders are fundamentally dystonic—or at most non-dystonic instead of syntonic.

People with obsessive-compulsive personalities are too critical of others and of themselves to be happy notwithstanding the syntonicity of their traits, at least some of them. Obsessionals perfectly exemplify those who believe they would be perfect if it were not for reality, namely others and the world as a whole, all of which reflects their egological solipsism.

Hence, Group II are not interested in self-change, since their attributes are congruent with their selfish desires and arrogant self-concepts and images, and, therefore, their attributes are ego-syntonic. Or, at least, the supposed "symptoms" of abnormality of Group II are not usually painful to them on a conscious level.

Given their conceitedness, the antisocial, paranoid, narcissist, and, to a far lesser extent, the obsessional are interested not in changing themselves but only in changing others to get them to conform to their egoistical interests. For this reason alone, Group II make very poor partners of any intimate sort since a good relationship requires the ability and desire for self-change if necessary and it invariably does, given that all human beings are cognitively, emotionally, and conatively flawed and bring these defects into their relationships. If such shortcomings are those that involve personality disorders, then such attachments are precluded or at minimum most precarious from the beginning.

Group III experience their qualities as painful and problematic on a conscious level. Hence, they wish to eliminate or transform their traits, arguably especially those that render them extremely vulnerable to (a)loneliness. Why would they not want to alter their qualities since the loneliness that suffuses them is comprised of exceedingly painful negative self-attributions? Such negative self-ascriptions and affects also repel and alienate others, making relatedness to the pathologically lonely Group III incredibly trying.

Group I, like all pathologicals, lack insight into their problems, but it is not caused by their self-conceit as is mainly the case of Group II, whose dearth of self-understanding and humility reinforce one another. Group III, as a totality, have more self-discernment and less hubris than, respectively, Groups I and II. Consequently, they stand a greater likelihood to ameliorate their negative traits, though they rather infrequently are able to sufficiently get beyond them and their dystonicity. The more a *DSM* trait is essential (primary), especially insofar as it is a genetic given, and the more numerous are the associate (secondary) traits of a personality, clearly the more difficult it is to transform them.

To the extent that Group III are neurotic and insofar as Neuroticism is sometimes thought to be a masochistic kind of pleasure, these four abnormals' traits may be said to have a kind of syntonicity. Such considerations depend on to what degree personality traits, especially those deemed abnormal, are voluntary and volitional. Neurotics can be innately predisposed to pessimism, in which case they can act in gloomy fashion and do so voluntarily though not volitionally, or freely, unless they choose to alter their glumness and other dystonic traits. It bears underlining that people, including normals, are often ambivalent about their qualities in that they are not always sure they are pluses or minuses.

In sum, and in contrast to those of the *DSM*, my three aggregates consistently reflect the distinctions regarding seriously (di)stressful attributes that the *Manual* holds are, along with significant functional impairment, the customary part of the personality package of abnormals. Those with personality aberrations whose objectively negative attributes, like hard-heartedness, cause them no (di)stress are patently more disturbed than those with personality abnormalities whose traits cause them psychic distress and displeasure. Nonetheless, the non-syntonic and non-dystonic schizoid or the non-dystonic, non-syntonic, and dystonic schizotypal of Group I are the most pathological personalities from a purely psychological perspective, for reasons stipulated above.

Consequently, the non-dystonics or mainly so (Group I) and the syntonics (Groups II) are, according to the above rationale, more mentally disturbed as a totality and as such are less amenable to therapy—and especially to self-therapy—than the dystonics of Group III. The more severely psychopathological are the traits, the less open to they are to successful therapeutic change. Aggregating the abnormals according to their candidacy for alterotherapy and autotherapy also adds to the coherence of their classification.

It is fitting to insert here the notion of criticality in terms of the pathological personalities and their groupings. Abnormals can be, first, neither critical nor uncritical regarding themselves and their traits since they are experienced as being non-dystonic or non-syntonic (Group I). These two aberrants are similarly disposed to others, although the schizotypal can be somewhat critical of self and others.

Second, pathologicals can be negatively uncritical of themselves and their traits, since they are syntonically felt, while they are concurrently hyper-critical of others and their qualities (Group II). Yet, obsessionals and, to a lesser extent, narcissists can be self-critical. However, the first fault themselves for not having attained self-perfection, whereas the second do so because they believe they have fallen from it.

Third, aberrants can be negatively critical of others and their attributes—yet sometimes highly and unreasonably laudatory of them as well, like the borderline and dependent—but are mainly hyper-critical of their own qualities and selves (Group III).

6. Conflict with Self or Others

The distinctions pertaining to syntonicity and criticality are linked to those concerning conflict with others and with self, and they constitute my sixth rationale for diverging from the *DSM* division. Group I are conflicted neither with themselves nor with others, although the schizotypal, unlike the schizoid, has some minimal inclination for both such clashes. Group II are extremely conflicted with others but little if at all with themselves. Group III are exceedingly conflicted with themselves but far less with others, except the borderline who can instantaneously vacillate between antagonism and acquiescence regarding them.

Both conflict with others and self-conflict can be positive or negative insofar as they respectively involve, for example, constructive or destructive criticism. The aberrants who have constant dissensions with others are negative because they undermine or even preclude normal relatedness to them. Those who experience self-conflict, namely Group III, have the most potential for normality since such an inner battle can lead to insight into the criteria for sound and sustained affiliation with others.

The chief danger for Group III is that their self-conflict can turn into or stem from the various forms of self-hatred described by Karen Horney, such as those of self-contempt and self-torment (1991, pp. 110–154). Such self-disgust and self-torture are obviously allied to Group III self-worthlessness, which can be both an effect and cause of their pathological loneliness.

Group I's largely non-conflictedness with others emanates from their indifference to the former except when the social isolation of the schizoid and schizotypal is imperiled. Non-conflict with themselves arises from Group I's absence of tension between their actual self and ideal self because they have no such exemplary self to speak of. These deviants, especially the schizoid, have neither inflated nor deflated views of themselves or others, which is due to their lack of self-conflict and to their lack of self and other criticism.

Individuals with Group II anomalies have inflated views of themselves and deflated ones of others. Group III have deflated views of themselves and inflated ones of others, with the exception of borderlines. Although their self-appraisal remains negative, borderlines waver between extreme over- and under-evaluations of others. This ambivalence re-merits their particular appellation of being betwixt and between various mental illnesses (originally neuroticism and psychoticism). Of all the pathologicals, the borderlines are the most conflicted with themselves and others.

If peril to others is considered due to an aberrant's hostility toward them, then the Group II lonerist tops the list of the ten abnormals. The Group III lonelies rank second, while the Group I absolute loners come in last.

If danger to self is the primary criterion for ranking disturbed personalities, then they can be ranked as follows: Group III, II, and I. Concerning grading the aberrants most dangerous to themselves within their own unit, the Group III dependent, for instance, vis-à-vis the avoidant, is a far more involved undertaking than doing so in terms of their particular aggregate's danger to others, such as that of the Group III histrionic in comparison to that of the Group II sociopath. One reason for this greater complexity is that danger to self in terms of self-injury and suicidal tendencies is largely contingent upon the extent to which a given abnormal is prone to depression and perhaps, above all, lonely depression. Danger and hostility to self, I believe, are very important factors in ascertaining the kind and depth of a personality disorder. Such perils in terms of the ten aberrants, along with their relationship to clinical depression and FFM dejection, constitute another reason for my departing from the *DSM* division.

In the case of personality disorders, being more prone to either nonlonely or lonely depression is less a sign of being psycho-ethically ill than being utterly incapable of them is. For instance, unless a person is not susceptible to being extremely down-hearted at least from exogenous factors, the individual is decidedly not normal. Bereavement does not usually terminate in clinical depression, but if it does, it is an example of the loneliness-generated type. (Of course, depression can also be caused by other external factors, for instance, imprisonment, loss of job, and persistent negatively felt climate conditions.)

As to the aggregates as such, Group I have not had or do not want ever to have any beloved, especially a one-and-only type, to bereave, which is a sure sign of their abnormality. Group II, in their monomania, have themselves as their abiding one-and-only. What they miss is the loss of anyone who served them in being "number one," a reflection of their egomania. Group III have as a, if not the, principal goal of their lives to get and keep this most singular, idolized, one-and-only beloved, short of which they may be subject to clinical depression of the lonely species.

The Group I schizoid is not given to either lonely or nonlonely depression. The schizotypal is prone to depression though apparently not its lonely species, and, accordingly, this aberrant is less ill than the schizoid. Such is the case insofar as the inability to be depressed is a more disturbed state than not possessing such a capability. Hence, and insofar as depression is mainly if not solely a psychological instead of a moral condition, it can be argued that the schizotypal is less abnormal than the schizoid. As to Group II, all save the paranoid are subject to some degree of depression but not the sort that stems from habitual endogenous loneliness. Group III, above all the borderline and dependent, are at extreme risk of inveterate depression, nonlonely but especially lonely types.

In sum, the order of the groups assailable by depression is as follows: Group III, II, and I. With reference to this scale, questions must be asked as to the nature, type, and cause of the depression concerning which there are abnormal species due to neuroticism and psychoticism. There are also normal and even supranormal sorts of depression, such as existential, in which there may be a kind of habitual sadness due to an altruistic concern for the unhappiness to which human beings as a whole are periodically and some persistently exposed.

The antithesis of such humane or humanitarian sadness is the depressed mood to which, for instance, sociopaths may be subject. Their dysphoria revolves solely about their failure to satisfy their selfish and anti-altruistic interests or their despondence in being apprehended and sanctioned for their illegal conduct (ibid., p. 647). Within Group III, the reasons for the dependent's neurotic depression are generally less acquisitive and self-centered than those of the borderline, a consideration which, in my judgment, makes the first less psycho-ethically unwell than the second.

7. Personality Disorders: Approach and Avoidance

A seventh reason, one affiliated with the fifth and sixth, for my deviating from the *Manual*'s taxonomy involves the approach/avoidance distinction. It is a differentiation concerning which the *DSM*, as in the case of the other reasons for my diverging with its clustering system, takes little if any cognizance (but, then, it is hardly obligated to do so given its program and accompanying parameters).

With at most minimal aptitude or interest in intimacy, Group I, being the social isolates and introverts that they are, stay away from others and give as little attention to them as possible.

Regarding social isolation, Group II avoid others in general due to disdainful indifference or move toward but against them in hostility (the narcissist and obsessional), in antagonistic aggressiveness (the paranoid), and in aggression and violence (the sociopath). Group II can be highly attached to a select few provided they further these lonerists' self-interests. Once such intimates are suspected of being disloyal, especially by paranoids, they become sworn enemies.

Despite their fondness for distainfully distancing themselves from others, Group II need to be with others to exploit (the sociopath), avenge (the paranoid), gain veneration (the narcissist), and exercise control (the compulsive). Otherwise, these four atomistic and negatively autonomous abnormals would prefer to be even more alone, socially and emotionally, given that their hearts and heads are mired in misanthropy.

Paranoids would be completely alone if they had their way. However, their egoism is such that they fancy themselves as being the center of others' consciousness. These pathologicals deplore but also desire such supposed vigilance; they perceive it as attesting to their self-imputed significance. The paranoids' endless repertory of unsavory qualities invites others' ill will that, in its wake, reinforces these aberrants' suspiciousness of them in addition to increasing their all-around self-engrossed mentality.

To some extent, paranoids must approach and associate with others if only to detect their putative plots against them and then to plan their revenge on these enemies. Some of these supposed machinations on the part of others might actually occur since they may go on the offense against the paranoids' malevolence. The paranoids' attitudes toward their adversaries are in accordance with individuals full of hubris, enviousness, and acrimony, qualities that also habitually infect other Group II individuals.

As lonelies, the histrionic and dependent of Group III approach others for purposes of intimacy but, like the borderline and avoidant, their doing so is motivated by habitual acquisitiveness. The avoidant, obviously the paradigm of the avoidance mentality, longs for intimacy but, if not guaranteed uncritical acceptance, will remain distant for fear of being reproved, condemned, and then cast out and away.

Avoidants are extremely afraid that they may be hurt and even destroyed by hostility in a relationship, perhaps especially the sort that tries to pass itself off as indissoluble. Unless, therefore, they have more or less complete confidence in others to sustain their inclusion and refrain from engaging in their excluding tendencies, avoidants remain remote socially and often physically. Like the other Group III individuals, they do so in a state perpetually permeated by or at the precipice of pathological loneliness.

Borderlines vacillate between avoidance and approach. When they do come in contact with others, it can be in either an attack-like fashion akin to Group II behavior or in the basically appeasing manner similar to their fellow Group III negatively homonomous pathologicals. In the offensive mode, the impetuous borderlines are liable to explode in the attempt to redress past putative maltreatment by their intimates for their supposedly being, according to the *DSM*, "neglectful, withholding, uncaring," and, above all, "abandoning" (p. 651).

Since all Group III abnormals are basically negatively dependent sorts of individuals, they favor approach to and submersion in others. In contrast, Group I relish continuous avoidance and separation from others. Group II prefer separation but will approach others when they need to use them for purely privatist goals.

Consequently, Group I evade others due to uninterest but their withdrawal is not out of scorn or enmity for them. Group II circumvent others but do so largely out of contempt such that they are not only non- but anti-gregarious. When Group II do in fact approach others, they often do so either in active (the sociopath and paranoid) or both active and passive (the narcissist and obsessional) aggressiveness.

Group III greatly desire to approach others such that the dependent does so in order to parasitically cling to them. The borderline will approach, withdraw, and then re-approach, depending on her or his mercurial moods. The histrionic will approach, withdraw, and then almost immediately approach someone else. The avoidant will approach but may permanently withdraw if genuine intimacy is not guaranteed and dismissal cannot be ruled out with the same sort of certainty.

8. The Dionysian and Apollonian Archetypes

An eighth reason for varying from the *DSM* disordered personality classification concerns the Dionysian and Apollonian archetypes. Among other vital entities, the higher Dionysian stands for the heart and emotion, especially a passion for living of which love and liberality are its most obvious ethical hallmarks. When the Dionysian becomes dissolute, reckless, lawless, and anarchic, it signals its lower species.

The higher Apollonian symbolizes the head and reason and specifically the dispassionate as found in justice, harmony, balance, guidance, and restraint, especially in reference to the passions. When the Apollonian becomes stifling, rigid, reactionary, and dictatorial, it bespeaks its lower species.

Normals inhabit the middle levels of the Apollonian-Dionysian spectrum. Those who habitually dwell at their top echelons, especially and arguably even exclusively that of the higher Dionysian, would be the supranormals. Only the lower Dionysian and lower Apollonian can be fully employed for the purpose of identifying and classifying pathologicals because any abnormal personality is, by definition, excluded from being classified as higher Apollonian or Dionysian.

With reference to the specific personality aberrants, the schizoid of Group I is a lower Apollonian; the schizotypal, a lower Dionysian. The sociopath and narcissist of Group II are lower Dionysians; the paranoid and obsessional, lower Apollonians. The borderline and histrionic of Group III are lower Dionysians; the dependent and avoidant, lower Apollonians. Consequently, if all ten aberrants were divided into two units representing the lower Apollonian and Dionysian, the first would feature the schizoid, paranoid, obsessional, dependent, and avoidant; the second, the schizotypal, sociopath, narcissist, borderline, and histrionic.

Within my aggregates' single foundation, namely their disposition concerning intimate interpersonality, is a triple diversity, depending on whether the aberrant is non-, dis-, or insufficiently related to relatedness itself. Moreover, within each of the three units, there are diversities that form complementarities, as is the case with each of the three aggregates containing one or more but, in any event, an equal number of lower Dionysians or lower Apollonians.

A pathological may be lower Apollonian on the expressed side of personality but a lower Dionysian on the unexpressed side, that, in turn, may be due its being suppressed, repressed, or otherwise denied. (More rarely is the opposite the case such that the lower Dionysian exists on the expressed side and the lower Apollonian on the suppressed of the individual.) Such is the situation with, for example, the paranoid and obsessional. On the surface, these two pathologicals display the authoritarian even the tyrannical lower Apollonian. Nonetheless, in their depths, they can evince the affective anarchy of the lower Dionysian through such frenzied emotions as rancor and rage that frequently burst forth in their behavior, especially that of the paranoid.

Normals are well-ordered individuals, whereas abnormals are termed disordered. Order itself is an Apollonian attribute that, if excessive, is also pathological, as epitomized by the obsessive aberrant. On the other hand, being insufficiently ordered signifies the lower Dionysian, as epitomized by the antisocial aberrant. The ability to obey the ideal self via self-mastery is an Apollonian aspect of supranormality. However, this self-discipline culminates in the freedom of the person to create or recreate its ideality all of which is a hallmark of Dionysian supranormality.

A well-ordered, or healthy, individual predominantly consists in being comprised of good—namely enjoyable, enduring, and psycho-ethically uplifting—interpersonal relationships. A properly ordered person refers to a higher Apollonian trait, but mental health, as do positive relationships, pertains even more to a higher Dionysian type of individual, whose self-order is creative instead of constrictive.

Obsessionals best exemplify a negatively orderly disordered individual. Indeed, their illness in great part lies in their fixation on order. This mania for control often generates its opposite since, being overwhelmed by the trivial, they tend to procrastinate. As a result, they wind up being disorderly and lower Dionysian. Again obsessives can, on the surface, be lower Apollonians, who manifest despotic tendencies toward others. But in their depths, they are controlled by affective anarchy and conative chaos, traits typical of other lower Dionysian types, such as schizotypals and borderlines.

As noted above, an argument can be advanced for the higher Dionysian being the best of personality archetypes. If so, then it falls to the lower Dionysian personality to be considered the worst. From this perspective, the lower Dionysian aberrants as a whole are more abnormal than the lower Apollonians, but in such cases it somewhat hinges upon which traits are most prominent.

In terms of the severity of the pathology within an aggregate, the Group I lower Dionysian schizotypal, is, for instance, more psychologically diseased than the lower Apollonian schizoid. This greater abnormality is seen in the fact that on the psychotic spectrum, the schizotypal is ordinarily considered being closer to the schizophrenic than is the schizoid. Being so with reference to this most severe Axis I mental illness is generally indicative of a greater mental pathology. I say generally because, in a significant sense, the schizophrenic may be less sick than the schizoid. As indicated earlier, the first, unlike the second, has some capability or at least some desire for relatedness, albeit highly restricted ones, all of which makes the schizotypal less ill than the schizoid.

As well, we can posit that the schizoid is more ill than the schizotypal since, unlike the first, the second exhibits FFM Openness to Experience, which allows for greater change for the positive. Additionally, the schizotypal manifests potentially positive FFM neurotic traits, such as anxiety, depression (despondence), self-consciousness, and vulnerability, in contrast to intrinsically negative FFM neurotic qualities, namely hostility and impulsiveness.

Unlike any other personality abnormality, the schizoid exhibits no neurotic traits, a condition generally more aberrated than one that contains some neurotic qualities above all those that are more potentially developmental (Costa and Widiger, 2002, p. 461). Obviously, to be neurotic the individual has to be alive. In being non-neurotic (and lower Apollonian), the schizoid is death-like and specifically robot-like. On the other hand, the schizotypal is highly neurotic (and lower Dionysian) and, therefore, highly alive and unrobot-like.

Consequently, these and other considerations, to be examined forthwith, are grounds for arguing for either the schizoid or the schizotypal being not only the more psychologically disturbed in Group I but more pathological than all the other eight aberrants in Groups II and III.

With reference to Group II, the lower Dionysian sociopath is the most psycho-ethically disturbed of all the aberrants, followed by the lower Apollonian paranoid who, from some perspectives, might be deemed more psychologically sick than the sociopath but less ethically so. The lower Dionysian narcissist is more psycho-ethically diseased than the lower Apollonian obsessional who is the least mentally/morally ill of the Group II personalities. This unit as a totality is more morally ill than Group I but less mentally so. Group II are both mentally and morally more unhealthy than Group III, save for the borderline who potentially is the pathological most purely psychologically sick of all the aberrants with the exception of Group I, hence, this aberrant's exceedingly high recidivism rate.

As to Group III more specifically, the lower Dionysian borderline is more mentally-morally pathological than the lower Dionysian histrionic. Both are more diseased than the lower Apollonian dependent and avoidant, the two abnormals who are the least psycho-ethically ill of all the disturbed personalities. The dependent is more aberrant in terms of moral commissions than the avoidant but the second is more disturbed in terms of omissions than the first.

Again, a case can be made that the histrionic is the least psychologically aberrant of all ten pathological personalities—not only those that constitute

Group III. The aberrant least subject to genetic factors is arguably the least ill, and the histrionic may well be just this kind of deviant. In general, the lower Dionysian is to the lower Apollonian as immoral action is to immoral inaction. As well, immoral behavior is worse than immoral non-behavior, though clearly both are bad. It is likely that human beings, when they fail in moral terms, tend to do so more by immoral omission than immoral commission.

Similarly and as Aristotle proposes, it "is more characteristic of" moral virtue "to do what is noble than not to do what is base" (1941b, 1120a11–13). Moral virtue is both higher Apollonian and Dionysian with the second being more elevated than first. Thus, the Dionysian (supra)virtue of love is superior to the Apollonian virtue of justice if only because the first incorporates the second and must do so if it is genuine love. For instance, philanthropists are not truly practitioners of altruism and charity, which are forms of universal love, if they are not just, and economically so to, for example, their employees. Such fairness requires their being recipients of a living wage. Love may cover a multitude of sins but not all of them such as injustice. In my view, no disordered person attains the level of justice, certainly not on the habitual level that constitutes a virtue, let alone virtue's perfection in the form of love, especially universal.

It bears repetition that either the lower Apollonian schizoid or the lower Dionysian schizotypal is the most pathological, psychically speaking, of the pathological personalities. Their ranking depends upon which facets of their mental trait illness are emphasized. However, these Group I aberrants are not the most pathological of the personalities when characterological considerations are factored in. That most anti-accolade belongs to the lower Dionysian sociopaths, especially the sadistic sorts. Their ethical depravity, as manifested in vicious maliciousness, is qualitatively different from the rest of the abnormals, including even the extremely unethical and at times extremely ruthless lower Apollonian paranoids. In typical Group II hauteur, paranoids may consider themselves as moral models, though not to the extent that the hyperconscientious but the pharisaical, moralistic lower Apollonian obsessionals do.

As well, the hypo-conscientious, irresolute, and usually dissolute lower Dionysian narcissists of Group II are liable, in their unmitigated sense of self-grandeur, to fancy themselves as being the epitome of moral probity. For instance, narcissists picture themselves as being no less than most suitable candidates for, if not already the incarnation of, "ideal love." In fact, they are simply the personification of their own idolatrous and vainglorious love of self, an addiction to self that, however, is not always beyond self-hatred (p. 661). As just implied, a case could be made for holding that the pathological personalities in terms of the four archetypes all differ in kind, especially the lower and higher Dionysian relative to one another.

Aberrated individuals, including even the lower Dionysian types—like the impulsive sorts, such as the sociopath and borderline—and the undisciplined kinds, to wit, the histrionic and again the sociopath—have inflexible traits, inflexibility being a lower Apollonian attribute. Thus, individuals who are customarily chaotic, or lower Dionysian, in their lifestyles, are, nevertheless, intransigent in the sense that they tenaciously persist in maintaining their tumultuous traits, including irresponsibility and unrestraint.

Thus, with respect to their inflexibility, Millon and colleagues claim that individuals with personality disorders have "intense and rigid traits." They say that these qualities "implicitly drive or control interpersonal situations," behavior that clearly impairs their connections to others. These researchers further contend that, as a consequence of their inflexible and maladaptive traits, such deviants are seldom able to change "the pathological themes which dominate their lives" (2000, p. 11).

Consequently, it can be put forth that, while the lower Apollonian aberrants are by definition unbending and unadaptive concerning their qualities, so also are the lower Dionysians whose traits, while they are typically riotous, are routinely unchangeably so. Consequently, the diseased personality is either oblivious or consciously opposed to any change in his or her personality traits (Groups I and II). Or, they are opposed to these qualities but relatively powerless to alter them without help and often even with it (Group III, especially the borderline). In whichever case, aberrated personality traits, including the most rambunctious and rebellious of them, are so inflexible as to be pathological for this reason alone.

Hence, all individuals with personality disturbances manifest aspects of the obstinacy of the lower Apollonian even though the traits themselves may be lower Dionysian in nature. Thus, the sociopath, who is by definition paradigmatically impulsive, a lower Dionysian trait, is largely unalterably so, a lower Apollonian feature. In general, change is to the changeless as the Dionysian is to the Apollonian.

Therefore, abnormals fail to attain and even less combine the positive aspects of the Apollonian and Dionysian. They are termed "disordered," that is, insufficiently ordered, which is a lower Dionysian trait. But they can also be hyper-ordered, a lower Apollonian trait, as uniquely occurs among the pathological personalities in the case of the obsessive-compulsives who, then, can be characterized as orderly disordered individuals. Normal personalities are fairly adaptable and pliant, which are Dionysian hallmarks, and yet they can be principled and firm, which are Apollonian.

According to Millon and colleagues, pathological personalities waste opportunities to improve and, thereby, "constantly create situations which replay their failures," usually with "only minor variations on a few related, self-defeating themes" (ibid.). Hence, individuals with personality abnormalities are their own worst enemies such that their "pathology pathologizes" in that their illness takes on a life of its own. It is in these senses that individuals with personality disturbances can be construed as failed personalities.

Dividing these failures into lower Apollonian and Dionysian symbols has some affinities with the *DSM* clusters. Its Cluster A contains the schizoid and paranoid, which are lower Apollonian types of personality, though its schizotypal is a lower Dionysian. Cluster B, the antisocial, borderline, histrionic, and narcissist, are lower Dionysian types. Cluster C, the avoidant, dependent, and obsessional, are lower Apollonian types.

Hence, while there is not a complete correspondence between the lower Apollonians and lower Dionysians with respect to the three *DSM* clusters and its ten aberrants, there is in the case of nine of them (the schizotypal being the only exception). This overall congruity, albeit not deliberate on the part of the *Manual*, is one of several reasons why I still find merit in its taxonomy.

The Dionysian signifies diversity and change; the Apollonian, unity and the unchanging. The more a personality can incorporate the Dionysian functional and dynamic into its structures without impairing their underlying Apollonian stability and integrity, the more evolved is its integration. The less it can do so, the more primitive is its unification.

9. Personality Integrations and Disintegrations: Negative and Positive

John Livesley maintains that the first failure of the aberrant personality includes the inability "to establish stable and integrated representations of self" and self-structure. He argues that this inaptitude is exemplified in the aberrant's lack of self-boundaries, self-coherence, and, in general, self-identity (1998, p. 142). In my judgment, some aberrants display negative kinds of integration such as those that are excessively unitary, like that manifested in lower Apollonian cohesiveness and homogeneity.

Hence, I agree with Kazimierz Dabrowski who, in concert with Andrew Kawczak and Michael Piechowski, distinguishes negative and positive personality integrations and disintegrations. These distinctions give rise to the ninth reason for my taxonomical variance from that of the *DSM*.

A personality that exhibits healthy psycho-ethical development attains what Dabrowski and colleagues designate secondary integration. It is based on altruistic inclinations in contrast to primary, in the sense of primitive, mental integrations emerging from egoistic drives. In between primary (negative) and secondary (positive) personality unifications, either of which can be total or partial, are negative and positive personality disintegrations, either of which can also be total or partial in composition. Integrations tend to be more permanent than disintegrations.

Constructive disintegrations break down negative lower-level integrations that, in their wake, may or may not lead to higher-level personality integrations. For instance, ignorance of the diversity and complexity of reality is a kind of primitive cognitive integration that often gives their possessors feelings of security and stability, albeit at the expense of truth. When this simplification is shattered by awareness of the world's complexity, it can be a prelude to a positive unification. Thus, such ignorance, in the sense of nescience, can be fragmented positively by becoming a "learned ignorance" à la

Socrates that can be a step to intellectual wisdom—metaphysics, according to Aristotle—arguably the most positive kind of cognitive integration

Correlatively, personality changes in terms of mental structures and functions, like the cognitive, that break apart higher-level integrations may be viewed as negative types of personality disintegration. These may lead to lower-level integrations (Dabrowski, Kawczak, and Piechowski, 1970, pp. 164–166, 171–174; see also Dabrowski, 1972, pp. 293, 296; McGraw, 1986, pp. 216–223). Positive disintegrations may involve regressions to earlier personality states, which become constructive if they promote personality progressions vis-à-vis the mental structures and functions of cognition, emotion, and volition. Accordingly, we can say that sometimes pathological personalities can be envisioned as being either habitually negatively integrated or negatively disintegrated. These abnormals seldom reach higher-level integrations not even partial and transitory sorts without first going through various positive disintegrations. It is virtually impossible for a disturbed personality to become so transformed that it undergoes a transition to the supranormality of secondary integration. This sort of transformation can be looked upon as the higher Apollonian being subsumed under the higher Dionysian.

The change from a secondarily integrated to a primitively integrated or negatively disintegrated personality would be even more infrequent, assuming that it ever occurs. This transition would involve, for example, the secondarily integrated saint, understood here as a spiritual (moral) paragon, degenerating into a paranoid, a negatively integrated personality, or a sociopath, a negatively disintegrated personality.

Once the psycho-ethically most elevated echelons of personality are reached, no lower one has any sustained appeal for an individual. Normals may become sub- or supranormals, but supranormals are unlikely to become normals and, of course, even less subnormals. They, in turn, may become normals, albeit relatively infrequently and, logically enough, even less frequently do subnormals become supranormals.

Disordered personalities sometimes have an attraction to become more elevated types or at least to have psycho-ethically superior traits, such as the narcissist's craving for ideal love (*DSM*, p. 658). As a rule, any desire to become a more morally mature person depends in great part upon the degree of dystonicity to which the individual is subject. Group II, such as the sociopath and paranoid, have syntonic traits as a whole. Hence, they are not enticed by more evolved stages of personality, objectively considered, chiefly because their arrogance, such as that which typifies the narcissists, has them believe that they are already at these lofty levels.

With respect to the notions of personality integration and disintegration, the five aberrants who evince exceedingly insufficient positive unity and stability are the schizotypal of Group I, the sociopath and narcissist of Group II, and the borderline and histrionic of Group III. Of this quintet, the borderline and especially the histrionic have the most capability for being positively disintegrated because their neuroticism, which is the central factor in their being fragmented and unbalanced, can itself be potentially constructive. Thus, neurotic traits, such as anxiety and vulnerability, can be instrumental in attaining higher-level integrations.

The five aberrants who display grossly insufficient personality diversification are the schizoid of Group I, the paranoid and compulsive of Group II, and the dependent and avoidant of Group III. These lower Apollonian types illustrate extremely but varying negatively integrated personalities. However, the dependent and avoidant, like their fellow borderlines and histrionics, also possess potentially positive neurotic traits that may lead to positive disintegration. This breakdown can then morph into a positive integration.

Space allows consideration of only four pathologicals in any detail, two of whom are negatively disintegrated, the schizotypal and the borderline, and two of whom are negatively integrated, the paranoid and schizoid. The schizotypal and borderline are most at risk for negative disintegration and the absence of a cohesive and firm self-identity. This lack includes those fragmentations that pertain to depersonalization, a dissociative disorder in which, according to David Rosenhan and Martin Seligman, the person feels "cut off from or unsure of his or her identity" (1989, p. 688). It is noteworthy that the *DSM* reports there being "a high rate of co-occurrence" between the schizotypal and borderline (p. 644).

Millon regards the schizotypal as having an "estranged" self-image," "permeable ego-boundaries" with "recurrent social perplexities, and illusions [along with] experiences of depersonalization, derealization, and dissociation" (1986, p. 694). These phenomena might be described as, respectively, personal identity alienation, reality decomposition, and personality splitting, all three being lower Dionysian and negatively disintegrating in nature.

Millon characterizes the borderline as displaying "an uncertain" self-image due largely to "confusions of an immature, nebulous, or wavering sense of identity" (ibid.). Additionally, the borderline has a "diffused intrapsychic organization," in which there are "periodic dissolutions of what limited psychic order and cohesion" this aberrant has to begin with (ibid., p. 709).

All these features are clearly evocative of the lower Dionysian and negatively disintegrated personality. The borderline's lack of a stable identity can be witnessed in its propensity, according to the *DSM*, for possessing "transient psychotic-like symptoms" (p. 644). Alternatively, the schizotypal is likely to have more enduring symptoms, the kind which approach being schizophrenic in composition.

Indeed, of the ten personality disturbances, the schizotypal is the closest to psychosis, in particular, schizophrenia. Leaving aside the "residual" and "undifferentiated" types of schizophrenia, those with this illness may be looked upon as being either negatively disintegrated and possessed of the most unbalanced Dionysian mental state disturbance (namely "disorganized" schizophrenia).

Schizophrenics may also be seen as negatively integrated and with the most disturbed Apollonian mental state disorder (to wit paranoid schizophrenia). Or, they may be envisioned as a combination of the most mentally ill Dionysian and Apollonian mental state illnesses (namely catatonic schizophrenia). All schizophrenics are lower Dionysian in the sense of being disordered, meaning departures from the ordered in the sense of the normal construed as the statistically average. In addition to this descriptive sense of normal, mental illnesses as a whole are usually considered as departures from some ideal and prescriptive sense of normal.

Millon depicts the schizoid as endowed with a "complacent" self-image (1986, p. 694). I would underline the fact that this self-satisfaction is not to be understood as smugness, like Group II aberrants' self-images, but instead as being pathologically passive and acquiescent. Millon further portrays the schizoid as evincing "an undifferentiated intrapsychic organization" that is marked, he says, by an "inner barrenness" and "internal structures best characterized by limited coordination and sterile order" (ibid., p. 698).

The above description of the schizoid well fits the lower Apollonian individual. It also fits a person with a negative, or primitive, personality integration and one who appears to be incapable of any kind of positive disintegration and, a fortiori, any positive, or secondary, integration. The schizoid represents the most negative of personality organizations and self-systems from a purely psychological perspective.

The negative integration of the non-neurotic schizoid is more pathological than the highly neurotic negative disintegration of the schizotypal. The reason is, again, that FFM neurotic traits of anxiety, depression, self-consciousness, and vulnerability are potentially positive in that they may lead to a constructive disintegration and even to a higher-level personality integration. Still, the schizotypal proceeding to such a more elevated stage of self-unification is likely very rare. Instead, it is perhaps more probable that this aberrant will further negatively disintegrate even to the extent of becoming psychotic, most likely the more fragmented kind of schizophrenic.

Consequently, schizoids have an utterly undifferentiated and an extremely unified overall personality structure. However, its unification is due to its narrow and simplistic sort of integration, especially in terms of affectivity. Contrarily, the schizotypals of Group I have an exceedingly differentiated but an exceptionally disunified, chaotic, or negatively disintegrated structure.

If the schizotypal disintegration is positive, meaning that it leads to a higher-level personality organization, then its possessor is more mentally sound than the primitively integrated schizoid who is essentially incapable of any positive self-fragmentation. The potentially positive disintegration of the schizotypal is manifest in the FFM supertrait of Openness to Experience in terms, for instance, of the traits of ideas and values. In such personality facets, the schizotypal displays a curiosity and quest for new meanings. This openness requires a shift away from the more crudely integrated personality, which characterizes the closed-minded and closed-hearted schizoid (Costa and Widiger, 1994, p. 329; 2002, pp. 461–466).

If the Axis II schizotypal's disintegration proves to be negative, this individual may become subject to psychotic disorders such as the schizophrenias, which can be construed as Axis I lower Dionysian mental state disturbances (p. 643). Although they may behaviorally sometimes manifest lower Apollonian traits like the catatonic's mutism, stupor, and overall rigidity, the disordered mental states of the schizophrenics as a whole are of a fundamentally lower Dionysian nature.

Millon portrays the paranoid as having an "inviolable" self-image and holding "a fixed hierarchy of tenacious memories, immutable cognitions, and irrevocable beliefs" (1986, p. 695). All these attributes attest to the paranoid's dogmatic and despotic kind of lower Apollonian mental makeup and a negatively integrated personality organization. Millon further depicts the personality structure of the paranoid as being "inelastic, constricted, and uncompromising," again, all lower Apollonian traits characteristic of a primitively integrated individual (ibid., p. 697).

Given their inflexible psychic condition, paranoids are, according to Millon, so unable to accommodate "changing circumstances" that "stressors are likely to precipitate either explosive outbursts or inner shatterings," both of which are lower Dionysian in nature (ibid.). Thus, paranoids are continuously at the precipice of succumbing to the dissolution of their personality, in which case they oscillate between a negative psychic integration and a negative disintegration. So construed and purely from a psychological instead of an ethical perspective, paranoids may be envisioned as being on the schizophrenic sequence.

From a purely psychic perspective, the schizoid is more primitively integrated, or structured, than the paranoid but ethically considered it is the reverse. The schizoid is highly non-ethical; the paranoid, extremely unethical. Hence, unlike the lower Apollonian schizoid, there is beneath the paranoid's unbending personality organization a cauldron of clashing lower Dionysian forces—usually negatively disintegrating psychic types—that are constantly erupting from their subterranean stronghold. These volatile emissions can be witnessed in the paranoid's unprovoked, objectively considered, invectives and other kinds of offensive behavior. This odious conduct stems from this aberrant's persistent jealousy, envy, rancor, spite, and deep-seated ill will, all typical of this pathological's *ressentiment*.

In sum, the schizoid and paranoid personalities manifest, at least on a conscious level, primitively organized psychic lower Apollonian integrations. They contrast with the disorganized and negatively disintegrated personality structures of the lower Dionysian schizotypal and borderline. An inflexible self-structure with immovable self-boundaries and narrow self-coherence à la John Livesley is indicative of a lower Apollonian negatively integrated personality. It may be symptomatic of an even deeper disturbance than one with a chaotic self-structure with its broader but looser cohesiveness and, therefore, its greater capability for a positive disintegration.

10. Personality: Autonomy and Homonomy

The tenth reason why I vary from the *DSM* taxonomy concerns the autonomy/homonomy distinction. Group I abnormals are negatively autonomous with the schizoids being passively and the schizotypals actively so with neither being aggressively so.

Group II paranoids, narcissists, and above all sociopaths are negatively actively independent save for the obsessive. This aberrant is predominantly actively independent, especially concerning perceived inferiors, but passively so relative to perceived superiors. The extreme independence of Group II is connected with the sociopaths' tendency to act out their autonomy in terms of aggression and even violence and for the paranoids to do so aggressively but usually without physical aggression. The narcissist is more assertive than aggressive but is often passively so, though not to the extent that the obsessional is when confronting perceived superiors (Costa and Widiger, 2002, p. 461–467).

Group III are negatively homonomous, although borderlines and avoidants fluctuate between negative homonomy and negative autonomy. Nonetheless, they, like their fellow histrionics and especially dependents, are also at base negatively dependent, meaning non-constructively attached to others. Avoidants are also negatively autonomous, but they would prefer being homonomous if they could find a union in which they would not be excoriated and then expelled. Group III tend not to engage in acts of aggression and even less those of violence, although the borderline can indulge in both, including directing violence toward themselves.

Hence, Groups I and II incline to social atomism; Group III, to social monism. SCRAM, as a philosophy of hyper-individualism, engenders conditions conducive to the emergence of the negatively autonomous and atomistically inclined Group II deviants, above all antisocials and narcissists. In partial reaction to them, SCRAM generates conditions propitious to the eliciting and arguably, at least in some cases, of actually causing the negatively homonomous and monistically inclined Group III.

Millon and colleagues claim that, as a general rule:

> personalities which are self-oriented [autonomous], such as the narcissist and antisocial, tend to develop paranoid traits under conditions of intense or prolonged stress, whereas personalities which are other-oriented [homonomous], such as the dependent and histrionic, develop traits which are more borderline. Accordingly, both dependents and histrionic personalities, for whom fantasies of fusion with [others] are an impor-

> tant feature, tend to develop symptoms related to identity diffusion and dissociation [for example, negative disintegration], though borderlines are usually more severe. (2000, pp. 261–262).

This passage is highly relevant to my views for a number of reasons. First, it supports my position that the antisocial, paranoid, narcissist, and by implication the obsessional, belong to the same personality unit (Group II). Second, it seemingly endorses my view that the borderline, histrionic, dependent, and by implication the avoidant, belong to the same personality aggregate (Group III).

Referencing the autonomy/homonomy issue, Erlene Rosowsky says:

> Patients with a severe PD, at any age, experience intense, rapid, broad swings in their interpersonal relationships. They vacillate between extremes of loving and hating, idealizing and devaluing, needing to be close [homonomy] and needing to be distant [autonomy], seeking dependence [homonomy] and independence [autonomy]. They act out the conflict between the fear of abandonment (threatening annihilation) and the fear of domination (threatening fusion). (1999, pp. 157–158)

If we are to adhere to their *DSM* characterizations, the swings in interpersonality and between loving and hating do not occur at all among Group I but most frequently do so among Group III, especially the borderline. As to the personality aberrant's fear of abandonment, it especially pertains to the Group III, preeminently the borderline and dependent.

Fright regarding abandonment refers to the anxiety of losing union, homonomy, and shared privacy; fear of domination, to that of losing separateness, autonomy, and individual privacy. Abandonment and maximal exclusion in general are the greatest apprehensions of the negatively homonomous and submissive (Group III). On the other hand, being subjugated and absorbed are the foremost fears of the negatively autonomous but non-dominating (Group I) and the negatively autonomous but dominating (Group II).

Still, anxiety concerning being forsaken to a personless existence is the foremost fright of all human beings since such a condition would be literally hellishly abominable. Ergo, the absence of positive homonomy is the utmost apprehension. Correlatively, the presence of positive homonomy is the ultimate consolation for the consummately social beings that are the human types, certainly the ones who are normal.

Contrary to the positions of SCRAM's social atomism, homonomy and interdependence are both a more basic need and metaneed than are autonomy and independence. They are insofar as human beings are reckoned to be thoroughly and irreversibly social mammals, both structurally and functionally.

Rosowsky is, I think, correct in stating that the disordered personalities may alternate between seeking the closeness of dependence (homonomy) and the distance of independence (autonomy). For instance, the Group II obsessional and the Group III borderline sway between deference and defiance vis-à-vis others. I do not hold that the obsessional vacillates between loving and hating (at least not with respect to the same individual), as Rosowsky appears to suggest by implying that all the aberrants do, though, I agree, that the borderline does and in paradigmatic fashion.

The sudden switch from (re)capitulation to recalcitrance is also supremely the case with the borderline. This individual, like the other Group III deviants, is more afraid of the prospect of being independent than dependent, all of which is the reverse for the obsessional.

According to Millon and colleagues, "the dependent shares a variety of traits with other personality disorders, most notably the histrionic, avoidant, masochist, and borderline" (2000, p. 223), the very pathologicals that form my Group III. I do not discuss the masochistic disorder since it is not (yet) one of the aberrants adopted by the *DSM*. Still, I would add that masochism is most associated with highly negatively dependent individuals as sadism is with the highly negatively independent individuals.

Sociopaths are the pathological personalities who appear to have the most inclination toward negative independence and sadism. Borderlines followed by obsessionals appear to combine the greatest propensity toward both masochism, a dependence disease, and sadism, an independence disease. Obsessionals are the least psycho-ethically disturbed of Group II, though this unit is the most disturbed of my three aggregates. Borderlines are the most psych-ethically disturbed of Group III, though this unit is the least mentally/morally sick of my three aggregates.

Pathologically dependent individuals, by definition, try to lose themselves in others. Thus, Group III, as essentially dependent types, may make people, including strangers and even enemies, the absolute center, parasitically understood, of their lives since they lack a true psycho-ethical center of their own. Though Group III, as perpetual lonelies and alonelies, make others crucial to their very being, they basically view them in a negative fashion. So, while they may sometimes waver between adoration and abhorrence of others, Group III, especially borderlines, usually exhibit the second attitude, though not to the degree or kind that Group II do.

Group III, who tend to be females, seek extreme inseparability and homonomy instead of separateness and autonomy. Hence, these aberrants have too fluid an identity, if any at all, and, as a result, incline toward negative disintegration. Group I and II tend to be males and have a propensity to seek extreme separateness and autonomy, and insofar as they do, they display an overly fixed and isolating type of negative integration, or self-identity.

Millon and colleagues relate that borderlines "frequently feel worthless and empty," traits typical of lonely people in general but especially of the Group III lonelies, again, paramountly borderlines (ibid., p. 433). But they contend that not every type of borderline exclusively seeks fusion, the ultimate in homonomy, with others. They state that though merging "brings a powerful intimacy which banishes feelings of emptiness and worthlessness," it "also leads to fear of engulfment" (ibid., p. 435). This sort of anxiety concerns the fear of completely losing any sense of independent identity, or autonomy. Hence, "the emptiness of not being attached to fantasies of fusion, usually idealization of a magic romantic figure" may, according to Millon and colleagues give way to the borderline's "fears of total dependence on someone else for a sense of self-worth and self-esteem" (ibid.). It does somewhat the same in terms of the other three Group III abnormals.

Millon and colleagues then state that intimacy heightens the borderline's apprehensiveness about being "vulnerable and exposed," which can subsequently lead to a wish for separation. Nonetheless, they contend that the quest for autonomy can render the borderline once again at risk not only concerning habitual feelings of emptiness and worthlessness, typical of loneliness, but depression. This condition is characteristic of Group III pathologicals as a whole. If borderlines feel locked into a situation of total dependence, they will not allow any relationship to become overly stable. Thus, Millon and associates claim that when attachments "become too normal or things are going too well" for this personality, they "must be sabotaged." In sum, borderlines are continually on the verge of fluctuating between extreme homonomy and autonomy, dependence and independence, passivity and frenzy, and fears of being fused and engulfed or, alternatively, forsaken and abandoned (ibid.).

We have seen that the *Manual* describes borderlines as possessing a pattern of unstable and intense relationships, owing to the fact, for instance, that they quickly sanctify others and then perhaps even more quickly satanize them. They will do so if the borderlines believe that others are about to make their greatest frights realities by abandoning them, the epitomy of negative independence (pp. 650–651).

Millon and colleagues mention that it is hardly surprising that the borderline often overlaps with a number of other disturbed personalities, who are in, fact, the histrionic, dependent, and avoidant of my Group III. Thus, these personologists state:

> The first diagnostic criterion [of the borderline's] frantic efforts to avoid abandonment resonates with the dependent and histrionic personalities. The dependent desperately needs an instrumental surrogate, without which feelings of panic quickly rise to the surface. The histrionic needs an instrumental surrogate as well, but also needs to feel physically attractive, to be the center of attention, and to believe that she herself is idealized by her companions. Abandonment is, thus, a double jeopardy for the histrionic, being both a separation and a commentary on the insufficiency of her attractiveness. The avoidant could also be included here, because this PD needs a mate who is willing to face a world where the avoidant feels shamed, defective, and incapable. (2000, p. 442)

The *DSM* states that borderlines have a capability for empathizing with and nurturing others but actualizes it only on condition that the second are available to fulfill "on demand" the needs of the first (p. 651). This borderline proclivity is clearly indicative of its acquisitive motivational pattern. The *DSM* notes that if this aberrant's needs are not immediately met, he or she frequently resorts to "extreme sarcasm, enduring bitterness, or verbal outbursts." All this conduct, according to the *DSM*, is often accompanied by rage, especially if the "caregiver or lover is seen as neglectful, withholding, uncaring, or abandoning" (ibid.). All such behavior manifestly impedes fulfillment of the borderline's insatiable hunger for a humane sort of homonomy and deliverance from (a)loneliness.

Like other (a)lonelies, including their fellow Group III abnormals, borderlines have a self-image mired in self-worthlessness. Unlike theirs, that of the borderlines is carried to the point wherein they deem themselves, as we have seen, according to the *DSM*, to be "bad or evil," all of which makes them constantly worry about being cast aside. The *DSM* appends that the borderlines' "abandonment fears" are associated with their "intolerance of being alone and a need to have other people with them." In which case, these pathologicals' pathological loneliness is rooted in an equally aberrated aloneliness (ibid.).

The *DSM* maintains that the borderlines' "chronic feelings of emptiness" may be so powerful that they may doubt that they literally exist at all (ibid.). This lived, or actual, doubt is, to be sure, antithetical to the Cartesian abstract sort of methodological solipsism. It is so since the doubt of the borderlines ends not in the affirmation of their existence but in its negation (including that of suicide). All this pushes these aberrants to the border of psychological solipsism, or psychosis.

Histrionics are, at source, highly dependent sorts but, like the borderlines, they often flitter between negative homonomy and negative autonomy. In the end, histrionics revert to their underlying negative dependence on others who are rapidly replaced by one another due to these aberrants' alleged superficial but, in any event, self-serving interest in them.

Histrionics are obviously anxious concerning any sort of exclusion, noninclusion, or indifference, since all threaten their being the center of attention and affection. Their seductiveness is, in part, a means to circumvent these menaces that imperil their sense of belonging. Their sexually inappropriate behavior is, in my view, largely rooted in their (a)loneliness, as are their craving the attention and other forms of acceptance and affirmation that beget their unseemly comportment.

Dependents are, as their name makes plain, negatively homonomous. They are totally adverse to any autonomy such that their only vacillation is between the different objects of their homonomy should they be jilted or otherwise jettisoned. Len Sperry maintains that, according to cognitive-behavioral formulations of their disorder, dependents have the distorted belief that they "are either totally connected to another and dependent or totally alone and independent" (1995, p. 82). So understood, these pathological personalities construe complete dependence as the only solution to their horror at the prospect of being isolated in abject autonomous separateness and separation.

Therefore, like borderlines, dependents are terrified at the mere thought of being maximally excluded. Instead of dreading being alone qua alone—though it usually takes the form of fear of abandonment, as is the case with borderlines—dependents are more afraid of being initially excluded as such instead of being included and then forsaken. They are so because, in their aloneness, dependents will have no one to nurture and protect them. At which point they become even more compliant with others' wishes however much these desires may conflict with their own.

Avoidants, as their name announces, move away from others and do so into a negative autonomy. In their depths, they are also exceedingly supine types of individuals, like the dependent sorts of personality they are. They would forfeit or, at least, substantially scale back any desire for independence if they could unite with others without fear of being demeaned or discarded by them.

Thus, the *DSM* observes that avoidants "become very attached to and dependent on those few other people with whom they are friends" (p. 663). The maximal exclusion of abandonment to sheer desolating aloneness constitutes the foremost fright of the Group III borderline to which this individual reacts with terror and rage. The maximal exclusion of rejection is the chief anxiety of the Group III avoidant to which this individual reacts with increased apprehensiveness and despondence.

I have proposed that those abnormals, in which a negative autonomy presides—namely, Group I and II—are more mentally ill qua personalities than those in which a negative homonomy prevails, namely Group III. As I have sought to demonstrate throughout this volume, the leading cause of their greater pathology is that individuals with Group I and II deviations are far more deficient with reference to interpersonal relatedness than those with Group III aberrations. Group I, especially the schizoids, are quantitatively deficient due largely to constitutional factors such as their extreme introversion. Group II are deficient by qualitative defectiveness mainly traceable to their contemptuous and hostile behavior that may become not only negligent but abusive in nature.

Mary Gordon has found that the common denominator of abusers and neglectors is lack of empathy (*The Montreal Gazette*, 5 July 2008). With reference to personality disorders, the loners of Groups I and the lonerists of II are, respectively, neglectors and abusers at least the latter are verbally. Group I and II are also, respectively, non-empathic and anti-empathic. As well, Group II are antipathetic in being antagonistic and uncompassionate individuals.

The lonelies of Group III are, save for the dependent, likewise bereft of empathy due to their general negativism toward others. My division of these disorders into loners, lonerists, and (a)lonelies and their disposition to empathy have no counterparts in the *DSM* and may be looked upon as further and major reasons for my variation from it.

In this chapter, I have considered reasons why I believe that the *DSM* taxonomy of personality disorders is sometimes lacking in clarity, consistency, and coherence. There are more grounds for my diverging from the *Manual*'s classification, especially those germane to its use of the categorical approach to its taxonomy of personality and its traits, matters, which now demand additional attention.

11. Deficiencies in Current Personality Disorder Theory

In this section, I will examine some of the problems, especially those concerning personality disorders, that still plague personologists, both researchers and clinicians. Stephen Strack contends that currently, "there are few areas of scientific inquiry as exciting as that of the interface between normal and abnormal personality," an investigation, he says, that "is still in its infancy" (2006c, p. 187). Robert Cloninger describes this inquiry not so much as being in its infancy but in a state of psychiatric "diagnostic dysfunction" (2007, p. vii).

Joel Paris goes so far as to assert, "few specialists in PD research doubt" that this *DSM* Axis II aberration "will eventually be replaced by a different system" (2000, p. 129).

Similarly, Katherine Fowler, William O'Donohue, and Scott Lilienfeld propose that the entire current personality disorder arrangement might well be supplanted since it has an array of problematic areas, which include the following:

(1) whether it possesses sufficient "predictive utility";
(2) whether it is best conceptualized as dimensions or categories;
(3) whether it is best served by a dimensional model, and if so, then which one (there are perhaps twenty different dimensional systems, including the FFM);
(4) its high comorbidity among classifications, which may put into question its "validity and/or existence as independent syndromes";
(5) its reliability and internal consistency;
(6) its construct validity;
(7) its lack of a clear method to best assess the personality disorders;
(8) its distinction from Axis I disorders;
(9) its possibly containing a gender bias;
(10) its lack "of well-conducted research" regarding "effective" therapies;
(11) its absence of agreement with reference to specific diagnostic criteria;
(12) its considerable symptom heterogeneity within a given diagnosis such that there may be "little or no overlap in symptoms among patients with the same diagnosis"; and,

(13) its etiological heterogeneity in variants of one and the same personality disorder (2007, pp. 6–12).

Since there is hardly enough space to address all or even a major portion of the issues enumerated by Fowler and colleagues regarding personality disturbances, only those most pertinent to my purposes will be examined. These concerns will, above all, continue to include these personality anomalies in terms of their *DSM* diagnostic features and, especially in this section, the usage of the categorical paradigm—in contrast to the dimensional and, more precisely, the FFM—vis-à-vis these traits. The next section will focus on the *DSM* personality disorder diagnostic features in reference to the FFM supertraits and traits and two taxonomies herein that reflect them, namely those of *The Manual* and mine.

John Livesley criticizes the *DSM* personality division, saying it is "one of the least satisfactory sections of contemporary psychiatric classifications" (1998, p. 137). For one thing, he faults the *DSM* for lacking a clear, consistent, and compelling "theoretical or empirical rationale for the selection of [diagnostic] categories" (ibid., p. 138n1).

More specifically, Livesley maintains that the *Manual*'s taxons form but "an arbitrary list drawn from diverse theoretical positions," such as "self-psychology, object-relations theory, and social learning concepts." Hence, in lieu of a diaphanous, cohesive, and cogent explanation for its choice of categories, the *DSM* has, according to Livesley, a jumble of theories at its foundation of its treatment of personality. He says that this disarray in effect makes personality disorder classification chaotically atheoretical (ibid.).

Though I concur with Livesley that the *DSM* does indeed have a profusion of personality notions at its base, which hinders its having a persuasive typology, this superfluity is somewhat understandable. One of the reasons for this perhaps benign interpretation is that it is widely conceded that the concept of personality possesses a singular richness, one that subsequently lends itself to a panoply of theoretical perspectives from which it can be approached and appraised.

However much the diversity of theoretical stances regarding personality and its variants may dismay personlogists, they are somewhat placated, and apparently not a little intrigued, by two facts. First, they above all others realize that the subject of their inquiries, namely the nature and diversity of personality itself, is among the most complex of conceptual issues and, second, it centers on the most crucial of practical matters.

My position on personality is anchored in the philosophy and psychology of personalism and my typology of the abnormal personality is rooted in a threefold departure from interpersonal relatedness, the essence of which is private and public intimacy. Moreover, my view of the etiology of personality aberration is that it arises from an exceedingly intricate blend of biological, psychological, social, and voluntary or volitional factors with a lack of connectedness in the form of shared inwardness being the proximate source of this personality disturbance.

12. Categorical and Dimensional Paradigms

Another major liability of the *DSM*, for Livesley, as it is for many other researchers and clinicians, is its utilization of a categorical instead of a dimensional paradigm for the elucidation of the personality disorders (ibid., p. 138n2). The question of the proper model with respect to personality and its traits and abnormalities—considered both in themselves and in their relation to states of aloneness—is so pivotal that it must be a chief consideration for this investigation.

It is generally held that the two principal perspectives on personality are the categorical (the absolute and non-continuous) and the dimensional (the relative and continuous). The categorical—the approach adopted by the *DSM*—maintains that individuals with personality deviations have essential (primary) and associate (secondary) criteria which form discrete diagnostic divisions (p. 633).

In employing a categorical model of pathological personalities, the *DSM* contends that personality disturbances differ in kind not only from one another but and, a fortiori, from non-psychopathological types of personality, namely from the normal and by implication from the supranormal. The *DSM* maintains that there are well-differentiated boundaries between each of the ten aberrations and between each of its three clusters. According to Fowler and colleagues these divisions allegedly "carve nature [human] at its joints," meaning categorically, more aptly than do individual diagnoses of the disorders (2007, p. 5).

With respect to the dimensional, or continuous (non-discrete), paradigm, the one most currently utilized, including by myself, is the FFM.

Roger Blashfield and Ross McElroy observe that of the two models, the dimensional is the more basic with the categorical being the former:

> with the additional assumption that patient data form descriptive clusters when plotted in the space defined by the dimensions. That is, a categorical structural model assumes that the descriptive data form densities [for instance, *DSM* clusters]. [It] also assumes that there are boundaries between clusters. A categorical model is a more complex, elaborated version of [the] dimensional. (1995, p. 409)

Gordon Parker contends that dimensional models are highly useful in that they furnish second-order data concerning personality aberrations, namely quantitative information, such as "the duration of impairment." Correspondingly, he maintains that the non-discrete paradigms do not provide first-order data, to wit qualitative information, which would reflect one personality disorder as being actually distinct from another (2006, p. 880). Parker states that a quantitative model is preferable to a qualitative one if, first, "the conditions to be defined and distinguished are truly aligned along a defining continuum," and second, "and possibly—as a default option—if a truly categorical condition resists delineation and measurement by categorical techniques." Parker proposes that dimensionalists contend that these two conditions are met by a quantitative approach to personality traits (ibid.).

On the other hand, Parker proposes that categorical models are to be favored over dimensional types in terms of yielding "definitional power" because the first reveal clearer lines of demarcation regarding disorders than the second (ibid.). Such well-defined boundaries, he submits, may be quite evident among purely physical diseases—although and as noted momentarily not all dimensionalists would concur—and even among Axis I mental disorders.

However, Parker then claims that such "pristine separations" do not obtain among personalities, including those which are abnormal and which pertain to Axis II disorders. They do not do, he says, since such aberrations flow into one another such that they are continuous and interdependent instead of being otherwise. Consequently, Parker concludes, "a dimensional model has to be preferred over any categorical model" with respect to personality or personality style, including the pathological (ibid., p. 885).

Livesley writes that it is not exactly fitting to speak of personality deviations flowing into one another in the sense of their overlapping since this comorbidity is supposed to refer "to the co-occurrence of distinct diagnoses." However, he argues, "there is no evidence that personality disorders are distinct," since, in fact, they merge into one another, as the dimensionalists hold (1998, p. 138n6).

Therefore, Livesley maintains that, if the *DSM* classifications, or categories, were actually qualitatively demarcated, they would be mutually exclusive from the beginning. However, he insists that they are not differentiated in kind, a fact that even the *Manual* acknowledges by noting their frequent comorbidity (ibid., p.138n7).

Livesley appends that the *DSM* categories lack not only exclusivity but exhaustiveness since they do not possess a complete enumeration of cases. He states that to gain such total itemization, the *DSM* resorts to the use of "'waste-basket' categories"—most notably the Personality Disorder Not Otherwise Specified (PDNOS)—which, Livesley concedes, when used judiciously, are justifiable. But it is not justified, he insists, in the case of the *Manual* because, for instance, it overuses the PDNOS classification (ibid.).

Recall that one study found that more than a fifth of clinical patients as a whole and almost a third of personality disordered patients in particular were described as having a *DSM* PDNOS (Lee, Livesley, and Morey, 1997, p. 176). These figures, dimensionalists argue, are indicative of the *DSM's* lack of clarity and conciseness in reference to the aberrated personalities' exclusiveness and exhaustiveness.

Lee Clark, John Livesley, and Leslie Morey ask whether there are specific traits that are qualitatively different such that they are applicable only to normal or abnormal (or supranormal) personality. Alternatively, they ask whether the relevant traits are themselves the same, but that abnormality results from trait extremity or inflexibility or from a particular combination of traits (1997, p. 218).

For perhaps most of those who advocate utilizing a FFM paradigm, it is not a matter of qualitatively different traits being ascribable to the abnormal personality. Instead, it is their extremism or lack of flexibility that is. For instance, Thomas A. Widiger and Timothy Trull state that, for the FFM, an aberrated personality is construed as "an extreme and/or aberrant variant" of the five supertraits of personality (presumably an aberrant variant does not mean departing from the quantitative sequence) (1992, p. 364). Paris proposes that not only are these abnormal personalities "exaggerations of normal traits," but "all medical illnesses lie on a continuum with normality" (1996, p. 1).

On the other hand, Widiger writes that with reference to the FFM conception of an aberrated personality it has been recurrently emphasized that it:

> is not simply an extreme variant of a normal personality trait. Dimensions of general personality functioning vary in their implications for maladaptivity, maladaptivity may arise through a particular constellation of personality traits, and maladaptivity will often be relative to a situational context in which it is important for a person to adequately function (2006, p. 182)

In any case, from the FFM perspective, it would be held that, for instance, the shyness experienced by an individual with an avoidant personality disorder within a small group compared with the social anxiety experienced within a large group differs solely in degree from the apprehensiveness that a normal individual suffers in such situations. Similarly, the FFM would propose that there is only a quantitative difference regarding a specific trait such as a boy's fear in playing rugby for the first time in comparison to that of his engaging in hand to hand combat in war.

With respect to one personality disorder versus another, for dimensionalists, like those who endorse the FFM model, the difference in mistrust between paranoid and schizotypal aberrants, for example, is only quantitative, however huge the dissimilarity might be. Likewise, the difference between the paranoid personality and the normal personality would be but quantitative. Contrarily, categorists would aver that at some point on the continuum, the change from the balanced and non-persecutory to the unbalanced and persecutory mentality of the paranoid becomes qualitative.

R. D. Laing opines that we are all but "only two or three degrees Fahrenheit" from mental unbalance. Consequently, he states that after but "a slight fever" the entire "world can begin to take on a persecutory," threatening reality, a mentality typical of the paranoid aberrant (1965, p. 46). It would seem that Laing, in using the word "degrees," is implying but a dimensional difference between normalcy and abnormalcy, or mental imbalance. Others would essay that Laing's example might be interpreted as being indicative of a change in caliber, or category.

Consequently, it might be asked of Laing whether at some point, literally speaking, between 98.6 and 106.6 or exactly on the latter, the thermometer records a physiological qualitative change in the individual such that self goes from physically non-sick and normal to sick and abnormal. Clearly, those who support a categorical paradigm would respond in the affirmative; the dimensionalists, apparently including Laing, in the negative.

Water freezes and thaws at specific temperature points such that it arguably takes on new properties in what is a "qualitative leap."

Consequently, it can be again asked whether there comes a line of demarcation along the quantitative progression pertaining to personality traits when their quantitative differences are sufficient to reflect "a qualitative leap," or transition, from normalcy to abnormalcy and vice versa.

It might be put forth that, on a continuum of 1 to 100, the difference between 1 and 5 is of a degree that involves relatively minor significance. However, categorialists might contend that the disparity between 1 and 99 is of such an enormous magnitude that it has a qualitative, major import. In turn, dimensionalists can reply that all the changes between 1 and 99 are but quantitative, whether taken one-by-one or altogether. If the change jumped immediately from 1 to 99, categorists might counter with the claim that such an instantaneous and colossal jump was of a qualitative type, certainly in effect.

In some views, mental, or subjective, traits are not quantifiable and therefore, are not measurable. They are surely not determinable in the way objective, corporeal traits, such as body heat via a thermometer, are registered. Moreover, in some quarters, they are not for the very good and perhaps obvious reason that the mind and its constituents are not material but spiritual, meaning, in this, case non-material (immaterial).

Even those who deny that any immaterial realm exists might assert that mental and material phenomena differ in kind such that the first, unlike the second, are not measurable or not adequately so by any physical device. Furthermore, it is frequently maintained that even if the mental were reducible to the physical, its traits are so subjective in nature that we do not have, assuredly not yet, any means of measuring them, even though their physiological effects may be quantifiable and, therefore, measurable.

To exemplify what to some is likely evident, the subjective coldness of schizoids is not discernible in the way the objective coldness of their hands is when submerged in frigid water (if at all). Nor is the mercurial emotional makeup of borderlines quantifiable and, therefore, measurable, in the manner that the mercury in a thermometer registers body heat when they are in a state, for instance, of rage. Thus, it is put forth that we can measure the physiological effects of rage but not its mental and specifically its emotional magnitude.

The metaphysical materialist—in contrast, for example, to the hedonist type—and those who subscribe to objectivism and scientism in general would deny that there is any qualitative difference in principle between subjective and objective states. They claim that the first are equivalent or at least reducible to the second. Similarly, for metaphysical materialists, personalities, along with their traits, can be equated or ultimately reduced to physical phenomena none of which by definition, according to them, have qualitative differences.

Michael Stone likens FFM personality traits to atoms, supertraits to molecules, and personality disorders to compounds (1993, p. 29). The analogy, while instructive, must not obscure the fact that personalities, be they normal or anormal, are living entities. As such, they are endlessly more complex and problematic, if not mystery-laden, than are any purely material phenomena like compounds. Categorialists argue that these factors require a qualitative approach. Moreover, non-materialist metaphysicians would contend that personality disorders are arguably far more unlike compounds and their constituents than like them, in which event they differ in kind rather than quantity.

Even among materialist metaphysicians, there are those who think that people and their mental traits are so unlike all other entities that, in effect, the depth of their differences constitutes a variation in kind. To some, that the mind can even ask what comprises differences in quantity and quality already assumes that human consciousness varies in kind from matter and the quantitative. One reason is the argument that only non-material beings could reflect on material objects and upon themselves as subjects and therein differentiate the two kinds of reality from one another.

To illustrate the viewpoint that personality traits vary but in degree, we can call upon Millon and colleagues. They propose that, since personality disorders are comprised of maladaptive traits, there are two ways in which personality illness can become more dire when "moving along the continuum from health to pathology." The first occurs when a trait becomes more intense, such that anger turns to rage and rage to outrage. The second takes place when the number of maladaptive traits themselves increases (2000, pp. 11–12).

Intensity and number, considered in themselves, are quantitative in nature, but they may also be construed as pertaining to the qualitative. Thus, when water changes from 211 to 212 degrees Fahrenheit, it boils, a process that might be considered as entailing a qualitative change within a material entity. As to number, it is one thing to count the units of material things and the changes within them, like the degrees of the heat of hot water, and another to count the units of arguably non-material beings and the changes within them. Whence, to some minds, the mind and its traits, such as kindness and callousness, are in se non-material entities and, as a result, are subject to qualitative changes.

Widiger states that personality, like intelligence, "is best described as a continuous variable with no discrete break in its distribution" that "would provide a qualitative distinction between normal and abnormal levels" (2000, p. 4). But what about the variation between the extremely subnormal IQ and a supranormal IQ? Categorialists would propose that these are instances of qualitative variation. On the other hand, according to dimensionalists, the gap between the most foolish and most wise is solely a matter of degrees and are, in principle, measurable.

The problem whether ethical and prescriptive traits vary in degree or kind between normals and anormals is even more polemical than those apropos of purely psychological and descriptive ones. It is significant that the first meaning of "normal" is the norm(ative), or the standard, principle, or model, according to which subjects are appraised and compared. The normal construed as average is a secondary meaning.

As well, once the prescriptive and normative are involved in personality traits, then the contrast of the best and supernormal—or, at minimum, the supramoral—with the worst and abnormal, whether categorically or dimensionally construed, is implicit.

Thus, not all personality traits are purely psychic in nature; many are moral as well. The fact that the word "quality" is used for "trait" suggests that the latter is already or can be *qualitative* in nature. The defenders of the categorical model might propose that even within the personality disorders themselves, there are differences in kind among their qualities, such as the sociopath's hard-heartedness and the dependent's soft-heartedness. Naturally, dimensionalists would beg to differ with such reasoning since they state that, at some point, hard can become soft even regarding mental, or subjective, phenomena.

We might inquire whether the unkindness of Carl in his occasionally teasing his sister Grace as compared to perpetually torturing her differs in degree, or whether these behaviors plead for a diversity in kind. Does the moral quotient of a sadistic sociopath such as Saddam Hussein, who symbolizes characterological depravity, and that of a saint such as Mother Teresa, who epitomizes ethical excellence, signify a variance in kind or degree?

There are any number of ethicians who maintain that the variations between moral wickedness and goodness, or between the extremely vicious and the extremely virtuous, differ in caliber, as do our examples, and they do so regardless of cultural variations. But can such differences be mediated quantitatively, or in degree, via the normal person—understood here as the statistically average individual? Mr. Average might be characterized as being good-willed but he is far from being fully virtuous and loving, though he is, hopefully, even more removed from being completely vicious and hateful.

It may be put forward, then, that there seems to be a qualitative jump between the abnormal and normal and between the normal and supranormal in terms of morality. But once the so-called ethically normal is inserted between the abnormal and supramoral, then all three moral conditions might be thought to differ only in degree. Such would be the case, therefore, with the variations among and between Jack the Ripper, John Doe, and St. Francis of Assisi such that at some point(s) they all shade into one another on the ethical spectrum.

As maintained above, the intentions of benevolence, equalization, acquisition, acquisitiveness, and malevolence can be construed as entailing variations in kind. If personality aberrations are habitually acquisitionally (Group I), acquisitively (Group III), or malevolently motivated (Group II), then it can be proposed that they differ in kind from each other and from normals and, a fortiori, from supranormals. The concepts of benevolence, malevolence, and everything in between are at once psychic and ethical traits, all of which categorialists would contend differ in kind. Of course, it can be proposed that entities which differ in kind may do so completely (for example, deities and devils) or partially (for example, saints and sociopaths).

In response to the charges that the *DSM* advocates a categorical model of personality and yet personality traits appear to join with one another on a continuum such that there are no clear boundaries between abnormal personalities and normals, in effect, it responds that personality disturbances differ not totally but only partially (see pp. 633–634). This position moves the categorical model of the *DSM* closer to the dimensional model. This paradigm can be said to have a relative view of disordered personality variations at least in terms of their three groupings and motivational traits. Yet, entities that are close or even next to one another may differ in kind and not only in degree, or so categorists might claim.

If the *DSM* espoused a categorical model, in which each aberrant was reckoned to be totally different from every other one, then it would look upon them as being so different from one another that they could not be aggregated into three clusters. If each pathological person—or any person for that matter—were envisaged as being completely different from every other person, then it would be impossible to have any clusters or even any ten personality disorders. In that case, each person would not only possess uniqueness but, according to scholastic philosophical parlance, "unicity," in which event every person would constitute both a numerical and ontological atomic, or indivisible and unshareable, species. However, to be denominated human beings, people must have something in common, namely the same universal essence, or nature. Qua persons, human beings have diversified, individuated essences. Still, this individuation is not so singular that it possesses unicity, as is predicated only of God in the most absolutely singular fashion.

Contrariwise, if the *DSM* were to employ a dimensional model that is totally relative, it could be proposed that each person would be so much like any other that there would be no differences or at least none of any consequence among them. In that case, persons would hardly be the singular and irreduplicable individuals they are customarily deemed to be. Thus, everybody would be so similar that no distinctions would exist among them, mentally or extramentally, to differentiate the abnormal, normal, and supranormal for there would be no basis, that is no norm, standard, or criterion, of any kind to do so.

It might be proposed that humans beings qua human differ only in degree, while qua persons, be they normal or anormal, they differ in kind. Nevertheless, irrespectively of the way individuals "objectively" vary from one another, they may feel or believe they do in sui generis form if only because they are not comparable objects but incomparable subjects, especially qua persons. Such variations arguably reach their positive affect top and negative emotional bottom in, respectively, the euphoria of love and the dysphoria of loneliness. However, at this point, it is desirable to examine the personality disorders in terms of neuroticism and loneliness, noting that the first can be both a cause and consequence of the second.

Eight

PERSONALITY DISORDERS, NEUROTICISM, AND LONELINESS

1. Neuroticism and Personality Disorders

The lonely are frequently perceived by others and often even by themselves as being mentally sub-par and specifically neurotic in the sense of their manifesting ongoing emotional insecurity, fragility, and instability. When extreme, these traits require therapeutic intervention. Unfortunately, neurotics are often not the best at helping themselves find a remedy for the anxiety and other traits that ail them. Moreover, discovering and realizing such an antidote to their affliction are by no means the same thing.

The research of Daniel Peplau and Letitia Perlman has found that, first, the lonely "score higher" than the nonlonely in terms of neuroticism; second, that "loneliness is associated with poor mental health" in general; and, third, "structured psychiatric examinations" reveal the lonely as having more "mental symptoms needing treatment" than the nonlonely (1984, p. 20).

Thomas A. Widiger and Timothy Trull state that those who rank above average in FFM Neuroticism:

> lack the emotional strength to simply ignore the hassles of everyday life and the emotional resilience to overcome the more severe traumas which are inevitable at some point within most persons' lives. Which particular mental disorder they develop may be due in part to other contributing variables (for example, gender, social-cultural context, childhood experiences, genetic vulnerabilities, and additional personality traits) which either direct the person toward a preferred method of coping (for example, bulimic, dissociative, or substance use behavior) or reflect an additional vulnerability (for example, a sexual dysfunction). (1992, p. 355)

These risk factors negatively impact lonelies' ability to relate to others and leave them disgruntled with the quantity but especially the quality of their relationships. Hence, the ongoing problem for lonely people is ordinarily traceable to their personality features—meaning trait, or endogenous, loneliness in contrast to state, or exogenous, loneliness. Many of these qualities are highly neurotic in nature, including an overall vulnerability itself.

This rather ubiquitous if not universal risk factor leaves the lonely susceptible to (dis)stress and the inability to deal with daily difficulties, all of which are germane to existential and other forms of negative aloneness. Though not all lonely people are neurotic, many are, but even more is the reverse the case, such that neurotics tend to be lonely and usually significantly so, depending on the number, the mixture, and severity of their neurotic traits.

Neuroticism is the only FFM supertrait that is intrinsically negative. Alternatively, the other four FFM domains, namely Extraversion, Openness to Experience, Conscientiousness, and especially Humaneness, imply the positive, as do their very names. The combination of Humaneness and Extraversion, especially its traits of warmth, gregariousness, and positive emotions, are the most indicative not only of health in all its forms, namely physical, mental, and spiritual, but of happiness. This singular state of joy and serenity substantially eludes the neurotic and the lonely, above all the neurotically lonely.

With respect to the personality abnormalities, the absolute loners of Group I are a mixture of extreme Neuroticism, the schizotypal, and extreme non-Neuroticism, the schizoid, the most non-neurotic of the ten aberrated personalities. The neurotic is characterized by negative emotionality; however, the schizoid is devoid of much if any affect whatsoever (Costa and Widiger, 2002, p. 461). In being emotionally cold, flat, and detached or, more accurately, non-attached, this aberrant is less functionally human than neurotics (all individuals are equally human in their essential structures). Hence, this absence of affect renders the schizoid more pathological than the highly neurotic individual who has a propensity to be exceedingly emotionally driven.

Even when an individual's emotions are negative, they are better psycho-ethically, all things considered, than the radical incapability of experiencing almost any emotion as in the case of the archetypal schizoid. At least the presence of neurotic emotionality implies a kind of vitality, whereas its non-presence suggests a kind robotic-like condition. Perhaps it is more accurate to say that the schizoid leads a zombie-like existence, in which case an individual is alive yet dead to the inner and outer worlds.

Schizotypals are, save for Group III aberrants as a whole, the most neurotic of the pathological personalities. Schizotypals are so specifically in terms of the Neuroticism traits of anxiety, self-consciousness, depressiveness, and vulnerability but not angry hostility toward others (and self) and impulsivity, arguably the two most negative traits of this FFM supertrait. So conceived, the schizotypal mirrors the Neuroticism of the relative loner, the avoidant of Group III (ibid.; 1994, p. 329).

However, the focal points of these two neurotic aberrants critically differ since, unlike the avoidant's, the schizotypal's contain little if any desire for being attached. Furthermore, the avoidant, unlike the schizotypal, is not on the so-called schizophrenic spectrum. On what may be titled "the neurotic spectrum," I would argue that the avoidant is the least neurotic with the borderline being the most and also being the most prone to psychotic symptoms after the schizotypal and schizoid.

Though schizoids are the least neurotic of all the abnormal personalities, they are the most purely psychologically disturbed of them. For one thing, these total loners are the most negatively integrated of the abnormals. For another, they are the lowest of the lower Apollonian. From the perspective of the most negatively disintegrated and, therefore, the lower Dionysian, schizotypals can be rated the most purely psychologically disturbed. As to Group II, these lonerists' Neuroticism is mainly manifested by their angry hostility toward others but not themselves.

In addition to their obdurate animosity, Group II's sociopaths are extremely impulsive and both susceptible and non-susceptible to despondence (depressiveness) and anxiety, depending largely on whether these antisocials believe they will be caught and suffer retribution for their illegal activities or what the *DSM* titles their Conduct Disorder.

The paranoids are neurotic in that they are extremely expressive of their antagonism toward others, but they also lack any potentially positive neurotic trait, like vulnerability. Paranoids are also the closest to psychosis of Group II, all of which makes them the most purely psychologically ill of that aggregate. Additionally, paranoids are the most ethically diseased of the deviated personalities save for sociopaths (ibid.). Narcissists are extremely self-conscious, vulnerable, and both subject and not subject to despondence (depressiveness), depending upon the current state of their self-esteem. Obsessionals are somewhat subject to self-consciousness and despondence but are also highly prone to hostility toward others, though it is often repressed or suppressed (ibid.).

I have stressed that those individuals with pathological personalities who most suffer from Neuroticism, namely Group III, are lonely (and alonely) to the point of being pathologically so. Much of this chapter will be focussed on these abnormals and their variegated negative states of aloneness, especially loneliness.

2. Loneliness and FFM Neurotic Traits

Group III personalities as a unit manifest high rates of Neuroticism, though not every one of this aggregate, save the borderlines, exhibit each trait in elevated fashion. For example, dependents do not display much impulsiveness and avoidants do not exhibit much angry hostility. In any case, all six Neuroticism traits are highly intrinsic to loneliness, an affliction, in turn, intrinsic to the pathology of Group III.

A. Anxiety

Paul T. Costa and Thomas Widiger state that anxious people are "fearful, prone to worry, tense, and jittery" besides being subject to a "free-floating" apprehensiveness (2002, p. 463). These qualities directly impede intimacy by, for example, sabotaging communication skills that, in turn, can lead to loneliness of various forms, including, obviously, the communicative kind itself.

Warren Jones remarks that the lonely have a host of social inadequacies that revolve around anxiety, including inhibited sociability such as demonstrated by "lower social risk taking, affiliative tendency, and sociability" (1982, pp. 240–241). He posits that the impairment of the lonely is more specifically witnessed in, for instance, their "problems with making friends, introducing themselves, participating in groups, enjoying a party, being friendly, and in relinquishing control" (ibid., p. 241).

Hence, the lonely person, according to Jones, is liable to engage in "coercive attempts to influence others" (ibid.), which may readily prevent relationships from starting or progressing. This coerciveness is, above all, predicable of the borderline, whereas the histrionic resorts mainly to seductiveness to control and manipulate others, a ploy not foreign to the dependent, while the avoidant's overall strategy is chiefly to circumvent people.

The worrisomeness of the lonely is also seen in that they tend to be fearful of self-disclosure that, in part, is also owing to their sentience of inferiority or at least inadequacy. These traits suggest that the anxiety of the lonely is rooted in their low sense of self-worth. This negative self-appraisal is exceedingly ascribable to all four of the pathologically lonely and neurotic Group III aberrants, especially the borderline.

In reference to the trepidation concerning self-divulgence and the lack of communication skills, Robert Bell and Michael Roloff observe that the lonely "may be inclined to discuss themselves in superficial ways" (1991, p. 61). This propensity for deficiencies of depth in self-disclosure is immensely inimical to emotional intimacy that, by its very nature, tends toward both profundity of feeling and self-revelation.

Peripherality in terms of self-divulgence is most predicable of avoidants and histrionics but for different reasons. Being utterly shy in non-intimate but especially in intimate situations, the extremely introvertive avoidants engage in shallow discourse because they fear drawing attention to themselves.

The consummately non-shy and extremely extrovertive histrionics do so because they resist engaging in any conversations other than cosmetic, often the erotically provocative sort. Completely unlike the timid avoidant, the histrionic worries about not being the center of attention and, according to the *DSM*, will, for instance, use dramatic, lively, and flirtatious words to get it (p. 655).

Intimacy is often a fertile source of anxiety for both normals and abnormals not only because its absence spells loneliness, but because people fear the self-disclosure this emotional contact necessitates. Thus, anxiety is sometimes the result of being apprehensive of both communicating and not communicating what is desired (and of getting and not getting it). Therefore, while people wish to share their interiority, they are simultaneously afraid to do so, in which case trust is required. This trait demands, among other things, that people believe that potential intimates are sincere and benevolently disposed toward them.

The lonely long for attachments but at the same time lack the positive personality traits—and often connection competencies—that would make them appealing intimates. Leonard Horowitz, Rita de Sales French, and Craig Anderson report that the prototypically lonely person finds it taxing to relate personal matters to others, commit to them, and what is most salient, tell others they love them (1982, p. 192).

Donald Saklofske, Richard Yackulic, and Ivan Kelly suggest that high scores in Neuroticism might be indicative of greater cognizance of shortcomings with respect to interpersonal contact (1986, p. 901). This awareness would render neurotics, like Group III abnormals, more susceptible to loneliness in general. Such sensitivity also suggests that the neurotics of Group III are less abnormal than the other two aggregates. Group I are unmindful of interpersonal shortages because they have little or no interest in intimacy. Group II are unmindful because they have largely repressed or suppressed any interest in connectedness or they are mindful of it but their derisive indifference and overt hostility militate against it.

This greater perspicacity on the part of the lonely with respect to a lack of relatedness is one factor in why it is held that some neurotic traits, namely anxiety, despondence, self-consciousness, and vulnerability but not angry hostility and impulsiveness are often considered at least potentially positive. This heightened neurotic perceptiveness to the exigencies of interpersonality is one reason that neurotics are sometimes considered less psychopathological than the statistically normal individuals who often lack such sensitivity.

To some ways of thinking, what is known as existential loneliness is constituted or at least augmented by the ongoing (dis)stress and anxiousness of everyday life due to a lack of intimacy, one that peaks and plateaus in import and intensity for normals. It may be the case that neurotic individuals, instead of normals, statistically defined, are more alert to the daily stresses that contribute to existential loneliness and to the anxiety and alienation that these pressures create. Still, neurotics are unable by definition, as we have just seen in the citation from Widiger and Trull, to handle such (di)stress without self-fragmenting.

John Cacioppo and William Patrick state that the lonely are much more attuned than the nonlonely "to social connection and social rejection in everything they see and do" (2008, p. 172). They state that though the lonely devote "more mental energy to the perception" of their environment, this "added effort comes from a defensive, self-protective posture, which tends to distort [their] perception" (ibid., p. 119).

Cacioppo and Patrick report on studies that indicate that the higher the level of loneliness, the lower is the accuracy of interpreting facial expressions (ibid., p. 161). On the other hand, the nonlonely are more relaxed with what is inside and outside of them, especially its interpersonal portion. As a result of their greater ease, they are more astutely aware of their surroundings and more adept at reading and rating them and less prone to the (dis)ease of the hypertension that afflict the lonely.

B. Angry Hostility

Costa and Widiger contend that hostility is exhibited by those who have a penchant "to experience anger and related states, such as frustration and bitterness" (2002 p. 463). These emotions are routinely imputed to the prototypically lonely, such as the Group III borderline and histrionic. Emotional isolates—due in part to their abiding feelings of worthlessness within themselves and unworthiness before others—are prone to generate anger and acrimony toward them.

The lonely are antagonistic vis-à-vis others in part because they feel that their fellow human beings have let them down relative to what these emotional isolates believe is their right to relatedness. These isolates feel that they do not get the respect and concern they believe is owed them as human beings or as unique persons and, yet, they are liable to believe they have forfeited the right to them. Hostility and bitterness are also highly predicable of the more or less non-neurotic and non-consciously lonely Group II abnormals. However, their acrimony is traceable to their exaggerated sense of self-worth and far more directed to others than to themselves, all of which is the reverse for the neurotic and lonely Group III aberrants. Eventually Group III's animus toward others almost always yields increased anger toward themselves and to a self-indictment for their plight. These negative self-ascriptions may well end up in belligerent behavior toward self, as in self-injury, and others, all of which is routinely the case with borderlines. Lonelies' prolonged feelings of guilt and shame pave the path for despondency that, in its wake, may lead to clinical depression.

People disposed to persistent ire, chiefly when directed toward themselves, typically possess low self-worth. This self-abasement, in turn, reinforces self-fulfilling expectations of being excluded, and these anticipations, in their wake, intensify hostility toward others. The lonely are characteristically unassertive, unobtrusive, and timorous wallflowers and, among the aberrant personalities, most markedly the avoidants followed by the dependents.

Yet, the lonely can also be highly assertive, intrusive, or brazen such as is customary with borderlines and histrionics. Eventually, however, these two more extrovertive aberrants become increasingly hopeless, de-energized, and ultimately introverted and despondent.

Jeffrey Young states that not only are the lonely disposed to believe that others are uncaring but that they are out to take advantage of them (1982, p. 393). This conviction is often well-founded since there is a wide assortment of lonely types among vulnerable individuals, including Group III, most notably the dependents. These pathologicals are easily victimized by intimacy pirates, such as the sociopaths of Group II. The Group III histrionics also victimize others or attempt to do so via their seductiveness. Still, there are grounds, according to the *DSM*, to believe that histrionics themselves have often been previously sexually victimized—or believe and act as if they had been (p. 656).

According to Chris Segrin, the lonely have consistently negative outlooks, including angry hostility, toward others, whether they be strangers the lonely have just met or long-standing intimates (1998, p. 230). Carol Marangoni and William Ickes report that lonely men are liable to produce more irate and rejecting appraisals of their women partners, express more hostility toward rejecting women, and display greater negative reactions when jettisoned by women. Somewhat ironically yet unsurprisingly, these same men actually anticipated being jilted or otherwise actively rejected by the women (1989, p. 103).

Daniel Perlman and Letitia Peplau report on research that "suggests that loneliness in males is associated with aggression toward women and proclivity toward rape" (1984, p. 20). These males—there is a most understandable resistance to designating them genuine men—ordinarily but not always have a very low sense of self-worth, as is the case with the lonely in general.

Emotional isolates may feel so worthless and empty that the only way they believe that they can feel significant and fulfilled—including the sense of being literally filled—in addition to feeling connected and real is to resort to violence. Rollo May avers that violence is "the ultimate destructive substitute which surges in to fill the vacuum where there is no relatedness," to wit the desolate land of the lonely (1969, p. 130).

It is evident that violence is the antithesis of intimacy and that anyone who thinks otherwise is, to paraphrase R. D. Laing, guilty of maximum self-mystification. It is a matter of received wisdom that where violence begins intimacy—especially with respect to love, according to Carl Gustav Jung—ends and vice versa.

Consequently, some lonelies are liable to resort to covert or overt coercive measures to gain the intimacy they crave. Their pressure upon people to relate intimately to them is largely traceable to the lonelies' desperation and to their externalization of their usually covert hostility.

We have seen that these lonelies' anger is mainly self-directed. However, it is reported that individuals who wind up hurting even killing their loved ones do so out of a jealousy embedded in loneliness. Such diverse thinkers as Margaret Mead and Jean-Paul Sartre maintain that jealousy does not register people's love for others but only their insecurity and, it could be added, their possessiveness. Naturally, if people were totally incapable of jealousy, they might be indifferent to their intimates. However, such non-interest is completely contradictory to the very nature of love. Of course, even the greatest love does not forever remain untarnished by egocentricity.

Received wisdom also holds that love overcomes jealousy at least its externalized behavior if not its actual feeling. Unfortunately, for the lonely, love, being loved and loving, is precisely what the lonely most need. Indeed, the chronically lonely are often non-loving in great part because they lack the sine qua non of love: habitual goodwill and its application in deeds and words. The foremost cause of being loved is loving, a fact that the lonely forget, ignore, or are simply unable to realize largely due to neurotic traits and their customary acquisitive motivational mould.

Carin Rubenstein and Phillip Shaver report that unpopular and, therefore, lonely boys, as a result of their having been subjected to peer ostracism and other forms of maximal exclusion, are liable "to act out" their aggressiveness via bullying. These authors report that such conduct on the part of these lonely youngsters is exhibited in their greater penchant for fighting, hostile language, possessiveness, and general disruptiveness (1982, p. 53).

Much though not all bullying, which today is a veritable epidemic in United States' secondary and even primary schools, ordinarily originates in feelings of inferiority and inadequacy, but they are masked by feelings and displays of bravado and other shows of putative superiority. These emotions are often ensconced in social and cultural sorts of loneliness—due to their being repressed or suppressed—that have explosively erupted into aggressiveness, aggression, and violence.

By using intimidation and force of various types, bullies try to achieve what they cannot accomplish by other means, since they are often lacking the social skills in general and intimacy skills in particular. Violence due to lack of communication competencies happens more often and at an earlier age than is customarily believed. In an episode of *Peanuts*, a little boy confided to his buddy that, because he did not know how to tell a little girl that he "liked her," he proceeded to "slug" her. Later, he will learn that violence is an expressway to multiform isolation instead of a short cut to real intimate unification.

As lonely children are often the objects of exclusion and non-inclusion by schoolmates and of torment by bullies, lonely adults are more likely to have had isolating experiences as children than the nonlonely. Arguably, this is caused, in part, because of the legacies of lonely and often neurotically possessive and narcissistic parents.

Twenty-eight thousand Americans die annually from gunshot wounds. Two hundred fifty million guns are privately owned by some eighty million individuals in "The Gun Nation," as America has been called. An American is twenty-two times more likely to be killed by a family member's gun than by an intruder's (National Geographic Channel, 8 July 2010). Therefore, the United States is inarguably one of the most violent as well as lonely, socially and culturally considered, countries in the world. These two dishonors, in my judgment, are greatly attributable to the influence of SCRAM. Violence patently drives and keeps people apart, as do all the five constituents of SCRAM, but predominantly its social atomism.

Fred Bruning decries how Americans increasingly are socially withdrawing from one another due in part to violence. He writes that "detachment is the disease of the 1990s," an illness that, if anything, has increased since then and is the trademark of Group II aberrants. Bruning appends, "when trouble starts we are on our own." . . . All for none is the battle cry" (1995, p. 15) and, it might be annexed, "none for all."

What triggered Bruning's denunciatory outcry was an incident in which Deletha Word, a thirty-three-year-old Michigan woman, was attacked by a man because she allegedly slightly dented his car fender. While being chased by the man, Word fell into the Detroit River and drowned. Approximately forty people stood by while the tragedy unfolded and "some cheered the attacker or laughed at the spectacle [as if] the assault had been staged for their entertainment" (ibid.). The physical, psychological, and moral isolations that pertain to Bruning's report are patently both a consequence of and contributor to violence and threats thereof.

Bruning further contends that social withdrawal and detachment are the result of a greedy and uncaring attitude that, in his assessment, is increasingly plaguing the United States:

> Let the ill cure themselves. Let the poor find their way out of despair. Let the minorities stop whining. Let the welfare clients suffer in silence. Let the corporations do as they please. Let the regulators retreat . . . . it's sink or swim . . . and don't even yell for help. (Ibid.)

In such conditions—ones that are so patently generated and exacerbated by SCRAM, especially its hyper-individualism—a person increasingly feels abandoned to loneliness. This forsakenness, unless countered by personalist/communalist movements, only augments the already widespread lonely extreme individualism that infects the United States. This extremism permeates the anti-government movements such as those of the "Militia Men," "Tea Party" advocates, and (neo)conservatives in general (in a representative democracy, the people *are* the government).

Sandy Close observes how, in large United States' cities, "the one young person who can go anywhere in the city unchallenged is the white skateboarder." She says the reason for this immunity is that this person represents the quintessential loner, who, Close claims, is "the ultimate assimilation into the individualist culture" of America (1995, p. 280). This cultural absorption is patently nominal since social isolates form no actual group and even less a community as such.

Americans may talk proudly about their social participation. Yet, they seem more frequently to commiserate about their isolation. For instance, Americans bemoan the fact that their compatriots are among the lowest regular voters in political elections. Besides, their friendliness and outgoingness in general are often offshoots of and substitutes for the lack of deeper and more enduring feelings found in genuine friendship and other forms of intimacy, as I documented in the first volume. On the other hand, many Americans had given up on achieving their laudatory goals or simply (re)turned to other objectives of SCRAM, like success with its insatiable quest for celebrity, wealth, status, power, and other emblems of esteem by self and others.

In this atomistic American arena, wherein the excluded and self-excluded have become the rule of inclusion, it is the most precarious period, Close believes, to be alone in the United States, since neither the public nor the private realm seems to care. The situation is well portrayed by the "protagonist in a Stephen King novel [for whom] the universe is one of random terror." Moreover, Close says, "the public realm is irrelevant, the family is too feeble to protect you," and, therefore, "you are intensely alone." What these outsiders, meaning the culturally, metaphysically, and cosmically alienated loners and lonelies, feel is, to put the matter in Close's words, "that the world is out of their control and that they are alone in it," a (a)lonely feeling indeed (ibid., pp. 280–281).

It is no secret to loneliness researchers that the chronically socially and culturally lonely and alienated often make willing candidates for movements and organizations based on hatred and violence and for individuals committed to spreading them. Illustrative of this research is Joachim Fest who documents how and why so many of the Nazis' rank and file were drawn from the emotionally isolated and estranged: the marginals and misfits of society (1970).

Adolf Hitler was proficient in using devices such as mass media and meetings to capitalize on Germany's social and cultural rejects and renegades. It is likely that such lonely and alienated outcasts attempted to find, in brutality, violence, and crime, an outlet for pent up hostility, truculence, and unhappiness that their diversified exclusion and non-inclusion had brought them.

I interpose here that Hitler himself was a colossally alienated individual. He was also a Group II lonerist in that he both feared and despised intimacy, all of which was, I believe, indicative of a variegated but largely repressed or suppressed loneliness, including cosmic and cultural, which imbued his unconscious. Indeed, this wickedly vicious individual was, in my view, a supreme and a quite conspicuous exemplification of all four Group II personality disorders that dys-synergically impacted one another.

Therefore, because chronically lonely people ordinarily have deflated self-worth and feel unrelated even unrelatable to others—or, at minimum, to those with whom they would like to associate—aggression and violence toward others may provide them a sentience of being a "somebody" instead of a "nobody." Hence, belligerence may lend these affective isolates a temporary feeling of self-importance. It may also provide them a sense of being in contact with others, however distorted and destructive these beliefs may prove to be because these convictions are inclined to make the violently lonely feel more emotionally and socially isolated.

Although regularly equated by the lonely and the nonlonely alike, the fear of being alone and of being lonely are distinct phenomena. Either can impel individuals, especially highly dependent, conformist types, into a negative group. It is well-known that such passive personalities may become an active part of a violent crowd. In which case, they lose their sense of propriety, responsibility, and dignity as individuals since they identify themselves with the mob and, therefore, no longer feel personally accountable for what they do or not do.

Obviously, aggression and violence have diverse geneses beyond loneliness, but they recurrently emerge in retaliation against a world perceived as inimical or indifferent to a person's meaning/intimacy needs. Moreover, in a culture where success and material values are uppermost, verbal proclamations to the contrary notwithstanding, violence may be sought by those who believe they do not have their fair share of such desiderata.

As a result, hostilities may be utilized by the lonely for their sheer notoriety to evade or escape their sense of futility, powerlessness, and anonymity. These feelings are accompanied by beliefs of not being recognized, appreciated, or understood (sentiments typically reflective of epistemic loneliness). Whereupon, aggression and violence may be adopted to quash, among other things, the convictions of the lonely that their presence is unnoticed, their absence is not missed, and that their entire existence is valueless. All this is the exact opposite of meaning/intimacy, preeminently the kind contained in being loved unconditionally with its conviction of being esteemed simply for the person one is apart from what she or he has or does now or later.

Save for the very elderly the most lonely individuals in the United States are those in adolescence and early adulthood. For many but not most of them, the severity of their affliction will increase as they age. These two younger groups also rank highest in belligerent behavior perhaps especially with respect to its random types.

As well, those who are unattached or detached are more prone to commit crimes in general not only in the United States but in most Western countries. For instance, in Canada, personal crime rates for the single, separated, and divorced have at times been at least twice the national average and three times higher than the rates for the married. As well, all the unmarried categories have higher rates of loneliness than those who live with a partner (*The Montreal Gazette*, 13 October 1989).

Sociological analyses of loneliness, according to Karen Rook, demonstrate that "social relationships serve to inhibit deviant behavior [and] provide support and companionship" (1984, p. 239). Those who live alone, alonists in my terminology, are "more vulnerable to psychological disorders" for reasons that include their "lack of social regulation." Rook notes that alonists are more liable "to engage in deviant behavior, including risky and self-destructive acts." The reason for this negative comportment is that those who live all by themselves often do not possess adequate social relationships and networks. The consequence of this inadequacy means that they have less "structure and input" to serve as guidelines in their daily lives (ibid., pp. 253–254).

Furthermore, there is considerable evidence, according to Peplau and Perlman, that loneliness is linked with "poor grades, expulsion from school, running away from home, engaging in delinquent acts," such as "theft, gambling, and vandalism" (1984, p. 20). Mass and serial murderers tend to be lonely and alienated individuals who externalize their rage, bitterness, and frustration (*USA TODAY*, 18 November 1991).

The criminal and cruel dyssocial personality, arguably the utmost embodiment of both legal and ethical deviancy, is sometimes thought to have experienced bonding problems as an infant. This early lack of contact-intimacy likely contributes to this egological solipsist's psychological involution and moral retardation.

In general, the lonely are incensed at others due to their being subject to a lack of belonging due to what amounts to Mark Leary's triad of exclusion, non-inclusion, and indifference. Though the lonely tend to increasingly view others negatively as their malaise mounts, they are concomitantly more prone to internalize the anger that they bear others and, thereby, take out their hostility more on themselves, as we have seen in the case of Group III. If they do so at all, Group I manifest the least hostility, anger, and bitterness toward others or themselves; Group II, the most toward others and the second least toward themselves.

The animosity of the lonerists of Group II against others is more generalized than that of the lonelies of Group III. For instance, paranoids evince a quasi universal contempt for people and for intimacy as well. If they do have any close bonds, paranoids must exercise, according to the *DSM*, "complete control" over them in order "to avoid being betrayed" (p. 635). When paranoids feel they are deceived and attacked, they furiously respond by even more aggressive counterattacking.

Obsessionals, like paranoids—and sociopaths and narcissists as well—bear hostility toward others in general. The *Manual* maintains that compulsives disdain intimacy as being insufficiently serious and, therefore, a waste of time. Thus, there is no place in the obsessionals' lives for leisure, the most proper domain of intimae (p. 669). Still, should they be involved in a close connection, compulsives, like the paranoids, also feel compelled to exert total domination over it (p. 671).

The extremely rare hostility that the loners of Group I might exhibit vis-à-vis others is ordinarily owing to their not being let and left alone emotionally, socially, and often physically as well. They display little or no anger and even less aggression toward others regarding any lack of intimacy due to their uninterest or unwillingness for anything so emotional, especially one so inward and involved.

I re-emphasize that my remarks concern a given personality disorder insofar as it pertains to the archetype or, as some would say, the pure type. Should the individual be subject to comorbidity things can be very different regarding, for instance, aggression and violence. Schizoids and psychopaths exhibit emotional coldness and as such lack normal feelings and affect. Both may evince little FFM self-consciousness such that they display an absence of normal and necessary shame and remorse. This deficiency may dispose schizoids to cease being non-social and become antisocial by being callously unfeeling in their conduct. They may also do so because of their ready deference to the wishes of others, including sociopaths.

With respect to loneliness being a frustrating longing, it is so because, as mentioned above, its chronic sufferers believe that no matter what they do or not do their intimacyless existence seems sealed by an unchangeable (pre)destiny or fate. For instance, Jones states that the lonely may be persuaded that "their interpersonal fate is being determined by a hostile and capricious social environment" (1982, p. 240).

In a strict sense, "capricious" refers to chance, acausality, or non-determined. Indeterminism is the theory that holds that one, some, or all events happen without any causes. What is putatively fated from the future, predestined from the past, or destined in the present refers to determinism, the position that all events, or occurrences, have necessitating causes. Self-determinism, commonly known as freedom or free will, is the radical capability to act or not act according to what an individual values. Persistent valuelessness is known as axiological nihilism, a scourge that typically affects the clinically depressed. It specifically plagues loneliness-induced depression since without the self's intimates, above all that titled herein "the one-and-only" sort, the self-world and even the world as a whole readily becomes valueless or meaningless (absurd).

Consequently, the lonely are liable to hold confused, even contradictory, views as to the origin of their affliction. Accordingly, they feel victimized by factors both inside and outside themselves that they regard as inexorable and unalterable. The lonely may also think that their nemesis somehow just happens to them as if it were a case of random, or causeless, misfortune.

At the beginning of their distress, the lonely have a penchant for accusing others or their overall objective milieu for posing problems to their relatedness. As time passes they possess an even greater propensity to reproach themselves for the protraction of their plight. The longer their isolation persists, the more the lonely turn their fury toward themselves. This wrath leads to increased guilt and may terminate in depression and even suicidal thoughts and actions, especially for borderlines (Perlman and Peplau, 1984, p. 20).

C. Depression

To signify depression as a FFM personality trait under the supertrait of Neuroticism, I will continue to use the words "depressiveness," "despondence," and "dejection" (and their adjectives). Clinical depression will continue to be called simply "depression" unless otherwise stated.

Neuroticism's despondence is the trait under which Costa and Widiger locate loneliness (2002, p. 463). It is a stance I support in the sense that emotional isolation, if it belongs anywhere among the thirty FFM traits, it does so under this FFM facet since the more grave is loneliness, the more it involves dejection, though it need not terminate in clinical depression. Yet, when this emotional isolation is significant, it often does end in this mental state illness. Even more than depressed loneliness, clinical depression ordinarily involves social and frequently physical withdrawal. Loneliness, in fact, is the most emotional expression of the radical and unchangeable sociality of human beings. However, this tribulation consists in the failure, partial or total, to realize this innate drive for togetherness.

Depressiveness in general is a personality trait that becomes pathological perhaps most under the aegis of grave loneliness. Depressiveness is especially manifest among Group III, who are arguably most vulnerable to loneliness, especially its dysfunctional species, clinical depression as a whole, and clinical lonely depression in particular.

Sharon Brehm remarks, "it's depressing to stay lonely, and being depressed makes it harder to engage in an active effort to improve our social life" via intimate relatedness, in which event all types of negative isolations easily emerge (1992, p. 338). Their reciprocal influence does not make loneliness and depression (clinical) identical experiences. On the contrary, it assumes their being distinct if not separate phenomena.

Hence, not all lonely are depressed nor are all depressed lonely. Nonetheless, the more profound and enduring the loneliness, the more likely it is to verge toward depressiveness and then toward outright depression (Perlman and Peplau, 1984, p. 21). Like the depressed, the lonely are sad. The depressed are not only archetypically mournful, but often extremely (a)lonely if only because they need others to help them manage and overcome their misery.

While I contend that one species of depression is essentially caused and comprised by loneliness, I consider depressiveness to be intrinsic to serious sorts of loneliness, but it lacks the degree or kind of the more all-encompassing despair and pessimism characteristic of depression. Consequently, I prefer, like most researchers on the subjects of depression and loneliness, to consider them different tribulations that often but do not necessarily intersect.

Loneliness is sometimes reckoned the common cold of normal malaises. Clinical depression is often known as the common cold among abnormal afflictions. Actually, it is the most common *DSM* major Axis I mental state disorder after anxiety psychopathologies. The World Health Organization has predicted that depression, after heart disease—an illness positively correlated with various longings of loneliness—will become the leading cause of disability worldwide by 2020 (*The Montreal Gazette*, 25 February 2006).

It is estimated that about 10 percent of the Americans who consult doctors for what they believe are physical problems are actually experiencing depression (so also is a large percentage of them undergoing loneliness and lonely depression). It is likewise estimated that around 10 percent of Americans are subject to "depression severe enough to require medical attention." A third of this 10 percent suffers it on a more or less enduring basis and most of the rest of the two thirds are subject to it in recurring bouts (Beers, 2003, p. 558).

It has been calculated that almost 15 million Americans suffer from clinical depression with women twice as likely to be exposed to this disorder as men (ABC, 22 March 2006). How much depression is due to loneliness and its cognates and results in them is presently difficult if not impossible to say, but it is reasonable to speculate that a significant portion is.

The aim for Americans to succeed is so stressful that failure is a potent source of their apparently widespread depressiveness and depression. For example, one of the most powerful pressures to "make it" for United States' students is to get and stay enrolled in colleges, especially the more prestigious types. A Kansas State University study published in 2003 relates that in America "the number of college-age students treated for depression doubled between 1981 and 2001." The University of Michigan Depression Center "estimated that as many as 15% of college students are depressed" (*USA TODAY*, 21 August 2006).

The same study revealed that nearly 20 percent of American high school students took prescription medications to cope with depression and various pressures (ibid.). Taking non-prescription and illegal drugs is a frequent means among all Americans to allay not only the effects of depression and anxiety but loneliness (in some views, the depressed and lonely necessarily experience anxiety but the reverse is not inevitably the case).

The *DSM* has been considering whether a separate personality disturbance category should be established for what it titles "the depressive personality disorder." This proposed pathological personality may have a predisposition for Depressive Dysthymic Disorder and possibly Major Depressive Disorder (p. 732). The depressive personality disorder may substantially overlap with other personality abnormalities but, according to the *DSM*, the incidence of any such comorbidity is currently not known (pp. 732–733).

The focus of this volume is almost exclusively on the unipolar depression disorders instead of those of a bipolar, or manic-depressive, nature and is carried out in conjunction with negative states of aloneness, predominantly loneliness. Moreover and unless otherwise stated, the unipolar disorders will all be congregated under one title, namely depression. It will stand for the following: major depressive disorder, dysthymic disorder, "depressive disorder not otherwise specified," and major depressive episode (in the above instances, depressive refers to depression and not to what I have titled FFM depressive).

Based on a review of the literature, David Rosenhan and Martin Seligman observed, "80% of suicidal patients are significantly depressed" and that "depressed patients ultimately commit suicide at a rate that is at least 25 times as high as control populations" (1989, p. 357). Loneliness stems from not having the (meta)needs of intimate attachment sufficiently, if at all, satisfied. When some form of seemingly invincible loneliness is linked with the absolute despair of depression, the likelihood of suicide climbs significantly.

Ann Ulmer, Lillian Range, and Gale Trioia have found that loneliness is often a more reliable predictor of suicide than is depression (1992, pp. 183–188). This is probably especially the case when the emotional isolation is of the grave type and believed to be interminable, as it tends to be.

Since meaning/intimacy is so absolutely indispensable to a person's being and well-being, its disappearance may render mental or extramental reality intolerable. To rid themselves of a terrifying sense of feeling alone and unsupported, to wit alonely, suicidals may violently take their lives perhaps believing, as the German proverb has it, "better an end with terror than terror without end" (Choron, 1964, p. 65).

Instead of leading to an all at once "active" suicide, a person's lifestyle may be steeped in a kind of "passive" or "chronic" suicide. The toll of this "suicide by installment" is, in terms of the sheer number of individuals it affects, immeasurably greater than "acute" or active suicides. In either case, grave loneliness is a frequent feature in suicidal ideation and action.

Costa and Widiger state that people susceptible to the FFM trait of depression (depressiveness) are not only prone to loneliness but to Neuroticism's "feelings of guilt, sadness, [and] hopelessness," affects which are themselves especially prominent among the lonely (2002, p. 463). The lonely are subject to guilt in the sense of self-blame since these isolates have a penchant for believing that they are mainly even exclusively responsible for their malaise due to their personal qualities, especially as their adversary advances in intensity and longevity.

We have seen that the lonely are also prone to enervating sadness so much so that it may morph to the melancholy of lonely unipolar depression. It may even become the so-called melancholia of bipolar depression, above all, if their tribulation is due to mourning and, a fortiori, bereavement. The temporalities of loneliness' yearning and missing can also contribute to and even cause depression. This mental state disorder entails a permanent loss or the perception thereof that makes it, respectively, like lonely bereavement and mourning. However, depression is unlike lonely yearning and missing insofar as they refer to perceived temporary instead of permanent absence.

Depression due to such lonely temporalities is sometimes dubbed exogenous in that it stems from outside losses but all, save bereavement-caused depression, may in the end be owing to endogenous personality traits. Thus, people who yearn for but fail to find a life-partner may be unsuccessful in their quest because of their negative qualities, such as self-centeredness, which alienate potential intimates.

Depressiveness is part of all the temporalities of significant loneliness, but it is preeminently an element of grief, understood as bereavement. Elisabeth Kübler Ross and David Kessler distinguish five stages of grieving: denial, anger, bargaining, depression, and acceptance (2005, pp. 7–28). In concert with most professionals and laypeople as a whole, they say that bereavement is "a normal, expected, and healthy" reaction to a permanent loss of a loved one (ibid., pp. 81, 83).

Kübler Ross and Kessler depict bereavement as a lonely, despairing, imprisoning, and an increasingly unshareable desolation:

> There is a wall where none existed before, standing between you and the rest of the world . . . . There is no port in this storm, and the one person who could bring you connection is the one person who is gone forever. And so you feel you will be forever lost. . . . A lack of an expressive outlet is one of the toughest parts of isolation. With anger, you can get mad at someone and yell. With sadness, you can cry. But isolation feels like being in a room with no doors or windows—a place with no way out. And the longer you get stuck there, the harder it becomes to share the pain and the sorrow which create the portals for your movement into the next phase of grief [(acceptance)]. In isolation, hope disappears, despair rules, and you can no longer glimpse a life beyond the invisible walls which imprison you. (Ibid.)

With reference to hopelessness, the lonely may feel largely incapable of changing the objective situation that generated their isolation. Still, they feel even more disconsolate and ineffectual about changing their subjective traits that might have triggered or directly caused their predicament. This despair is both a cause and an effect of the lonely's sentience of self-inefficacy. The longer loneliness lingers, the more its sufferers are apt to incriminate themselves for their tribulation; the more they do, the more hopelessness seizes their being.

Unlike depression, yearning and missing can end abruptly because it can take but an instant for people to fill the void in their heart and have their wounds healed. These immediate changes rarely if ever occur in mourning or bereaving.

Nonetheless, existential loneliness is considered as not subject to any elimination, especially instantaneous, since it is held to be co-extensive with life. Yet, it may be the case that this loneliness *of life* is postulated mainly or even solely by those, for instance, who constantly experience the other nine forms of loneliness *in their lives*.

Both trait and state loneliness, or the emotional isolation traceable, respectively, to internal personality traits and external conditions, can be predisposing, precipitating, and maintaining factors in depression. Sometimes endogenous depression is distinguished from exogenous depression in a way analogous to trait and state loneliness. Some researchers believe endogenous depression appears to have a heritable factor, unlike loneliness, although the traits, especially those of FFM Neuroticism, which dispose a person for this tribulation, are often viewed as heritable. Exogenous depression is sometimes known as the melancholia, which is occasionally conceived as not having any "apparent precipitating event" (Beers, 2003, p. 559).

There continues to be much debate about the etiology, nature, and nosology (classification) of depression disorders, including the typology devised by the *DSM.* This controversy also involves the question whether these disorders are better understood from the binary, or categorical, paradigm or, alternatively, from the unitary, or dimensional (see Parker, 2006, pp. 879–886).

Loneliness is a frustrating longing, owing to the belief that it will not soon if at all cease, which increases the anger and desperation of its sufferers. If they feel certain that their condition will persist indefinitely, then desperation may lead to despair. This defeatism may subsequently yield to depressiveness that, in its wake, may cede to depression with its concomitant hopelessness.

However, instead of ending in utter sorrow and despair, depression may result in its possessor having no feelings whatsoever. This aridity distinguishes it from loneliness and the depression generated by loneliness both of which tend toward being searing in terms of affective intensity.

If the longing does lead to despondence and, a fortiori, to lonely depression, then its sufferers may said to pine, or waste, away because they believe that union or reunion with a potential or actual intimate is impossible. This languishing may give way to the suicidal thoughts and gestures. In such cases, emotional isolates may seek death as the final release from their loneliness, depression, or their fusion.

For the *DSM,* if this "loss of a loved one" goes on for more than two months and is "marked by functional impairment, morbid preoccupation with worthlessness, suicidal ideation, psychotic symptoms, or psychomotor retardation," it can be regarded as depression construed as a major depressive episode (p. 327).

According to the *Manual,* symptoms of major depressive episode usually develop "over days to weeks" and often persist for six months or longer if untreated (ibid., p. 325). While, for instance, a loss of a job may immediately propel a person into a state of exogenous, or reactive, depression, a new job may soon and possibly immediately end this affliction. Contrastingly, the loss of a best friend and its ensuing lonely depression does not end quickly let alone straight away since such an intimate by definition cannot so readily if ever be replaced.

The *DSM* states that a major depressive episode includes lowered mood and "diminished interest or pleasure" in day-to-day activities; negative changes in appetite, weight, sleep, and energy patterns; "psychomotor agitation or retardation"; decreased self-worth and increased guilt; a lessening of the "ability to think or concentrate, or indecisiveness"; and, finally, "recurrent thoughts of death (not just fear of dying), recurrent suicidal ideation without a specific plan, or a suicide attempt or a specific plan" for taking one's life. The *Manual* appends that the above symptoms are "not better accounted by bereavement," a temporal species of loneliness (p. 327; see Brehm, 1992, pp. 336–338).

All of the aforesaid symptoms of depression may be found in significant sorts of loneliness. However, they are not usually as debilitating because they do not, as a rule, pertain to a person's total life as is frequently the case with depression. Still, existential loneliness, above all when pathological, is an enfeebling affliction that affects a person's whole life qua life and not simply segments of it. Nonetheless, existential loneliness is frequently weak in intensity and often of an unconscious condition. Contrarily, depression is typically strong in intensity and of a conscious condition.

Moreover, the impact of life as loneliness is diluted in the sense that it is usually fused with other tribulations such as alienation. While depression is also often mixed with other travails, including loneliness, it generally stands all by itself or pulls these other afflictions into self so much so that it operates like a single disorder.

Finally, existential loneliness is not considered to be any kind of mental state or trait disorder but contrarily, is deemed to be a normal part of life. Depression is a mental state disorder, although it may and often does contribute to existential loneliness. FFM depressiveness is a mental trait problem but not a disorder as such.

Exogenous depression can also occur as a result of the ramifications of physical illnesses such as infections (for example, AIDS, viral pneumonia), hormonal disorders (for example, Addison's disease, Cushing's syndrome), connective tissue disorders (for example, rheumatoid arthritis), neurologic disorders (for example, brain tumors, dementia, or stroke), nutritional disorders (for example, pernicious anemia), or cancers (for example, abdominal, pancreatic), none of which as such causes loneliness at least not directly (Beers, 2003, p. 558). Yet, insofar as such illnesses physically and socially isolate people, they can be instrumental in producing or protracting emotional isolation.

Behaviorally considered, the lonely may act desperately at times by, for instance, engaging in reckless sex and using chemical substances (legal and illegal drugs are common causes and consequences of both loneliness and depression). The lonely usually dodge what is dangerous and opt for the supposed safety of more or less pure passivity, such as that provided by food, sleep, or television, all typical self-medicating devices of the depressed as well. Whether active or increasingly passive, the mentality of the lonely still contains hope and motivational force in terms of self-efficacy. Contrarily, depression inclines toward an all-pervasive hopelessness, helplessness, and loss of motivation and feelings of self-empowerment.

The *DSM* does not refer to loneliness vis-à-vis depression (or to schizophrenia or other psychotic disorders). Yet, it is instructive that when it discusses this mood disorder concerning its cultural contexts, the *Manual* notes that, among Middle Eastern countries, it is often construed as pertaining to "problems of the 'heart'" and among the Hopi aboriginals of northeastern Arizona as "being 'heart-broken'" (p. 324). These usages suggest depression's being linked to if not equated with loneliness by two very different cultures. As symbolizing the affective order in general, the heart can be properly associated with the affect disorder of depression and when broken with lonely depression.

Roy Baumeister and Mark Leary distinguish between general depression and social depression, the second being "dysphoria about the nature of an individual's social relationships" (1995, p. 506). So defined, social depression is allied to social loneliness. Unlike general depression, which refers to grave dissatisfaction with life as a whole, loneliness pertains to that regarding inadequate relatedness to personations (an inadequacy that may lead, nonetheless, to existential loneliness).

Yet, the majority of people's interactions and especially their relationships are what matter most—certainly "when the chips are down" or "it is crunch time." Consequently, a quantitative deficit but above all a qualitative defectiveness in relatedness can hugely and adversely influence attitudes toward life as a whole. Much of this attitude has changed with the triumph of SCRAM since relationships assume a less prominent part of the lives of SCRAM proponents to their great though not always conscious sorrow.

Depression is all-embracing in that it can be the felt loss of all meaning. Hence, it can be the loss of anything under the sun and even the sun itself, due to the absence of natural light, as occurs in the case of seasonal affective disorder (SAD). The loss of some specific source of value, like youth or health, can generate the feeling that all is lost and meaningless. In this case, depression is due to a perceived permanent loss of meaning in a person's life in general, though it may be triggered by the disappearance of a specific value, such as an individual's livelihood.

In contrast, loneliness is the temporary or permanent lack of that specific meaning that is intimate, but, above all, that intimacy that is meaningful. Nevertheless, if people lose the meaning (value) which is congealed in their most intimate other(s), then they can lose not only the meaning(fulness) in their own intrapersonal and interpersonal worlds but in the world as a whole. As a consequence, they can suffer not only existential but metaphysical and cosmic loneliness, which are universal in nature but only as to intimate/meaning but not meaning as a whole, either of which can put people at the threshold of lonely depression.

Therefore, the loss of a heart mate can make a person have no heart for life as a totality, in which case the individual may become subject to lonely depression. In turn, this can readily result in suicidal thoughts or actions. It is at this point when feelings of loneliness and depression are most likely to coincide and then reinforce one another.

If, therefore, depressed individuals have lost interest in intimacy, then they cannot be said to be lonely—at least not according to its cognitive discrepancy model. Nonetheless, loneliness may have contributed to the onset of depression and may remain an unconscious but active element within it. Contrary to the adage that what individuals do not know about themselves cannot hurt them, being unaware of being lonely can hurt or even kill them. People can literally die from lonely heartbreak and may do so without being attuned to what specifically ailed them; such is the nature of some malaises, including loneliness (Lynch, 2000, p. 43).

David Rosenhan and Martin Seligman report on a study that found "64% [of depressed patients] simply lost . . . their feeling for other people," in which case they were or at least were no longer lonely, certainly not consciously so. These authors also reported "92% [of the depressed had no] gratification from some major interest in their life," in which event they were at risk of persistent boredom (1989, p. 309).

Since depression necessarily tends toward an all-inclusive life-dissatisfaction, it may at least initially present itself as the boredom constituted by lack of meaning in a person's activities and overall interests. The lonely also commonly experience monotony, which comes about because they find their activities unsatisfactory; they do not sufficiently share intimate/meaningful activities—or do not so in an intimate and meaningful manner—with those for whom they long. It is the interpersonal intimacy itself that, above all, bestows or bolsters the meaning inherent in such shared activities and intimate sharing and that brings, among other desiderata, focus, energy, novelty, and excitement to them.

The depressed are supreme candidates for ennui, a kind of world-weariness and listlessness due to an all-comprehensive life dissatisfaction. As the world is felt as being dead to them, these individuals become dead to the world with the result that they are especially vulnerable to thoughts of the deathly and death itself, including the self-perpetrated. As characterized by the *DSM,* the borderline, histrionic, dependent, and avoidant are all subject to depression as they are, in my judgment, to pathological loneliness.

James Reich essays that chronic depression has several characteristics in the way it frequently presents itself in disordered personality patients. When they are not in a major depressive episode, the depression in these "patients is defined by emptiness, loneliness, fear of abandonment, low self-esteem, and pessimism" (2005, p. xvii). As I have indicated above, fear of abandonment is part of aloneliness and the other three traits are ingredients of habitual loneliness. However, as a totality, these phenomena pertain only to Group III, especially the borderline and dependent.

Theodore Millon and Roger Davis with Carrie Millon, Luis Escovar, and Sarah Meagher state that the connection:

> between depression and dependency is well researched . . . . Cognitive theorists frequently emphasize feelings of hopelessness and helplessness as two key components in depression. The connection is obvious: subjectively at least, hopeless persons have nothing to which to look forward, and helpless persons have no means of putting their life on course. Both characteristics are closely related to the dependent personality. Because dependents have few competencies of their own, they may have

> only a few strained relationships and a sense of utter helplessness. Likewise, with no possibility of ever learning how to master the complexities of life on their own, they easily become mired in hopelessness. Real abandonment may prompt the dependent to plead for reassurance and support. Excessive guilt and self-condemnation are also common as means of evoking sympathy while preempting further expressions of criticism from former protectors. Once a person is depressed, dependency complicates the road to recovery. (2000, p. 226)

Though both the lonely and the depressed tend to be passive types, loneliness itself causes people to be desperate in the sense of frantic in the search for an intimate. Yet, as this quest increasingly falters, the more people lose their sense of self-efficacy and, as a result, they become more and more acquiescent. Cacioppo and Patrick contend:

> Where loneliness and depression converge is in a diminished sense of personal control which leads to a passive coping. This induced passivity is one of the reasons that, despite the pain and urgency which loneliness imposes, it does not always lead to effective action. Loss of . . . control leads to lack of persistence, and frustration leads to what the psychologist Martin Seligman has termed "learned helplessness." (2008, p. 83)

Consequently, the lonely can vacillate between frenzied impassionateness and extreme impassiveness, whereas the passiveness of the depressed usually becomes only more entrenched in apathy and inertia with the passage of time. Consequently, the more loneliness moves toward depression, the more it also becomes passive and indolent.

Unlike those of Groups I and II, the aberrants of Group III are essentially extremely dependent, often clinically depressed, or at least highly despondent, and as a whole neurotic and pathologically lonely. These traits are, first, frequently interconnected and, second, have traditionally been attributed, whether for bio-psychological or socio-cultural reasons, more to women than men. Consequently, it is not surprising that Group III aberrants tend to be women; Groups I and II, men.

D. Self-Consciousness

Costa and Widiger describe FFM self-consciousness as an anxiety-laden self-awareness predicable of those liable to experience excessive "shame and embarrassment." They maintain that such individuals are likely to be "uncomfortable around others, sensitive to ridicule, and prone to feelings of inferiority" (2002, p. 463). Self-consciousness is highly ascribable to the lonely, the neurotic, and to Group III, most noticeably the avoidant.

Lasting loneliness is a humiliating condition since it implies that its experiencers are undesirable companions. Hence, the lonely are often deemed to be failures since they do not succeed in realizing the most elemental exigency of human beings qua persons: intimate sociality.

Sometimes the self-image of the lonely is so low, their plight so desperate, and their personality so negatively dependent that they will accept anyone as an intimate. One lonely eighteen-year-old relates that she had a boyfriend during her early adolescent years but confesses she "didn't like him much" (Rubenstein and Shaver, 1982, p. 62). The implication seems to be that she had "settled" for him because she was lovelorn, meaning desolate and forsaken, in that she had no one else in her "life," meaning her "love life."

Generally speaking, worthlessness is to shame as unworthiness is to guilt, both of which are highly predicable of the chronically lonely and Group III pathologicals. Nonetheless, these individuals, despite or even because of their self-consciousness and attendant feelings of sunken self-worth and self-worthiness, may try to force others to like or love them. In such instances, their customary passiveness yields to pushiness, possessiveness, hyper-active hastiness, and the failure to discriminate real relatedness from pseudo-relatedness.

Not all lonely people have low self-worth, especially if they look upon their affliction as caused by external factors. Yet, if outwardly generated loneliness persists, it tends to produce the belief in its sufferers that they are the cause of their adversary and even of the external conditions that activated their internal traits. Thus, protracted external (state) loneliness has a penchant for fostering internal (trait) loneliness. Consequently, this malaise is felt as being self-induced predominantly in the sense of being the legacy of negative personal qualities.

For example, poverty is conducive to creating social loneliness, perhaps especially when it is felt as a result of being excluded, non-included, or objects of indifference. However, this tribulation eventually tends to become a matter of self-blame on the part of the poor who increasingly consider it an effect of their personal traits. This conviction is frequently initiated or at minimum reinforced by SCRAM, which indicts the poor both for their economic plight and their affective adversity in the form of loneliness. It does so because SCRAM perceives the indigent as poachers, parasites, and other free-loaders and, therefore, emblematic of their being losers and all around-failures.

Some lonelies believe that if others really knew them, they would find them not only acceptable but highly attractive due to their personality pluses. Given their relatively high self-appraisal in comparison to most lonelies, these few believe that they have, above all, themselves to give. This bestowal primarily pertains to their unique selves and to their singular set of qualities, assuming that the self its distinct from its attributes. These lonely yet fairly self-assured individuals may be benevolently disposed to others. Because they are good-willed, their nemesis does not, as a rule, consign them to more or less habitual feelings of shame, inferiority, inadequacy, shyness, and social anxiety associated with negative self-consciousness (positive self-awareness is linked to self-confidence, self-reflection, and self-reflexion).

Contrarily, not all people who believe they are good-willed and even loving are saved from loneliness. Many of them are of the mind that they constantly strive to be caring and personable. Nonetheless, they are equally certain that what they get in return from these efforts is indifference, degrading pity, strong dislike, and even hatred. Unfortunately, most neurotically, like most habitually trait lonely individuals, are too wrapped up in themselves to go out to others via benevolence and active concern (beneficence). The painfulness of their predicament is another factor that tends to rivet their consciousness on themselves in non-constructive fashion.

E. Impulsiveness

Impulsiveness means the incapability of individuals to manage their "cravings and urges" (Costa and Widiger, 2002, p. 464). The inability regarding impulse-control on the part of the lonely is evinced by their desperation-driven rashness concerning relatedness, in which case they may become "intimacy-addicts." They indiscriminately pursue various forms of contact with anyone and everyone, as in the case of so-called sex-addicts.

René Bruemmer states that sex addicts, who comprise approximately 3 percent of the population, "have lost control over their sex lives." He says that their fixation, for example, may concern only the Internet, but "for their partners, it feels like an affair" (*The Montreal Gazette*, 5 December 2009). Studies indicate that those "who spend a lot of time with on-line porn are prone to increased loneliness, dissatisfaction in their relationships, and sexual impairment." These studies also indicate that, in 2008, "there were 420 million pages of porn on the Internet" and about "1000 new porn sites are created every day." Still, it is reported that almost 70 percent of Americans regard the Internet favorably, especially insofar as it provides them a positive kind of contact with other human beings (CBS, 21 December 2008).

The lonely are also compliant candidates for addictions to drugs such as alcohol—the usual chemical of choice for the seriously emotionally isolated who use such substances to palliate their painful feelings. The lonely Group III aberrants, above all the dependents and borderlines, are especially ready recruits for substance abuse. They are also at high risk for becoming relationship-addicts, in which case any connectedness is perceived as being preferable to being isolated.

The term "dependent" is routinely used to characterize those individuals subject to various sorts of addiction. This compulsive conduct is bound to make their habituates even more lonely. For example, such behavior renders these isolates more anxious, depressive, if not outright depressed, in addition to being more self-engrossed. These traits, in turn, repel actual and potential intimates and thereby reinforce the (a)lonelies' unwanted separation from such individuals.

Alternatively, the lonely may impulsively flee intimacy due to their apprehensiveness concerning being close to others, a flight most obviously prominent among Group III avoidants. Or they may frantically pursue, for example, one erotic contact and then suddenly drop it in search for another escapade to escape, among other things, their loneliness, all of which is the history of histrionics.

The many reasons why intimacy can be frightening include fear of engulfment or various sorts of maximum exclusion, such as abandonment; lessening or total loss of independence and freedom; embarrassment concerning self-disclosure; loss of privacy, and trepidation concerning the painfulness that is the lot of those whose connections have gone awry due to betrayal or simply have gone away due, for example, to boredom.

F. Vulnerability

Costa and Widiger depict vulnerability as a liability to suffer stress such that those who score high in this trait feel "dependent, hopeless, or panicked when facing emergency situations" (2002, p. 464). All these are vintage traits of the lonely since their affliction is felt as a kind of ongoing crisis that is increasingly perceived as insurmountable. As this isolation approaches feeling of insuperability, their sufferers easily becomes panicky. They become alarmed even terror-stricken at the prospect of losing an intimate or never gaining—or at least not adequately so—the one(s) sought. In facing emergencies, the lonely are liable to become distraught and frenetic. Eventually they may become despairingly apathetic because the majority of those subject to chronic loneliness are prone to being passive and despondent personalities to begin with.

Jules Henry contends, "vulnerability and loneliness are inseparable." He claims that individuals feel exposed when they are "unprotected, easily hurt, and trapped, or misled." Henry goes on to say that people are lonely because "they feel vulnerable, and they are vulnerable because they are alone." Or they believe they are, in which event, to use my terminology, their loneliness is rooted in aloneliness. Consequently, "whoever is alone is vulnerable because there is no one on whom he can rely" (1980, p. 95), a feeling most predicable of Group III, and especially, of course, of the dependent aberrant.

Thereupon, Henry states that the lonely person eventually perceives "the world as made up of things, not people," since objects, such as drugs, "acquire supreme importance because they can be relied on" relatively speaking (ibid.). Materialitis and the obsession regarding buying, possessing, hoarding, consuming, and discarding of objects, or "stuff," are frequently due to just this kind of loneliness/aloneliness and feelings of defenselessness.

Some lonely individuals, like the supremely fickle histrionics, are—mostly due to their acquisitiveness—also disposed to scrap one subject after another. Yet these Group III abnormals perceive themselves both as the sources and recipients of objectifications. Histrionics will do almost anything to secure others' attention, a compulsion that compromises their autonomy, dignity, and integrity but that temporarily relieves them of (a)loneliness.

Normal human beings are fairly able to be both vulnerable and invulnerable in positive fashion. For instance, they can be sensitive to others without being soft-hearted. They can also forge ahead on their own despite being criticized by others without becoming hard-hearted. All Group III are negatively vulnerable in the sense of being fundamentally weak-hearted and overly sensitive sorts of personalities. The borderline can be hard-hearted but this trait usually masks a more soft-hearted, thin-skinned psyche or alternates with it.

Groups I and II as a whole are more or less negatively invulnerable in that they are coldly insensitive to others and, respectively, non-hearted and hard-hearted. This innate (Group I) and largely acquired (Group II) impregnability prevents these pathologicals—especially the schizoid and to a lesser but still formidable extent, the schizotypal—from being susceptible to loneliness at least on a conscious level. However, it also renders them more psychopathological than Group III. Group II especially seek to make themselves invincible and triumphant regarding others. These endeavors are part of their pursuit of the domination of and independence from people save when they can be used in various fashions. Little wonder Group II aberrants are anti-intimacy since such connectedness is the paragon instantiation of cooperation and inter-independence.

3. The Negativism of Lonelies and Neurotics

The lonely and the neurotic are customarily considered to be unduly critical of others. Still, both groups—whose members highly overlap—are usually even more disapproving of themselves. The lonely often assess others negatively because the first anticipate being appraised in like manner by the second. For example, Jones reports that the lonely tend to rate themselves and their partners' personality negatively (1982, p. 247). Naturally enough, these unflattering evaluations cause self-alienation even as they alienate others, including potential and current intimates. In this manner, alienation and self-alienation may be said to generate, respectively, interpersonal and intrapersonal (intraself) loneliness.

Jones has found that the lonely disapprove of people "collectively and individually," which, he says, is especially the case with "lonely males." Given their criticism of others and themselves, it is not altogether surprising when Jones states that, in comparison to the nonlonely, the lonely have a propensity to dislike themselves and others (ibid., p. 238). Habitual self-aversion and disaffection vis-à-vis others are proven paths to estranging them and thereby initiating or increasing at least indirectly the likelihood of loneliness.

In addition, Jones reports that the lonely may lack positive feedback from others, which itself generates feelings of self-devaluation and negative self-consciousness. This lack of desirable feedback also deepens the lonelies' anticipation of rejection that, in its wake, aggravates their feelings of self-abasement (ibid., pp. 246–247).

Robert Bell and Michael Roloff have found that loneliness is positively associated with "self-deprecating information" (1991, p. 69.). Such self-disparagement is an alienating turn off for others since people do not generally like it when individuals habitually disapprove of themselves especially in overt fashion.

All this dissatisfaction with self, and with and by others, contributes to the vicious circle in which the lonely are entangled. These isolates are past masters at creating the downward spiral that their affliction takes and that they so desperately yearn to escape. They do so unless, of course, they enjoy wallowing in self-pity and other forms of masochism that many lonely appear to do, especially the dependent types of Group III.

Research suggests, "loneliness correlates inversely with acceptance of others" (Jones, 1982, p. 239). Lonely people "expect too much from others or are looking for perfect mates and friends and," as a result, "fail to take advantage of available interpersonal resources" at hand (ibid., p. 247). Lonely individuals often are so more due to their displeasure with the imperfect relationships they have than because they may have no ongoing attachments whatsoever. In such cases, missing is more lonelifying than yearning.

In part, the desire for a perfect intimate is derived from the lonely individual's sentience of lowliness, inadequacy, and imperfection in general. To a considerable degree, as well, looking for Mr. Right and other embodiments of Ms. Perfect is an element of the idealization process. This unfolding is routinely involved in various kinds of intimacies, especially romantic types. Idealization in general is what makes human beings what they are: ideal-forming social mammals.

Hence, regarding relationships, it is far from easy to discern when idealization is appropriate. It goes against the grain to settle for a mediocre friend or lover. Still, it goes even more against human nature to be perpetually lonely. As a result, in their desperation, the lonely may lower their standards and settle for anything or anyone who relieves their accursed agony.

The positivity of idealization is to be distinguished from the negativity of idolization, to which the lonely are extremely inclined. This kind of misguided veneration often stems from the inability or unwillingness to accept others (or self) as they are. Thus, the lonely may simultaneously develop or reinforce their negative attitude toward others and yet quasi-adore them, an ambivalence typical of (a)lonely borderlines.

Love accepts self and the other(s). Nonetheless, this acceptance (and and validation) does not preclude the loving from wanting loved ones from becoming the best they can be. The best, of course, is moral goodness, which itself is measured by the purity (the absence of self-centeredness), commitment, extension, and other such qualities of love itself. Love is commonly said to alone possess the kind of immediate and direct insight that grasps the unique essence of a person and the fusion of its actual and ideal selves.

Jones also notes that the lonely are given to "less expressed inclusion of others" even as the first are less included by second. The lonely bear not only less "affection for others" but greater "difficulties in being friendly," "empathic," and responsive toward them, and less apt to engage in "intimate disclosure" (ibid.). Thus, lonely avoidants, though they intensely long for intimacy, may talk about everything else except such inwardness insofar as their timidity does not preclude them from communicating at all.

Lonely people are highly susceptible to frustration and anger—two emotions exercising reciprocal negative influence upon each other. The lonely are studies in exasperation, owing to their belief that their predicament will continue despite their or others' efforts to the contrary. This conviction is federated with the lonelies' ever-increasing conviction that they are powerless to alter their affliction, especially when embedded in addictions. Lack of this self-empowerment contributes to their tendency toward anger, FFM despondence, and often clinical depression so characteristic of Group III.

4. Loneliness and the Negativism of Pessimism and Cynicism

In its strictest sense, pessimism is the doctrine that maintains that the actual world is not only bad but the worst conceivable, that human beings are born into this most sad state of affairs, and they cannot escape it. From an ethical perspective, pessimism contends that the world is evil and replete with unhappiness or at least they outweigh what is good and felicitous. In short, pessimism stresses the gloom and doom, meaning the misery of reality and the hopelessness of changing it.

Like the depressed, the lonely have a pessimistic attributional style in that, according to Sharon Brehm, both exhibit an inclination to explain their unhappiness in terms of causes that are subjective, trait, or endogenous instead of objective, state, or exogenous; enduring instead of transient; and multiple instead of single (1992, p. 338). Still, the lonely attributional style is not as global in scope as that of the clinically depressed tends to be.

Stephen Davis, Helen Hanson, Roger Edson, and Charlene Zieglere have found that loneliness is positively correlated with pessimism and inversely correlated with optimism. Pessimism is negatively associated with a shortage of self-esteem, while optimism is positively related with it (1992, pp. 245–246). Obviously, optimism and pessimism are negatively related.

The lonelier people become, the more they tend not only to gravitate toward pessimism but cynicism (the reverse is also true). Cynicism is the doctrine that claims human beings are motivated solely by self-interest, which means, in the language employed herein, that all their intentions are acquisitional, acquisitive, or selfish. Hence, cynicism entails a disbelief that others are benevolently motivated with the consequence that all genuine intimacy, including love, is viewed as illusory or even feigned. The opponents of cynicism claim that such a view chiefly reflects the externalization of the ill will and self-centeredness of its proponents.

Cacioppo and Patrick state:

> The cynical worldview induced by loneliness, which consists of alienation and little faith in others, in turn, has been shown to contribute to actual social rejection. This is how feeling lonely creates self-fulfilling prophecies. If you maintain a subjective sense of rejection long enough, over time you are more likely to confront the actual social rejection, which you dread. (2008, p. 175)

Concerning cynicism, Jones remarks, "loneliness correlates inversely with acceptance of others, just world beliefs, and belief in the trustworthiness, altruism, and favorability of human nature" (1982, p. 239). Lonely individuals' negativism toward self and others is both a cause and a consequence of cynicism, which expects the worst in and from everyone, and of pessimism, which expects the worst from everything, both of which, especially the first, pave the way to misanthropy.

Marangoni and Ickes propose that the lonely, as a consequence of their negativistic outlook on human nature as a whole, have, logically enough, decreased hopes about finding a partner, at least a suitable sort (1989, p. 103). The lonely are also less sanguine with reference to the likelihood of the continuation of a future relationship should they be able to initiate one. Naturally, real love requires its pursuers to be caring if they are to help prevent the loneliness of an unhappy relationship. Unfortunately, the gravely lonely (trait loneliness) tend to be devoid of an indispensable condition of caring, namely benevolence, at least on a highly sustained basis. I underline here that the cynicism of the lonely Group III pathologicals is provisional and a posteriori, whereas that of the lonerist Group II is permanent and a priori.

The cynicism of the lonely can be readily seen in their general attitude and overall behavior. For instance, Jones reports that the lonely exhibit "inhibited sociality" and are inordinately "self-focused" in comparison to the nonlonely or ephemerally lonely (1982, p. 241).

Echoing findings of Jones, Chris Segrin relates that the lonely manifest poor "partner attention," owing to their pre-occupation with self. He says that this self-engrossment is manifested in the lonelies' failure "to send messages of involvement or concern" to others as a whole, including even their partners. In comparison to the nonlonely, the lonely partake, for instance, "less in conversations with strangers and roommates" and "engage in less self-disclosure with opposite-sex-partners" (1998, p. 229).

Lack of self-divulgence is often traceable to the lonelies' inadequate communication and social skills, all of which is typical of Group III, especially the avoidant. The lonely are highly given to anxiety and self-consciousness, traits that impede social adeptness.

Deficient consideration of others, though it often originates from the lonely's self-engrossment, also results from their negative perception of others. This viewpoint is frequently traceable to the lonelies' belief that others view them unfavorably, which is ordinarily the case if the first seem unwilling to give up their negative outlook on the second. These negative perceptions, then, involve the lonelies' self-identity (their view of themselves) and their meta-identities (their view of others' view of them) (Laing, Phillipson, and Lee, 1966, pp. 5–6, 19).

Marangoni and Ickes refer to data that also suggests that, unlike the non-lonely, the lonely customarily rate themselves and others, including their partners, negatively. Because the lonely also expect to be rated negatively, their sense of shame and discomfiture is enlarged (1989, p. 103). Accordingly, their self-worth further sinks while their infelicitous isolation soars.

Similarly, Jones states that the lonely "engage in extensive self-derogation." They anticipate negative appraisals from others, including being rejected, a belief that exacerbates the lonelies' low self-regard. This negative self-appraisal leads the lonely to think that they will be kept or left out in the future (1982, p. 246–247). Thoughts of being excluded and unincluded increase the anger that the lonely bear others. Though such feelings may be placed in abeyance by the lonely, they frequently surface in their moody and other negative behavior.

Brehm comments that because the lonely are inclined to consider themselves as "unworthy and unlovable," they are liable to foresee themselves as being "uncomfortable in risky social situations." This unease can cause the lonely to decrease their social contacts, all of which reduces their opportunity to gain the relatedness they need to vanquish their adversary (1992, p. 333).

With their interactions in decline, the lonely may appear to be removed from and uninterested in contacts with others. This seeming aloofness and indifference may encourage people to stay away from the lonely. Whereupon, others' retreat from the lonely causes them to feel further rebuffed and to judge their fellow human beings even more unfavorably.

The reduction in social contacts may also decrease the lonelies' social skills, a contraction that is programmed to further diminish their already limited opportunities for social intercourse. As Segrin observes, it is ironic that the lonely who, by definition, want "more intimate and meaningful contact with others simultaneously emit messages of disinterest and non-involvement" to them (1998, p. 230).

As have other researchers, such as Jones, Segrin hypothesizes that this seeming ambivalence may be due to the interaction of the negative views the lonely have of others and their expectation of being on the receiving end of such negative attitudes themselves. If all this is so, it is logical that the lonely would be "avoidant, detached, and somewhat withdrawn in social interactions" (ibid.), (of course, none more than the avoidant aberrant). In their desperation for connections, the lonely constantly scan their surroundings for possible intimates. However, they are also fearful of such interaction since closeness makes these isolates vulnerable to a host of possible dangers, including being forsaken.

Not all lonely are timorous types, habitually withdrawn from others, like the avoidant aberrant. Extraverts, like the supremely so histrionic, may also be given to loneliness. The occurrence of this affliction depends on the gap between what is needed and desired in terms of intimacy and what is achieved. Extraverts may have a bigger chasm than introverts in these respects.

Still, given their seeming constitutional inclination toward optimism, the more gregarious individuals are not dissuaded by periodic relational failures. They make renewed efforts to nullify the gap between their longings and attainments vis-à-vis intimacy. Alternatively, the lonely have a propensity toward introversion and pessimism and thereby sow the seeds of the interpersonal failures that they wish to elude.

Segrin essays that the lonely are "trapped in an emotional and cognitive conundrum" since they seek closer attachments but yet maintain their negative attitudes toward others. Such outlooks virtually guarantee an undesirable outcome for the lonely in what becomes a magnification of their arguably a fortiori misery (ibid.).

Jones also finds that the lonely are less "attracted" to others, both those in general and in particular, including "dyadic partners" (1982, pp. 246–247). Moreover, he, like Segrin, maintains that the lonely "less frequently indicate a desire for continued contact." To be sure, it is this very closeness that the lonely must obtain if they are to eliminate their tormentor (ibid., p. 247).

According to Jones' findings, the lonely not only have fewer social exchanges but often choose not to have them lest they be rejected, a decision preeminently prevalent among avoidants (ibid.). In order not to be perceived as incarnating what the Italians call a "*bruta figura*" (disgraceful impression), the lonely reject others before they themselves suffer the shame of being rejected or otherwise maximally excluded. Jones also reports that the lonely project their shortcomings onto others, whom they then deem too imperfect for relationships (ibid.). All this explains at least in part why the lonely tend not to want to socialize with "losers" like themselves but often are forced to do so because the "winners" do not want to associate with them. In sum, the lonelies' somewhat cynical disapproval and disavowal of others originate from their own self-dissatisfaction and self-repudiation.

The lonely who are isolated due to their personality traits are far more likely to be non-benevolent than are those whose loneliness stems from external factors. In whichever case, the lonely want to be liked and loved by others if they are to rid themselves of their nemesis. However, their lack of being well-disposed to others largely prohibits the realization of these desires. This counterproductive attitude drains not only the lonely but others' good graces, including their tendencies to empathize and sympathize with these isolates.

People's spontaneous compassion for the lonely often ends almost as quickly as it begins once they believe that these isolates have brought their tribulation on themselves or have at least implicitly chosen to continue it by being habitually non-benevolent. This lack of goodwill is especially reflected in their negativism, as expressed, in their pessimism and cynicism.

As a result, people time and again—and likely in good faith and with goodwill—advise the lonely "to get over" their problem. Thus, these isolates are routinely urged to get beyond their problem with relatedness by getting together with others, even other lonelies. Naturally, it is hard for the lonely to overcome a motivational pattern like any kind of non-benevolence that, by definition, is more or less locked into prolonged self-preoccupation. It is especially difficult to defeat a pattern that has degenerated into the sort of self-indulgence inherent in sustained self-pity, which is itself both a cause and an effect of such self-absorption.

To further consider the pessimism of the lonely, we return to Jones whose research indicates, "lonely students held a more pessimistic view of matrimony" and, as a result, "were less likely to believe that most people marry for love" (1982, p. 239). It may be conjectured that because the lonely tend not to be benevolent, they have a propensity to project this lack of goodwill onto others, all of which inclines the lonely not only to pessimism but cynicism.

Jones further relates that in terms of their own marriage and divorce, lonely students—or, at least, the lonelier of them, especially women—expected the following: "a low probability of having married by age 30, a greater likelihood of their own divorce," and "less of a probability of remarriage should their marriage end in divorce." If these same students were to become divorced, they "also expected greater negative reactions such as hostility" from others (ibid., pp. 239–240).

Since Jones wrote the above a generation ago, many people have not married before age thirty. In part, these individuals refrained from doing so because they saw their parents—who generally wed in their twenties—separate or divorce at extremely high rates. These under thirties want to avoid these lonelifying and other negative conditions.

Jones also found that the lonelier the student, the greater the likelihood "that he or she anticipated getting married because of loneliness, parental pressure, or a need for security and dependency" (ibid., p. 240). Such expectations have a way of proving true for the lonely in that what they most fear, namely increasing emotional isolation, becomes a fact. Hence, the greater the loneliness, the more likely it is to increase in the future as does the fear of this affliction.

The lonelier the student, according to Jones, the less would this individual imagine marrying "for love" (ibid., p. 240). This belief is possibly an even more pessimistic position—or "realistic," according to cynicism—than the view that romantic love alone is necessary for a lasting and happy marriage is an overly optimistic one. Assuredly, marrying primarily, not to mention solely, to get away from or get out of loneliness is not the best reason to enter this kind of bond.

Being afraid of loneliness, meaning aloneliness, is a far more common motivator than people would like to believe. It is so since when marriage and other unions are based primarily on such self-interest—namely that of avoiding feeling negatively alone—they are not benevolently grounded, at least not primarily so. In addition, if they are not people think that they are not the kind of marriages undertaken principally and, a fortiori, exclusively "for love."

Abraham Maslow distinguishes two sorts of love: "needing love," which is non-benevolent and false, and "unneeding," "growth-motivated," or "self-actualizing" love, which is benevolent and true (1968, pp. 41–42). The first type is a poverty-stricken need for love, what Maslow calls a "deficit-motivated" love, like the acquisitive neediness of the pseudo-love characteristic of FFM Neuroticism.

Thus, people can love others, rather paradoxically, because they perceive them as not being needy in a negatively dependent fashion. Accordingly, people want to be loved purely or at least primarily for themselves. Maslow states that needing love:

> is the sort which is customarily studied and is a hole which has to be filled, an emptiness into which love is poured. If this healing necessity is not available, severe pathology results; if it *is* available at the right time, in the right quantities, and with the proper style, then pathology is averted. Intermediate states of pathology and health follow upon mediate states of thwarting or satiation. If the pathology is not too severe and if it is caught early enough, replacement therapy can cure [it]. . . . The therapeutic and psychogogic effects of experiencing [unneeding love] are profound and widespread. (Ibid.)

Needing love, therefore, amounts to a kind of acquisitive desire, the habitual motivational pattern of Group III. Maslow maintains needing love is based on jealousy, possessiveness, hostility, anxiety, fearfulness, insecurity, insatiability (due to love-starvation), hyper-dependence, and self-worthlessness (ibid., pp. 42–43), all hallmarks of FFM Neuroticism and loneliness. They are also traits typical of Group III, the most neurotic and lonely of the pathological personalities.

It is often these dystonic qualities that incite aberrant personalities, such as the borderlines, histrionics, dependents, and avoidants to seek therapy (Group III comprise the unit most likely to do so). Alas, these traits are also the very ones that so often sabotage the success of "the therapeutic alliance" and other forms of interpersonal relatedness.

Still, in comparison to Group II and especially Group I abnormals, Group III have a considerable potentiality for "unneedy," or genuine, love. It can be actualized if they are genuinely loved themselves. But, then, their negative attributes frequently repel potential intimates, all of which instigates or aggravates their loneliness. Regrettably, these neurotics themselves often had neurotic caretakers in their formative years. As a result, they became convinced of their unlovability and often of their inability to love, all of which propelled them toward Maslow's specious and needing kind of love.

Receiving love, above all its unconditional brand, is the main method to gain unneeding, or mature, love. Children ordinarily have to get love before they can habitually give it, though they seem naturally disposed toward benevolence and, therefore, to love itself. Obviously, it takes more intimacy skills and other proficiencies plus more positive psychomoral attributes to love than it does to be loved.

Nonetheless and somewhat ironically, the chief way for adults to gain unconditional love from others is to give it to them but not seek it for themselves, at least not primarily so. Unfortunately, unconditional love is often confused with its antithesis such as that by way of excess, or so-called "hyper-love," which is a coddling kind brought about by, for example, "hyper-parenting," meaning the constantly hovering over their children. In any case, genuine love is not only unconditional but conditional—namely the kind that both presupposes and yet inspires the fulfillment of the obligations of justice, the objective foundation of interpersonal relations.

Pathological love sickness is the sort seen in grave loneliness, the kind so rampant among Group III. They are by far the most neurotic and "needy" of the abnormals. However, the absence of such deficiency-motivated "love" can signify the existence of even more profoundly pathological personalities. Such is the case with the non-loving Group I and the anti-loving and unlovable, hatred, and malice prone Group II.

5. The Ranking of the FFM Neurotic Traits and the Personality Disorder Groupings

A central consideration for my aggregating the personality disorders in the way I do is that Group III are much more subject to Neuroticism than Group II and especially Group I. However, Group III, save the borderline, are less at risk of psychoticism than Groups II and above all Group I.

The *DSM* states that borderlines may "develop psychotic-like symptoms," such as hallucinations, especially during stressful periods (p. 652). These episodes would, in my estimation, preeminently pertain to the borderlines' fright at the dissolution of their relationships and none more than those that would end in the loneliness of abandonment.

Hence, borderlines—in that they rank at the very top of the scale in terms of all six traits of Neuroticism—may be seen as the most neurotic of the psychotically disposed of the abnormals and the most psychotically inclined of the neurotics (Costa and Widiger, 1994, p. 329; 2002, p. 461). This combination significantly accounts for the extreme difficulty encountered by others, including clinicians, in dealing with borderlines and their extremely high rate of clinical recidivism among the pathological personalities. The histrionic, dependent, and avoidant of Group III are also highly neurotic, like the borderline, though they mainly lack their sibling's extreme impulsiveness and hostility to self and others.

Depending to a large extent as to what is the motivation and who is their focus, self or others, neurotic traits, in my judgment, are not of the same degree or level of negativity among themselves. I regard Neuroticism's anxiety, depressiveness, self-consciousness, and vulnerability as the least damaging traits, all of which highly characterize dependents and avoidants and, to a lesser extent, histrionics.

Angry hostility and impulsivity, the two most negative traits of Neuroticism, most typify the borderlines and Group II sociopaths but for different reasons. Borderlines' antagonism and disinhibitedness are ordinarily most vehemently brought out in connection with their frustrations and failures vis-à-vis intimate relationships. Accordingly, they are unlike sociopaths whose impulsiveness and lack of self-discipline mainly concern the goals intrinsic to success, such as power, profit, and status.

While FFM neurotic traits are abnormal, nonetheless, the complete absence of some of them, such as vulnerability, can be more indicative of a pathological personality than their presence. Recall that of the FFM superstraits, only the six traits of Neuroticism imply intrinsic negativity. The other four, Extraversion, Openness to Experience, Humaneness, and Conscientiousness, and their traits suggest positivity or at minimum neutrality.

This said, the shortage of FFM self-consciousness, as in the cases of the Group I schizoid and Group II sociopath, point to, in my judgment, a greater psycho-ethical sickness than the surfeit of self-consciousness typical of Group III. This trait involves feelings of shame and inferiority, each of which betokens a kind of attention to others that is utterly missing, for instance, in the schizoid of Group I and the sociopath of Group II. Nor do these two abnormals manifest guilt for their (in)actions, though the schizoid is not usually thought of as being morally blamable for not feeling remorse, whereas the sociopath is.

As a whole, no Group I or Group II aberrant, save the obsessional to some extent, displays guilt for their (in)actions. Nor do these two units, with the exception of the Group I schizotypal, exhibit Neuroticism's self-consciousness construed as humiliation and inferiority. Narcissists of Group II may be subject to these feelings when they think of themselves as being toppled from their self-appointed pedestal of superiority. All Group III deviants exhibit Neuroticism's self-hostility due to the self-blame and guilt associated with Neuroticism's despondence in addition to the shame and self-worthlessness of its self-consciousness.

Furthermore, even when Groups I, II, and III exhibit the same Neuroticism trait such as anxiety, the objects of their apprehensiveness markedly differ. For example, the consternation of Group I concerns being in the presence of others when they invariably want to be let and left alone, whereas that of paranoids of Group II pertains to their constant mistrust of others. The trepidation of Group III principally refers to their feeling of being objects of exclusion, non-inclusion, or derisive indifference.

6. Four Ways of Allying Loneliness with Personality Traits and Disorders

In this chapter, I have elaborated the way loneliness relates to personality traits and how it factors into personality disturbances, especially Group III. To summarize, I turn to the research of Peplau and Perlman, who propose that personality traits may contribute to loneliness in four, often reciprocally, related ways. First, these psychologists state that personality attributes may lessen individuals "social desirability" and, as a result, may limit their "opportunities for social relations" (1982, p. 9). For example, avoidants' self-consciousness in the sense of timidity make others uncomfortable in their presence. This annoyance inclines people to circumvent the company and companionship of avoidants, in which case they have alienated others and lonelified themselves.

Second, personality traits may influence individuals' "own behavior in social situations and contribute to unsatisfactory patterns of interaction," that, because they are insufficient in terms of generating intimacy, produce loneliness (ibid.). Borderlines' proneness to tantrums subverts their interactions with others. All the disturbed personalities by definition engage in behavior which precludes (Group I), invenoms (Groups II), or neurotically mars (Group III) intimate relatedness.

Third, personality attributes may affect how individuals respond to alterations "in their actual social relations and so influence how effective they are in avoiding, minimizing, or alleviating loneliness" (ibid.). Dependents' low self-appraisal disposes them to interpret their partners' desire to be alone as a personal slight, making these pathologicals all the more self-deprecating in addition to more submissive and depressive. These traits, in turn, render dependents less effective in dealing with their lonely isolation, especially that germane to abandonment and fears thereof.

Lonely neurotics, like dependents, often seem to engage in a kind of "self-chosen loneliness," as Paul Tillich terms it (1980, p. 550). It is as if they enjoy its painful isolation and isolating pain. Still, no one chooses anything painful in and for itself, especially what is arguably the most excruciating sort: emotional isolation. In general, no one wants anything negative in and for itself least of all what is emotionally most negative and most self-negating in the sense self-nullifying, namely loneliness.

Finally, Peplau and Perlman maintain that "personal factors may predispose people to loneliness and make it harder for them to overcome" its occurrence (1982, p. 9). Histrionics' generalized vulnerability and extreme self-consciousness make them easy prey for emotional isolation. Their inability to withstand delayed emotional and other forms of gratification make it difficult for histrionics to tolerate and overcome the sadness and anguish of loneliness, especially when they are physically or socially segregated. To what extent, if any, personality traits, whether abnormal or anormal, are voluntary or volitional, are matters calling for a separate chapter.

Nine

PERSONALITY CONSTITUENTS: CHOICE, COMPELLMENT, AND CHANCE

1. Self-Determinism (Freedom)

Volume I, Chapter Nine, "Loneliness and Freedom," was devoted to the notions of causality in the forms of determinism (necessitarianism) and self-determinism (freedom), both of which are distinguished from acausality, or indeterminism (randomness, chance, fortune, or luck). In this volume, attention will be especially accorded these phenomena in terms of personality and personality disorders.

Normal human beings are customarily considered as being endowed with the ability to determine in the sense of choose or not choose (liberty of exercise) their course of life and the means thereto (liberty of specification). However, the goal of human life as a whole, namely happiness, is generally held to be determined in the sense of its being innate and unalterably so. Still, the contents of such beatitude and the ways thereto are usually reckoned as being subject to self-selective processes, or alternatives. Hence, freedom is known as self-determinism and signifies that the self is the ultimate originator, or cause, of at least some of its internal acts and external actions.

2. Determinism (Necessitarianism)

Self-determinism is contrasted with the sort of determinism known as necessitarianism, the view that the self is compelled to act or not act and as is so either by force of internal factors, such as the biological and psychological, or by external ones, such as the social, cultural, political, economic, and historic. For libertarians, in this context meaning self-determinists, the inner and outer milieus affect the self in the sense of conditioning and influencing it. Nonetheless, these factors do not completely compel the individual to act or not act and do so in one way instead of another.

Freedom is also known as free will, especially when conceived as arising from the putative power or faculty of the self to choose (I say putative because determinists consider such a volitional power as an illusion, although a necessary one, according to some). So understood, freedom is often viewed as a permanent "structural" entity of the self, whereas its actual acts, or choices, refer to freedom considered as "functional."

While persons can be conceived to either have the capability for choice or not, freedom is not totally absolute. It is restricted by its internal and external milieus, which are also subject to free alteration to some extent. Consequently, all the self's choices, however, that pertain to the extramental world are situated and contextualized among other freedom-endowed subjects as well as freedom-less subjects and objects. These external entities can hamper or help the realization of freedom but perhaps even more so can inner factors such that truth(fulness), for instance, can "make a person free(er)."

Mental entities that impede freedom include negative personality traits such as FFM impulsiveness (a lower Dionysian quality) and those that assist it, such as FFM self-discipline (a higher Apollonian attribute). Paul T. Costa and Thomas A. Widiger state that low self-discipline and high impulsiveness are both instances of lack of self-control (and autonomy in the sense of self-rule and positive independence). Individuals "high in impulsiveness cannot resist doing what they do not want themselves to do." Those who are "low in self-discipline cannot force themselves to do what they want themselves to do" (2002, p. 467).

Acts that are instinctive and automatic in their inception are considered voluntary but not volitional, though the first may eventually be subject to the second's reflection, deliberation, and control. Voluntary acts may be construed as being compatible with a person's biopsychological givens, but they are, strictly speaking, unchosen, meaning they are involitional, at least initially.

Volitional acts may or may not be opposed to the voluntary, that is, to what "comes naturally," such as when a person who is constitutionally introvertive decides, respectively, to become extrovertive or more introvertive. Accordingly, volitional acts, or choices, may confirm and ratify voluntary acts and, to a lesser extent, disconfirm and sometimes repudiate them. Most inner acts and external actions, in sum, activities, that emanate from the self are voluntary instead of volitional in the sense that they are not consciously and deliberately willed.

Therefore, in this series, volitional activities are to be conceived as being carried out intentionally, at least tacitly and implicitly so. Abulia is a motivational disorder wherein people are incapable of volitional activity, meaning lacking in willpower or initiative. .

When freedom is held to be inborn or quasi-inborn, such that it is a permanent structure of the self, by definition, it cannot be lost. However, freedom in terms of its functions can progress or regress even to the point that the self perceives itself as no longer free (or chooses to relinquish freedom). In which event the person may experience abulia.

If people believe they have the radical capability for volitional inner acts and external actions but have an extreme fear or dread of making such choices, or decisions, they may be said to experience decidophobia à la Walter Kaufmann (1973, p. 273). Still, defenders of freedom argue that decidophobia is, at bottom, chosen or at least its continuation is. To some of these freedom advocates, all personality traits, be they normal or not, are volitional in that at some point, the self chooses whether to remain, for instance, decidophobic. In short, self-determinists claim that the self decides to determine itself to be determined, or necessitated, via some rejection of freedom on a structural or functional level.

3. Indeterminism (Chance)

Both self-determinism and determinism—sometimes known, respectively, as soft and hard determinism—contend that every event has a cause. So defined they are distinguished from indeterminism, the theory that maintains that one, some, or all events do not have causes. Indeterminism, determinism, and self-determinism or a combination thereof may be applied to reality as a whole or to its parts. For example, some may hold that the universe as an entirety is a chance event as to its origin but that all its parts are necessitated. Or they may claim that the totality of the parts are chaotic and indetermined with respect to one another but are necessitated within themselves.

Chance is often considered an unintended or unforeseen event. Nonetheless, for determinists, whether hard or soft, such an occurrence still has causes whether they are temporally antecedent or concomitant concerning their effects. Hence, such fortuity is held by determinists and self-determinists to be an effect of nescience. This means that chance is simply the absence of knowledge or awareness of something, in this instance, of the mental or extramental existence of causality.

4. The Limits of Self-Determinism

Many internal factors exist—such as personal shortcomings, including cognitive ignorance, conative lethargy, and emotional anxiety—that can negatively impact freedom. Dealing with such factors pertains to self-determination in the sense of self-resolve. This firmness of freedom, often titled willpower, is not to be confused with determinism construed as necessitarianism.

Self-determination can not only mean a person's resolve to commit or omit doing something, but the ability to stipulate and specify what exactly the individual wills (liberty of specification). When individuals "decide" instead of being determined (necessitated) that they will play golf instead of soccer, such is a self-determination of a decision that evinces their ability to choose between specific alternatives.

Therefore, to what degree or level an individual can determine, or constitute, itself by its choices hinges upon several considerations. For instance, it depends upon the efficacy of its will, meaning its conative willpower, and other inner constituents of freedom, such as the cognitive and its clarity and comprehension vis-à-vis ends and means. This resoluteness includes the will to invigorate the power of the will itself in the sense of giving or actualizing its impetus and steadfastness. Naturally, such willpower is itself held to be unwilled by necessitarians, since they claim that any such effort—be it inborn or attained—is completely (pre)determined.

Though it is generally put forth that the self can, in some measure, freely change itself, it is not ordinarily held that it entirely creates itself through its choices, that is, "from scratch," or *ex nihilo* à la Jean-Paul Sartre. However, he seems to mean that no previous condition forces the self to choose in the fashion it does (1948, pp. 26–30).

Sartre claims that the self *is* what it *does*, and what it does, it *chooses* to do at least implicitly. Yet what choice has done it can undo, including changing the self's personality traits (ibid.). These changes do not occur by simple fiat but by self-determination. Hence, the self can undo addictions to chemical substances, to possessions ("stuffitis") or to relationships, such as "love-addictions," including those to self as in the cases of egocentricity in general and narcissism in particular.

Nevertheless, even those who maintain that the self is not solely the sum of its choices à la Sartre may argue that every choice affects the total self, including each of its traits, but it does not do so in necessitating and direct fashion. Thus, becoming a habitual liar, such as the prototypical psychopath, affects the whole self. Yet, doing so does not mean that the self is exclusively the assemblage of its lies.

Whatever might be the truth relative to Sartre's notion of the self and its literally being its free choices, it seems undeniable that every self is a distinct "psychobiological" entity. It is, moreover, a unique being situated in a singular social environment that can expedite or retard the emergence and expansion of freedom.

Determinists, at least implicitly, hold that no one, normal or anormal, can be credited or discredited psychologically or morally for what they do or not do because freedom does not exist in reality save its being an illusional mental state or a verbal reference thereto. Whereupon, determinists may argue that destiny from the present, predestiny from the past, or fate "from" the future compels them to be, for instance, upholders of freedom or its deniers, as well as saints or sociopaths. In fact, when apprehended for criminal wrongdoings, dyssocials are notorious for bemoaning being forced by internal or external factors for being the way they are and acting the way they do.

On the other hand, some sociopaths boast of being the epitome of freedom in doing what they choose to do. However, in reality, they are among the foremost examples of impulsiveness and lack of discipline in the form of license or irresponsibility (and often licentiousness and hedonism as a whole).

Other determinists propose that people should be held responsible for their (in)actions, even though they are not and cannot be freely chosen. They argue, for instance, that legally right and morally good conduct should be encouraged even though it is necessitated. Correlatively, its contrary should be discouraged even though it is also necessitated, since it is a more salutary policy, practically considered, for individuals and society. According to this logic, people are to be deemed responsible for their traits and behavior, be they normal, abnormal, or supranormal, even if they are not formally and intrinsically free.

Some students of these issues insist that they are not the sorts that can or even need be answered in any conclusive manner. They stress that the point is to feel or function as if the self were free. These pragmatic libertarians do so because they maintain that conducting ourselves *as if* we are the forgers of our fate and the designers of our destiny have positive consequences in terms of health and happiness. These effects are deemed better or less bad than acting as if we were the "playthings" of a universe in which indeterminism and determinism take place simultaneously or successively in the mental and extramental worlds.

People may be inclined by constitutional factors or elect to indulge in a life of non-choice, a kind of perpetual passivity, one clearly typical of Group III dependents. Such individuals are also prone to the abdication of freedom via addictions such as chemical, but especially addictive relationships and relationship addictions. Consequently, if abulia is considered abnormal, then freedom may be considered the normal state of human beings. Hence, to be mentally and morally healthy requires being able to exercise liberty of choice and the absence of psycho-ethical diseases, above all, abulia and decidophobia themselves. Correlatively, the habitual absence of freedom signifies the negation of the basis of a healthy personality and even the elimination of the very concept of personality itself.

Abulia is also abnormal statistically considered since it appears that most people consider themselves and are so envisaged by others as self-determining up to a point (including the point wherein personality is arguably necessitated by temperament and other constitutional factors). Those who defend freedom may claim that individuals who suffer from abulia may at some point have chosen to act as if they were necessitated. They may do so to avoid being held responsible and accountable for their lives, including being so due to their personality traits.

Self-determinists may also maintain that those who subsequently become accustomed to believing themselves to be unfree are no longer disposed to bring themselves to think and, a fortiori, act as if they were unnecessitated. In this way, abulia becomes a kind of self-fulfilling prophecy, but one that, at base, is arguably volitional. It is chosen in the sense of being a matter of election and then one of acquiescence and even bad faith, meaning willed self-deception.

Perhaps for most people, changing personality traits is also held to be subject to their initiative, a freedom that assumes a kind of self-criticality. The meaning of "critical" can suggest what is crucial and decisive; so construed, it is especially germane to freedom and personality. Normal people, by definition, learn to accept their traits and themselves in addition to those of others. Nevertheless, unlike abnormal personalities, normals can be decisive and hopeful regarding changing these attributes if they perceive them to be impairing or dystonic.

Without some degree of hope, people would cease choosing at all and would thereby cave into the indecisiveness and irresponsibility that are generally ascribed to both determinism and indeterminism but for different reasons. A life in which necessitarianism reigns reflects the rigidity of the lower Apollonian, in which everything is fixed or fixated and nothing is permitted outside that which is dictated. A life that is indeterministic reflects the chaos of the lower Dionysian, in which "anything goes" and "everything is permitted." However, the more people experience shame and especially guilt, the more they are said to be self-determining or at least the less necessitated.

Self-determinism at its acme signifies the rule of the higher Dionysian after it has subsumed into itself the higher Apollonian. Freedom, when it stresses willpower, pertains to the higher Apollonian. When it stresses the spontaneity of willpower after it has been perfected by self-discipline, freedom pertains to the higher Dionysian.

5. Mental State and Mental Trait Disorders: Causality and Acausality

Issues regarding self-determinism and its contrary (determinism) and their contradictory (indeterminism) are exceedingly intricate and polemic in reference to mental disorders, especially pertaining to personality disorders. Allen Frances, Widiger, and Melvin Sabshin state:

> Psychopathology is not thought to occur as a result of free will or choice. The psychodynamic, neurochemical, social learning, and other models of psychopathology are deterministic. Persons who suffer from schizophrenia, depression, phobias, or personality disorders are not thought to have chosen these disorders. (1991, p. 22)

It is hardly disputable that anyone initially or explicitly chooses to have a mental state disorder. No one elects to be schizophrenic, depressed, or phobic since such *DSM* Axis I disturbances are both dystonic and impairing and, thereby, involitional. One seeming exception to the dysphoric and the enfeebling elements of these psychopathologies might arguably be the manic phase of bipolar depression. However, this so-called euphoric period is, by definition, embedded in and by the inveterate and debilitating gloom of major depression. The grandiosity that is sometimes found in the manic phase of this illness is routinely beset by a delusional sense of inflated empowerment and yet a willpower decimated by compulsions, such as those involved in reckless gambling and driving habits. Whereupon, it is safe to assume that few if any Axis I disorders are chosen in any fashion. Still, there are those who argue that some of these aberrations may be a matter of an implicit original election or at minimum a tacit implicit ratification of them via acquiescence; individuals may choose by default to become or remain, for instance, phobic or depressed as being, for example, a lesser evil.

Others claim that some types of schizophrenics, such as the paranoid, have at least implicitly chosen some of their inner qualities and external conduct in part as defenses to deal with other human beings whom they perceive as dangerously malevolent. Nonetheless, the origination and prolongation of their diminished and frequently lost contact with mental and extramental reality, as well as their reduced motivational power and social functioning are almost invariably looked upon as necessitated (Beers, 2003, p. 582).

Whether and how (in)voluntariness and (in)volition apply to individuals with Axis II mental trait disorders, such as those of personality, are far more debatable than they are concerning Axis I mental state disorders. Personality traits are far more often judged to be subject to the voluntary and even the volitional than those personality qualities, for instance, predicable of schizophrenic, depressive, or phobic disorders.

Moreover, freedom is ascribable to person(ality) as such and, consequently, more likely pertinent to disorders of personality in contrast to mental state disorders, such as schizophrenia. Thus, being sociopathic or narcissistic is a psychopathology a person *is*, whereas being schizophrenic or phobic is a mental illness an individual *has*. Of course, all mental disorders inhere solely in persons, but they do not do so qua persons as is the case with Axis II mental trait disorders.

Obviously, a major question concerning personality and its traits vis-à-vis self-determinism and related issues is the role heredity plays in them. Jeffrey Magnavita reports that anywhere from "30% and 50%" of personality variation is inherited (2004a, p. 16). Nonetheless, to what extent, if any, trait heritability is a matter of determinism such that all personal qualities are biologically, psychologically, or otherwise strictly necessitated is the subject of ongoing debate.

Jennifer Bartz, Alicia Kaplan, and Eric Hollander maintain that parents directly bequeath:

> to their children genes which contribute to specific personality profiles (for instance, cold and controlling); moreover, early environments are complicated by the fact that they are *influenced* by the parents' own genes. Basically, parents create an environment for the children due to their own genetic propensities, and because parents also pass on these genes to their children, the children are going to be especially responsive to these environments. (2007, p. 239, emphasis added)

Many of those who adhere to FFM perspectives on personality claim that personality traits are heritable. However, they do not always agree to what extent these qualities differ in their degree or level of genetic grounding. Nor do they always concur as to whether such a foundation consists in strictly necessitating determinants or simply (pre)conditioning and influencing propensities. FFM proponents do appear to agree more concerning the ranking of the five supertraits with respect to heritability. Hence, there is considerable consensus among them that Extraversion is the most heritable supertrait followed by Neuroticism—some, though apparently fewer in number, reverse the order —Openness to Experience, Conscientiousness, and Humaneness. But even as to this gradation, dimensionalists disagree as to what measure it is based on necessitarianism.

6. Freedom and Normality of Personality

Normals tend to believe that they have largely chosen their traits either explicitly or by accepting or rejecting those that may have been or perceived to have been initially inherited. This said, it can be proposed that what in significant part separates normal from abnormal personalities is precisely the fact that the first are held to be free or more fully so, objectively considered, regarding their traits than the second. Of course, normals may not always *feel* that these qualities are volitional or totally so.

Alternatively, it is essayed that the more abnormal individuals are qua persons, the less they are free, objectively considered. Subjectively, these pathologicals may feel being extremely non-necessitated and even free, all of which is especially the case with sociopaths. Sociopaths mistake qualities or choose to do so, like disinhibitedness, as the higher-level type of spontaneity predicable of the freedom of the higher Dionysian. In short, these lower Dionysian personalities confuse irresponsible libertinism with responsible liberty, and insofar as they manifest *DSM* Conduct Disorder, impunity and lawlessness with autonomy.

Hence, the degree or level concerning which people are subjectively and objectively free or necessitated in part accounts for their being reckoned, respectively, normal or abnormal to begin with. Yet, it bears underscoring that freedom and necessity can synergize. This kind of fusion was considered a kind of "eminent," or elevated, necessity among scholastic philosophers such that they held that at its highest level, this blending was reflected in God. Accordingly, they argued that whatever "he" does so he does so necessarily, providing he does so willingly.

Such higher-level determinism/self-determinism analogously occurs, for instance, in the superior athlete or artist. They perform what are, objectively considered, demanding undertakings with a sort of spontaneous discipline as if doing so were a felicitous confluence of the voluntary and volitional or what is sometimes designated, respectively, first and second nature.

In terms of ethics, this fusion of spontaneity and self-control has its counterpart in supremely virtuous individuals who find dealing with what is morally difficult (the Apollonian) relatively easy (the Dionysian). As deficient, psycho-ethically speaking, no abnormal personality approaches and, a fortiori, attains such a blend of necessity and freedom. They fail by either being overly determined (for example, the schizoid). Or they do so by being overly undetermined (for example, the schizotypal, though at base, this aberrant is also necessitated such that what appears voluntary or volitional is strictly predetermined).

Traits that are heritable can be psycho-ethically negative or positive in potentiality. Hence, there are, genetically speaking, both bad and good "seeds." But the question regarding them remains as to whether heritability is deemed strictly necessitating or only more or less conditioning; the second is compatible with freedom; the first is not (unless construed as eminent necessity).

Rather recently Laura Baker wrote:

> what was known over a decade ago about genetics of psychopathology during adulthood, including personality disorders, remains true today. Genetic *influences* [my emphasis] are at least moderate for clinical diagnoses for the major Axis I disorders, including schizophrenia, unipolar and bipolar depression, and for many Axis II disorders, including antisocial and schizotypal disorders....More important, there has been *no major gene found for any of these mental disorders*. Instead, most clinical mental disorders appear to be polygenic (that is influenced by many different genetic elements). (2006, p. 257)

It may be asked whether Baker is contrasting moderate genetic influences with strong influences that are tantamount to necessitating factors. Additionally, it is one thing to posit that the sources of mental disorders, be they state or trait, are necessarily inherited. It is quite another to propose that once inherited their possessors must without exception function in deterministic, or unfree, fashion. Still, it could be argued, though it rarely if ever is, that there is an all-comprehensive necessitating trait or capability that is inherited that predetermines all other mental traits. On the other hand, it could be posited (though likely even more rarely) that there is an all-embracing self-determining trait which is inherited that renders all other mental traits subject to freedom.

Magnavita ponders the possibility of whether there will be a gene that will be discovered as the cause of pathological personalities (and, we might add, normal and supranormal types). He concludes that finding such a gene is improbable since "there are certainly multiple genes which *predispose* our neuro-biological system and that which who we are and how we behave" (2004a, p. 16, emphasis added).

I have two comments regarding the above. First, Magnavita does not reduce personalities, disordered or otherwise, and their internal qualities to their external conduct, as do metaphysical, in contrast to methodological and therapeutical, behaviorists. When behaviorism is understood as the "objective" way to understand and alter human conduct, it is known as methodological instead of metaphysical. Second, predisposing and precipitating factors may influence these personality anomalies but by definition do not cause them.

It is instructive that, in the above citation, genes, which are often thought of as necessitating, appear to imply what is merely influencing of that which is neuro-biological. The latter itself is often deemed determining, especially when construed as being part of a system. In any event and as a general rule, the more heritable is a trait or a set of such, the less it is amenable to therapy. They are so unless, for example, such attributes, like the flexibility in the Humaneness trait of cooperativeness, are themselves among those considered heritable.

Widiger essays:

> It is frankly surprising that psychology, as a science of human behavior, has devoted very little attention to even trying to confirm or refute the existence of free will, let alone attempting to determine [ascertain] what proportion of our behavior is within volitional control (2006, p. 181)

I have the following animadversions concerning Widiger's remarks. First, psychology, obviously etymologically considered, is the study of the psyche, or mind, and not behavior as such. If, however, the mind is construed solely as its embodied functions in response to external stimuli, then psychology is aptly known as the study of behavior. This school rejects the concept of the mind as consciousness and, a fortiori, as unconsciousness. So construed, behaviorism is a kind of metaphysical materialism. In which case, as a non-material entity, freedom is precluded from being construed as a proper object of study, certainly of the scientific genre, because it is held to be non-existent, objectively speaking.

Second, if psychology is the study of behavior as just described, then it is not at all surprising that it has allocated scant if any attention to affirm or deny the existence of freedom or free will. Nor is it surprising that it does not attempt to ascertain what if any behavior is volitionally freely controllable (my critique of behaviorism appears in the first volume). Ultimately any theory of the mind and behavior is rooted in philosophical psychology that, in turn, is linked to metaphysical, epistemological, and axiological, including ethical, considerations. All science has philosophical assumptions, implications, and ramifications, as arguably many even most scientists themselves *freely* admit.

7. Personality Disorders and Choice

Being atheoretical, the *DSM* does not endorse any school of psychology. Nor does it discuss freedom in any systematic fashion vis-à-vis mental illness, certainly not with respect to Axis I mental state disorders or Axis II mental trait disorders of personality. Nevertheless, *The Manual*'s entire enterprise assumes that freedom is a property of normality. The *DSM* does sometimes explicitly, albeit rarely, raise the issue of freedom. A case in point is when it precises that dependents experience difficulty in making decisions and, therein, often fail to take the initiative and responsibility for major aspects of their lives (pp. 665, 668).

Thus, *The Manual* appears to view dependents as disturbed in part because they are quasi-decidophobics. This failure in terms of decision-making in general can itself be viewed as presupposing self-determinism in that individuals are responsible for their being irresponsible due to not making choices when they are obliged to do so. In short, people decide not to decide (as Sartre and many others before and after this perhaps most passionate defender of human freedom have argued).

Furthermore, dependents exhibit a sense of guilt and shame in not being responsible. These two subtraits fall under the FFM trait of self-consciousness, a trait that typifies dependents and Group III aberrants as a totality (Costa and Widiger, 2002, p. 463).

Obsessive-compulsives, like dependents, albeit for very different reasons, have extraordinary difficulty in making choices (*DSM*, p. 669). The second are insufficiently responsible; the first are overly so in the sense of being maniacally dutiful. For instance, obsessive-compulsives are so focused on trivia that it causes them to lose the purpose of the business at hand and its role in the "bigger picture."

Similarly, obsessive-compulsives do not exhibit a deficiency of freedom's deliberation but an excess. These abnormal personalities' very name(s) indicates necessitation since it can be argued that their mental traits as obsessive are determined and their behavior as compulsive is as well. (Some metaphysical behaviorists propose that the mental is simply internalized behavior.)

Yet, insofar as obsessive-compulsives' traits are syntonic, it can be proposed that they in fact *feel* they have chosen their attributes at least in the sense of volitionally sustaining them. Obviously, syntonicity and its contrary (dystonicity) and its contradictory (non-dystonicity or non-dystonicity) refer to the subjective appraisal of the objective status of traits that in themselves are self-determined, determined, or at minimum highly influenced. Insofar as obsessionals regard their traits as syntonic, it may be contended that they ultimately elect to be necessitated, in which case they enjoy their self-imposed fixations. Alternatively, those with the Axis II obsessive-compulsive disorder find their traits tormentingly intrusive, or ego-alien (dystonic).

It remains problematic, therefore, whether any trait—be it more or less neutral, meaning non-syntonic (non-pleasurable) and non-dystonic (non-displeasurable), syntonic (pleasurable), or dystonic (painful)—is originally or eventually voluntary or volitional, or contrarily, involuntary and involitional. The more dystonic the trait, the more it implies the unchosen (the involitional) or at least the non-chosen (the involuntary); the more syntonic, the more it is chosen or at least freely continued.

The question, then, is not whether an individual's kind of personality—and, for present concerns, the abnormal ones in particular—or its traits has causes, for there clearly are and arguably without exception. Instead, the question should be, "What kind of causal relationship prevails among personality qualities?" Are they are a matter of self-determining or determining factors? If so, to what extent are they absolutely necessitating and endlessly so? Are the causes merely influencing or possibly merely occasioning?

To my knowledge, no personologist subscribes to indeterminism (causelessness) with reference to personality traits. People, abnormal or otherwise, just do not "just happen" to be the kinds of individuals they are or think, believe, or feel they are. They are so owing to internal factors, arguably chiefly genetic sorts, and external environmental factors in addition to those of a voluntary and volitional nature. However, they not only *are*, but *ex-ist*, that is, they also choose to stand outside or at least alongside necessitating factors such that they become who they are, in part, by choice. For example, they do not choose their temperament, but they can decide how it functions in their lives and, to some extent, they can alter it.

Some personologists propose that a person can, in some measure, reconstitute itself by modifying inherited traits, including the necessitating sort (acquired traits ipso facto change the self or its traits, depending if the first is held to be distinct from the second). If the self is solely the sum of its traits, then changing all of them would obviously mean creating an entirely new self.

Yet, even altering one trait would effect, at least indirectly, a change in all the rest however imperceptibly. Just as nature abhors a vacuum, so also does human nature and perhaps especially so with respect to personality attributes. Everything seems to be connected to all else, be it that pertaining to the body, mind, or the putative soul. All this seems to argue for necessitarianism or at minimum strong influentialism and conditionalism in terms of personality structures and functions.

Nor do personologists, to my knowledge, hold that individuals, especially pathological ones, can completely change themselves let alone all at once, assuming that they want to do so. This assumption refers solely to the dystonic Group III abnormals. Still people may be able to alter some of their traits at least in terms, for instance, of intensity and range.

Logically enough, when individuals decide that they can act freely (in theory or in practice), these choices themselves are those that most affect, at least indirectly, all their remaining qualities. These prior decisions are akin to the "original choice" à la Sartre since they set the pattern for further choices or non-choices. Consequently, this initial decision(s) *determines* whether the self will act freely or not act at all. For Sartre, the original choice includes the possibility that the self will try to hide its freedom from its awareness, all of which is clearly a free act itself (1948, pp. 42–43).

If there were no pattern to the self and its traits, we could hardly speak of personality, meaning the unification of attributes in an ongoing, numerically one individual. Even the most fragmented of lower-level Dionysians has a kind of ontological unity in its psychological chaotic diversity.

On the other hand, personality, together with its original and subsequent choices—and their eventual habitual trait configuration—, cannot be construed as themselves being set in stone. They are not altogether resistant to reconstitution. The determinist will counter that any such Sartrean original choice is itself, like all later choices and their resulting personality compositions, necessitated. Sartre would respond that freedom is directly experienced; necessitarianism, he insists, is only a theory about experience and one not faithful to it. For Sartre—at least the so-called "early," or explicitly pre-Marxist, version of this existentialist—people get the kind of personality they choose and, indeed, deserve from an ethical perspective.

To exemplify these matters, at some juncture, dependents choose to abdicate their freedom and act as if determinism were their (pre)destiny or fate, an original choice that renders their lives inauthentic, for volitionists, like Sartre. As well, the kinds of anxiety and self-consciousness exhibited by the dependents and Group III aberrants in general suggest that they are implicitly aware of being free. Yet, these highly neurotic personalities are so anguished by this awareness that, to re-invoke Sartre, they *choose* to try to conceal their freedom from their consciousness (ibid., pp. 31–32).

The Neuroticism traits of anxiety, self-consciousness, vulnerability, and despondence—even the last's extreme instantiation in clinical depression (endogenous)—are sometimes understood as being not only freely perpetuated but freely initiated if only because they are held as being lesser evils. In this manner, Neuroticism traits are sometimes considered as relatively positive, though they are deemed dystonic and impairing, absolutely speaking.

8. Personologists: Self-Determinism versus Determinism

Insofar as universal psychological determinism is embraced, no trait is a matter of freedom, objectively considered, though people may feel free, subjectively construed, but, then, determinists argue that such feelings are also necessitated. Nonetheless, this kind of mental involitionality is not endorsed by every school of psychology, as might be inferred from the Frances and colleagues quote given above (1991, p. 22). Several non-deterministic models vis-à-vis abnormal mental attributes and the psychopathological in general, include those germane to the personality disorders. These perspectives include the relational, (inter)personalist, humanist, existentialist, and as a whole the phenomenological.

Even neuroscientific psychological camps, which emphasize the heritability of traits, need not adhere to necessitarianism. For example, they can maintain that such attributes are simply extremely (pre)conditioned in the sense of strongly influenced instead of absolutely determined. These issues greatly hinge on which views of the mind and its relationship to the body, and specifically the brain, that an individual or a school of thought espouses.

Gordon Claridge states that, unlike psychiatric patients, healthy individuals are held to be "more in control of their behavior and felt experience, leaving room for a more dualistic perspective on brain/mind relationships." Note that Claridge does not imply that the pathological personality has no freedom but only less than the normal (2006, p. 142).

As to the mind/body relationship, those who hold that the mind is the brain and that the brain is totally material would then logically conclude that no human beings, normal or otherwise, freely control their traits or behaviors because nothing material is ordinarily *thought* of as being endowed with freedom. Whatever is totally material is usually envisioned as being wholly necessitated. I say usually because many theorists contend that some kinds of matter, most notably the type the brain putatively possesses, are, to some extent, free from necessitarian laws.

Some propose that the mind and the brain are so different in degree if not in kind that even within the material order these two entities are not reducible to one another. In such instances, the brain can be looked upon as being biologically necessitated and unfree; the mind, unnecessitated and free. Still, how two such different material entities—and, a fortiori, how the mind as an immaterial and the brain as material—would be able to interact with one another, if they do so at all, is a further and exceedingly disputed issue (Titus, 1970, pp. 168–174).

Claridge holds that the reductionism of mind to the determinist, materialist biological model in psychology has not occurred because "a greater range of explanatory models—social [interpersonal], humanist, cognitive, existentialist," ones that are among the types predominantly invoked in the present study:

> have continued to flourish, having little or no need to call upon physiological data. Biological [necessitating] models, can, therefore, claim no particular priority in general psychology, though they are highly relevant here [namely regarding personality aberration] because of the real part they have played in trying to explain the connection between personality and psychological disorders. (2006, pp. 142–143)

Additionally, Claridge contends that the psychological and philosophical debates concerning the nature of the mind and brain and their relationship will likely continue. He admonishes:

> It will be a mistake to fall further and further into the common trap of confusing correlation for cause as data pour daily out of genetics, neurochemical, and neuro-imaging laboratories, demonstrating [necessitating] relationships between brain process and every conceivable psychological state, trait, or propensity. (Ibid., p. 159)

Self-determinists, then, can respond to deterministic claims in myriad manners. One of which is that most human beings can readily testify to the experience of freely reacting to and modifying their given personality configuration, even if it seems to be, or is, necessitated at the outset. Necessitarians can reply that such experiences are merely chimerical. Self-determinists, in return, can propose that such interpretations themselves rest on denial of what is evident and, more importantly, self-evident, namely the immediate experience of freedom, especially in terms of actual choice.

Determinists appear to be *determined*, at the very least in the sense of resolved, to deny the reliability and validity of what normals consider their primordial, pervasive, and persistent experience of being free. In which case, it may be said that necessitarians *decide* a priori to make experience itself conform to their theoretical views instead of the reverse.

Furthermore, determinists are often reluctant to admit that some kind of necessity forces them to reject the existence of freedom either in a priori or a posteriori fashion. People who deny the "objective" reality of free choice usually do so relative to its nature, properties, and limits instead of its sheer objective existence (of course, freedom exists only in subjects and arguably only those that are persons).

According to self-determinists, individuals, including abnormals, can, therefore, somewhat alter the legacies of heredities, such as those of temperament. In which case, neither biology nor physiology is a matter of predestiny and destiny, construed, respectively, as the beliefs that the past and present necessitate the self or it traits. Accordingly, an extrovert can to some extent choose to become less gregarious and a neurotic less vulnerable.

Still, a total transformation of negative personality traits to ones positive is most unlikely if not impossible (or from positive to negative traits). In part, what renders traits negative is precisely their strong resistance to change even when they are felt as dystonic.

It is sometimes said that neurotics prefer their condition to its opposite. For example, dependent aberrants almost like being sheepishly submissive as much as they dislike it. Neurotics characteristically complain that they cannot help themselves being and acting the way they are and do (assuming being and acting are not ultimately the same). All this is in keeping with the position that Neuroticism is heritable and necessitatingly so and usually felt as being so.

Whatever changes are made to the inherited, necessitarians avow that it is genetic or environmental factors themselves that (pre)determine the depth and breadth of any such trait change or that of the personality considered as distinct from its traits. Accordingly, determinists claim that volition is a matter of deception—even self-deception—such that, and contrary to Sartre, the postulation of freedom is itself a matter of bad faith and inauthenticity. Naturally, any kind of deception cannot, for involitionists, be actually chosen but only seemingly so.

Once theorists and therapists find themselves beyond the research and clinical contexts, they are situated in the court of public and world opinion and occasionally in the legal court as well. In these arenas, it is quasi universally assumed that human beings are to a varying degree—depending on, for instance, internal factors such as age and external ones such as family conditions—responsible for their traits or, at minimum, for these qualities' repercussions in terms of behavior. It is so unless the individuals have the kind of mental disorders, such as schizophrenia, that are ordinarily viewed, both by professionals and laypersons, as being largely or even wholly necessitated. As a result, they are construed as being out of a person's control (the gravity of all mental disorders is generally rated in terms of their unchangeability).

This said, even determinists may claim, if only for pragmatic reasons, that human beings, including those with personality disorders, must be held legally and morally accountable for their actions. Self-determinists generally if not universally contend that, to the extent that people are not free, they are not responsible for their traits or behavior. Some libertarians hold that individuals can be held responsible for their behavior but not their internal traits (the reverse position is far less often endorsed).

9. Self-Determinism, Determinism, and Heritability

Joel Paris states, "although biological, psychological, and social factors are all necessary, none of them by themselves [is] sufficient to produce PDs" (1996, p. xviii). For strict, or hard, determinists, any of these three elements is sufficient to generate these aberrations. In the judgment of self-determinists, while the previously mentioned three factors may be necessary, none, taken separately or jointly, is sufficient to create any kind of personality, abnormal or otherwise because such factors do not take into consideration the voluntary, volitional, and axiological (normative) elements, or their absences, that go into personality formation.

Paris continues, "biological factors, by shaping individual differences in personality traits, would *determine* the specific forms which personality pathology can take" (ibid., emphasis added). Shaping of traits is ordinarily construed as a kind of influencing instead of a strictly determining, or necessitating, factor with respect to personality attributes, pathological or otherwise. Shaping, viewed as a type of conditioning, is compatible with freedom, whereas necessitating, by definition, is not.

Paris essays that all individuals are characterized by specific personality traits "derived from both temperament and social learning" (ibid.). In which case, they stem from the genetic and given on the one hand, and the nongenetic and acquired on the other (unless social learning is itself deemed necessitated and necessitating). Paris continues, "research indicates that genetic factors have a much stronger influence on traits than on disorders" (ibid.).

Although what Paris relates appears to be true, categorialists (as opposed to dimensionalists) would contend that "a much stronger influence" in itself does not constitute a necessitating factor, since however potent the first is, it differs in kind from the second.

John Livesley and Kerry Jang state, "personality appears to be inherited as a large number of genetic dimensions" (2000, p. 137). Yet, these super-traits (for example, Extraversion) "are not inherited directly" (ibid., p. 145); only the individual traits are (for instance, Extraversion's gregariousness).

Self-determinists might concede that traits are initially inherited but, for them, genetics does not automatically entail being unchangeable. They argue, for instance, that individuals are at liberty to interpret and to change the meaning they assign to their heritable qualities. For example, if I am seemingly born with a passion for details, I can choose to make this proclivity a plus by becoming a debater or a minus by becoming maniacal about minutiae, like the obsessional.

Volitionists argue that it is our freely formed attitudes toward our traits—and our person distinct from them—that are decisive (and deciding). They propose, for instance, that obsessionals in the end elect to be compulsive in their behavior in that they, at least implicitly, choose to view themselves as being compelled. Such views are tantamount to the notion of Georg Wilhelm Friedrich Hegel and at times, Friedrich Nietzsche, who hold that freedom consists in knowing that and how we are necessitated.

Paris expands upon his preceding positions by stating that various societal factors might: "*influence* the prevalence of personality" traits but their chief consequence:

> lies in their interactions with psychological risks. The most important of these interactions involve the prevalence of family breakdown and of parental psychopathology. . . . Psychological and social factors would have a more nonspecific effect in *determining* [my emphasis] whether underlying vulnerabilities lead to overt disorders. (1996, p. xviii, emphasis added)

It appears that by "determining," Paris means not necessitating but influencing or stipulating, meaning fixing, the boundaries as to whether such underlying risks go on to become overt personality disorders. Moreover, the very notion of "risk" suggests that which has a higher probability of being threatening instead of that which is certainly endangering. The concept of vulnerability conjures up not certainty but instead mere possibility or at most probability all of which is even more in keeping with the volitionist's notion of shaping.

Paris then states, "genetically influenced personality traits determine the specificity of PDs" (ibid., p. 98). It is not clear how something can be genetically influenced if "genetic" signifies the necessitating. Nor is it evident how that which is only influencing can be determining. Perhaps by "determine" Paris means to set boundaries, or limits, in which case, the words "determine the specificity" appear to be redundant. He additionally remarks:

> Biological variability would be the factor *determining* [my emphasis] which type of disorder could develop in any individual, while psychological and social factors would affect the threshold at which these personality traits become maladaptive. This diathesis[predispositional]-stress model views psychological and social factors in the PDs as precipitating instead of causative. (Ibid.)

Again, it is not manifest whether Paris is using "determining" in the sense of necessitating, influencing, or stipulating. It appears that in the above text, the biological necessitates but the psychological precipitates. Precipitation can be considered a kind of contributing and influencing factor but not a necessitating cause in the emergence of a personality disorder.

Rebekah Bradley, Carolyn Zittel Conkline, and Drew Westen maintain that though "personality traits are clearly heritable, the extent to which genetic transmission contributes to the development" of abnormal personalities and their qualities is itself not altogether evident (2007, p. 174). They urge caution "in making distinct attributions to nature or nurture in the etiology" of any "psychiatric disorder" because what starts out "as a biological vulnerability may lead to a cascade of environmental events" and, correlatively, "what may begin as an environmental effect may become 'hard-wired'" (ibid., p. 180).

We have seen that vulnerabilities are ordinarily construed as being conditioning, or influencing, factors instead of necessitating inevitabilities, whereas being hard-wired suggests the reverse. Consequently, Bradley and colleagues appear to be saying that either nature or nurture can be conditioning or necessitating with respect to pathological personalities but they advise vigilance in any and all cases of such predications vis-à-vis the biological and social.

Gordon Parker proposes that high—some would say total—heritability of personality traits does not mean that genes necessitate external behavior since, "there may be numerous opportunities for environmental modification of gene activity" (1997, p. 356). He appears to be arguing that nurture can reduce and possibly remove the necessitating aspects of nature. It may be added that genes do not strictly necessitate all mental attributes. Some are arguably also subject to alteration by other inner milieu factors, including choice itself. If genetic factors did necessitate internal traits, then it might logically be argued that what appears to be freely chosen actions, or behavior, are an illusion for they would have been in fact predetermined by unchosen internal acts. Human beings' customary conviction that they are free would, therefore, rest on a fiction. If so, then normality would be defined by abnormality instead of the reverse, all of which itself would be illogical or at least irregular.

Some believe that whatever is inherited is necessitated. Others hold that the heritability of personality traits does not ipso facto signify that genes dictate such qualities. High or even total hereditability of traits does not mean that genes necessarily (pre)determine all internal acts or external actions. Epigenetics is the science that examines the ways the external milieu can alter DNA and shape the manner in which genes act and influence conduct. Externals and experience, including that of choice, could produce chemical changes in the DNA and, thus, possibly elicit changes in the human psyche's structures and functions. These modifications would especially hold sway if the mind is deemed to be the brain. Still even if it is not, such changes could at least indirectly influence the psyche.

Daniel Goleman states that it is not possible, biologically considered, for genes to function independently of their milieus for they "are *designed* to be regulated by signals from their immediate surroundings." They include, he says, "hormones from the endocrine system" in addition to "neurotransmitters from the brain—some of which, in turn, are profoundly influenced by our social interactions" (2006, p. 151). Such interactions when habitually negative impact personality traits.

It may be proposed that whether the supertraits or their traits are deemed heritable, directly or indirectly so, individuals, especially if viewed as distinct from their attributes, still have some say as to what extent these qualities will affect the composition of their personality or at minimum continue to do so. Therefore, personality is always a project in process. Nevertheless, it is not totally so such that there is neither a psychological nor an ontological unity or continuity to the self if we subscribe to the more common view among personologists and people in general about these matters.

Robert Carson analogizes that genes are like the computer hardware of our personality, whereas the external environment is similar to the software (Smith Benjamin, 1996 p. 10). His comparison is fitting in important ways, but it leaves out the element of human (s)election in (re)molding personality and character. To some extent, volition can alter both our genes' influence via, for instance, biological engineering and our external environment via social engineering.

For self-determinists, people can mediately and indirectly transform themselves and their traits through internal decisions. They can do so immediately and directly if they are construed as being comprised by their attributes. If there are no choosers but only choices, then somehow one choice would have to choose the next choice. Or, somehow the totality of choices would be engaged in choosing, all of which seems contradictory even incoherent.

As well, human beings cannot be understood as "intelligent" computers or reducible thereto unless we already have endorsed a metaphysics that holds that the mind is compressible to the body—and specifically the brain and central nervous system—and the body to a machine endowed with artificial "intelligence." It is human beings themselves who choose to invent computers and their hardware that, subsequently, may be envisaged, respectively, as the determined to the self-determining (analogously considered, computer hardware is to software as the determined is to the determining).

The majority of personologists, along with human beings generally, appear to think of individuals as being made up of both inherited and chosen traits. However, the components and consequences of freedom are ordinarily seen as being less broad and deep in the abnormal personality, if they are present at all. As a general rule, the more psychopathological the personality disorder, the more necessitated or, if you will, the less volitional. The more necessitated the personality aberration, the more mentally, if not morally ill, and less responsive to therapy it is.

On the other hand, the more voluntary the trait, the more pathological it and its possessor may be. Thus, the more the schizoid becomes voluntarily withdrawn, the more ill is such an individual. However, the more voluntary is the trait, the less it may be a matter of morality, if it is at all. The reasons for these positions is that schizoid voluntariness is ultimately a matter of constitutional necessitation.

Even if a trait is initially inherited, it does not mean that it cannot be freely transformed if not in kind, such as, stinginess to generosity, then at least in degree, that is from the more to the less stingy or vice versa. Again, determinists propose that such changes envisioned as volitional are only seemingly so. They submit it is our ignorance of the unchanging laws that underlie and dictate any inner trait or outer behavior that might lead us to think we are free.

By most accounts, both self-determinism and determinism are givens, though, of course, not simultaneously concerning the same entity or in the same proportions. Human beings are free within some realms of their personality but necessitated in others. Preferring fish to meat may be volitional, but if we are to survive, then eating some kind of food is a matter of necessitation. Yet, people can perhaps always choose what the (in)voluntary and (in)volitional signify in terms of their meanings and values. In doing so, they can freely transcend their unfreedom, as it were, in this case their alleged supertrait or trait necessitation.

That psychotherapists become health professionals, favor some method(s) of treatment instead of others, and attempt to improve their patients all strongly suggests that at, minimum, they implicitly adhere to the reality of self-determinism with respect to themselves and to their patients. This said, some therapists, though I suspect very few, may insist that what seems to be a "chosen profession" on their part and what seem to be free efforts by them and their patients regarding helping and being helped, are themselves embedded in various sorts of necessitarianism.

If biological factors ultimately necessitate not only FFM traits but supertraits and even personality disorders themselves, it might be contended that clinicians and all other interested parties should forget about any kind of therapy unless the original necessitating factors are themselves subject to change from within or from without. Nevertheless, individuals, including clinicians, could still attempt to help others or themselves upon the belief that they were unable to act otherwise due to one or more sorts of determinism, especially biological, psychological, and societal types.

10. Personality Disorders: Freedom, Necessitarianism, and Chance

Perhaps the reader has heard the story about a sociopathic convict who, while on parole, took part in a series of armed robberies (the very notion of parole implies volition in that it entails a prisoner's word of honor to fulfill certain obligations while released from incarceration). After being caught by the police, the convict pleaded innocent (pleading itself presupposes volition), because, he swore (an act that also implies freedom), that he simply could not keep himself from acting differently.

After duly *deliberating*, the judge sentenced the man to do further time in a penitentiary for his crimes despite his plea that he was inwardly compelled to act as he did. The judge claimed, like the convict, to also be necessitated such that no verdict other than the one rendered was possible. The convict caught the drift of the judge's logic and was reduced to silence (or chose to be) as he once again was led away to prison. Metaphorically speaking, this story is the epitome of condemnation to necessitation.

Being the utterly remorseless individuals that sociopaths are, they are hardly likely to think of penitentiaries as places for doing penance for their actions (the notion of penitence of any sort itself seems to imply freedom). Besides, these antisocials, being consummate cynics and self-deceivers, are liable to believe that they are no more guilty—irrespective of how dishonest and callous they know they are—than others are for their negative traits.

A sociopathic serial murderer who had an abusive or neglectful parent(s), perhaps especially a father, a not altogether infrequent occurrence, will ordinarily still be held morally guilty by the public and legally culpable by the courts. The criminally antisocial's negative upbringing might be considered a mitigating, though not customarily an exculpatory, factor in assessing the measure of the individual's personal responsibility.

Recall that antisocials so habitually lie that they become a kind of prevarication themselves. In which case, they no longer feel themselves to be self-deceivers but truth tellers. All this may explain their lack of anxiety in deception regarding themselves and others. It may also explain why sociopaths are able to "deceive" mechanical detectors of lies. Hence, such antisocials may be described as ontological or ontical liars in that their very being is comprised of what is mendacious. So much so is the case that they can be masters at fooling others by their feigned sincerity or appearing to be what they are not. Sartre might refer to such dyssocials as paradigms of bad faith (1956, p. 63).

Are people born, for example, truthful or mendacious, or at least so inclined? The more a trait is germane to the sphere of morality, the less it is held to be a matter of necessitation. Still, there are personologists who back the doctrine of characterological determinism, in which case whatever people are, ethically considered, they are born and remain so, unless necessitation causes them to become otherwise.

Others claim that there are both good and bad seeds from a moral perspective. But, then, what is seminal by definition is subject to being freely cultivated and nurtured, for better or worse, though to what degree or kind remains a pivotal part of ongoing debate. The more a pathological personality is viewed as aberrant across cultures, or universal, the more arguable it is that such abnormality is biologically necessitated as least concerning its origins.

I stand with those who have grave reservations about including histrionics on the list of the abnormals if we adhere exclusively to the *DSM* depiction of them unless being severely deficiently related to others is a sufficient condition of this mental trait disorder. In any case, histrionics appear to be the least necessitated of all the pathologicals and much more a product of volitional and environmental than heritable factors, especially if heredity is considered as totally compelling.

Some cultures bring out the traits of particular aberrants such as the histrionic more than others do. I have submitted that SCRAM educes or strengthens Group II deviants or their types and traits, especially the sociopathic and narcissistic sorts. Partially as reactions to these two types of pathologicals, SCRAM is an ethos that fosters the emergence and magnification of Group III aberrants, such as the histrionics.

Group I are, in my judgment, the most necessitated and, thus, the least volitional if they are to any degree whatsoever, all of which renders them the most unreceptive to curative processes (assuming that the less necessitated is the aberrant, the more treatable is its aberration). Group I pathological traits are the most voluntary in the sense that they function in accordance with their inborn or quasi so propensities.

All this does not prevent schizotypals from experiencing some of their traits as highly dystonic, for example, anxiety and depressiveness. Hence, subjectively viewed, the schizotypal and especially the schizoid may not feel at all necessitated, at least not in any undesirable fashion.

Group III are the least necessitated as a totality if only because they are the closest to Humaneness, the supertrait most amenable to the volitional. Insofar as Group III are subject to Neuroticism, especially its more negative traits, such as hostility toward others, they are necessitated or at least greatly influenced. They are so given that Neuroticism is usually considered most subject to determinism after or along with Extraversion. Given that Neuroticism traits are largely experienced as dystonic in addition to being impairing, their possessors, among all the abnormals, most desire to change their qualities.

Group II pathologicals occupy a middle position with reference to the necessitation and self-determination of personality qualities, both in terms of their being (in)voluntary and (in)volitional and their therapeutic alteration.

The traits of these aberrants are typically ego-syntonic; as such, their possessors resist altering them. Plus, one of the traits of Group II, especially the among sociopaths, paranoids, and narcissists is overt arrogance, a quality that itself generally vehemently opposes any attribute alteration.

Those traits that are not necessitated are usually held to be open to self-determinism at least in principle. To exemplify that at least some aberrant personality traits may be subject to freedom, we can turn to the dependent and Group III as a whole, who are all accustomed to feeling highly remorseful, a subtrait of their FFM despondence (Costa and Widiger, 2002, p. 463). Remorse, or guilt, suggests that their experiencers feel penitent and culpable as to their negative internal acts and external actions precisely because they believe they had some degree of choice in these matters, if not as to their inception, then as to their continuation.

Group III feel not only regretful but shameful, a subtrait of FFM self-consciousness, with respect to their negative traits in general. Feeling humiliated is often held to presuppose freedom. But, more commonly embarrassment is predicated of individuals who, at least at the outset, have little if any control over their feelings and behavior, especially if they should have. Whether we are more belittled by what is a matter of necessity via constitutional factors, choice, or even chance is a complex and contestable concern.

Further to Group I, they do not feel guilty or embarrassed regarding their traits or behavior, though the schizotypal is subject to some degree of shame. By and large, the ability to experience humiliation and especially remorse are indicative of less psycho-ethical illness than the inability to do so.

As to Group II, sociopaths and paranoids feel both guiltless and shameless regarding their traits and actions. Narcissists feels remorseless but sometimes are humiliated by theirs. Obsessionals may feel both contrition and shame with reference to their qualities and conduct, but they routinely blame others more than themselves for the consequences of these two emotions unless their pretentious and cold dutism demand their doing otherwise. The more subject to shame but especially guilt is a deviated personality, the less mentally disturbed the personality is. From this perspective, Group I are the most diseased; Group III, the least.

Objectively considered, Group II can be looked upon as being less necessitated than Group I but more than Group III, largely depending to what extent Neuroticism is deemed determining. If Neuroticism is notionalized as highly necessitating, then Group III, the most neurotic of the aberrant personalities, can be appraised as being more necessitated or at least highly influenced by heredity than Group II.

In any case, Group III are likely apt to feel they are more necessitated, or less free, than Group II or even Group I. Subjectively considered, Group II may believe they are not only unnecessitated but, in their arrogance, as being eminently free and endowed with omnipotence, or infinite power of the will. Group III tend to think of themselves as powerless. Group I are largely indifferent to power or self-empowerment save when it comes to maintaining their social if not physical isolation.

It is routinely put forward that abnormal personalities are almost by definition less free, or more necessitated, than normals. A sign of this necessitation or at least strong inclination is that these deviated personalities' negative traits and comportment persist regardless how socially impairing or negatively maladaptive they may be. Nonetheless, irrespective how much of personality is genetically determined, it largely *decides* what such necessitation will signify in its life, even though that decision itself may be (pre)determined.

By some accounts then, the more abnormal individuals are, the more necessitated they are, and vice versa. Correlatively, the freer individuals are, the more normal and, a fortiori, supranormal they are and vice versa. Yet, regarding eminent necessity or eminent freedom, in the case of supranormal individuals, the more necessitated they are, the more free they are and vice versa, such that there is a synergic fusion of the determining and self-determining.

Necessitarians concede that people can feel emotionally free not only superficially but profoundly; that is, at a "gut level," they cognitively think that they are free, and conatively will or will to believe that they are free, but, according to determinists, they are only so subjectively considered. They contend, for example, that if the individual feels guilty about being irresponsible, this sentience of self-blame is itself compelled, objectively considered.

Whether any personality is free, it is likely better, both mentally and morally, to regard the individual as being endowed with choice, because freedom of choice, or more exactly, the choice of freedom corresponds to what is considered normal experience and to the demands of authenticity. Again, doing so also makes pragmatic and practical sense in terms of health and happiness.

The degree to which persons are adjudged to be free is crucial since construing the self as being overly free is sometimes more detrimental to self-determinism than being the opposite. The danger of excessive freedom in terms of autonomy is especially so in the case of the hyper-individualist Group II, above all the antisocials. The danger of deficient autonomy is especially predicable of Group I.

All these issues impact on therapy, a subject that is the touchstone of the pathological personality and its traits being self-determined, determined, indetermined, or a combination thereof.

Ten

AMENABILITY TO PERSONALITY CHANGE: THEORIES, THERAPIES, AND THERAPISTS

1. Personality Change

This chapter focuses on personality change in general and changing abnormal personality in particular, especially via autotherapy (self-treatment), therapy, or other healing or curative procedures. Personality alteration is seldom a radical transformation be it cognitive, emotive, or conative. Generally, people change gradually and, arguably, for the better, in the sense of psycho-ethically, as they become adults.

It is commonly held that we are born innocent and become otherwise as we age. Nonetheless, genuine innocence, in the sense of freedom from egotism, especially that kind which is harmful to others, comes only after people have met and overcome internal and external challenges and achieved what is sometimes known as second innocence. It is secondary from a temporal perspective but primary from a psycho-ethical slant.

Consequently, most contemporaries are not likely to subscribe to Jean-Jacques Rousseau's view that human beings were originally unselfish "noble savages" and even quasi savants due to their being "natural solitaries." Rousseau declared that people become immature mentally and morally when they abandon their idyllic aloneness and congregate with others in dehumanizing society, for example, Paris, which he titles a "vast desert of people" who live a "frightful" sort of loneliness (Sayer, 1978, p. 53).

Thus, Rousseau envisages immaturization as a switch from the constructive aloneness of social and physical (external) solitude to the destructive aloneness of emotional isolation which takes place within a throng of other lonelified and alienated individuals. Many people hailing from non-urban areas are still apt to look upon urbanites, who currently comprise more than half the world's population, as inhabiting "dens of iniquity" and decadence.

Nor has the reverse position apropos of human development gained much acceptance as formulated, for example, by Thomas Hobbes in his view that originally human beings were anything but innocent. Indeed, he conceived their being utterly selfish, ignoble, and ignorant savages. These bellicose individuals lived outside any civil society in a putative State of Nature wherein they existed, Hobbes writes, in "continual fear and danger of violent death." He famously characterizes the life of these belligerents as being "solitary" in the sense of alonely because of their fear of an existence that was "poor, nasty, brutish, and short" and remained so unless and until they agreed to come together and form a civil(ized) society (1953, p. 248n21).

Thus, the Hobbesian putative social contract was undertaken solely to avoid the aforesaid perils and hardships in being alone-ly and not because human beings were no longer basically selfish and malevolent. They continued to be entirely egocentric and combative but the fear of the state and specifically governmental sanctions was designed to keep their inhumaneness from resurfacing.

Notwithstanding the widespread view that becoming mature entails a gradual psycho-ethical transformation, total and instantaneous transitions, for good or evil, are sometimes believed to occur. An example is found in conversion of the previously ruthless Saul of Tarsus (St. Paul) to righteousness (Acts, 9:1–19). Contrarily, a fictional illustration from good to evil is that of Dr. Jekyll's metamorphosis into Mr. Hyde (Stevenson, 1886).

Saul's case is thought to be supernaturally caused, while Jekyll's was attributed to an illicit potion with preternatural powers. In neither case, then, was the change a natural occurrence. In the order of nature, there are few if any such complete personality metamorphoses, moral or psychological, that go from worst to best and even less from best to worst. Such total transitions occurring even incrementally over a long period of time are considered extremely exceptional.

Because personality aberrations principally pertain to disorders people *are* instead of *have*, it is exceedingly hard to transform them since what is more intrinsic resists alteration more than what is less so and, a fortiori, what is extrinsic. Hence, it is generally easier to change behavior than the mentality behind it.

Studies repeatedly suggest that even for normals any major psycho-ethical alteration is far from frequent. For example, Misty Harris reports on research that found that elementary school teachers' assessments of their students concerning their core personality traits proved to be accurate forty years later (*The Montreal Gazette*, 29 July 2010).

Paul T. Costa, Nicholas Patriciu, and Robert R. McCrae state that modification of personality in terms of FFM traits comes predominantly in two ways with the first being psycho-ethical evolution as the individual ages:

> Personality may change spontaneously through intrinsic maturation. As people move from adolescence to midlife, they usually decline in Neuroticism (N), Extraversion (E), and Openness to Experience (O) and increase in [Humaneness] (H) and Conscientious (C). (2005, p. 538)

A decline in Neuroticism is generally constructive—except in cases of positive neurotic disintegration—as are the inclines in Humaneness and Conscientiousness. Decreases in Extraversion are positive if people become less gregarious due, for instance, to their becoming more engaged in solitude, though it and Extraversion's sociability are, in principle, reinforcing constructive correlatives. Insofar as Extraversion pertains to the traits of warmth and positive emotions, its lessening is negative.

A decline in Openness to Experience can also be positive or negative, depending on which of its traits is at issue. Thus, a drop in the Openness to Experience trait of positive values is negative. A lessening in the trait of feelings may be positive if it is a change from the lower Dionysian Openness to Experience to the higher Dionysian Openness to Experience. This transition requires that, for example, the feelings be subject to Conscientiousness's discipline, an Apollonian component, so that they become, for example, more controlled, purified, and sublimated but without losing their original spontaneity and overall vitality.

As for the second change in personality traits, Costa and colleagues note that it can occur through:

> interventions (for example, pharmacotherapy) which alter the biological basis to traits. . . . It is often possible, however, and sometimes far easier to reshape characteristic maladaptations directly; for instance, cognitive intervention can restore an accurate self-image, assertiveness training may build social skills, and behavior modification can alter self-destructive behavior. (Ibid.)

Jeffrey Magnavita maintains that personality disorders "begin to crystallize in the early twenties then realize a more permanent form in the thirties." In this vein, he states that, for the preponderance of personologists, personality as a whole is "essentially fixed by age 30" (1997, p. 6). Nevertheless, Magnavita concedes, "the potential for in-depth personality restructuring *does* exist" among abnormals provided "the appropriate candidate is matched with the optimal approach" (ibid., p. 7).

As a rule, the more their personalities are abnormal, the more difficult it is to get such individuals into therapy and to remain there. Still, even with suitable patients who have an array of positive self-change motivations and mechanisms along with ideal therapists and therapies, substantive recomposition of pathological personalities is a most formidable feat, outside or inside the clinical context. Many individuals with personality disorders are highly incorrigible, such as the arrogantly defiant and devious sociopaths. Recidivism rates are high, especially, for example, among the manipulative and tempestuous borderlines. Naturally, the least success is evident among pure types that, possess all of the *DSM* diagnostic criteria for their particular disorder (pp. 649–650, 654). Obviously, the more personality traits are (pre)determined instead of (pre)conditioned, the less significant alteration by self or others is possible.

Michael Stone conceives personality as "fundamentally an aggregate of the ways in which" human beings "habitually" and "enduringly" relate to others. Second, Stone contends that "these 'ways,' taken one by one, are the individual *traits* of personality" (2006, p. 2). This said, he sets forth some "guidelines for evaluating treatability factors in personality disorders." They include harmonious interpersonal relatedness (ibid., pp. 32–36); absence of Axis I mental state disorders; a resolve to enter and continue treatment; and favorable life conditions, such as the necessary monetary, educational, and employment resources (ibid., pp. 41–42).

To be sure, all the aberrated personalities are extremely taxing to reform; perhaps at most they can be slightly reshaped. Richard Zweig and Jennifer Hillman remark that "It would seem, therefore, that the view that 'A zebra does not change its stripes'" is valid enough. Still, they adduce the corollary that "subtle shadings into 'a horse of a different color' would be heuristically useful" (1999, p. 49).

Yet, personality shaping has its limits, including those involving temporal types. Stone stipulates that personality, with respect to both its normal and abnormal traits, especially as it commences to "crystallize in its final shape around thirty, is highly resistant to change." He then writes that, as time passes, people with greatly "maladaptive traits (or a full-fledged disorder)" do not so much change themselves. Instead, they begin to configure "the world around them so as to be in greater conformity with the disorder" and thereby try to justify their aberration (1993, p. 156). At that point, any profound and enduring self-reconfiguration is most probably out of the question due largely to the intransigence and overall egocentricity on the part of the deviated personality.

Stone's animadversions apropos the changeability of personality disorders deserve greater scrutiny:

> The therapist who works with PDs is more cabinetmaker than carpenter. We do not build and reshape so much as polish and sand down with #600 paper: with luck and elbow grease we can smooth the surface. The shape stays as it was. Still this sanding down can accomplish a great deal. So long as the personality is more than half acceptable to others (something that is hard to measure precisely), treatment can bring about modifications which render someone much easier to live with or to work with. This can occur with just *minor* changes, which scarcely affect the basic personality profile. It is a question of thresholds: the fundamental nature of the personality will remain unaltered, but the intensity of the more bothersome traits may lessen. [A person] can become less pessimistic, less disdainful, less reckless . . . with [his or her] mate, etc. [We] could plot the final result as . . . similar peaks and valleys, but each one lower in amplitude. . . . At the end of the treatment, the personality profile was, in its contours, just the same as it was in the beginning, but the amplitudes of the negative traits were lower. . . . Under ideal treatment circumstances, modest quantitative changes can spell impressive qualitative changes for the better, while the basic personality tendencies remain pretty much as they were. (Ibid., pp. 160–161)

It appears that most personologists believe that any positive features an aberrant personality might have can be toned up and negative ones toned down. Still, the underlying structure of a personality disorder, especially the kind inhabiting Groups I and II, cannot be substantively revamped perhaps not even with the most appropriate therapies and adept, empathetic, sympathetic, and caring therapists.

Hence, it is possible that, as Joel Paris and others have put forth, most disordered personality therapy does not cure at all. Instead it makes minimal improvements such that pathological personalities change from more to less degrees of sickness. In short, they become less ill but not actually healthy. However, Stone has just suggested that sufficient quantitative trait changes can yield qualitative results. Consequently, people might hold that if therapy can help the sadistic serial murder to become "merely" a murderer, and the murderer to become simply nonmurderous, and the nonmurderous to become merely cruel, and the ruthless to become less callous, then it has to be considered somewhat successful. Admittedly, therapeutic triumphs vis-à-vis pathological personalities seem to be sparse.

One reason for infrequent therapeutic success relative to aberrant personalities is that they present both mental and moral hurdles. I have proposed that rarely if ever is there any lasting "skipping" of psycho-ethical motivational categories such as a leap from selfishness to acquirancy by omitting acquisitiveness. Even graduating to a higher stage within a category is difficult to permanently accomplish, such as going from habitually malicious patterns of action to simply malevolent intentions.

Hence, for the malevolently motivated and maliciously acting sociopaths, to become only acquisitive and remain so without reverting to their habitual ill-will and maleficence would be a therapeutic coup. Still, such a change is hardly even close to a complete cure.

Nonetheless, disturbed persons are commonly viewed to be sometimes malleable provided they have the right environment, including the therapeutic. Even the sociopath, according to the *DSM*, may "remit as the individual grows older, [especially] by the fourth decade of life" (p. 648). Given their complete disinhibitedness, including their proclivity to aggression and violence, in addition to their spur-of-the-moment suicide—sociopaths have, in general, a shorter life expectancy than normals and even other aberrant personalities. Accordingly, these exceedingly reckless individuals have less time for any positive transformation.

A convincing case can be made for the position that psycho-ethically normal people have at minimum a fairly abiding concern for their fellow human beings. They are not only benevolently disposed toward a few individuals but to most of them unless the latter consistently and flagrantly forfeit the grounds for that solicitude that generally takes the forms of empathy and sympathy. Consequently, the more ingrained the egocentricity, the harder it is to make the next move upwards; correlatively, the less egocentric, the easier it becomes. Whereupon, it would be less challenging to change from acquirancy to benevolence than it is from acquisitiveness to acquirancy and, a fortiori, from selfishness to acquisitiveness.

Stated otherwise, it is easier for good people to become better than it is for bad ones to become less bad. Truly iniquitous antisocials, such as sadistic killers, seldom if ever reform such that they become psycho-ethically good. Nevertheless, these master con artists may, most unfortunately, convince others to believe they have. For many a personologist, such as Stone, these types of murderers may be forgiven but they must never be forgotten in the sense of not remembering to keep them incarcerated or, in any case, vigilantly monitored (1993, 434–486). Stone remarks that the possible remediation of such barbarous individuals is a moot point for in:

> the face of incurable destructiveness, it would be better if psychiatry gave up the illusion of a cure, and recognized that in this situation the welfare of a society weighs more in the balance than the liberties of the offender. (Ibid., p. 486)

The capability for human beings to change non-human objects and conditions is profound, widespread, and often wondrous. However, this aptitude is far less visible vis-à-vis human subjects and their existential condition, though hope for such change should obviously not be abandoned.

2. Amenability to Therapy

According to Stone, amenability to therapy requires introspectiveness and empathy (traits highly lacking in Group I and II) in addition to adequate, even above average, intelligence (ibid., pp. 42–44). In terms of character and spirituality, these provisions involve moral integrity and common decency in general and, more specifically, hopefulness, forbearance (patience), and what amounts to the six traits of Humaneness, all of which are spiritual (ethical) qualities (ibid.). These views are compatible with my position that personality disorders are quintessentially psycho-ethical deviations concerning relatedness to other persons.

Thus, the most elementary cause of inability or unwillingness of disordered personality patients to change their mentality or behavior is, at base, their non-relatedness, dis-relatedness, or grossly deficient relatedness to others.

Erlene Rosowsky writes that the aberrated personalities "are typically those who are among the most challenging to treat, regardless of venue, clinician, or the patient's age." These abnormals are widely perceived as being "over-demanding, long-suffering, malignant, and hateful" in addition to being disabled or impaired (1999, p. 153).

David Bernstein and David Useda state that with respect to the personality aberrants:

> Clearly, their mistrust, antagonism, introversion, rigidity, and other features present challenges for psychotherapists, given that therapy usually is predicated on an individual's ability to form a trusting relationship with the therapist and to examine the self's own assumptions about itself, others, and the world. (2007, p. 56)

As a totality, the ten personality anomalies have literally hundreds of other features that make them highly undesirable patients (and intimates) and candidates for creating a trusting alliance with the clinician. For example, the literature regards the paranoid as being abrasive, arrogant, callous, cantankerous, combative, competitive, confrontational, contemptuous, cynical, dissembling, dogmatic, domineering, embittered, envious, grudge-holding, humorless, hypercritical, illiberal, ill-willed, inconsiderate, incorrigible, jealous, mean, mean-spirited, monomaniacal, obnoxious, obstinate, overbearing, pretentious, pusillanimous, rancorous, self-righteous, slanderous, smug, spiteful, sullen, unapologetic, uncooperative, unsociable, vengeful, vindictive, vituperative, willful, and, of course, mindlessly and inveterately suspicious (Stone, 1993, pp. 100–102).

Obviously, these qualities are not the kind that therapists relish for any sort of alliance with their patients. This affiliation is itself a moral coalition since it requires, for example, sincerity, loyalty, and confidentiality, features critically lacking in pathological personalities. Of the paranoid traits listed, only suspiciousness in evinced by the schizotypal, but this individual's mistrust of others is mild and somewhat understandable and justified in comparison to that of the paranoid's.

Theodore Gradman, Larry Thompson, and Delores Gallagher explain that psychotherapy and pharmacotherapy rely on interpersonal collaboration and persuasion to achieve results. They underscore that pathological personalities make poor, even horrendous, candidates for therapy precisely because they are such uncooperative and unpersuadable individuals They emphasize that those with personality deviancies also have greater problems in creating "a good working therapy alliance and exhibit greater attrition and poorer compliance with both somatic and psychological treatments." Consequently, when these abnormals do remain in therapy, they require more extended treatment than is usually needed for other types of patients (1999, p. 69).

Likewise, Richard Zweig and Jennifer Hillman report that individuals with personality anomalies are "widely viewed as more likely to form a tenuous therapeutic alliance, to be noncompliant, or to refuse mental health treatment" (1999, p. 31). Louis Charland notes that the therapist strives to make the client "be more honest, less manipulative, and less resentful and vindictive" (2006, p. 124). These traits are among those most resistant to change and are especially prevalent among Group II.

Robert Ruegg and Allen Frances relate that aberrant personalities make extremely undesirable patients because they are linked to delayed recovery from Axis I and medical illness, misdiagnosis and mistreatment of medical and psychiatric disorder, malpractice suits, medical and judicial recidivism, dissatisfaction with and disruption of psychiatric treatment settings (1995, pp. 16–17). Not only are these aberrants highly troublesome patients, but they are routinely involved in a host of behavioral and social problems—not surprisingly especially the antisocial—that often land them, frequently most reluctantly, in therapy to begin with. These problems include, according to Ruegg and Frances:

> crime, substance abuse, disability, increased need for medical care, suicide attempts, self-injurious behavior, assaults . . . institutionalization, underachievement, underemployment, family disruption, child abuse and neglect, homelessness, illegitimacy, poverty, [and] socially transmissible diseases. (Ibid., p. 16)

Not unexpectedly sociopaths are the deviants who most resist therapy, unless they can use it for their own selfish and duplicitous purposes, for example, conning health professionals to avoid or abate legal punishment, especially incarceration.

When in treatment, sociopaths—usually only after being compelled by various persons *of* authority, such as police, or *in* authority, such as psychiatrists—are the most detestable and dangerous of patients. They are followed in resistance to therapy by the other Group II aberrants and in the order stated above, namely the paranoid, narcissist, and obsessional.

Katherine Fowler, William O'Donohue, and Scott Lilienfeld go so far as to claim that except for a few treatments for the borderline that "have promising empirical support, there are few *documented* effective interventions for personality disorders." Yet, they then state, "clinical lore regarding the intractability of some personality disorders," (such as the antisocial) "has led to marked pessimism surrounding therapeutic intervention, possibly further contributing to this inertia" (2007, p. 11, emphasis added). These statements appear to reason that acknowledging the lack of therapeutic personality disorder success only increases the failure rate.

Freedom signifies the apertures to act and to do so with alternatives, whereas determinism shuts these self-determining openings. Hence, if personality necessitation itself involves the ability to take advantage of opportunities to change, as encapsuled in the FFM supertrait of Openness to Experience, then it could, rather ironically, be argued that the more necessitated is the personality disorder in terms of Openness to Experience, the more amenable it is to therapy.

Thus, if the necessitating trait pertains to that found in Openness to Experience's trait of *actions*, then the individual may be "willing" to enter the realm of the unfamiliar in terms of activities in which event treatment is more likely. Similarly, if the necessitating trait refers to Openness to Experience's *ideas,* then the individual is "willing" to engage in "new and perhaps unconventional" thought processes, then treatment is more likely (Costa and Widiger, 2002, p. 465).

The less freely caused or continued is the aberration, the less probable is the individual amenable to therapy in general.

Group III would, in my judgment, be the best prospects for amelioration, given that, as a totality, they are, for instance, the least psycho-ethically necessitated of the personality aberrations. Group I would be the worst candidates, surely from a purely psychic perspective. As a combination of the psychic and ethical, Group II, especially the sociopath, are the worst prospects for ameliorative procedures.

The Group II narcissists and obsessionals are less purely psychologically compelled than the Group I aberrants but are more so than Group III. The obsessional, representative of the lower Apollonian, is more dutiful, deliberate, and all-around conscientious than all the other pathological personalities put together, including the highly irresponsible narcissist, emblematic of the lower Dionysian.

For these reasons alone, the obsessional is more favorably disposed toward therapy than the narcissist. If the positive aspects of the FFM supertrait of Conscientiousness were the only elements involved in therapy, the obsessional would clearly be the leading aspirant of all the abnormals for treatment (ibid., p. 461).

In principle, the fewer *DSM* diagnostic criteria for a specific personality disorder a person has, and the lower their ranking, the more amenable that person is to personality change. For example, the person who has only five of the nine requisite criteria to qualify for being a *DSM* borderline, is far more likely to experience therapeutic remediation than is one who has all nine (pp. 672–673). It also follows that the more such criteria pertain to nature, the less changeable is the aberrant; the more they pertain to nurture, the more modifiable. By definition, those diagnostic criteria that are able to be modified by choice are, in principle, the most alterable.

The first personality disorder listed in each of my aggregates is the more (Group I) or most pathological (Groups II and III) of its members; correlatively, the last mentioned is the least. Consequently, Group I are the least amenable to therapy and its schizoid less so than the schizotypal, if, for example, the first's integration remains negative and the second's disintegration can become positive. Group II are more responsive to therapy than Group I with the sociopath being the least and the obsessional the most. Group III are the most successful concerning therapy with the borderline being the least and the avoidant the most.

All the above rankings could change contingent upon numerous factors. For instance, if the schizotypal is reckoned closer to psychosis than is the schizoid, then the first would obviously be less treatable than the second. Also, if the avoidant is reckoned to be more genetically determined or strongly influenced than, for instance, the dependent, then the second would be more amenable to therapy not only in relation to Group III but as compared with all the personality disorders, other factors remaining equal.

Some deviants are especially problematic to rank with respect to their amenability to therapy, a sign of which is that they are difficult to aggregate. The obsessional and borderline are the two abnormals, in my view, most problematic to place in units, everything considered.

The Group II obsessional, the aberrant closest to Group III, the unit most amenable to therapy—a proximity that, by itself, makes the compulsive the most open to therapy of Group II—has traits that are especially promising for psycho-ethical improvement namely, those of Conscientiousness, such as dutifulness and achievement striving.

On the other hand, the obsessive's excessive commitment to duty (dutism) and achievement striving in the form of perfectionism, hostility toward others, iciness, arrogance, recalcitrance, unease in and scorn for matters intimate, and overall trait syntonicity argue against its conduciveness to ameliorating interventions.

Insofar as obsessionals are extremely inflexible, dictatorial, scornful, self-righteous, and accusatory, they are less treatable than the Group III borderlines. Borderlines are also exceedingly difficult to improve in part due to their manipulativeness, emotional turbulence, and overall unpredictability. However, borderlines, unlike obsessionals, are mainly self-accusatory about their traits and tribulations. As might be expected, self-blame is a quality that is less resistant to change than faulting others for one's problems. The obsessional-compulsive's traits, like those of the other Group II deviants, are syntonic. On the other hand, the traits of the borderline and the other Group III pathologicals are dystonic. Thus, the painful traits that constitute Neuroticism—the supertrait that, in turn, most typifies Group III—could be construed as being qualities adopted by these individuals as being lesser evils. Thus, their high ranking in Neuroticism's vulnerability due to the stress in their pursuit of connectedness is looked upon by Group III as being less painful than the loneliness that occurs due to having abandoned any such quest for intimacy.

Syntonic qualities are, by definition, more resistant to change than dystonic attributes. However, the traits of obsessionals are the least syntonic of Group II, given, for instance, their high rate of Neuoticism, which is another reason I rank compulsives as I do.

A major impediment for the treatment of obsessionals is that they have features of the lower Apollonian on the conscious level and lower Dionysian on the unconscious level such that they have a double dose of negative qualities. When their more inhibited, subterranean side surfaces, obsessionals' lack of warmth, altruism, cooperation, and tender-heartedness may explode into a ferocious yet systemic maleficence.

Alternatively, borderlines are almost entirely lower Dionysian sorts and, consequently, do not have a kind of dual personality dilemma that faces obsessionals. Still, given their torrential and titanic temperaments, they can suddenly switch moods, especially concerning their intimates. As well, borderlines are at least neutral regarding Openness to Experience's adaptability, which all therapies require by definition. This supertrait manifestly makes borderlines more amenable to treatment than the closed-minded, self-righteous, stubborn obsessionals.

Those who are uncritical of themselves are less open to therapy than those who are. Self-criticality itself can become pathological, as in the case of borderlines in their constant focus on their being bad, even evil. To the extent that a personality disorder involves such hypercriticality, the less successful will the aberrant be, therapeutically considered. Those who are especially subject to successitis, such as Group II, strongly resist entering therapy because, for them, it already implies gross failure and humiliation. Insofar as therapy is a source of stigmatizing shame it will be resisted by all non-masochistic individuals.

Additionally, Group II tend to dislike others (and vice versa) perhaps especially those who, like clinicians, are both in authority, due to their position and its specific powers such as administrative, and are authorities, due to their expertise. For those aberrants not so much concerned about success, entering therapy need not imply self-failure but may even suggest a kind of achievement. Furthermore, Group III, certainly in comparison to Group II, are less hostile to others, including therapists. Yet, borderlines, in their typically ambivalent manner, are both aggressive and appeasing and, correspondingly, hyper- and hypo-critical of others, probably especially of those who evaluate them, like clinicians.

The schizotypal and especially the schizoid of Group I in addition to the paranoid and above all the sociopath of Group II are less open to therapy than the borderline. However, these four deviants are far less likely to show up volitionally for any kind of therapy, not to speak of remaining in it, in comparison to the borderline, the aberrant most found in clinical settings.

The borderlines' belief that they might not exist is consonant with the pathologically lonely individuals' persuasion that, in a lived sense—meaning a practical versus a merely theoretical fashion—they are all alone in the world. Because human existence is innately and irremediably a matter of co-existence, and specifically interpersonal relatedness and sociality in general, their aloneness makes borderlines excruciatingly vulnerable to feelings of nonbeing. It need not be stressed that those with convictions of their "no-thingness" are a major challenge to therapy of any sort.

I propose that the paranoid is far less necessitated than the schizoid or schizotypal, another reason why I do not aggregate these three pathologicals in the same unit, as does the *DSM* in its Cluster A. I consider borderlines to be less necessitated than these Group I personalities and the paranoids of Group II. Still, borderlines are more necessitated than their fellow Group III aberrants, the histrionics, dependents, and possibly the avoidants. This appraisal concerning the avoidants is partially contingent upon to what extent they are not considered being a Group I type of abnormal.

Sociopaths are the most immorally psychotic and egologically solipsistic of all the aberrants. In my outlook, they can more fittingly be denominated immoral psychotics than paranoids can be appropriately termed psychological psychotics. The sociopath's antisociality is as egologically solipsistic as the schizophrenic's delusions are psychologically solipsistic. The egological (immoral) and psychological (psychotic) types of solipsism are actual, or lived, sorts and, therefore, are exceedingly resistant to therapy because psychotherapy in itself is a de facto admission by the patient of not being all alone in the universe.

Contrastingly, the metaphysical, epistemological, and methodological brands of solipsism—the kinds that can be designated philosophical—are ordinarily contemplated exclusively in theoretical terms and, as such, require no therapy, at least none which is conventional.

There are good grounds to think that antisociality, especially when it refers to psychopathy, may be biologically based, including that which pertains to physiological abnormalities such as those involved in brain dysfunctionality (Rosenhan and Seligman, 1989, pp. 502–504). However, there are also solid reasons to believe that sociopathy arises at least partially from a negative environment, such as in families where rampant abuse or neglect occurs (ibid., pp. 496–500). Still other sociopaths and psychopaths may simply choose to initiate or perpetuate the traits they have, such as their habitual mercilessness, because they perceive these qualities as promoting their egoistical objectives.

Paris writes, "findings that all the traits which are less influenced by genetic factors relate to problems in intimacy should be encouraging to therapists" because "difficulties with intimacy are common in practice, and may be more amenable to psychological interventions" (1996, pp. 165–166) (Paris apparently holds that genetic factors might only influence instead of necessitate).

Everything considered from both the psychological and characterological perspectives, the least treatable, if they are at all, are the schizoids, schizotypals, sociopaths, and paranoids, and usually in that order, depending on the attributes stressed and their severity. They are followed by the narcissists and then either the borderlines or obsessionals, again contingent upon which prototypical traits are in question and their gravity. However, the borderlines are the most liable to relapse. This propensity, in some respects, attests to both their greater and lesser receptivity to treatment than, for example, narcissists.

Finally, and in the following order, the most treatable are histrionics, and avoidants, although this ranking can be altered, again contingent upon the attributes at issue and their seriousness. Since a good portion of the robustness of the traits is its degree of geneticity, if avoidants are viewed as being more biologically than environmentally produced, they will to that extent be more like the schizoids and especially the schizotypals of Group I, who are the worst candidates for ameliorative methods. Correspondingly, avoidants will be less like the Group III aberrants who as a totality are those abnormals most open to and the least unsuccessful regarding personality improvement.

Stone considers the personality disorders "*generally* more amenable" to therapy to be the histrionic, avoidant, and dependent" (2006, p. 80), all of whom belong to my Group III, and the obsessional of my Group II. As is evident from what I have just written, I agree with Stone except I would add my Group III borderline to his list. However, if this aberrant's more psychotic-like traits become highly active in the therapeutic setting, I would relegate the borderline to my least amenable category. That category contains the two aberrants most disposed toward "mental" psychosis, namely the schizoid and the schizotypal; the aberrant most inclined to a mixture of mental and moral psychosis, the paranoid; and the abnormal most susceptible to "pure" ethical derangement, the antisocial.

Still, an argument can be made that moral "madness" is embedded in a kind of mental insanity (or the reverse, though it is less arguable). Consequently, the unequalled egological solipsism, or actual versus theoretical automania, of the archetypal antisocial is so viciously egocentric that it places its possessor outside the mentality of all humanity. In this case, I would contend that the sociopath differs from all other pathologicals in kind, certainly ethically considered.

If narcissism is taken to mean self-centeredness in general, then all pathological personalities are narcissistic, especially Group II, in which the narcissistic aberrants are themselves housed. The greater the self-centeredness of an individual, the more opposed to therapy is the disorder. In the psycho-ethical order of egocentricity, it becomes graver as it goes from the acquisitional of Group I, to the acquisitive of Group III, and finally to the malevolent self-centeredness of Group II.

Nonetheless, the ego-centeredness of Group I is not egoistical as it is in the case of Group II. There is a profound sense in which the schizotypal and above all the schizoid seem to lack any interest in their egos. They do so except to keep themselves away from others and even themselves in that they are bereft of the introspection on their selves or their behavior. On the other hand, Group II are full of the introversion that characterizes such consummately self-centered loners.

Individuals with pathological personalities generally have little if any insight into their own problems in part because many of them do not look upon their traits as problematic, especially for themselves. The more they do, the less disturbed as a rule they are, and the less so, the more they are suitable for self and other-based therapy.

Group I have the least grasp of their difficulties; Group III, the most, all of which may be one reason why the second tend to be neurotic and the first psychotic-like. The more understanding the aberrant has of its difficulties, the more dystonic it may become, but through that very process, the more it may become amenable to therapy. Still, mere understanding of personal problems is not sufficient to make people able or willing to change their qualities. Even the strong desire to change is rarely enough to bring it about since, among other things, suitable therapies and therapists are also often required.

The more a personality aberrant experiences shame and guilt, the more treatable is that individual in principle. Group I aberrants, especially the schizoids, experience little if any of these two feelings largely because they are impoverished in terms of affectivity. They are remiss especially regarding socially directed emotions such as shame and guilt in that they are total social isolates. Nor are the sociopaths and paranoids of Group II vulnerable to significant embarrassment and self-blame largely because of these lonerists' gross contempt for others. Narcissists are subject to little guilt but often to much shame. Obsessionals experience both self-embarrassment and self-reproof, another reason they are the most treatable of Group II aberrants. However, it is the highly dystonic Group III pathologicals who are most susceptible to feelings of humiliation and self-reproach.

Depending on the diagnostic criteria emphasized, Group III borderlines, in some significant respects, are more psycho-ethically sick than either narcissists or obsessionals and, as a result, are less susceptible to therapy than both these Group II aberrants. For instance, even more so than do narcissists and especially obsessionals, borderlines lack FFM straightforwardness and cooperativeness, traits clearly crucial to therapeutic success (Costa and Widiger, 2002, p. 461).

Though they are less neurotic than Group III, Group II as an ensemble are closer to psychosis than Group III. As such, they are less suitable for therapy than Group III, save the borderline who, we recall, is more psychotically inclined than any of the Group II aberrants, with the possible exception of the paranoid. This deviate is, as stated above, widely viewed as being on the schizophrenic, or psychotic, sequence, along with the schizoid and schizotypal of Group I. I re-stress that I do not take this perspective, at least not insofar as the paranoid is portrayed by the *DSM*. Nonetheless, I have placed the paranoid second only to the sociopath as being the most psycho-ethically diseased of the pathologicals.

Of all the abnormals, the schizotypal is probably the closest to psychosis. I note that *The Manual* states that there is "considerable co-occurrence" between schizotypals and borderlines (p. 642) (both aberrations have, according to some, a strong biological basis). Borderlines can be subject to temporary psychosis, as manifested, according to the *DSM*, in "transient paranoid ideation" and "dissociative symptoms (for example, depersonalization)" and "psychotic-like symptoms (for example, hallucinations, body-image distortions, ideas of reference, and hypnagogic phenomena") (pp. 651–652).

This said, schizotypals have more enduring psychotic-like symptoms than borderlines. The first have symptoms more cognitive in nature and the second have more affective types. The emotional life of schizotypals is extremely inhibited and non-intimate; that of the borderlines is extremely disinhibited (impulsive) and explosively and indiscriminately intimate (p. 644).

Neurotic traits are, in principle, more often deemed indelible than psychotic-like qualities are, unless the latter are part of an individual's personality. Trait disturbances, such as those of pathological personalities, refer to what the persons *are* and their attributes are often genetically based. Mental state disorders, such as schizophrenia, refer to what people *have* in the sense of what they acquire unless they are predisposed toward this debilitating illness by their traits. What a person innately is can be changed less than what a person acquires.

Mental state disorders, like schizophrenia, are generally more amenable to pharmacological treatment than are mental trait disorders. If personality disorder aggregates are interpreted in more probabilistic, prototypal fashion, instead of being construed as archetypes as my aggregates are, then, for instance, the narcissists of Group II might be more amenable to therapy than the avoidants of Group III. Again, this conduciveness is contingent upon which of their diagnostic features, their intensity, time of onset, and the like, most prevail concerning these two personality disorders.

Group I, especially schizoids, avoid therapists as befitting the total social isolates they are. Group II, as hostile lonerists, to wit partial social isolates, also ordinarily dodge clinicians in the order listed, namely the sociopath do so the most and the obsessional the least. Group III, as lonelies, seek therapy and may be attracted to its practitioners for the intimate attention and sometimes the affection and companionship they may provide.

3. Personality Alteration and the Five Factor Model

Writing from the perspective of the FFM, Robert R. McCrae and Paul T. Costa claim that personality traits do not significantly change and are "found in all cultures studied so far." Nonetheless, they point out that cross-cultural investigations suggest that people, perhaps mainly after thirty years of age, can experience some decreases in FFM supertraits of Extraversion, Neuroticism, and Openness to Experience in addition to increases in Humaneness and Conscientiousness, at least on a "very modest pace" (1999, p. 144). Increases in Humaneness and Conscientiousness and a decrease in Neuroticism are reasons to be more optimistic about human nature and its amenability to therapeutic intervention.

A decrease in FFM Openness to Experience is generally negative and is undesirable in particular regarding therapy, both self and other-directed, since it requires, among other things, being open to change by definition. The only aberrants who score higher than average in Openness to Experience are the Group I schizotypal, the Group II narcissist, and the Group III histrionic. Their Openness to Experience fantasy, for example, is utterly capricious instead of creative and, in general, negatively unfettered as to objective reality testing. Being positively unbounded involves Openness to Experience via the inventiveness of the higher Dionysian (Costa and Widiger, 1994, p. 329; 2002, pp. 461, 465–466).

Therefore, while their fantasizing might get the schizotypal, narcissist, and histrionic into therapy because they dream of bettering their condition, their lack of discrimination and discipline might cause them to drop out early, or, in any case, prevent them from attaining the desired results. These deviants' shortage of the Apollonian qualities required for the therapeutic alliance, such as self-control, reliability, and straightforwardness, clearly hinders therapeutic success for these aberrants.

The *DSM* schizotypals in particular score high, for example, not only in fantasies but ideas. Unfortunately, their ideas are quasi-psychotic, marked by paranoid ideation and magical, odd, or illusory thinking. All these are often externally exhibited in the schizotypals' exceedingly irregular even bizarre speech (p. 645).

The *DSM* narcissists score high in fantasies but theirs revolve about idolized selves such that they have recurrent reveries about "unlimited success, power, brilliance, beauty, or ideal love," which makes them the paradigm case of SCRAM's successism (p. 661). These narcissistic mental attributes and extramental conduct are hardly conducive to being changed for the better. However developed their cognitive abilities are, narcissists remain puerile if not infantile with reference to their emotional and conational development.

In my judgment, the FFM dimensions can be ranked from the most self-determining to the most involitional or involuntary. From various perspectives and in the order given, Humaneness, Conscientiousness, and Openness to Experience are arguably the most subject to self-determinism. These three supertraits are, in my view, the most conducive to therapy. Neuroticism is ordinarily appraised as being the most negative or the least positive of the supertraits. It is also usually rated, along with Extraversion, the most necessitated, and, consequently, the least subject to change or amenable to therapy over the life-span (Rubenstein and Shaver, 1982, pp. 133–135).

Humaneness, the FFM supertrait most subject to self-determinism, and Extraversion, when combined with Humaneness are, in my view, the nucleus of psycho-ethical health and happiness. Extraversion may decrease over the years, but if it is a constructive change, it can involve a greater attending to not only external but internal solitude. Concomitantly, the decrease in Extraversion can contain a lesser need for the servile type of gregariousness à la Nietzsche and, for instance, the craving for popularity or celebrity (1989a, pp. 110–117nn199–202).

People can, for example, score high in Humaneness and Neuroticism, as do dependents, such that the first makes them less necessitated or at least less conditioned and, therefore, more accessible to therapy, while the second renders them more necessitated and, thus, less open to it. Within a given supertrait, some traits are more necessitated or at least more conditioning than others. For example, within Neuroticism, anxiety is often reckoned more necessitatingly heritable than vulnerability and, therefore, in principle, less treatable. Anxiety can be looked upon in general as a condition even a cause of vulnerability but the second also fosters the first.

Traits of Humaneness and Conscientiousness are especially considered ethical or moral and subject to volition. As such, they are considered amenable to change, therapeutic and otherwise. As a totality, Group III have the potential to be closest to Humaneness, that, because it is the least heritable of the supertraits, is the most elective of them. Humaneness is also the most positive of the FFM dimensions, including the therapeutically considered. Patently, those who are, for example, more benevolent, trusting, cooperative, and kind, are more suited for a healing alliance, which in part is a moral contract, than those who are not. Manifestly as well, the more they have such Humaneness traits, the less likely are people to need to enter therapy compared to those who have no-Humaneness (Group I) and especially anti-Humaneness (Group II) qualities.

Whereas their Neuroticism qualities are generally held to argue against Group III being self-determining and conducive to therapy, their Humaneness attributes argue for them. The narcissist and obsessional have the most neurotic traits of Group II. This similarity is another reason why I have ranked these two Group II aberrants closest to the Group III, and in particular next to the borderline, where once again its title is fitting.

Borderlines are the most neurotic, both intensively and extensively, of not only Group III but of all the deviants (Costa and Widiger, 2002, p. 461). As a result, they are among if not the most difficult to treat of all those aberrated personalities who are apt to seek counseling, at least those who do so relatively freely.

Antisociality has been analyzed as a behavioral disorder and as such, it can be reckoned to be a voluntary or volitional aberration. David Rosenhan and Martin Seligman state that antisocials are "*capable* of exercising will and of conducting themselves properly, but simply *choose* not to do so" (1989, p. 494). This choice of conduct adds to antisocials being the most untreatable of the aberrants, save the most necessitated of them, which are arguably the schizoids and schizotypals.

On the other hand, some dyssocials appear not to understand what (im)morality requires. Insofar as such comprehension is considered a necessary condition of the ethical, antisocials cannot be said to act volitionally, or freely. However, they do act voluntarily insofar as their actions reflect their natural predispositions and inclinations, if not necessitations. Naturally, the more antisociality is envisioned as being inborn, the less it is viewed as being accessible to therapy as a whole.

Consequently, antisocials can be thought of as possessing the will, or the faculty of freedom, but lacking the willingness to change their mentality or conduct. However, these socially sick individuals do not ordinarily regard what is culturally considered to be amoral, immoral, or anti-moral traits as dystonic. All this argues for some antisocials as having a mind-set that renders them highly unsusceptible to any kind of therapy.

In sum, sociopaths are the deviants most lacking in Conscientiousness and being the most immoral, amoral, and antimoral of aberrant individuals. Of all the pathological personalities, they are, therefore, the most vociferously and belligerently resistant to therapy unless they can somehow use this process to further their own brutal selfishness.

Extraversion as a totality is perhaps the most unchangeable of supertraits. When its traits are positive and when allied to those of Humaneness we have the combination of factors most relevant to happiness insofar as it relates to the actualization of human sociality in the forms of socialness and sociability.

Those who have various kinds of difficulties with relatedness, which is the case with all the personality disorders, may be candidates for therapy depending on how they are disposed toward changing their hearts through the release of inwardness that must occur in therapy.

Changing the heart of the person wherein intimacy symbolically resides and that signifies the individual's values and value-hierarchy—which, in turn, are predominantly the provinces of Humaneness and Openness to experience—is admittedly among if not the most trying of tasks. Still, nothing transforms a person more than being the recipient of intimacy, especially of unconditional love. Unfortunately, those most in need of personality change are often those most lacking in such caring affirmation and validation.

The more, therefore, people are open to gaining and maintaining genuine connections with others, the better candidates they are for beneficial therapy. But, then, the more disposed they are toward true ties with others, the less likely they are to have a pathological personality to begin with. Hence, the more an aberrant has a need, capability, and desire, plus the will to obtain and sustain inwardness and the communicative abilities to express it, the less grave is the personality pathology, and the more it is modifiable by suitable therapy, mutatis mutandis.

According to these criteria, personality pathologies rank in the following order vis-à-vis the weightiness of their problems with intimacy and lack of receptivity and success relative to treatment: Groups I, II, and III. Individuals with Group II and especially Group I anomalies are those who most rarely enter therapy. If they do, they are the least able to be helped with the possible exception of some sub-types of the obsessional for reasons mainly attributable to this aberrant's Conscientiousness.

These six Group I and II abnormals do not seek aid in great part because their traits are either nondystonic or nonsyntonic (Group I) or syntonic (Group II). I append that schizotypals' traits are also dystonic. Alas, their extreme social anxiety and suspiciousness keep them away from others in general and clinicians in particular.

These two aggregates are close-minded and heartless either in being devoid of heartfelt emotions and emotions in general (Group I, especially schizoids) or are closed-minded and hard-hearted (Group II, especially sociopaths). Group III are the most likely to seek treatment because their traits are dystonic. They are the most apt to be assisted because they are not only the most open-minded but the most open-hearted of these abnormals.

Since a radical transformation of personality is rare, obviously, even the transition from violent to nonviolent selfishness is exceedingly taxing, and from it to the kind of acquisitiveness that deliberately ignores the needs of others is perhaps even rarer.

All such motivational habits, like acquisitiveness, vary in degree and more probably in kind from one another. The shift from one positive pattern to another is demanding for even the normal person. Being mired in a negative motivational pattern is a constituent of the disordered person, a regularity that patently resists therapeutic transformation.

4. Loneliness and Amenability to Therapy

In terms of loneliness and therapy, the deviants least likely to be found in the clinical population, surely on a chosen basis, are those of Group I, the personalities who are bothered neither by emotional isolation nor by any sort of isolation for that matter. Second in least prevalence are those of Group II who are largely untroubled by loneliness in conscious fashion, except in the ways stipulated above, though they can be extremely affected by aloneliness, especially in a nonconscious manner. Group III are by far the most common patients in the clinical population and are the most disturbed by loneliness and aloneliness, above all in a highly conscious way.

In reference to Group II, sociopaths, as do paranoids, display hostility not only to the notion of therapy but to therapists, as they do to human beings in general. If sociopaths are defined as being involved in Conduct Disorder, then these antisocials in general and insofar as they appear in "prison and forensic settings" will have, according to the *DSM*, an especially high resistance to therapy and mental health professionals as a whole (pp. 646, 648).

As for the narcissists, they are likely ambivalent regarding therapy and therapists. They relish the attention paid them in clinical contacts but resent the humiliation involved therein.

Concerning obsessionals, they can—given their propensity to be conscientious, especially in the sense of dutifulness and self-discipline—be more amenable to loneliness-therapy than the other Group II deviants. As being the least aberrated and least opposed to therapy of Group II, the obsessionals are next to the least disordered aggregate of the disordered. They are Group III individuals since, for one thing, these four abnormals are the those most apt to seek "intimacy-therapy."

Many gravely lonely and alonely individuals, such as Group III, are disposed to pursue individualized clinical care for the very company and companionship of the mental health personnel such treatment provides them. In the process, they may find the means to cope with their adversaries. They may also seek group-therapy for the same reasons.

5. Optimal Therapies

I look upon the relational and, more specifically, the interpersonal as being the optimal therapies concerning personality abnormality. These approaches regard personality traits as being more flexible than most other curative or healing interventions. They do so in part because such traits are more highly dependent on social and cultural conditions which, by definition, are more alterable, all things considered, than those qualities derived more from, for example, biological factors.

Judith Jordan, who accentuates social and cultural relational theories of therapy, states, "the healing of chronic disconnections depends heavily on establishing good, safe connections," instead of "analyzing or reworking personality traits or simply eliminating bothersome symptoms" (2004, p. 125). I agree with Jordan in that the absence of genuine relatedness is the essence of personality abnormality. Nonetheless, I think that creating safe and sound connectedness very much depends on altering the troublesome traits that impede relatedness. Jordan seems to underestimate the biopsychological factors that operate within personality, especially the abnormal.

Consequently, it is my position that "analyzing and reworking" aberrant traits is central to interpersonal therapy and establishing close contacts and relatedness in general. Even so, it remains, as a rule, easier for individuals to alter their external than their internal environment along with its traits. I leave aside for consideration the inner self-changes that can be wrought by devices, such as those of a pharmaceutical nature. However, these alterations to personality are ordinarily quite temporary and seldom deal effectively with the impediments to stable and substantive relationships.

Despite my just registered reservations with her outlook, I largely share the position put forth by Jordan, to wit that the governing goal of therapy is:

> to bring people back into connection through mutual empathy and empowerment. As chronically [non or] disconnected individuals begin to find ways to represent themselves more fully and authentically in relationship with the therapist, they begin to experience *empathic possibility*, the hope that another human being will understand, resonate with, and respond positively to them. The work of therapy is to honor the patient's strategies of disconnection while safety in connection is created. Slowly, the patient relinquishes strategies of disconnection and begins to

move out of shame and isolation into the fullness of authentic connection. (Ibid., p. 132)

The pathologicals most biologically based—the schizoid and schizotypal—are not "dis"connected from others for they never were connected to them, save perhaps to their primary caregivers during their earliest years. Subsequent to this period, these social isolates were unable or, at minimum, uninterested or unwilling to make connections. Moreover, these Group I deviants seldom if ever experience shame and unwanted isolation in feeling unconnected, given their being the non-plus-ultra voluntary absolute loners.

In any case, the *DSM* states that the schizoid is "uncommon in clinical settings." It does not even speculate as to the occurrence of the schizotypal apparently because this abnormal's clinical presence is even more rare than the schizoid's (pp. 639, 643). Their clinical infrequency is likely due to their not being interested in dealing with other patients and therapists. Even if they were so inclined, we have seen that very little, if anything of significance, can be done to change their personality.

I have contended that relationship failures are the central contributors and sometimes the causes of Group II and III anomalies to begin with. For Group I, these failures are not, in my estimation, the origins or abettors but the results of their pathologized personalities.

Similarly, Jeffrey Johnson, Judith Rabkin, Janet Williams, Robert Remien, and Jack Gorman consider failure in relatedness as a "defining feature" of the diseased personality (I regard it as the defining feature). It is a position which these researchers claim forms a consensus among personality disorder personologists (2000, p. 52).

Since I construe pathological personalities as essentially serious deficiencies in interpersonality, I have advocated that interpersonal approaches be the fulcrum and link of all deviated personality therapies, with the possible exception for those best treated pharmacologically. However, even then the interpersonal, among other approaches, can be reckoned highly desirable and often absolutely necessary to be used in conjunction with those which are pharmaceutical, above all if positive and long term personality changes are intended.

Aaron Pincus and Michael Gurtman state that the fundamental principle to which interpersonalists adhere with reference to the personality disorders is that proposed by Harry Stack Sullivan. It is, they state, that the abnormal personality is "inherently expressed via disturbed interpersonal relations" (2006, p. 86). Accordingly, the basic and unifying therapy for these deviations is—or should be, in my view, as in Sullivan's—the interpersonal.

Leonard Horowitz maintains that "Of all the theoretical approaches to psychopathology, the interpersonal approach is the one most compatible with all the others" (2004, p. 3) because:

> first, like the biological approach, it assumes that innate differences in an [individual's] temperament can cause differences in interpersonal interactions [and] are sometimes magnified by interpersonal processes. Second, like the cognitive-behavioral approach, the interpersonal approach emphasizes the role of cognitions in interpersonal interactions. . . . Third, the interpersonal approach, like the humanistic approach, emphasizes the self, dyadic relationships, communication, empathy, and social support. . . . Finally, the interpersonal, like the psychodynamic approach, emphasizes motivation and motivational conflict. . . . Because it harmonizes with other theoretical approaches, the interpersonal is integrative: it draws from the wisdom of the other approaches to systematize our understanding of psychopathology. Contemporary trends in clinical psychology tend to overemphasize the biological and cognitive-behavioral, so the interpersonal approach may help restore a more balanced weighting of theoretical mechanisms. (Ibid., pp. 3–4)

However, people need not only look to professional clinicians for help in dealing with their problems. Abraham Maslow reminds us that all human beings, preeminently through the social provisions they furnish one another, are potentially lay therapists for, he says, they have invariably:

> gone for advice and help to others whom they respected and loved. There is no reason why this historical phenomenon should not be formalized, verbalized, and encouraged to the point of universality by psychologists. . . . Let people realize clearly that every time they threaten someone or humiliate or hurt unnecessarily or dominate or reject another human being, they become forces for the creation of psychopathology, even if these be small forces. Let them recognize that every person who is kind, helpful, decent, psychologically democratic, affectionate, and warm, is a psychotherapeutic force even though a small one. (1970, p. 254)

Unfortunately, individuals with personality disorders are isolated emotionally, socially, and even physically because they are unloved and unloving (and vice versa).

Irrespective of my position that personality disorders arise from serious interpersonal relational deficiencies and my recommendation that their optimal treatment, therefore, would be interpersonal, cognitively expert and empathic clinicians are likely to employ a federation of remedial stratagems to produce a sustained positive personality change in their patients.

Personality deviations also involve intrapersonal shortcomings, but even these are almost always affected and sometimes effected by relatedness deficiencies, especially those concerning primary relationships and the individual's social support system. (For example, almost all paranoid traits are interpersonal in nature.)

Recall that nine of the ten *DSM* personality disorders are defined essentially in terms of interpersonal features. The only aberration not so notionalized is the obsessional. Still, even obessionals have primary features that are implicitly demarcated vis-à-vis other persons because "pre-occupation with order, perfectionism, and control" predominantly concerns subjects (objectified) instead of pure objects.

Clinton McLemore and David Brokaw claim that all significant "intrapsychic and behavioral 'events'" involve other people, whether they are real or imagined (1987, p. 271). This view endorses the position that the elemental and, indeed, defining experiences of people refer to their interpersonal relationships. They, as emphasized throughout this book, generate the gist of personality.

Consequently, I hold, in concert with McLemore and Brokaw (ibid.) and personalists as a whole, that personal identity is both in its elemental and elevated aspects essentially interpersonal in nature. Also, as I have postulated, relationship-failures are the central contributors to, and sometimes the causes of Group II and III anomalies to begin with. For Group I, these failures are, instead, the results of their pathologized personalities. McLemore and Brokaw concede, however, that an aberrated personality cannot be reduced to poor interpersonal functioning since the latter might be, for example, a reflection of "intrapsychic difficulties" (ibid.).

According to McLemore and Brokaw, changing from intimacy-foiling to intimacy-fostering interactions usually demands resolving feelings toward "introjected" persons, such as a parent or sibling. They also aver that intimacy-enhancing interactions require a "corrective interpersonal experience" that, at some point, will likely involve interpersonal group therapy (ibid.). However, individual clinical therapy is also interpersonal, but with different dynamics to some extent, depending in part on the personality and professionalism of the therapist.

McLemore and Brokaw contend that what professionals or other helpers actually do through their personal style of interaction is far more crucial for those whom they help than is usually believed. Optimal interaction style is simultaneously close and personal (subjective), yet distant and objective. The helper can be thought of as being like a true friend who at once is empathetic, sympathetic, loving and uncritical, but, nonetheless, objective and critical. They maintain that this rapport distinguishes interpersonal therapy from behavioral kinds since the second essentially focus on a person's "environmental contingencies," commonly construed as being objective in nature (ibid.).

Nevertheless, for some types of personality anomalies, especially Group I and the antisocial and paranoid of Group II, therapy of whatever sort may prove largely ineffective regardless how knowledgeable, artful, understanding, or caring the therapist may be. Paris states, "the general goal of [personality disorder] treatment must be to aim for rehabilitation instead of a cure"

(2003, p. 482), which, I believe, is especially the case with the pathological personalities just mentioned.

McLemore and Brokaw hold that an effective diagnostic method will:

> enable helper and helpee to *see* (a) what other people are doing (or have done) to the helpee; (b) how the behavior of others (past or present) prompts/pulls dysfunctional behavior from the helpee; (c) how the helpee continues to train others to reinforce his or her disordered pattern; and (d) what the helpee must do in order to end this self-perpetuating cycle of dysfunctionality. (1987, p. 271)

McLemore and Brokaw essay that interpersonal approaches envisage the therapist as a "participant observer" in the clinical relationship. Only by their actual involvement are clinicians able to help the individual's "self-defeating cycles" (ibid.). In this manner, therapists strive to observe the patient from the inside, so to speak, all of which is the nucleus of empathy, especially the intuitive types.

McLemore and Brokaw contend that the true power of the interpersonal models of therapy rests in their ability "to *predict* behavorial sequences" (ibid.). Pincus and Gurtman maintain that therapists strive to work on behalf of patients to promote their best interest, an undertaking that subsequently requires "a positive therapeutic alliance" (2006, p. 103). This partnership, according to Charland, involves the sort of effective therapy that necessitates the usual moral obligations between clinician and client, namely, he says, "veracity, privacy, confidentiality, and fidelity" (2006, p. 123). We recall that Charland maintains that the therapist tries to make the patient less dishonest, less manipulative, and less resentful and vindictive" (ibid. p. 124), all traits representative of Group II aberrants.

Magnavita and many other mental health experts have proposed that with optimal therapies, considerable improvement can be had concerning at least some deviant personalities. These, in my view, would be Group III and, to a lesser extent, the obsessional of Group II. The borderline, histrionic, dependent, and avoidant are the four aberrants who put a high premium on intimacy and love, though they are acquisitive, needy, and neurotic sorts. Still, being focussed on the most important of questions is closer to normalcy than, for instance, having most or even all the answers to lesser concerns.

6. Optimal Therapists

Gerald Klerman and Myrna Weissman refer to those who describe effective psychotherapy as a process akin to "optimal parenting" in which case caring is combined with "non-possessive warmth." They propose that such "ideal" therapy would provide "a cognitive explanation of distortions of past relationships" (1986, p. 432), such as those that are familial, a view akin to that of McLemore and Brokaw, described above.

Of course, optimal parenting involves optimal love, meaning an unconditional yet discriminating and justice-based conditional love (Fromm, 1962, pp. 38–46, 49–52). Hence, optimal love is a whole-hearted but also a discerning, judicious, and demanding love or what is commonly known as "tough love."

Thus, optimal parenting is a type of intimate caring expressed via FFM Humaneness traits. It is a rather common view that many individuals with Group II and Group III abnormals were largely deprived of such optimal love by one or both their parents.

It is widely contended that what most changes persons for the better is optimal love, both loving and being loved. What most changes the person for the worst is maximal hatred. It entails a loathing of love and a love of, or craving for, misanthropy. In terms of the ten pathological personalities, this hatred of human beings is, in my view, solely found in the most wicked of Group II antisocials and paranoids and sometimes in comorbidities formed with the other Group II pathologicals, namely the narcissists and obsessionals.

Treating pathological personalities is arguably the most challenging of undertakings, for clinicians, for reasons given above. Logically enough, among or quite possibly *the* optimal personality disorder therapists would be those best at employing optimal therapy, which, as just proposed, is the interpersonal. However, and perhaps the crucial component of all therapy, especially the interpersonal, is the personality of the therapist. Stone tells us that the chief instrument therapists use in is their own personality.

Jordan states that the ideal qualities of what she terms the "therapeutic personality" clinicians would include "warmth," a foremost attribute of all intimacy, positive regard à la Carl Rogers, "empathic imagination"—or "the ability to objectively see another's experience"; and "kindness, clinical sensibility, and artistry" (2004, p. 1290). Given that disturbed personality therapy concerns human beings qua their personalities, such clinicians would especially require a competency that contains people skills. Therapists would need to possess such abilities since pathological personalities are the most morally troublesome and among the most psychologically troubled of patients.

In terms of attachments as such, Jordan specifically stresses the need for clinicians "to learn about relationships, relational failures, chronic disconnection, relational images" and "re-establishing empathic possibility" in addition to "relations resilience" (ibid.).

Magnavita maintains that optimum therapeutic traits involve a trust "in the healing capabilities of the human psyche and body." These qualities require "an ability to tolerate the uncertainty, vulnerability, and ambiguity of oneself and of the healing relational matrix." Further, an optimum therapist necessitates having "a continuous desire to evolve as a human being and healer," and, finally, "flexibility and consistency" (2000. p. 79). He proposes:

> The restorative or healing aspect of the therapeutic relationship is the quality of the therapeutic alliance. Regardless of the therapeutic approach, the most important factor in predicting therapeutic change is the quality of the therapeutic relationship. (Ibid., p. 10)

This quality is obviously greatly affected by the traits of the therapist, who, most regrettably, may occasionally also have a pathological personality. Perhaps no amount of professional screening can prevent every psycho-ethical aberrant from infiltrating the ranks of clinicians. Nor can any such safeguard likely preclude highly immoral individuals from teaching or preaching matters of a moral nature in academic and ecclesiastical settings.

Rosenhan and Seligman review literature that suggests that, regardless of its orientation, genuine therapy has necessary preconditions on the part of the clinician, none of which, however, are sufficient to guarantee therapeutic success (1989, p. 642). These pre-requisites can be summarized as follows:

The first is warmth, which is part of the nonjudgmental and non-intrusive caring by the therapist for the patient both as a human being and unique person (ibid., p. 641). However, being nonjudgmental does not mean that the therapist completely overlooks the patient's moral defects. If, for instance, the disordered individual is persistently mendacious, manipulative, and hard-hearted in relationships, including those in the clinical setting, then ignoring these negative traits by the clinician will likely set the therapeutic alliance back.

Perhaps a more contentious consideration is whether the patient can or should ignore the negative traits of the clinician, above all those that damage the "partnership." A positive submissiveness—possibly a better word is docility—on the part of the patient is required to "accept" the therapy. But accepting any quality of the clinician however uncaring and incompetent would be considered a negative sort of submissiveness, assuming the patient has the ability to recognize these negative traits in the clinician.

The second precondition of genuine therapy is, according to Rosenhan and Seligman, empathy—construed as the effort of the therapist to understand the patient's experience and to do so, they annex, with sensitivity and accuracy on a "moment-to-moment encounter" (ibid.). It goes without saying that therapists must avoid letting their empathy and other aspects of concern become so subjective that they lose their objectivity. Naturally, patients may be ambivalent concerning empathy on the part of the clinician if they want to preserve their privacy, a niche that can both obstruct and expedite intimacy.

The lonely patient may even hope that the therapist will become a friend or lover, if only "rented" types. Alternatively, patients may envisage therapists as utterly removed "scientific" observers with no personal interests in them. Each of the ten types of personality disorders arguably necessitates appropriate mixtures—cognitive, emotive, and physical—of proximity and distance on the part of the therapist and patient.

The third precondition for successful therapy is genuineness and the need for therapists to be sincerely and profoundly themselves instead of being officious or pretentious (ibid., p. 642). Clinicians cannot simultaneously be requisitely warm and empathic yet pompous and phony. In addition to realness and sincerity, an optimal therapist manifests all the other five FFM traits of Humaneness. If the therapist is perceived as inhumane, the likelihood of successful therapy is minimal.

Pitirim Sorokin insists that the crux of therapeutic methods consists in the opposite of "the atmosphere of rejection, enmity, reproof, and punishment the patient is usually living in." He insists that the worst therapy is marked by "an impersonal, cold, often inimical ambience" and by "punitive" therapists. Sorokin indicts such clinicians for looking upon their patients as "irresponsible, dangerous, stupid, and inferior" individuals (1967, p. 63).

Sorokin further comments that, irrespective of the absence of certainty and the presence of "the contrariety of the curative results of various psychiatric methods," psychiatrists appear to agree that the central therapeutic factor in all the treatments and techniques is the "'acceptance' of the patient by the therapist" (ibid.). Nonetheless, the acceptance of patients need not include approving their unlikable and unlovable traits, assuming that such qualities are distinct from their persons.

Sorokin maintains that the chief (re)habilitative elements require "the rapport of empathy, sympathy, kindness, and love established between the therapist and the patient" (ibid. p. 63). Up to here many therapists might well agree. Nonetheless, clinicians might view what he next proposes quite differently:

> Since the real curative agent in mental illness is love in all its various forms, this explains why many eminent apostles of love have been able to cure the mental disorders of legions of persons, though these altruists did not have any specific psychiatric training . . . The need for an important role of scientific training is not cancelled by the thesis that love is the main agent. To do its work effectively, love needs to be competently guided, channelled, and used. For the geniuses [of love, namely altruists], their supraconscious [their humane ideals] supplies the guidance. For the ordinary therapists, their scientific training performs this function. Stressing the importance of either supraconscious or scientific guidance of love, then, the curative power of love remains indispensable for practically all successful therapeutic treatments of mental disorders (Ibid., pp. 64–65)

Alas, the number of such deeply caring and expertly competent therapists is allegedly relatively few. The most demanding professions do not always attract the most humane and accomplished of individuals. On the other hand, the number of con artists is legion and their repertory of artifices even more multifarious.

7. Therapies, Therapists, and the Normative

In terms of personality, the norm can refer to the ideal, in which case it carries a qualitative and prescriptive meaning, or it can signify the statistically average, in which event it bears a quantitative and descriptive meaning. In clinical settings, "normal" ordinarily applies explicitly to the psychological and descriptive domains. Often, however, it also refers, at least implicitly, to the axiological (and specifically the ethical) and prescriptive spheres. Accordingly, I characterize personality disorders as psycho-ethical and mental-moral aberrations.

Nancy Nyquist Potter contends:

> Meaningful relationships are central to living a flourishing life. It is hard to imagine a moral life without friendships, love, and companionship; personal attachments are part of morality as well as [psychological] well-being. One indicator of mental illness is the relative absence of meaningful relationships or difficulty in maintaining them. People diagnosed with borderline personality disorder often have unstable interpersonal relationships, and this difficulty is likely to cause the patient significant distress and suffering. This anguish is both psychological and moral, because relationships are both psychological and moral. A link does exist between moral life and mental health (2006, pp. 153–154)

I agree with Potter except that, unlike her, I construe serious psycho-ethical failures in terms of meaning/intimacy relatedness as not simply one indicator of pathological personalities but as their necessary ingredients.

Without doubt, the injection of the ethically normative into personality therapy can be hazardous if only because it may degenerate into the moralism that is detrimental to therapeutic effectiveness. Indeed, pontificating is itself immoral since it entails dogmatic posturing about what is most essential to becoming and being human: moral integrity, meaning goodness, which, in turn, is chiefly constituted by a justice-included altruistic love.

It is one thing to make necessary evaluations of patients' mental-moral traits but quite another to be judgmental—harsh or condemnatory concerning the patients themselves. It is quasi-axiomatic that we can dislike and disapprove of people's moral shortcomings yet affirm, even love them, assuming once more that personality is distinct from its attributes. However, when people are evaluated, even in caring fashion, with respect to their qualities, they often think of this process as being a denunciation of their persons.

Though therapists might be encouraged to be neutral as to their patients' ethical status, they routinely engage in evaluations that are at minimum implicitly prescriptive. In any case, it may be even more dangerous and immoral to exclude moral concerns from both the therapeutic and theoretical provinces of personality. Psychology and psychiatry are not entirely free from the axiological and evaluative nor ought they be. Of course, to declare that they are value free is itself a value judgment.

Lee Clark states that, in the last analysis, "the clinical and moral" domains "cannot be separated without altering the essence of being a particular person" (2006, p. 185). Like their patients, clinicians are, before anything else, persons. But, unlike patients, therapists are professionally entrusted with helping disordered patients qua persons.

Though the normative as moral cannot be separated from the normative as psychological, they are distinguishable and must be understood as so. Clark further writes:

> part of clinical training is learning to keep judgments based on personal moral values from clouding clinical judgment. Presumably, such training is needed precisely because moral failing and [psychological] dysfunction may non-exclusively describe the same behavior. If all behaviors were either one or the other, and clinicians should and need concern themselves with only clinical behaviors, then clinical training should focus instead on learning to discriminate moral from clinical behaviors. (Ibid.)

Nevertheless, clinicians' excluding purely private values is one thing; excluding all values is quite another. Undoubtedly, most therapists would argue that purely subjective norms should be kept out of the therapeutic setting, whereas objective ones should be kept in. This obligation is easy to say but far from easy to fulfill.

All this is not to imply that therapists must be students of and, a fortiori, experts in moral philosophy. Still, it stands to reason that clinicians and their patients would be well served if the first can discern the major moral consequences of the theories they at least implicitly use in their practices.

Unfortunately and as Drew Westen and Jonathan Shedler contend, clinicians are sometimes apt "to dismiss research as irrelevant" to their practice. Some of them might well view research and theories germane to moral philosophy as the most irrelevant of all. On the other hand, Westen and Shedler state that "researchers tend to view clinicians as sloppy, unsystematic, and unscientific in their thinking" (2000. p. 124). Theory is a guide and blueprint for practice but the first is no substitute for the second; to think that it is so is akin to confusing a map of a city with the city itself.

Whereas involving moral elements in therapy runs the risk of being discredited for being judgmental, it might well be immoral to omit them. Indeed, the clinical alliance itself calls for ethical qualities, such as honesty, patience, perseverance, and courage in general. Sound judgments in the sense of accurate ethical evaluations vis-à-vis moral shortcomings are necessary if, in fact, personality traits are not only descriptive psychological attributes but prescriptive ethical features. Still, the therapist need not resort to explicit language that is highly evaluative in nature, above all the sort that is accusatory.

Hence, while therapeutic evaluations can be uncaringly and harshly critical, there is also the other unwanted extreme of their being uncritically caring. In such cases, the patients may think that they have license to do anything, ethically construed, both inside and outside the clinical setting. Ideally and as in other relationships, clinical judgments—valuations, assessments, or appraisals might be better terms—should be neither hyper- nor hypo-critical but critical in the sense of competent in addition to solicitous.

If the therapeutic alliance is a moral partnership with an implicit moral contract and requiring moral traits, such as truthfulness and loyalty, then both the therapist and patient must hold one another accountable for failing to honor commitments. However, people with personality disorders are, in my estimation, not only psychological but moral aberrants. Accordingly, they find fulfilling any moral contract hugely problematic. Some patients are in treatment—and involitionally so, especially antisocials—precisely because of their unwillingness to be faithful to the demands of any mutual agreement.

How to create and adhere to this accountability are part of the art and virtue of optimal therapists. Again, clinicians are more bound to the alliance and its obligations than their patients since the second are in counseling—and as a rule, ultimately freely so—to be served by the first.

Just before having all but completed this volume, I read Charland's article in which he argues that the *DSM* contains "theoretical entities which denote two very different kinds of syndromes," namely the clinical (psychological) disorders of Clusters A and C and the moral disorders of Cluster B (2006, p. 117).

Charland proposes that the *DSM* Cluster B abnormals represent ethical deviations and that those individuals possessing them should be held responsible for their actions. He concedes that doing so "might appear reactionary and reprehensible to some" in that it would seem to be "a return to an era when clinical conditions were mistaken for moral conditions." Consequently, Charland contends that in such times patients "had to bear the weight of moral stigma and blame" (ibid.).

If individuals with personality disorders are truly responsible for their actions, then their unacceptable conduct, perhaps especially that which unfolds in the clinical context, should not be countenanced by therapists. Of course, it is unlikely that any professional therapist today would recommend that pathological personalities be stigmatized in the sense of being labeled as hopeless reprobates and treated accordingly. At any rate, being held responsible and accountable for morally unacceptable behavior is hardly the same as being disgraced, denounced, and branded for being nonmoral or immoral.

I insert here that I maintain that, first, all the personality disorders—and, therefore, not only those of *DSM* Cluster B, as Charland maintains—but also Cluster A, especially its paranoid, and Cluster C entail ethical aberrations. As I have many times documented throughout this work, the *DSM* portrays the ten personality disorders as having numerous traits that are clearly not only psychologically negative but also unethical in composition.

Second, and following from my first position, I propose that all those with pathological personalities are morally responsible for their (in)actions. Though I do so in varying extent, with Group I being the least and Group II or III being the most responsible, depending to what degree their traits and (in)actions are actually volitional. To the measure that Group I are voluntary but not volitional in their conduct, they are not ethically responsible—or so it is often argued—though they may be legally so.

Charland further states, "the moral aspects of the Cluster B disorders," namely the antisocial, borderline, histrionic, and narcissist, "are an integral part of the *DSM* conception of those disorders," and not, he stresses, merely "a fabrication or recommendation" on its part (ibid., p. 118). I agree with Charland here except I have proposed that moral aspects permeate the diagnostic features of Cluster A and C and not only those of Cluster B.

Charland also maintains that Cluster B disorders entail "the *explicit* use of moral terms and notions, while the language of Cluster A and C does not." Nonetheless, this usage is not accidental because as just noted, according to Charland, Cluster B disorders "are fundamentally moral in nature while Cluster A and C disorders are not" (ibid., p. 119). Hence, he seeks "to uncover and expose those normative assumptions, that are philosophically concealed by the neutral clinical descriptive language" of the *DSM's* Cluster B (ibid., p. 118).

However, the *DSM* does, in fact, explicitly employ moral language and concepts vis-à-vis all it clusters. For example, if Cluster A is inspected even cursorily, then it will be manifest that the *Manual* constantly uses moral and other normative discourse and notions in its characterization of the paranoid. And it does so concerning the other personality deviants in all three clusters and not only in Cluster A.

Though Charland has mainly in mind the borderline of Cluster B, he proposes that, for all the other three abnormals in this *DSM* aggregate, therapy is "really a moral contract" and "a moral treatment" (ibid., p. 124). Nonetheless, it appears that, for Charland, the clinical compact, irrespective of the cluster in question, contains what he has termed the customary duties between clinician and patient. Recall that these obligations entail, for Charland, such moral traits as truthfulness, privacy, confidentiality, and loyalty. His position would seem to imply at minimum that all ten of the pathological personalities and not only those of Cluster B are involved in moral issues by being engaged in therapy to begin with, given its aforesaid moral contract.

Charland contends that the moral cure on the part of the Cluster B individuals demands their "moral willingness, moral change, and moral effort," all of which presupposes that such individuals possess the requisite volition (ibid.). In fact, he claims that, with respect to Cluster B deviants, "it is impossible to imagine successful treatment or cure" which, in their case, is not "tantamount to a moral conversion" (ibid., p. 122).

I am in accord with Charland's argumentation provided this moral therapy is located within an interpersonal kind of therapy. Pathological personalities are essentially psycho-moral failures concerning interpersonal relatedness. They are defects owing to different levels of egocentricity. In my estimation, self and or/other centeredness is the fundamental consideration of morality and interpersonality.

Still, it appears that Charland would hold that pathological personality treatment can be successful even being short of a total recovery. Hence, it can be ameliorative without being panaceac, a view that I likewise support. I do since I am in agreement with the likes of Stone and Paris that curing individuals with personality disturbances—especially if they possess all the traits delineated in each of the ten *DSM* aberrations—is largely if not entirely out of the question. This unlikelihood is especially so concerning Group I and II, save for the obsessional, and the borderline of Group III. Nonetheless, a most felicitous environment in the form of a social support system can arguably work wonders though perhaps not miracles.

In my judgment, a full moral conversion (metanoia)—the aforesaid reconstitution of the mind and especially the heart—a synonym for goodness, which when unqualified means moral goodness—begins with a life of simple justice. It then moves on to justice motivated by benevolence followed by mixed benevolence and finally pure benevolence. It thereupon graduates to love, above all its universalization in altruism.

Any moral cure apropos of those with personality disorders would require a motivational level that transcends a life habitually motivated by the acquisition of Group I, the malevolence of Group II, and the acquisitiveness of Group III. Morally considered, I doubt if any individual with a personality disturbance in which he or she has all the *DSM* diagnostic features of the disorder in question—to wit a pure, or archetypal, personality disorder—reaches and, a fortiori, remains at the motivational level immediately above it. For instance, my research and reflection lead me to conclude that the malevolently inclined sociopath very rarely attains and stays at an acquisitively motivated level. The lower the level of motivation, the less frequently a personality aberrant climbs to the next level and continues there.

Consequently, it is my view that those with pathological personalities seldom and some never persist in a psycho-ethical zone in which they are morally completely healed, meaning cured. To be cured of the non-moral or immoral aspects of their illnesses, abnormal personalities would have to ascend to and abide in a state of justice motivated by benevolence or at minimum a state of simple justice. It is the level that I believe is required for normality and morality. Again, the lower the level of motivation from which a disturbed personality starts, the less likely is a movement upwards let alone a full conversion possible.

Charland then posits:

> once the moral contract is established, therapy can move on to more clinical matters, where the clinician's professional skills and expertise are paramount. Yet, nothing in the professional clinician's training arsenal seems designed to prepare [the therapist] to be a moral being, which is the starting point of [the] professional therapeutic relationship with [the] client. Some sort of moral authority or guiding role is required for this aspect of therapy, but standard clinical training does not usually provide anything of the sort. (Ibid.)

Clinicians must be moral beings and highly so, given their exceedingly important moral role in the promotion of their patients well-being. However, they need not be moral authorities, or experts, in moral philosophy—especially not in terms of a formal and systematic training therein—no matter how useful and desirable such expertise might be vis-à-vis any pathological personality treatment. Still, it would be highly desirable were therapists able to discern the major moral ramifications—if not their presuppositions—of the psychological theories they explicitly or implicitly use in their practices.

Additionally, given all the above, it seems reasonable to propose that those clinicians who concentrate on dealing with individuals with pathological personalities would have to be among if not the most moral of therapists. It may happen that not especially moral clinicians could be adequate aberrated personality therapists provided they had the other (pre)requisites such as professional competence.

It appears to be case that therapists qua therapists are not usually trained to be highly moral beings, even though the clinical coalition does demand a host of moral traits on their part. These qualities would include all those listed above as essential ingredients of the optimal therapist.

It may also be true that in their training clinicians are not provided a kind of moral authority, or set of guidelines, to help gain or increase such ethical attributes for their own moral improvement as human beings. Just learning the psychological components of clinicianship is a formidable undertaking not to mention understanding those that arguably constitute a kind of moral education. Still and as indicated earlier, clinicians have their own code of professional ethics, and quite apart from it they are expected by their patients and people in general to be deeply humane individuals.

We can know a great deal about morality in an abstract fashion and thereby be a kind of moral authority ourselves. However, such knowledge is not a sufficient condition for making us moral beings, meaning moral as to our persons. It is well-known that we can use our knowledge of moral principles and issues for extremely immoral purposes. Similarly, clinicians may be exceedingly conversant with various theories and techniques about clinicianship, including its moral components, yet still not only be ineffective but damaging in terms of the art—and arguably the moral virtue—of therapy. However, people generally concede that becoming and remaining humane and ethical, are the greatest challenges any human being must face.

CONCLUSION

In this book, I have predominantly examined personality, especially the disordered, in terms of states of aloneness. In Chapter Two, I outlined various kinds of feeling and being alone, including alonism (residing alone); and lonism (social withdrawal), which can be total (absolute loners) or partial (relative loners that I denominate lonerists). In addition, aloneness takes the form of reclusion (reclusiveness), seclusiveness (seclusion), isolation, and desolation. Aloneness can be positive, such as solitude, negative, such as loneliness, or neutral, such as the kind of ontological aloneness in which case human beings are reckoned alone simply owing to their being numerically separate individuals.

Edward Bulwer-Lytton relates that poets consider the word "aloneness" to signify the most icy, hopeless, mournful, and deathly state of existence (Dusenbury, 1967, p. 8). No wonder aloneness is something to be feared and dreaded, an anxiety I have titled aloneliness. Its key component, as the word a-loneliness suggests, is the aloneness of loneliness, which I have contended is the most frightening state of feeling alone, for it is the most desolating of human afflictions and, therefore, the phenomenon most described and analyzed in these two volumes.

Those who suffer these sorts of aloneness I have designated aloners, which include alonists, lonists (loners), lonerists, reclusives, "seclusives," isolates, desolates, solitaries, lonelies, and alonelies.

By conceptually and linguistically differentiating types of aloners, I intend to add clarity and coherence to what are often highly confused phenomena and to relate these distinctions to the notion and division of personality.

I have contended that aberrant personalities are quintessentially negative isolates unlike, for instance, solitaries who are positive types. As social and often physical isolates, the schizoids and schizotypals of Group I are quasi total loners in that they strive to be left alone as much as possible. As such, they are not alonelies. However, Group I are not scornful of or hostile toward others but simply apathetically indifferent to them. This non-interest in their fellow human beings can be most glaringly witnessed in their apparently having little if any capability, desire, or willingness for intimacy. Accordingly, these Group I lonists are not lonelies neither on a conscious nor unconscious level.

The sociopaths, paranoids, narcissists, and obsessionals of Group II are the kind of partial loners I have termed lonerists. While these disturbed personalities are not as a rule physically isolated from others, they often are socially isolated in that they are contemptuously indifferent or actively hostile to people in general. Since they are opposed to intimacy, or at least are inclined to repress or suppress the desire for it save to serve their selfish interests, Group II personality anomalies tend not to be lonelies at least not on a conscious basis. Still, one of their ongoing interests is to avoid being or feeling alone in which case they use others to quell their fright of aloneness and to that extent Group II are alonelies.

The borderlines, histrionics, dependents, and avoidants of Group III are not usually socially or physically volitionally isolated from others though they are emotionally and unhappily so. Moreover, they are so in intense and prolonged fashion, all of which makes these four aberrants lonelies, indeed ordinarily in a pathological manner. Furthermore, their alarm regarding loneliness and negative states of aloneness in general renders these desolates consummate alonelies.

Human beings are entirely social beings even if they are those kinds of reclusive isolates designated hermits or anchorites. The heart of sociality is intimacy, a requisite that is both elementary and advanced. Normal human beings are essentially embodied inwardnesses who seek connections, above all intimate kinds, to others. They do so chiefly with respect to other persons but also personifications and personalizations. Normals are relatively effective in terms of their efforts to obtain and sustain relatedness.

On the other hand, abnormals are profoundly ineffective concerning relatedness in that they are either non-related to others (Group I), disrelated (Group II), or related but inadequately (Group III) in terms of initiating or maintaining social connectedness as a whole. In reference to intimate connections in particular, Group I are non-intimacy types; Group II are anti-intimacy; and Group III are pro-intimacy but their neuroticism and overall self-centeredness impairs any heart to heart affiliation with others.

Because I hold that these ten negatively isolated kinds of individuals are not only psychological but moral aberrants, I explicitly depart from the *DSM* notion and classification of the disordered personality. I have provided more than ten other reasons to account for this departure. However, the most fundamental reason is that I conceive mental/moral failures in relatedness to others in general and in particular as being a sufficient condition for predicating abnormality of a person.

Contrastingly, the *Manual* looks upon deficiencies in relatedness as not being a necessary let alone a sufficient condition for being titled a pathological personality. Yet, in my judgment, the *DSM* defines at least implicity each of the ten specific personality disorders in terms of negative relatedness. Moreover, it has at least a fivefold basis for its aggregating these aberrants into three clusters. In contrast, I have but a single substratum for my three groupings: a grave absence of connectedness to other persons.

Therefore, I endorse the view that persons are paramountly their interpersonality, meaning that they are the sum and, above all, the network of their temporary interactions but especially their more or less permanent ties. Because people are principally constituted by their interpersonality, a gross failure in such connectedness is indicative of their being failed, meaning disordered, personalities. However, only the dystonic Group III aberrants habitually perceive themselves as personality failures. This perception stems largely from their low sense of self-worth and feelings of emptiness that are intrinsic to their severe indeed their pathological loneliness.

Consequently, I have proposed that, though the treatment of individuals with sick personalities urges an array of models and methods, it is especially fitting that interpersonal therapies should assume the primary underlying and integrating role in ameliorative regimes for these disturbed human beings.

This work also engages in an analysis of five social factors that are conducive to predisposing, precipitating, and maintaining negative kinds of personality and aloneness. I have formed these factors into an acronym titled *SCRAM* since when they are present, intimacy scurries away and in its absence, loneliness and other sorts of unwanted aloneness scamper in and fill the person with unhappiness via, for instance, sadness and self-abasement. The constituents of SCRAM are: *S*uccessitis, *C*apitalitis, *R*ivalitis, *A*tomitis, and *M*aterialitis.

While SCRAM views unwanted aloneness to be the hallmark of losers, it nonetheless imprisons people in undesirable types of isolation, including pathological sorts be they of the Group I loner, the Group II lonerist, or the Group III lonely variety. Indeed, its five egocentric institutions cause SCRAM to be the nemesis of social association, including its intimate species.

Thus, despite its protestations to the contrary, SCRAM is a philosophy of life, or worldview, that engenders self-centeredness, the trait that characterizes all the personality aberrants and the trait most opposed to genuine intimacy and above all to love. It is this emotion that most delivers a person from unwanted aloneness, paramountly that of loneliness, the most painful and depressive of afflictions. Thus, Sophocles avers:

> One word
> Frees us of all the pain and weight of life.
> That word is love. (1970, p. 373n214)

WORKS CITED

American Psychiatric Association. (1987) *Diagnostic and Statistical Manual of Mental Disorders* (*DSM-III-R*). Third Edition revised.Washington, D.C.

———. (1994) *Diagnostic and Statistical Manual of Mental Disorders* (*DSM-IV*). Fourth Edition.Washington, D.C.

———. (2000) *Diagnostic and Statistical Manual of Mental Disorders, Text Revision* (*DSM-IV-TR*). Washington, D.C.

Angyal, Andras. (1958) *Foundations for a Science of Personality*. Cambridge, Mass.: Harvard University Press.

Aristotle. (1941a) *The Basic Works of Aristotle*. Edited by R. McKeon. Translated by Benjamin Jowett. New York: Random House.

———. (1941b) *Nichomachean Ethics*. Translated by W. D. Ross. In McKeon, *The Basic Works of Aristotle*.

———. (1941c) *Politics*. Translated by Benjamin Jowett. In McKeon, *The Basic Works of Aristotle*.

Arnold, Matthew. (1967) "Isolation. To Marguerite." In *Matthew Arnold: Poetry and Prose*. Edited by John Bryson. Cambridge, Mass.: Harvard University Press.

Baker, Laura. (2006) "Methods for Understanding Genetic and Environmental Influences in Normal and Abnormal Personality," pp. 257–281. In Strack, *Differentiating Normal and Abnormal Personality*.

Bartz, Jennifer, Alicia Kaplan, and Eric Hollander. (2007) "Obsessive-Compulsive Personality Disorder," pp. 325–351. In O'Donohue, Fowler, and Lilienfeld, *Personality Disorders*.

Baumeister, Roy, and Mark Leary. (1995) "The Need to Belong: Desire for Interpersonal Attachments as a Fundamental Human Motivation," *Psychological Bulletin*, 117:3, pp. 497–529.

Beers, Mark H., Ed. (2003) *The Merck Manual of Medical Information*. Second Home Edition. New York: Pocket Books.

Bell, Robert, and Michael Roloff. (1991) "Making a Love Connection: Loneliness and Communication Competence in the Dating Marketplace," *Communication Quarterly*, 39:1, pp. 58–74.

Berdyaev, Nikolai. (1938) *Solitude and Society*. Translated by George Reavey. London: Geoffrey Bles.

Berg, J. H. van den. (1972) *A Different Existence: Principles of Phenomenological Psychopathology*. Pittsburgh: Duquesne University Press.

Bernstein, David, and David Useda. (2007) "Paranoid Personality Disorder," pp. 41–62. In O'Donohue, Fowler, and Lilienfeld, *Personality Disorders*.

Blashfield, Roger, and Ross McElory. (1995) "Confusions in the Terminology Used for Classificatory Models," pp. 407–416. In *The DSM-IV Personality Disorders*. Edited by John Livesley. New York: Guilford.

Bradley, Rebekah, Carolyn Zittel Conkline, and Drew Westen. (2007) "Borderline Personality Disorder," pp. 167–201. In O'Donohue, Fowler, and Lilienfeld, *Personality Disorders*.

Brehm, Sharon. (1992) *Intimate Relationships*. Second Edition. New York: McGraw–Hill.

Brontë, Charlotte. (1980) *Jane Eyre*. Woodstock, New York: Beekman.

Browne, Thomas. (1970) *Christian Morals*, p. 95n1. In *International Thesaurus of Quotations*.

Bruning, Fred. (1995) "The Moral Bankruptcy of America in the 90s," *Macleans*, 108:37 (11 September), p. 15.

Cacioppo, John, and William Patrick. (2008) *Loneliness: Human Nature and the Need for Social Connection*. New York: Norton.

Charland, Louis. (2006) "Moral Nature of the *DSM-IV* Cluster B Personality Disorders," *Journal of Personality Disorders*, 20:2, pp. 116–125.

Charny, Israel. (1996) "Evil in Human Personality: Disorders of Doing Harm to Others in Family Relationships," pp. 477–495. In Kaslow, *Handbook of Relational Diagnosis and Dysfunctional Family Patterns*.

Chesterfield, Lord (1970). *Lord Chesterfield, Letters to His Sons*, p. 466n680. In *International Thesaurus of Quotations*.

Choron, Jacques. (1964) *Death and Modern Man*. New York: Macmillan.

Clark, Eloise. (1968) "Aspects of Loneliness: Toward a Framework of Nursing Intervention," pp. 33–40. In *Developing Behavioral Concepts in Nursing*. Edited by Loretta Zderad and Helen Belcher. Atlanta: Southern Regional Educational Board.

Clark, Lee. (2006) "The Role of Moral Judgment in PersonalityDiagnosis," *Journal of Personality Disorders*, 20:2, pp. 184–185.

Clark, Lee, John Livesley, and Leslie Morey. (1997) "Personality Disorder Assessment: The Challenge of Construct Validity," *Journal of Personality Disorders*, 11:3, pp. 205–231.

Claridge, Gordon. (2006) "Psychobiological Models and Issues," pp. 137–164. In Strack, *Differentiating Normal and Abnormal Personality*.

Cloninger, Robert (2006) "Differentiating Personality Deviance, Normality, and Well-Being by the Seven-Factor Psychobiological Model," pp. 65–81. In Strack, *Differentiating Normal and Abnormal Personality*.

———. (2007) Foreword, pp. vii–xv. In O'Donohue, Fowler, and Lilienfeld, *Personality Disorders*.

Close, Sandy. (1995) "The Public-Private Divide: Interview with a Vampire, et al.," *The Nation*, 261:8, pp. 280–281.

Coker, Linda, and Thomas Widiger. (2005) "Personality Disorders," pp. 201–227. In *Psychopathology: Foundations for a Contemporary Understanding*. Edited by James Maddux and Barbara Winstead. Mahwah, N. J.: Erlbaum.

Corin, Ellen, and Gilles Lauzon. (1992) "Positive Withdrawal and the Quest for Meaning: The Reconstruction of Experience Among Schizophrenics," *Psychiatry*, 55, pp. 266–278.

Costa, Paul, Nicholas Patriciu, and Robert McCrae. (2005) "Lessons from Longitudinal Studies for New Approaches to the *DSM-V*: The FFM and FFT," *Journal of Personality Disorders*, 19:5, pp. 533–539.

Costa, Paul, and Thomas Widiger. (1994) Introduction, pp. 1–10, and "*DSM-III-R* Personality Disorders and the Five-Factor Model," Appendix A, p. 329. In *Personality Disorders and the Five-Factor Model of Personality*. First Edition. Edited by Costa and Widiger. Washington, D.C.: American Psychological Association.

———. (2002) "Description of the Revised NEO Personality Inventory (NEO-PI-R) Facet Scales," Appendix D, pp. 461–467. In *Personality Disorders and the Five-*

Factor Model of Personality. Second Edition. Edited by Costa and Widiger. Washington, D.C.: American Psychological Association.

Cowburn, John. (1967) *The Person and Love: Philosophy and Theology of Love*. New York: Alba House.

Dabrowski, Kazimierz. (1972) *Psycho-Neurosis Is Not an Illness*. London: Gryf.

———, Andrew Kawczak, and Michael Piechowski. (1970) *Mental Growth through Positive Integration*. London: Gryf.

Davis, Stephen, Helen Hanson, Roger Edson, and Charlene Zieglere. (1992) "The Relationship between Optimism-Pessimism, Loneliness, and Level of Self-Esteem in College Students," *College Student Journal*, 26:2, pp. 244–247.

De La Rie, S. M., I. J. Duijsens, and C. R. Cloninger. (1998) "Temperament, Character, and Personality Disorders," *Journal of Personality Disorders*, 12:4, pp. 362–372.

Denton, Wayne. (1996) "Problems Encountered in Reconciling Individual and Relational Diagnoses," pp. 33–45. In Kaslow, *Handbook of Relational Diagnosis and Dysfunctional Family Patterns*.

Derlega, Valerian, and Stephen Margulis. (1982) "Why Loneliness Occurs: The Interrelationship of Social-Psychological and Privacy Concepts," pp. 152–165. In Peplau and Perlman, *Loneliness*.

Dersken, Jan. (1995) *Personality Disorders: Clinical and Social Perspectives*. New York: John Wiley & Sons.

Donne, John. (1953) *Anniversary*, p. 186nn27–28. In *The Oxford Dictionary of Quotations*.

Dowson, Jonathan, and Adrian Grounds. (1995) *Personality Disorders: Recognition and Clinical Management*. Cambridge: Cambridge University Press.

Dusenbury, Winifred. (1967) *The Theme of Loneliness in Modern American Drama*. Gainsville: University of Florida Press.

Eliot, T. S. (1950) *The Cocktail Party*. London: Faber and Faber.

Erdberg, Philip. (2004) "Assessing the Dimensions of Personality Disorder," pp. 78–89. In *Handbook of Personality Disorders*.

Ferreira, Antonio. (1962) "Loneliness and Psychopathology," *American Journal of Psychoanalysis*, 22:2, pp. 201–207.

Fest, Joachim. (1970) *The Face of the Third Reich: Portraits of the Nazi Leadership*. Translated by Michael Bullock. New York: Pantheon Books.

Fowler, Katherine, William O'Donohue, and Scott Lilienfeld.(2007) "Personality Disorders in Perspective," pp. 1–19. In O'Donohue, Fowler, and Lilienfeld, *Personality Disorders*.

Frances, Allen, Thomas Widiger, and Melvin Sabshin. (1991) "Psychiatric Diagnosis and Normality," pp. 3–39. In *The Diversity of Normal Behavior: Further Contributions to Normatology*. Edited by Daniel Offer and Melvin Sabshin. New York: Basic Books.

Fromm, Erich. (1962) *The Art of Loving*. New York: Harper & Row.

———. (1966) "The Application of Humanist Psychoanalysis to Marx's Theory," pp. 228–245. In *Socialist Humanism*. Edited by Erich Fromm. Garden City, N.Y.: Doubleday.

———. (1968) *Man for Himself: An Inquiry into the Psychology of Ethics*. New York: Fawcett.

Fromm-Reichmann, Frieda. (1980) "Loneliness," pp. 338–361. In Hartog, Audi, and Cohen, *The Anatomy of Loneliness*.

Gerstein, Lawrence, Harry Bates, and Morey Reindl. (1987) "The Experience of Loneliness among Schizophrenics and Normal Persons," *Journal of Social Behavior and Personality*, 2:2, pp. 239–248.

Goleman, Daniel. (2006) *Social Intelligence: The New Science of Human Relationships*. New York: Bantam Books.

Gradman, Theodore, Larry Thompson, and Dolores Gallagher. (1999) "Personality Disorders and Treatment Outcome," pp. 69–94. In Rosowsky, Abrams, and Zweig, *Personality Disorders in Older Adults*.

Guntrip, Harry. (1973) "Sigmund Freud and Bertrand Russell," *Contemporary* Psychoanalysis, 9:35, pp. 263–281.

Hammer, Max. (1972) "A Therapy for Loneliness," *Voices*, 8:1, pp. 24–29.

Hartog, Joseph, J. Ralph Audy, and Yehudi Cohen, Eds. (1980) *The Anatomy of Loneliness*. New York: International Universities Press.

Hatfield, Elaine, and Richard Rapson. (1993) *Love, Sex, and Intimacy*. New York: Harper Collins.

Hazo, Robert. (1967) *The Idea of Love*. New York: Praeger.

Heidegger, Martin. (1962) *Being and Time*. Translated by John Macquarrie and Edward Robinson. London: SCM.

Heinemann, F. H. (1965) *Existentialism and the Modern Predicament*. New York: Harper & Row.

Henry, Jules. (1980) "Loneliness and Vulnerability," pp. 95–110. In Hartog, Audi, and Cohen, *The Anatomy of Loneliness*.

Hobbes, Thomas. (1953) *The Leviathan*, p. 248n21. In *The Oxford Dictionary of Quotations*.

Horney, Karen. (1991) *Neurosis and Human Growth: The Struggle Toward Self-Realization*. New York: Norton.

Horowitz, Leonard. (2004) *Interpersonal Foundations of Psychopathology*. Washington, D.C.: American Psychological Association.

Horowitz, Leonard, Rita de Sales French, and Craig Anderson. (1982) "The Prototype of a Lonely Person," pp. 183–205. In Peplau and Perlman, *Loneliness*.

Johnson, Jeffrey, Judith Rabkin, Janet Williams, Robert Remien, and Jack Gorman. (2000) "Difficulties in Interpersonal Relationships Associated with Personality Disorders and Axis I Disorders: A Community-Based Longitudinal Investigation," *Journal of Personality Disorders*, 14:1, pp. 42–56.

Jones, Warren. (1982) "Loneliness and Social Behavior," pp. 238–252. In Peplau and Perlman, *Loneliness*.

Jordan, Judith. (2004) "Personality Disorder or Relational Disconnection?" pp. 120–134. In Magnavita, *Handbook of Personality Disorders*.

Kant, Immanuel. (1964) *The Metaphysical Principles of Virtue* (Part II of *The Metaphysics of Morals*). Translated by James Ellington. Indianapolis: Bobbs-Merrill.

Karren, Keith, Hafen Brent, Lee Smith, and Kathryn Frandsen. (2002) *Mind/Body Health: The Effects of Attitudes, Emotions, and Relationships*. Second Edition. San Francisco: Benjamin Cumming.

Kaslow, Florence, Ed.. (1996) *Handbook of Relational Diagnosis and Dysfunctional Family Patterns*. New York: Guilford Press.

Kaufmann, Walter. (1965a) *Hegel: Reinterpretation, Texts, and Commentary*. New York: Doubleday.

———. (1973) *Without Guilt and Justice: From Decidophobia to Autonomy*. New York: P. H. Wyden.

———, Ed. (1965b) *The Portable Nietzsche*. New York: Viking Press.

Keats, John, (1970) "*Lamia*," p. 470n14. In *International Thesaurus of Quotations*.

Klerman, Gerald, and Myrna Weissman. (1986) "The Interpersonal Approach to Understanding Depression," pp. 429–456. In Millon and Klerman, *Contemporary Directions in Psychopathology*.

Krueger, Robert, and Jennifer Tackett. (2003) "Personality and Psychopathology: Working Toward the Bigger Picture," *Journal of Personality Disorders*, 17:2, pp. 109–128.

Kübler Ross, Elisabeth, and David Kessler. (2005) *On Grief and Grieving: Finding the Meaning of Grief Through the Five Stages of Loss*. London: Simon & Schuster.

Laing, R. D. (1965) *The Divided Self: An Existential Study in Sanity and Madness*. London: Penguin.

———. (1967) *The Politics of Experience*. New York: Ballantine.

———, H. Phillipson, and A. Lee. (1966) *Interpersonal Perception*. New York: Springer.

Leary, Mark. (1990) "Responses to Social Exclusion: Social Anxiety, Jealousy, Loneliness, Depression, and Low Self-Esteem," *Journal of Social and Clinical Psychology*, 9:2, pp. 221–229.

Leising, Daniel, Doreen Sporberg, and Diana Rehbein. (2006) "Characteristic Interpersonal Behavior in Dependent and Avoidant Personality Disorder Can Be Observed within Very Short Interaction Sequences," *Journal of Personality Disorders*, 20:2, pp. 319–330.

Livesley, John. (1998) "Suggestions for a Framework for an Empirically Based Classification of Personality Disorder," *Canadian Journal of Psychiatry*, 43:2, pp. 137–147.

———, and Kerry Jang. (2000) "Toward an Empirically Based Classification of Personality Disorder," *Journal of Personality Disorders*, 14:2, pp. 137–151.

Lynch, James. (1977) *The Broken Heart: The Medical Consequences of Loneliness*. New York: Basic Books.

———. (2000) *A Cry Unheard: New Insights into the Medical Consequences of Loneliness in America*. Baltimore: Bancroft.

———, and William Convey. (1979) "Loneliness, Disease, and Death: Alternative Approaches," *Psychosomatics*, 20:10, pp. 702–708.

Macmurray, John. (1991) *Persons in Relation*. London: Faber & Faber.

Magnavita, Jeffrey. (1997) *Restructuring Personality Disorders: A Short-Term Dynamic Approach*. New York: Guilford.

———. (2000) *Relational Therapy for Personality Disorders*. New York: John Wiley & Sons.

———. (2004a) "Classification, Prevalence, and Etiology of Personality Disorders," pp. 3–23. In *Handbook of Personality Disorders*.

———, Ed. (2004b) *Handbook of Personality Disorders: Theory and Practice*. New York: John Wiley & Sons.

Marangoni, Carol, and William Ickes. (1989) "Loneliness: A Theoretical Review with Implications for Measurement," *Journal of Social and Personal Relationships*, 6:1, pp. 93–128.

Maslow, Abraham. (1968) *Toward A Psychology of Being*. Second Edition. New York: Van Nostrand.

———. (1970) *Motivation and Personality*. Second Edition. New York: Harper & Row.

May, Rollo. (1953) *Man's Search for Himself*. New York: Norton.

———. (1969) *Love and Will*. New York: Norton.

May, Valerie. (1999) "Survey 2000," *National Geographic*, 196:6, pp. 130–133.

McCrae, Robert and Paul T. Costa. (1990) *Personality in Adulthood*. New York: Guilford.

———. (1999) "A Five-Factor Theory of Personality," pp. 139–153. In *Handbook of Personality: Theory and Research*. Edited by Lawrence Pervin and Oliver John. New York: Guilford.

McGraw, John G. (1986) "Personality and its Ideal in K. Dabrowski's Theory of Positive Disintegration: A Philosophical Interpretation," *Dialectics and Humanism*, 1, pp. 211–237.

———. (1991) "On Loneliness: A Tentative Typology and its Implications in Art Therapy and in Imagery Process," pp. 135–163. In *Art Media as a Vehicle of Communication*. Edited by Irene Jakab. Brookline, Mass.: The American Society of Psychopathology of Expression.

———. (1992) "God and the Problem of Loneliness," *Religious Studies*, 28, pp. 319–346.

———. (1999) "Loneliness: The First of All Evils," pp. 145–158. In *The Problem of Evil*. Edited by Sandra Wawrytko. Amsterdam: Rodopi.

———. (2010) *Intimacy and Isolation*. Volume 1, Intimacy and Aloneness. Amsterdam: Rodopi.

McLemore, Clinton, and David Brokaw. (1987) "Personality Disorders as Dysfunctional Interpersonal Behavior," *Journal of Personality Disorders*, 1, pp. 270–285.

Miedema, Baukje, and Sue Tatemichi. (2003) "Gender, Marital Status, Social Networks, and Health: Their Impact on Loneliness in the Very Old," *Geriatrics Today*, 6, pp. 95–99.

Mijuskovic, Ben. (1979) *Loneliness in Philosophy, Psychology, and Literature*. Assen, The Netherlands: Van Gorcum.

Millon, Theodore. (1986) "Personality Prototypes and Their Diagnostic Criteria," pp. 671–712. In Millon and Klerman, *Contemporary Directions in Psychopathology*.

———, and George Everly. (1985) *Personality and its Disorders: A Biosocial Learning Approach*. New York: John Wiley & Sons.

Millon, Theodore, and Roger Davis. (1996) *Disorders of Personality: DSM-IV and Beyond*. Second Edition. New York: John Wiley & Sons.

Millon, Theodore, Roger Davis, Carrie Millon, Luis Escovar, and Sarah Meagher. (2000) *Personality Disorders in Modern Life*. New York: John Wiley & Sons.

Millon, Theodore, and Seth Grossman. (2004) "Psychopathic Assessment Can Usefully Inform Therapy: A View from the Study of Personality," pp. 24–55. In *Handbook of Personality Disorders*.

Millon, Theodore, and Gerald Klerman, Eds. (1986) "The Interpersonal Approach to Understanding Depression," pp. 429–456. *Contemporary Directions in Psychopathology*. New York: Guilford.

Morgan, Russ, Larry Stock, and James Cavanaugh. "You're Nobody 'Til Somebody Loves You." (San Antonio, Tex: Southern Music, 1944).

Mounier, Emmanuel. (1970) *Personalism*. Translated by Philip Mairet. Notre Dame: Notre Dame University Press.

Nietzsche, Friedrich. (1965a) *Thus Spoke Zarathustra*. In Kaufmann, *The Portable Nietzsche*.

———. (1965b) *Twilight of the Idols*. In Kaufmann, *The Portable Nietzsche*.

———. (1968) *The Will to Power*. Edited by Walter Kaufman. Translated by Kaufmann and R. J. Hollingdale. New York: Random House.

———. (1974) *The Gay Science*. Translated by Walter Kaufmann. New York: Vintage Books.

———. (1989a) *Beyond Good and Evil*. Translated by Walter Kaufmann. New York: Random House.

———. (1989b) *Ecce Homo*. Edited and Translated by Walter Kaufmann. New York: Random House.

———. (1991) *Untimely Meditations*. Translated by R. Hollingdale. Cambridge, UK: Cambridge University Press.

O'Donohue, William, Katherine Fowler, and Scott Lilienfeld, Eds. (2007) *Personality Disorders: Toward the DSM-V*. Thousands Oaks, Calif.: Sage.

Paris, Joel. (1996) *Social Factors in the Personality Disorders*. New York: Cambridge University Press.

———. (2000) "The Classification of Personality Disorders Should Be Rooted in Biology," *Journal of Personality Disorders*, 14:2, pp. 127–136.

———. (2003) "Personality Disorders Over Time: Precursors, Course, and Outcome," *Journal of Personality Disorders*, 17:6, pp. 479–488.

Parker, Gordon. (1997) "The Etiology of Personality Disorders: A Review and Consideration of Research Models," *Journal of Personality Disorders*, 11:4, pp. 345–369.

———. (2006) "Through a Glass Darkly: The Disutility of the *DSM* Nosology of Depressive Disorders," *The Canadian Journal of Psychiatry*, 51:14, pp. 879–886.

Peplau, Letitia, and Daniel Perlman. (1982) "Perspectives on Loneliness," pp. 1–18. In *Loneliness*.

———, Eds. (1982) *Loneliness: A Sourcebook of Current Theory, Research, and Therapy*. New York: John Wiley & Sons.

Perlman, Daniel, and Letitia Peplau. (1982) "Theoretical Approaches to Loneliness," pp. 123–134. In Peplau and Perlman, *Loneliness*.

———. (1984) "Loneliness Research: A Survey of Empirical Findings," pp. 13–46. In *Preventing the Harmful Consequences of Severe and Persistent Loneliness*. Edited by Letitia Peplau and Stephen Goldston. Rockville, Md.: National Institute of Mental Health.

Pincus, Aaron. (2005) "A Contemporary Integrative Interpersonal Theory of Personality Disorders," pp. 282–331. In *Major Theories of Personality Disorders*. Second Edition. Edited by John Clarkin and Mark Lenzenweger. New York: Guilford.

———, and Michael Gurtman. (2006) "Interpersonal Theory and the Interpersonal Circumplex: Evolving Perspectives on Normal and Abnormal Personality," pp. 83–111. In Strack, *Differentiating Normal and Abnormal Personality*.

Poe, Edgar Allan. (1978) "The Man of the Crowd," pp. 505–518. In *Collected Works of Edgar Allan Poe*. Edited by Thomas Mabbott. Cambridge: Harvard University Press.

Potter, Nancy Nyquist. (2006) "What Is Manipulative Behavior Anyway?" *Journal of Personality Disorders*, 20:2, pp. 139–156.

Rayburn, Carole. (1986) "Loneliness and the Single, the Widowed, and the Divorced," pp. 29–46. In *Psychotherapy and the Lonely Patient*. Edited by Samuel Natale. New York: Haworth.

Reich, James. (2005) Introduction, pp. xiii–xix. In *Personality Disorders: Current Research and Treatments*. Edited by James Reich. New York: Routledge.

Reid, William, and Michael Wise. (1995) *DSM-IV Training Guide*. Levittown, Pa.: Brunner/Mazel.

Rifkin, Jeremy. (2004) *The European Dream: How Europe's Vision of the Future Is Quietly Eclipsing the American Dream*. New York: Tarcher/Penguin.

Riggio, Ronald. (1986) "Assessment of Basic Social Skills," *Journal of Personality and Social Psychology*, 51:3, pp. 649–660.

Rook, Karen. (1984) "Research on Social Support, Loneliness, and Social Isolation," *Review of Personality and Social Psychology*, 5, pp. 239–264.

Rosenhan, David, and Martin Seligman. (1989) *Abnormal Psychology*. Second Edition. New York: Norton.

Rosowsky, Erlene. (1999) "The Patient-Therapist Relationship and the Psychotherapy of the Older Adult with Personality Disorder," pp. 153–174. In Rosowsky, Abrams, and Zweig, *Personality Disorders in Older Adults*.

———, Robert Abrams, and Richard Zweig, Eds.(1999) *Personality Disorders in Older Adults: Emerging Issues in Diagnosis and Treatment*. Mahwah, N.J.: Lawrence Erlbaum.

Rubenstein, Carin, and Phillip Shaver. (1982) *In Search of Intimacy*. New York: Delacorte.

Ruegg, Robert, and Allen Frances. (1995) "New Research in Personality Disorders," *Journal of Personality Disorders*, 9:1, pp. 1–48.

Ryff, Carol, and Burton Singer. (1998) "The Contours of Positive Human Health," *Psychological Inquiry*, 9:1, pp. 1–28.

Sadler, John, and Bill Fulford. (2006) "Normative Warrant in Diagnostic Criteria: The Case of *DSM-IV-TR* Personality Disorders," *The Journal of Personality Disorders*, 20:2, pp. 170–180.

Sadler, William. (1978) "Dimensions in the Problem of Loneliness: A Phenomenological Approach," *Journal of Phenomenological Psychology*, 9:1–2, pp. 157–187.

Saklofske, Donald, Richard Yackulic, and Ivan Kelly. (1986) "Personality and Loneliness," *Personality and Individual Differences*, 7:6, pp. 899–901.

Sangster, James, and Craig Ellison. (1978) "Mental Illness, Loneliness, and Helplessness," *Mental Health Society*, 5, pp. 284–295.

Sartre, Jean-Paul. (1948) *Existentialism and Humanism*. Translated by Philip Mairet. New York: Haskell House.

———. (1955) *No Exit and Three Other Plays*. New York: Vintage Books.

———. (1956) *Being and Nothingness: An Essay on Phenomenological Ontology*. Translated by Hazel Barnes. New York: Philosophical Library.

Sayre, Robert. (1978) *Solitude in Society: A Sociological Study in French Literature*. Cambridge, Mass.: Harvard University Press.

Schwartz, Richard, and Jacqueline Olds. (1997) "Loneliness," *Harvard Revue of Psychiatry*, 5, pp. 94–98.

Segrin, Chris. (1998) "Interpersonal Communication Problems Associated with Depression and Loneliness," pp. 215–242. In *Handbook of Communication and Emotion: Research, Theory, Application, and Contexts*. Edited by Peter Andersen and Laura Guerrero. New York: Academic Press.

Smith Benjamin, Lorna. (1996) *Interpersonal Diagnosis and Treatment of Personality Disorders*. New York: Guilford.

Smyth, Alice Mary, Ed. (1953) *The Oxford Dictionary of Quotations*. Second Edition. London: Oxford University Press.

Sorokin, Pitirim. (1950) *Altruistic Love: A Study of America's "Good Neighbors" and Christian Saints*. Boston: Beacon.

———. (1967) *The Ways and Power of Love*. Chicago: Gateway.

Sperry, Len. (1995) *Handbook of Diagnosis and the Treatment of the DSM-IV Personality Disorders*. Bristol, Pa.: Brunner/Mazel.

Stevenson, Robert Louis. (1886) *The Strange Case of Dr. Jekyll and Mr. Hyde*. London: Longmans, Green.

Stone, Michael. (1993) *Abnormalities of Personality: Within and Beyond the Realm of Treatment*. New York: Norton.

———. (2006) *Personality-Disordered Patients: Treatable and Untreatable*. Washington, D.C.: American Psychiatric Association.

Storr, Anthony. (1988) *Solitude: A Return to the Self*. New York: Ballantine Books.

Strack, Stephen, Ed. (2006a) *Differentiating Normal and Abnormal Personality*. Second Edition. New York: Springer.

———. (2006b) "Introduction," pp. xvii–xxvii. In *Differentiating Normal and Abnormal Personality*.

———. (2006c) "Problems and Pitfalls in Designing Research on Normal-Abnormal Personality," pp. 187–207. In *Differentiating Normal and Abnormal Personality*.

Strack, Stephen and Maurice Lorr. (1997) "The Challenge of Differentiating Normal and Disordered Personality," *Journal of Personality Disorders*, 11:2, pp. 105-122.

Suedfeld, Peter. (1982) "Aloneness as a Healing Experience," pp. 54–67. In Peplau and Perlman, *Loneliness*.

Sullivan, Harry Stack. (1953) *The Interpersonal Theory of Psychiatry*. New York: Norton.

Swan, Jim. (1985) "Difference and Silence: John Milton and the Question of Gender," pp. 142–168. In *The (M)other Tongue*: *Essays in Feminist Psychoanalytic Interpretation*. Edited by Shirley Garner, Clair Kahane, and Madelon Sprengnether. Ithaca, N.Y.: Cornell University Press.

Teilhard de Chardin, Pierre. (1965) *The Making of a Mind*. New York: Harper & Row.

Tillich, Paul. (1980) "Loneliness and Solitude," pp. 547–553. Hartog, Audi, and Cohen, *The Anatomy of Loneliness*.

Titus, Harold. (1970) *Living Issues in Philosophy*. Fifth Edition. New York: Van Nostrand Reinhold.

Tripp, Rhoda Thomas. (1970) *The International Thesaurus of Quotations*. (1970) Edited by Rhoda Thomas Tripp. New York: Harper & Row.

Trull, Timothy, and Christine Durrett. (2005) "Categorical and Dimensional Models of Personality Disorders" *Annual Review of Clinical Psychology*, 1, pp. 355–380.

Ulmer, Ann, Lillian Range, and Gale Trioia. (1992) "Loneliness and Depression Related to Reasons for Living in Military Personnel," *Death Studies*, 16:2, pp. 183–189.

Voltaire. (1970) *Candide*, 471n45. In *International Thesaurus of Quotations*.

Wakefield, (2006) "Personality Disorder as Harmful Dysfunction: *DSM*'s Cultural Deviance Criterion Reconsidered," *Journal of Personality Disorders*, 20:2, pp. 157–169.

Weinberg, Kirson. (1967) "The Relevance of the Forms of Isolation to Schizophrenia," *International Journal of Social Psychiatry*, 13:1, pp. 33–41.

Weiss, Robert. (1973) *Loneliness: The Experience of Emotional and Social Isolation.* Cambridge, Mass.: The Massachusetts Institute of Technology.

Weissman, Myrna. (1993) "The Epidemiology of Personality Disorders: A 1990 Update," *Journal of Personality Disorders*, 7:1, pp. 44–62.

Westen, Drew, and Jonathan Shedler. (2000) "A Prototype Matching Approach to Diagnosing Personality Disorders," *Journal of Personality Disorders*, 14:2, pp. 109–126.

Widiger, Thomas. (2000) "Personality Disorders in the 21st Century," *Journal of Personality Disorders*, 14:1, pp. 3–16.

———. (2003) "Personality Disorder and Axis I Psychopathology: The Problematic Boundary of Axis I and Axis II," *Journal of Personality Disorders*, 17:2, pp. 90–108.

———. (2005) "A Dimensional Model of Personality Disorder," *Current Opinion in Psychiatry*, 18, pp. 41–43.

———. (2006) "Tough Questions of Morality, Free Will, and Maladaptivity," *Journal of Personality Disorders*, 20:2, pp. 181–183.

Widiger, Thomas, and Timothy Trull. (1992) "Personality and Psychopathology: An Application of the Five-Factor Model," *Journal of Personality*, 60:2, pp. 363–393.

Willick, Martin. (1993) "The Deficit Syndrome in Schizophrenia: Psychoanalytic and Neurobiological Perspectives," *Journal of the American Psychoanalytic Association*, 41:4, pp. 1137–1138.

Winter, David, and Nicole Barenbaum. (1999) "History of Modern Personality Theory and Research," pp. 3–27. In *Handbook of Personality: Theory and Research.* Edited by Lawrence Pervin and Oliver John. New York: Guilford.

Young, Jeffrey. (1982) "Loneliness, Depression, and Cognitive Therapy: Theory and Application," pp. 379–405. In Peplau and Perlman, *Loneliness.*

Zweig, Richard, and Jennifer Hillman. (1999) "Personality Disorders in Adults," pp. 31–53. In Rosowsky, Abrams, and Zweig, *Personality Disorders in Older Adults.*

Appendix A

SCRAM: Five American Social Illnesses

In Volume I, I described five destructive social trends that I maintain to have increasingly dominated the United States since the 1970s. This series argues that these practices, which are tantamount to social institutions, are among the chief external contributors to negative kinds of personality and unwanted aloneness among Americans.

This quintet of societal arrangements can be represented by the acronym, SCRAM, which also symbolizes the reality that, when these trends are present, most markedly in their totality, relatedness rushes away. In the absence of relatedness, loneliness and other sorts of unwanted aloneness fill the void with negative emotions such as anxiety and negative self-attributions, such as self-worthlessness.

The constituents of SCRAM are the following five quasi-fixations:

"*S*uccessitis," or "successism," the dishonorable and runaway ambition to gain, for instance, popularity, celebrity, power, status, and wealth;
"*C*apitalitis," or "economic atomism," the unregulated, rapacious "free market" capitalism, the kind that triggered the present world financial crisis;
"*R*ivalitis," or "rivalism," the unmitigated self-aggrandizing attempt to conquer or even crush all competitors ("competivitis");
"*A*tomitis," or social atomism, or hyper-individualism ("individualitis");
"*M*aterialitis," or "anti-spiritual materialism," including its "affluenza," "possessionitis," "consumeritis," "stuffitis," and "discarditis."

These practices, understood as social diseases—hence, the suffix "itis" attached to them—build barriers instead of bridges to others in that they moat the person in self-centeredness. This egocentricity is the most salient psycho-ethical shortcoming of all those with personality disorders.

The five ingredients of SCRAM are dys-synergic in nature. As such, each generates greater negative personality and aloneness when it functions in concert with one or more of the other four SCRAM constituents than when it operates on its own. Thus, the egocentricity of SCRAM's social atomism becomes more ruinous to interpersonal relatedness when allied to the self-centeredness, for example, ascribable to the self-absorption typical of successism. Atomitis, or hyper-individualism, is the ground and glue of the other four factors of SCRAM.

Not only is it a common consequence, but SCRAM is also a formidable factor in causing a litany of unethical personality qualities not the least of which are enmity, envy, and greed. This triad of immoral traits poses a triple threat to authentic interpersonal relatedness, the lack of which is, in my judgment, also the principal part of aberrated personalities. Such disturbed individuals are, in my reckoning, the legacy of mainly acquired negative ethical traits and largely biologically based deficient psychological qualities.

As an ensemble, these detrimental characteristics isolate abnormal personalities from one another and from normal personalities. The present probe strives to identify how and why SCRAM can be heavily blamed for the social conditions, which assist in starting and strengthening negative psycho-ethical personality features that flourish in individuals with disturbed personalities (vol. 1, chap. 1, sec. 2).

With respect to loneliness, whereas it is by definition a paradigmatically profound personal and private experience, care must be taken not to confuse the locus of this tribulation, which is always internal, with its external conditions, promoters, and producers, such as the five elements of SCRAM.

Abraham Maslow avers that, though social institutions do not condemn a person to pathogenic consequences, they nurture them. On the other hand, he states that "the good society is the one that has its institutional arrangements set up" so "as to foster, encourage, reward, [and] produce a maximum of good human relationships and a minimum of bad" ones (1970, p. 255).

If Maslow is right—and there is ample evidence from an abundance of sources, to argue that he is—then the institutional arrangements which comprise SCRAM are conducive to maximizing bad and unhealthy relationships. In such circumstances, intimacy is a main casualty of these five pathogenic societal forces and loneliness and other negative states of aloneness are their inescapable consequences. Indeed, loneliness is demonstrably now a prominent part of the psyche of Americans who, despite their deserved recognition for being warm and outgoing, have increasingly become isolated not only emotionally but socially and often even physically from one another. Alas, they increasingly constitute a nation of internal exiles cut off and divorced from one another, predominantly traceable, in my judgment, to SCRAM.

Appendix B

Five Factor Model of Personality (FFM)

Diagnostic Features

The FFM assembles personality traits into a quintet of broad factors: Neuroticism, Extraversion, Openness to Experience, Agreeableness (Humaneness), and Conscientiousness. FFM considers these supertraits, also known as dimensions, classes, or domains, as the building blocks of personality in all its normal and anormal, meaning abnormal and supranormal, variations. Each of the five supertraits is made up of six traits—in sum, therefore, thirty facets. They are set forth by Paul Costa and Thomas Widiger as follows:

Neuroticism ("the chronic level of emotional adjustment and instability" and the proneness "to psychological distress"): anxiety, angry hostility, depression, self-consciousness, impulsiveness, and vulnerability.

Extraversion ("the quantity and intensity of preferred interpersonal actions, activity level, need for stimulation, and capability for joy"): warmth, gregariousness, assertiveness, activity, excitement seeking, and positive emotions.

Openness to Experience ("the active seeking and appreciation of experiences for their own sake"): fantasy, aesthetics, feelings, actions, ideas, and values.

Agreeableness [Humaneness] ("the kinds of interactions a person prefers along a continuum from compassion to antagonism"): trust, straightforwardness, altruism, compliance [cooperativeness], modesty [humility], and tender-mindedness [tender-heartedness].

Conscientiousness ("the degree of organization, persistence, and motivation in goal-oriented behavior"): competence, order, dutifulness, achievement striving, self-discipline, and deliberation. (see vol. 1, chap. 1; Costa and Thomas Widiger, 1994, p. 329; 2002, pp. 461–467).

All six of these FFM personality traits are manifestly ethical in essence. The supertrait of Humaneness is arguably the barometer of ethics especially in terms of altruism and love as a whole. In addition, the FFM supertrait of Conscientiousness involves other moral virtues. Its traits of dutifulness pertains to justice; self-discipline, to temperance; and deliberation, to prudence, meaning sound, even wise judgment in practical matters and day-to-day ethical exigencies (vol. 1, p. 83).

Thomas A. Widiger envisions:

> the FFM as the principal approach in general personality research, with wide-reaching applications in the fields of health psychology, aging, and developmental psychology. Empirical support for the FFM is extensive, including convergent and discriminant validity at the domain [supertrait] and facet [trait] levels across self, peer and spouse ratings, temporal stability across many years, consistency with genetic structure, and substantial cross-cultural replication. Adaptive and maladaptive variants of each of the two poles of the facets have been described, and highly convergent FFM descriptions have been provided by researchers and clinicians. The FFM is an especially robust model which has succeeded well in representing diverse collections of the traits of alternative models within a single, integrative, hierarchical structure. For example, dimensions of the *interpersonal* [my emphasis] complex (agency and affiliation) are rotated variants of FFM Extraversion and Agreeableness [Humaneness]. (2005, p. 42)

Michael Stone considers the FFM dimensional—versus the *DSM* categorical—model to be an all-inclusive conceptual matrix and taxonomy of personality. He does so in that Stone contends it is valid "across cultures and the millennia" with the exceptions being "only minimal and superficial" (1993, p. 115).

Robert McCrae and Paul Costa claim that the FFM model contains "virtually all the traits identified in common speech and in scientific theories of personality" (1990, p. vi). Ergo, it may be deduced that the FFM perspective is eminently accessible to the general populace over and above its utility for professional personologists both researchers and clinicians.

McCrae and Costa further hold that the FFM notion of personality, narrowly envisioned, "is an empirical generalization about the covariation of personality traits." But, more broadly construed, "the FFM refers," they say, "to the entire body of research that it has inspired, amounting to a reinvigoration of trait psychology itself" (1999, p. 139).

Nevertheless, McCrae and Costa posit, "neither the model itself nor the body of research findings with which it is associated constitutes a theory of personality." On the other hand, they insist that the FFM fits any theory of personality, all of which, they emphasize, is not the case with the *DSM* and its categorical model which itself employs a plethora of personality theories (ibid.).

Appendix C

DSM-IV Personality Disorders

1. Introduction

DSM-IV uses a five-axis multi-axial assessment, "each of which refers to a different domain of information that may help the clinician plan treatment and predict outcome" (p. 25):

Axis I	Clinical Disorders Other Conditions that May Be a Focus of Clinical Attention
Axis II	Personality Disorders Mental Retardation
Axis III	General Medical Conditions
Axis IV	Psychosocial and Environmental Problems
Axis V	Global Assessment of Functioning

The listing of Personality Disorders and Mental Retardation on a separate axis ensures that consideration will be given to the possible presence of Personality Disorders and Mental Retardation that might otherwise be overlooked when attention is directed to the usually more florid Axis I disorders. (p. 26–27)

Axis II
Personality Disorders
Mental Retardation

Paranoid Personality Disorder	Avoidant Personality Disorder
Schizoid Personality Disorder	Dependent Personality Disorder
Schizotypal Personality Disorder	Obsessive-Compulsive Personality Disorder
Antisocial Personality Disorder	Personality Disorder Not Otherwise Specified
Borderline Personality Disorder	Mental Retardation
Histrionic Personality Disorder	
Narcissistic Personality Disorder	

A Personality Disorder is an enduring pattern of inner experience and behavior hat deviate markedly from the expectations of the individual's culture, is pervasive and inflexible, has an onset in adolescence or early adulthood, is stable over time, and leads to distress or impairment. The Personality Disorders . . . are listed below:

Paranoid Personality Disorder is a pattern of distrust and suspiciousness such that others' motives are interpreted as malevolent.

Schizoid Personality Disorder is a pattern of detachment from social relationships and a restricted range of emotional expression.

Schizotypal Personality Disorder is a pattern of acute discomfort in close relationships, cognitive or perceptual distortions, and eccentricities of behavior.

Antisocial Personality Disorder is a pattern of disregard for, and violation of, the rights of others.

Borderline Personality Disorder is a pattern of instability in interpersonal relationships, self-image, and affects, and marked impulsivity.

Histrionic Personality Disorder is a pattern of excessive emotionality and attention seeking.

Narcissistic Personality Disorder is a pattern of grandiosity, need for admiration, and lack of empathy.

Avoidant Personality Disorder is a pattern of social inhibition, feelings of inadequacy, and hypersensitivity to negative evaluation.

Dependent Personality Disorder is a pattern of submissive and clinging behavior related to an excessive need to be taken care of.

Obsessive-Compulsive Personality disorder is a pattern of preoccupation with orderliness, perfectionism, and control.

Personality Disorder Not Otherwise Specified is a category provided for two situations: (1) the individual's personality pattern meets the general criteria for a Personality Disorder and traits of several different Personality Disorders are present, but the criteria for any specific Personality Disorder are not met; or (2) the individual's personality pattern meets the general criteria for a Personality Disorder, but the individual is considered to have a Personality Disorder that is not included in the Classification (e.g., passive-aggressive personality disorder). (p. 629)

The Personality Disorders are grouped into three clusters based on descriptive similarities. Cluster A includes the Paranoid, Schizoid, and Schizotypal Personality Disorders. Individuals with these disorders often appear odd or eccentric. Cluster B includes the Antisocial, Borderline, Histrionic, and Narcissistic Personality Disorders. Individuals with these disorders often appear dramatic, emotional, or erratic. Cluster C includes the Avoidant, Dependent, and Obsessive-Compulsive Personality Disorders. Individuals with these disorders often appear anxious or fearful. It should be noted that this clustering system, although useful in some research and educational situations, has *serious limitations* and *has not been consistently validated.* Moreover, individuals frequently present with co-occurring Personality Disorders from different clusters (p. 629–630; emphasis added).

Personality traits are enduring patterns of perceiving, relating to, and thinking about the environment and oneself that are exhibited in a wide range of social and personal contexts. Only when personality traits are inflexible and maladaptive and cause significant functional impairment or subjective distress do they constitute Personality Disorders. (p. 630)

Personality Disorders must be distinguished from personality traits that do not reach the threshold for a Personality Disorder. Personality traits are diagnosed as a Personality Disorder only when they are inflexible, maladaptive, and persisting and cause significant functional impairment or subjective distress. (p. 633)

2. General Diagnostic Criteria for a Personality Disorder

A. An enduring pattern of inner experience and behavior that deviates markedly from the expectations of the individual's culture. This pattern is manifested in two (or more) of the following areas:

(1) cognition (i.e., ways of perceiving and interpreting self, other people, and events)

(2) affectivity (i.e., the range, intensity, lability, and appropriateness of emotional response)

(3) interpersonal functioning

(4) impulse control

B. The enduring pattern is inflexible and pervasive across a broad range of personal and social situations

C. The enduring pattern leads to clinically significant distress or impairment in social, occupational, or other important areas of functioning.

D. The pattern is stable and of long duration, and its onset can be traced back at least to adolescence or early adulthood.

E. The enduring pattern is not better accounted for as a manifestation or consequence of another mental disorder.

F. The enduring pattern is not due to the direct physiological effects of a substance (e.g., a drug of abuse, a medication) or a general medical condition (e.g., head trauma). (p. 633)

A. Cluster A Personality Disorders

Diagnostic Criteria for 301.0 Paranoid Personality Disorder

A. A pervasive distrust and suspiciousness of others such that their motives are interpreted as malevolent, beginning by early adulthood and present in a variety of contexts, as indicated by four (or more) of the following:

(1) suspects, without sufficient basis, that others are exploiting, harming, or deceiving him or her

(2) is preoccupied with unjustified doubts about the loyalty or trustworthiness of friends or associates

(3) is reluctant to confide in others because of unwarranted fear that the information will be used maliciously against him or her
(4) reads hidden demeaning or threatening meanings into benign remarks or events
(5) persistently bears grudges, i.e., is unforgiving of insults, injuries, or slights
(6) perceives attacks on his or her character or reputation that are not apparent to others and is quick to react angrily or to counterattack
(7) has recurrent suspicions, without justification, regarding fidelity of spouse or sexual partner

B. Does not occur exclusively during the course of Schizophrenia, a Mood Disorder With Psychotic Features, or another Psychotic Disorder and is not due to the direct physiological effects of a general medical condition.

Note: If criteria are met prior to the onset of Schizophrenia, add "Premorbid"; e.g., "Paranoid Personality Disorder (Premorbid)" (pp. 637–638).

Diagnostic Criteria for 301.20 Schizoid Personality Disorder

A. A pervasive pattern of detachment from social relationships and a restricted range of expression of emotions in interpersonal settings, beginning by early adulthood and present in a variety of contexts, as indicated by four (or more) of the following:

(1) neither desires nor enjoys close relationships, including being part of a family
(2) almost always chooses solitary activities
(3) has little, if any, interest in having sexual experiences with another person
(4) takes pleasure in few, if any, activities
(5) lacks close friends or confidants other than first-degree relatives
(6) appears indifferent to the praise or criticism of others
(7) shows emotional coldness, detachment, or flattened affectivity

B. Does not occur exclusively during the course of Schizophrenia, a Mood Disorder With Psychotic Features, another Psychotic Disorder, or a Pervasive Developmental Disorder and is not due to the direct physiological effects of a general medical condition.

Note: If criteria are met prior to the onset of Schizophrenia, add "Premorbid"; e.g., "Schizoid Personality Disorder (Premorbid)" (p. 641).

Diagnositc Criteria for 301.22 Schizotypal Personality Disorder

A. A pervasive pattern of social and interpersonal deficits marked by acute discomfort with, and reduced capacity for, close relationships as well as by cognitive or perceptual distortions and eccentricities of behavior, beginning by early adulthood and present in a variety of contexts, as indicated by five (or more) of the following:

(1) ideas of reference (excluding delusions of reference)

(2) odd beliefs or magical thinking that influences behavior and is inconsistent with subcultural norms (e.g., superstitiousness, belief in clairvoyance, telepathy, or "sixth sense"; in children and adolescents, bizarre fantasies or preoccupations)

(3) unusual perceptual experiences, including bodily illusions

(4) odd thinking and speech (e.g., vague, circumstantial, metaphorical, over-elaborate, or stereotyped)

(5) suspiciousness or paranoid ideation

(6) inappropriate or constricted affect

(7) behavior or appearance that is odd, eccentric, or peculiar

(8) lack of close friends or confidants other than first-degree relatives

(9) excessive social anxiety that does not diminish with familiarity and tends to be associated with paranoid fears rather than negative judgments about self

B. Does not occur exclusively during the course of Schizophrenia, a Mood Disorder With Psychotic Features, another Psychotic Disorder, or a Pervasive Developmental Disorder.

Note: If criteria are met prior to the onset of Schizophrenia, add "Premorbid"; e.g., "Schizotypal Personality Disorder (Premorbid)" (p. 654).

B. Cluster B Personality Disorders

Diagnostic Criteria for 301.7 Antisocial Personality Disorder

A. There is a pervasive pattern of disregard for and violation of the rights of others occurring since age 15 years, as indicated by three (or more) of the following:

(1) failure to conform to social norms with respect to lawful behaviors as indicated by repeatedly performing acts that are grounds for arrest

(2) deceitfulness, as indicated by repeated lying, use of aliases, or conning others for personal profit or pleasure

(3) impulsivity or failure to plan ahead

(4) irritability and aggressiveness, as indicated by repeated physical fights or assaults

(5) reckless disregard for safety of self or others

(6) consistent irresponsibility, as indicated by repeated failure to sustain consistent work behavior or honor financial obligations

(7) lack of remorse, as indicated by being indifferent to or rationalizing having hurt, mistreated, or stolen from another

B. The individual is at least age 18 years.

C. There is evidence of Conduct Disorder . . . with onset before age 15 years.

D. The occurrence of antisocial behavior is not exclusively during the course of Schizophrenia or a Manic Episode (pp. 649–650).

Diagnostic Criteria for 301.83 Borderline Personality Disorder

A pervasive pattern of instability of interpersonal relationships, self-image, and affects, and marked impulsivity beginning by early adulthood and present in a variety of contexts, as indicated by five (or more) of the following:

(1) frantic efforts to avoid real or imagined abandonment. *Note:* Do not include suicidal or self-mutilating behavior covered in Criterion 5.

(2) a pattern of unstable and intense interpersonal relationships characterized by alternating between extremes of idealization and devaluation

(3) identity disturbance: markedly and persistently unstable self-image or sense of self

(4) impulsivity in at least two areas that are potentially self-damaging (e.g., spending, sex, substance abuse, reckless driving, binge eating). *Note:* Do not include suicidal or self-mutilating behavior covered in Criterion 5.

(5) recurrent suicidal behavior, gestures, or threats, or self-mutilating behavior

(6) affective instability due to a marked reactivity of mood (e.g., intense episodic dysphoria, irritability, or anxiety usually lasting a few hours and only rarely more than a few days)

(7) chronic feelings of emptiness

(8) inappropriate, intense anger or difficulty controlling anger (e.g., frequent displays of temper, constant anger, recurrent physical fights)

(9) transient, stress-related paranoid ideation or severe dissociative symptoms (p. 654).

Diagnositc Criteria for 301.50 Histrionic Personality Disorder

A pervasive pattern of excessive emotionality and attention seeking, beginning by early adulthood and present in a variety of contexts, as indicated by five (or more) of the following:

(1) is uncomfortable in situations in which he or she is not the center of attention
(2) interaction with others is often characterized by inappropriate sexually seductive or provocative behavior
(3) displays rapidly shifting and shallow expression of emotions
(4) consistently uses physical appearance to draw attention to self
(5) has a style of speech that is excessively impressionistic and lacking in detail
(6) shows self-dramatization, theatricality, and an exaggerated expression of emotion
(7) is suggestible, i.e., easily influenced by others or circumstances
(8) considers relationships to be more intimate than they actually are (pp. 657–658).

Diagnostic Criteria for 301.81 Narcissistic Personality Disorder

A pervasive pattern of grandiosity (in fantasy or behavior), need for admiration, and lack of empathy, beginning by early adulthood and present in a variety of contexts, as indicated by five (or more) of the following:

(1) has a grandiose sense of self-importance (e.g., exaggerates achievements and talents, expects to be recognized as superior without commensurate achievements)
(2) is preoccupied with fantasies of unlimited success, power, brilliance, beauty, or ideal love
(3) believes that he or she is "special" and unique and can only be understood by, or should associate with, other special or high- status people (or institutions)
(4) requires excessive admiration
(5) has a sense of entitlement, i.e., unreasonable expectations of especially favorable treatment or automatic compliance with his or her expectations
(6) is interpersonally exploitative, i.e., takes advantage of others to achieve his or her own ends
(7) lacks empathy: is unwilling to recognize or identify with the feelings and needs of others
(8) is often envious of others or believes that others are envious of him or her
(9) shows arrogant, haughty behaviors or attitudes (p. 661).

C. Cluster C Personality Disorders

Diagnostic Criteria for 301.82 Avoidant Personality Disorder

A pervasive pattern of social inhibition, feelings of inadequacy, and hypersensitivity to negative evaluation, beginning by early adulthood and present in a variety of contexts, as indicated by four (or more) of the following:

(1) avoids occupational activities that involve significant interpersonal contact, because of fears of criticism, disapproval, or rejection
(2) is unwilling to get involved with people unless certain of being liked
(3) shows restraint within intimate relationships because of the fear of being shamed or ridiculed
(4) is preoccupied with being criticized or rejected in social situations
(5) is inhibited in new interpersonal situations because of feelings of inadequacy
(6) views self as socially inept, personally unappealing, or inferior to others
(7) is unusually reluctant to take personal risks or to engage in any new activities because they may prove embarrassing (pp. 664-665).

Diagnostic Criteria for 301.6 Dependent Personality Disorder

A pervasive and excessive need to be taken care of that leads to submissive and clinging behavior and fears of separation, beginning by early adulthood and present in a variety of contexts, as indicated by five (or more) of the following:

(1) has difficulty making everyday decisions without an excessive amount of advice and reassurance from others
(2) needs others to assume responsibility for most major areas of his or her life
(3) has difficulty expressing disagreement with others because of fear of loss of support or approval. *Note:* Do not include realistic fears of retribution.
(4) has difficulty initiating projects or doing things on his or her own (because of a lack of self-confidence in judgment or abilities rather than a lack of motivation or energy)
(5) goes to excessive lengths to obtain nurturance and support from others, to the point of volunteering to do things that are unpleasant
(6) feels uncomfortable or helpless when alone because of exaggerated fears of being unable to care for himself or herself
(7) urgently seeks another relationship as a source of care and support when a close relationship ends

(8) is unrealistically preoccupied with fears of being left to take care of himself or herself (pp. 668–669).

Diagnostic Criteria for 301.4 Obsessive-Compulsive Personality Disorder

A pervasive pattern of preoccupation with orderliness, perfectionism, and mental and interpersonal control, at the expense of flexibility, openness, and efficiency, beginning by early adulthood and present in a variety of contexts, as indicated by four (or more) of the following:

(1) is preoccupied with details, rules, lists, order, organization, or schedules to the extent that the major point of the activity is lost
(2) shows perfectionism that interferes with task completion (e.g., is unable to complete a project because his or her own overly strict standards are not met)
(3) is excessively devoted to work and productivity to the exclusion of leisure activities and friendships (not accounted for by obvious economic necessity)
(4) is over-conscientious, scrupulous, and inflexible about matters of morality, ethics, or values (not accounted for by cultural or religious identification)
(5) is unable to discard worn-out or worthless objects even when they have no sentimental value
(6) is reluctant to delegate tasks or to work with others unless they submit to exactly his or her way of doing things
(7) adopts a miserly spending style toward both self and others; money is viewed as something to be hoarded for future catastrophes
(8) shows rigidity and stubbornness (pp. 672–673).

Diagnostic Criteria for 301.9 Personality Disorder Not Otherwise Specified

This category is for disorders of personality functioning that do not meet criteria for any specific Personality Disorder. An example is the presence of features of more than one specific Personality Disorder that do not meet the full criteria for anyone Personality Disorder ("mixed personality"), but that together cause clinically significant distress or impairment in one or more important areas of functioning (e.g., social or occupational). This category can also be used when the clinician judges that a specific Personality Disorder that is not included in the Classification is appropriate. Examples include depressive personality disorder and passive-aggressive personality disorder (p. 673).

ABOUT THE AUTHOR

JOHN G. MCGRAW was born in Minneapolis and attended St. John's College Preparatory School in Collegeville, Minnesota. He received his Bachelor of Arts in Political Science from the University of Notre Dame (South Bend), a Baccalaureate and Licentiate in Philosophy from the Pontifical Institute of Philosophy (Chicago), and a Doctorate in Philosophy from the Angelicum University (Rome). McGraw taught philosophy and interdisciplinary courses at Loyola of Montreal, where he was a Member of the Board of Trustees, President of its Faculty Association, and Chair of its Department of Philosophy. He is currently Professor Emeritus at Concordia University (Montreal)—a 1974 amalgamation of Loyola and Sir George Williams University of Montreal—where he served as Chair of its Department of Philosophy and a Member of its Board of Governors. McGraw has authored numerous articles and book chapters in philosophy, psychology, and sociology, as well as a volume in Interdisciplinary Studies. In addition to the present volume in the Rodopi Value Inquiry Series on personality and states of aloneness, Professor McGraw is currently working on a study on the life and works of Friedrich Nietzsche. He is married to Patricia McDermott O'Connor, a Professor of Philosophy and Humanities. They have two children, Sheiline and Désirée.

NAME INDEX

SUBJECT INDEX

VIBS

The **Value Inquiry Book Series** is co-sponsored by:

Adler School of Professional Psychology
American Indian Philosophy Association
American Maritain Association
American Society for Value Inquiry
Association for Process Philosophy of Education
Canadian Society for Philosophical Practice
Center for Bioethics, University of Turku
Center for Professional and Applied Ethics, University of North Carolina at Charlotte
Central European Pragmatist Forum
Centre for Applied Ethics, Hong Kong Baptist University
Centre for Cultural Research, Aarhus University
Centre for Professional Ethics, University of Central Lancashire
Centre for the Study of Philosophy and Religion, University College of Cape Breton
Centro de Estudos em Filosofia Americana, Brazil
College of Education and Allied Professions, Bowling Green State University
College of Liberal Arts, Rochester Institute of Technology
Concerned Philosophers for Peace
Conference of Philosophical Societies
Department of Moral and Social Philosophy, University of Helsinki
Gannon University
Gilson Society
Haitian Studies Association
Ikeda University
Institute of Philosophy of the High Council of Scientific Research, Spain
International Academy of Philosophy of the Principality of Liechtenstein
International Association of Bioethics
International Center for the Arts, Humanities, and Value Inquiry
International Society for Universal Dialogue
Natural Law Society
Philosophical Society of Finland
Philosophy Born of Struggle Association
Philosophy Seminar, University of Mainz
Pragmatism Archive at The Oklahoma State University
R.S. Hartman Institute for Formal and Applied Axiology
Research Institute, Lakeridge Health Corporation
Russian Philosophical Society
Society for Existential Analysis
Society for Iberian and Latin-American Thought
Society for the Philosophic Study of Genocide and the Holocaust
Unit for Research in Cognitive Neuroscience, Autonomous University of Barcelona
Whitehead Research Project
Yves R. Simon Institute

Titles Published

Volumes 1 - 210 see www.rodopi.nl

211. Tuija Takala, Peter Herissone-Kelly, and Søren Holm, Editors, *Cutting Through the Surface: Philosophical Approaches to Bioethics*. A volume in **Values in Bioethics**

212. Neena Schwartz: *A Lab of My Own*. A volume in **Lived Values, Valued Lives**

213. Krzysztof Piotr Skowroński, *Values and Powers: Re-reading the Philosophical Tradition of American Pragmatism*. A volume in **Central European Value Studies**

214. Matti Häyry, Tuija Takala, Peter Herissone-Kelly and Gardar Árnason, Editors, *Arguments and Analysis in Bioethics*. A volume in **Values in Bioethics**

215. Anders Nordgren, *For Our Children: The Ethics of Animal Experimentation in the Age of Genetic Engineering*. A volume in **Values in Bioethics**

216. James R. Watson, Editor, *Metacide: In the Pursuit of Excellence*. A volume in **Holocaust and Genocide Studies**

217. Andrew Fitz-Gibbon, Editor, *Positive Peace: Reflections on Peace Education, Nonviolence, and Social Change*. A volume in **Philosophy of Peace**

218. Christopher Berry Gray, *The Methodology of Maurice Hauriou: Legal, Sociological, Philosophical*. A volume in **Studies in Jurisprudence**

219. Mary K. Bloodsworth-Lugo and Carmen R. Lugo-Lugo, *Containing (Un)American Bodies: Race, Sexuality, and Post-9/11 Constructions of Citizenship*. A volume in **Philosophy of Peace**

220. Roland Faber, Brian G. Henning, Clinton Combs, Editors, *Beyond Metaphysics? Explorations in Alfred North Whitehead's Late Thought*. A volume in **Contemporary Whitehead Studies**

221. John G. McGraw, *Intimacy and Isolation (Intimacy and Aloneness: A Multi-Volume Study in Philosophical Psychology, Volume One)*, A volume in **Philosophy and Psychology**

222. Janice L. Schultz-Aldrich, Introduction and Edition, *"Truth" is a Divine Name, Hitherto Unpublished Papers of Edward A. Synan, 1918-1997.* A volume in **Gilson Studies**

223. Larry A. Hickman, Matthew Caleb Flamm, Krzysztof Piotr Skowroński and Jennifer A. Rea, Editors, *The Continuing Relevance of John Dewey: Reflections on Aesthetics, Morality, Science, and Society.* A volume in **Central European Value Studies**

224. Hugh P. McDonald, *Creative Actualization: A Meliorist Theory of Values.* A volume in **Studies in Pragmatism and Values**

225. Rob Gildert and Dennis Rothermel, Editors, *Remembrance and Reconciliation.* A volume in **Philosophy of Peace**

226. Leonidas Donskis, Editor, *Niccolò Machiavelli: History, Power, and Virtue.* A volume in **Philosophy, Literature, and Politics**

227. Sanya Osha, *Postethnophilosophy.* A volume in **Social Philosophy**

228. Rosa M. Calcaterra, Editor, *New Perspectives on Pragmatism and Analytic Philosophy.* A volume in **Studies in Pragmatism and Values**

229. Danielle Poe, Editor, *Communities of Peace: Confronting Injustice and Creating Justice.* A volume in **Philosophy of Peace**

230. Thorsten Botz-Bornstein, Editor, *The Philosophy of Viagra: Bioethical Responses to the Viagrification of the Modern World.* A volume in **Philosophy of Sex and Love**

231. Carolyn Swanson, *Reburial of Nonexistents: Reconsidering the Meinong-Russell Debate.* A volume in **Central European Value Studies**

232. Adrianne Leigh McEvoy, Editor, *Sex, Love, and Friendship: Studies of the Society for the Philosophy of Sex and Love: 1993–2003.* A volume in **Histories and Addresses of Philosophical Societies**

233. Amihud Gilead, *The Privacy of the Psychical.* A volume in **Philosophy and Psychology**

234. Paul Kriese and Randall E. Osborne, Editors, *Social Justice, Poverty and Race: Normative and Empirical Points of View.* A volume in **Studies in Jurisprudence**

235. Hakam H. Al-Shawi, *Reconstructing Subjects: A Philosophical Critique of Psychotherapy.* A volume in **Philosophy and Psychology**

236. Maurice Hauriou, *Tradition in Social Science.* Translation from French with an Introduction by Christopher Berry Gray. A volume in **Studies in Jurisprudence**

237. Camila Loew, *The Memory of Pain: Women's Testimonies of the Holocaust.*. A volume in **Holocaust and Genocide Studies**

238. Stefano Franchi and Francesco Bianchini, Editors, *The Search for a Theory of Cognition: Early Mechanisms and New Ideas.* A volume in **Cognitive Science**

239. Michael H. Mitias, *Friendship: A Central Moral Value.* A volume in **Ethical Theory and Practice**

240. John Ryder and Radim Šíp, Editors, *Identity and Social Transformation, Central European Pragmatist Forum, Volume Five.* A volume in **Central European Value Studies**

241. William Sweet and Hendrik Hart, *Responses to the Enlightenment: An Exchange on Foundations, Faith, and Community.* A volume in **Philosophy and Religion**

242. Leonidas Donskis and J.D. Mininger, Editors, *Politics Otherwise: Shakespeare as Social and Political Critique.* A volume in **Philosophy, Literature, and Politics**

243. Hugh P. McDonald, *Speculative Evaluations: Essays on a Pluralistic Universe.* A volume in **Studies in Pragmatism and Values.**

244. Dorota Koczanowicz and Wojciech Małecki, Editors, *Shusterman's Pragmatism: Between Literature and Somaesthetics.* A volume in **Central European Value Studies**

245. Harry Lesser, Editor, *Justice for Older People,* A volume in **Values in Bioethics**

246. John G. McGraw, *Personality Disorders and States of Aloneness (Intimacy and Aloneness: A Multi-Volume Study in Philosophical Psychology, Volume Two),* A volume in **Philosophy and Psychology**

CPSIA information can be obtained at www.ICGtesting.com
Printed in the USA
LVOW091347180412

278127LV00004B/21/P

9 789042 034945